BOMBS AWAY!

OTHER BOOKS WRITTEN OR EDITED BY
STANLEY M. ULANOFF

ILLUSTRATED GUIDE TO U.S. MISSILES AND ROCKETS

FIGHTER PILOT

MATS—THE STORY OF THE MILITARY AIR TRANSPORT SERVICE

BOMBS AWAY!

ILLUSTRATED HISTORY OF WORLD WAR I IN THE AIR

MAN IN A GREEN BERET

THE UNHEARD OF ACE—CAPTAIN W. C. LAMBERT, RFC

AIR COMBAT CLASSICS

WINGED WARFARE
  by Lieutenant Colonel William A. Bishop

ACE OF ACES
  by Captain René Fonck

FIGHTING AIRMAN—THE WAY OF THE EAGLE
  by Major Charles J. Biddle

FLYING FURY
  by Major James T. B. McCudden

WIND IN THE WIRES
  by Captain Duncan Grinnell-Milne

THE RED BARON
  by Rittmeister Manfred Frh. von Richthofen

ACE OF THE IRON CROSS
  by Oberleutnant Ernst Udet

UP AND AT 'EM
  by Lieutenant Colonel Harold Hartney

BOMBS AWAY!

TRUE STORIES OF STRATEGIC AIRPOWER
FROM WORLD WAR I TO THE PRESENT

EDITED BY

STANLEY M. ULANOFF, COLONEL, USAR

FOREWORD BY

Lieutenant General Ira C. Eaker, USAF (RET.)
World War II Commander of the Eighth Air Force
and the Allied Mediterranean Air Force

DOUBLEDAY & COMPANY, INC., GARDEN CITY, NEW YORK

Grateful acknowledgment is made for permission to use the following:

Excerpt from *Zeppelin, The Story of Lighter-Than-Air Craft* by Ernst A. Lehmann, translated by Jay Dratler. Copyright 1937 by Longmans, Green & Company. Copyright renewed © 1965 by David McKay Company, Inc. Used by permission of David McKay Company, Inc.

Excerpt from *Wings of the Morning* by Ian and Payne Cameron. Copyright © 1962 by Ian Cameron. Reprinted by permission of William Morrow and Company, Inc. and David Higham Associates, Ltd.

Excerpt from *Stuka Pilot* by Hans-Ulrich Rudel. Copyright 1958 by Ballantine Books, Inc. Used by permission of the publisher and author.

Excerpt from *Mission Completed* by Sir Basil Embry. Used by permission of Curtis Brown Ltd.

Excerpt from *Bombers Across* by Edgar J. Wynn. Copyright 1944 by E. P. Dutton & Co., Inc. Used by permission of the publisher.

Excerpt from *Memoirs of World War I* by Brigadier General William Mitchell. Copyright 1928 and renewed 1956 by Lorraine Lester and Associates. Copyright © 1960 by Lucy M. Gilpin. Used by permission of Random House, Inc.

"An American Fights for France" by Norman Prince. Used by permission of the author.

"I Led the Attack on Pearl Harbor" by Mitsuo Fuchida, from *Proceedings*, September 1952. Reprinted by permission of *Proceedings;* copyright © U. S. Naval Institute.

"First American Fighter Bombers" and "A Raid on Ostend" from *The Lafayette Flying Corps*, edited by Nordhoff Hall. Reprinted by permission of Kennikat Press, Port Washington, N.Y.

"Hit the Silk" by William N. Hess. Used by permission of the author.

"Torpedo Bombers Sink the *Repulse*" by Cecil Brown, from *From Pearl Harbor into Tokyo*. Copyright 1945 by the Columbia Broadcasting System, Inc. All rights reserved.

"Safety in Numbers" by W. A. McCarthy, *"Phyllis* Had the Stuff" by Charles W. Paine, "Hell Over Bizerte" by H. M. Locker, "Attack on Ploesti" by John S. Young, "Regensburg Mission" by Beirne Lay, Jr., "Portrait of a Guy Looking for an Island" by Bert Stiles, "Last Mission" by Allan H. Gillis, "Revenge Was Sweet Off Midway" by Walter C. Sweeney, Jr., "A Raid on Balikpapan" by Richard S. Reynolds, *"Old 26* Comes Home" by Robert V. Guelich and William G. Mors, "Men of the B-29's" by Kenneth B. Wolfe, "From Kansas to Tokyo" by Milton R. Krims, "Action in the Solomons" by Hulburt Burroughs, "Bombing the Red Hornets' Nest" by Robert B. Almach, and "I Was a Korean Sharpshooter" by Billie G. Beach. All reprinted by permission of *Air Force Space Digest.*

Excerpt from *Global Mission* by Henry "Hap" Arnold. Copyright 1949 by H. H. Arnold. Used by permission of Harper & Row, Publishers.

Excerpt from *Brave Men* by Ernie Pyle. Copyright 1943, 1944 by Scripps-Howard Newspaper Alliance; copyright 1944 by Ernie Pyle; copyright © 1971 by Holt, Rinehart & Winston, Inc. Used by permission of the publisher.

Photo Credits:

All the photographs in this volume have been provided by the United States Air Force, with the following exceptions: National Archives, photos 1, 2, 4, 7, 11, 17, 18, 24; McDonnell-Douglas Aircraft Corp., photos 16, 19, 51, 52, 53; Airfix, photo 37; J. F. Huber, photo 61; The United States Navy, photos 46, 54, 67. We wish to express our appreciation to these individuals and organizations for their permission and cooperation.

ACKNOWLEDGMENTS

An anthology like *Bombs Away!* requires the cooperation of many people. I was most fortunate in having had the help of some of the finest who gave unstintingly of their time and efforts. Bomber crew members, American, Allied, and former enemies alike, shared their combat experiences with me (and hence with you) and those who had written them down, whether in letters, diaries, reports, or published magazine articles and books, freely contributed them to this volume. Their names head the articles they wrote and are listed in the table of contents.

Chief among these was Lieutenant General Ira C. Eaker, USAF (Ret.), World War II Commander of the mighty Eighth Air Force, and of the Allied Mediterranean Air Force, who not only contributed an article but consented to write the Foreword, as well.

Another old friend, Jack Loosbrock, editor of *Air Force Magazine-Space Digest,* as he did with my earlier effort, *Fighter Pilot,* kindly gave me permission to borrow from his great publication's vast store of material.

Certainly not to be forgotten are the personnel of the Magazine and Book Branch of the Office of the Assistant Secretary of Defense (Public Affairs). Its chief, Colonel C. V. Glines, now in Alaska; Lieutenant Colonel Gene Gurney, now in Hawaii; Lieutenant Colonel Bob Webb; and Anna Urband broke down the barriers of old security classifications to get me the material I requested. Along with that fine crew I must mention Bill Nigh of the National Archives, who tracked down those elusive records I needed.

I could not complete these acknowledgments without at least mentioning my editor, Harold Kuebler.

Again to the U. S. Air Force I owe much gratitude for the wonderful photos they furnished. Unless otherwise noted, all of the photos in this volume were contributed by the USAF itself or from their collection at the National Archives.

To all of those others, too numerous to mention, who contributed to this book, I give my heartfelt thanks—and to the Xerox Corporation whose wonderful machine spared me hours upon hours of typing, my sincerest appreciation.

The original efforts on *Bombs Away!* began a few years ago and many of those mentioned here may be in other jobs and other places and have new and higher ranks and titles; nevertheless, my gratitude for their efforts in my behalf goes with them.

To my mother MINNIE D. ULANOFF
who saw her fiancé and her brother
off to France in the First
World War and who sent two sons
and two more brothers to war in
that second great world conflict. One of these sons was a
USAAF Bombardier Officer.

CONTENTS

LIST OF ILLUSTRATIONS

WORLD WAR I

1. Avro 504 K.
2. DH-4.
3. DH-9A.
4. The Salmson 2-seater.
5. A crew of the 96th Aero Squadron returning from a raid.
6. Handley-Page 0/400.
7. Caproni CA 33.
8. Curtiss HS2.
9. Gotha GIII.
10. Crash of a German Zeppelin.
11. The Kettering Aerial Torpedo.

WORLD WAR II

12. Boeing B-17 *Flying Fortresses* of the 390th Bomb Group.
13. Consolidated B-24 *Liberators* over Ploesti.
14. Boeing B-29 *Superfortresses* over Burma.
15. Doolittle's North American B-25
    Mitchells leave the deck of the Aircraft Carrier *Hornet*.
16. Douglas A-20 *Havoc*.

THE CREWS

FOREWORD

I commend Colonel Stanley M. Ulanoff's book, *Bombs Away!* It is a remarkable collection of essays and expressions on military operations, with particular emphasis on bombing. It is very timely now on account of the discussion of bombing propriety and effectiveness in the Vietnam War.

Those who today question our bombing effort in Vietnam can find in this book the historical answers to their queries.

Bombs Away! can make a real contribution to our future national security plans. Any thoughtful reader of this book will question the wisdom of reducing the bomber segment of our strategic forces and placing our principal war deterrence upon missiles never tried and proved in warfare.

I congratulate Colonel Ulanoff and his publishers for providing this compilation of historical sketches, always interesting and sometimes vitally significant for future political-military policy.

As I read *Bombs Away!* I was reminded of an experience in World War II when I commanded the U. S. Eighth Air Force in England. Prime Minister Winston Churchill said to me late in 1943, "General, you have been showing me photographs of German fighter plane factories demolished by your bombers. What do you make of this intercept of a German message our intelligence people recently handed me?" The paper he passed to me was a radiogram from Albert Speer, Munitions Minister, to Chancellor Hitler, reporting that fighter production during the past month had increased by 15 percent.

I suggested to the great British war leader that perhaps the Germans meant us to intercept that message. This looked to me like a propaganda effort to lead us to discontinue our bombing.

The P.M. considered this suggestion for a time and then said, "We shall see, we shall see, time will tell. In the meanwhile, General, whenever you can bring me more photographs of flattened German factories you will be most welcome."

Bombs Away! again reminds us that the bomber can be in the future as it has been in the past, the most effective way to disarm the enemy by destroying his war-making potential, his weapons-making capacity. There is a direct relation between the means to wage war and the will to wage war.

The bomber is now, therefore, and I predict will long continue to be one of the prime deterrents to any future nuclear war.

IRA C. EAKER
Lieutenant General, USAF (Ret.)

INTRODUCTION

Throughout the history of human conflict (which is about as old as man, himself) *homo sapiens* and his forbears have constantly sought better weapons of destruction to use against their neighbors—either to defend themselves and their homes or simply to attack their fellow man.

The first of these weapons was most probably the human hand, or perhaps a chance rock or a tree branch used as a club. As man became more "civilized," or more intelligent, he strove to develop weapons with which he could attack his enemy from a greater distance, preferably out of the reach of his adversary and without being seen himself. The rock, undoubtedly, was the forerunner of those "long-range" missiles.

As time passed, man found several ways to jettison that stone at his adversary. You will recall how, with his tiny slingshot, "little David" defeated the bigger, more powerful, and better armed Goliath. David's weapon, however, was relatively crude in comparison to the ballista and the catapult which were developed later. These monsters could launch tons of rocks over a great distance.

Simultaneously man also created a number of methods of reaching his enemy with that stick, while standing off at a reasonably safe distance. By fashioning the branch into a spear or javelin he could throw it at his opponent. In time man invented the bow and thus became able to mechanically propel that same stick and send it flying at his foe. Still later his genius improved the weapon and came up with the more powerful, and certainly more sophisticated, crossbow.

But the greatest advance up to that time came with the invention of gunpowder and the subsequent development of firearms. Nothing equaled this discovery for centuries until 1903 when Wilbur and Orville Wright invented the flying machine. Now man had a truly revolutionary delivery system for his gunpowder and any other subsequent weapons that might come along.

The airplane was barely ten years old when, like the drummer boy of the Civil War, it went off to war. And like the drummer boy its earliest function was not what might be called an entirely belligerent one—it went aloft completely unarmed.

When an assassin's bullet put an end to the life of the Archduke Franz Ferdinand of Austria and triggered World War I, France and England had a number of Blériot IXs, the same type of primitive aircraft in which their namesake first flew over the English Channel in 1909. France also had some other frail box-kite like flying machines such as the Farmans and Voisins. The Germans too, had several different types of aircraft. Principal among these was a low-wing monoplane type, manufactured by several different companies but all known as *Taube*, which, attesting to their peaceful nature means *Dove* in German.

Both sides used these tiny canvas and wood aircraft as *scouts*. They took the place of the foot soldier or cavalry that historically preceded an army to scout out the enemy's forces and his positions, to the front and to the flanks. The airplane was a natural for the job. It could do it better, quicker, and more efficiently. It became the "eyes of the army." And in short order it went on from the simple observation or reconnaissance function to spotting and adjusting artillery fire, and aerial photography.

History has not recorded which aviator fired the first shot at his airborne enemy[1] and thus began aerial warfare. In the be-

[1] Actually, the first was a rifle fired by a U. S. Army officer from an airplane piloted by Glenn Curtiss in 1910, over Sheepshead Bay in Brooklyn, N.Y. Two

ginning, pilots and observers of the opposing sides would wave and smile at each other as they flew over the front lines and went about their reconnaissance work. It is quite possible that on one of these flights, the German, Frenchman, or Englishman didn't return the greeting. Or perhaps his smile wasn't warm enough. At any rate, miffed at this apparent slight to his honor, the aggrieved one brought along a pistol or carbine on his next flight, and let go with a blast at the first unsuspecting adversary who happened along. The news spread like wildfire and soon all of the airborne scouts were carrying weapons on their observation missions.

Before not too long flexible machine guns were mounted on the 2-seater aircraft for the use of the observer. And in a short while the ingenious among the single-seater pilots devised methods of mounting a fixed machine gun between the cockpit and the propeller, synchronized to fire between the propeller blades.[2] Now all the pilot had to do was point his aircraft at the adversary and squeeze the trigger.

Here was born the fighter pilot—in a natural transition from the scout-observer.[3] (The French called their fighter planes *avions de chasse* or hunting aircraft; the Americans—pursuit planes; and the Germans fought in *Jagdstaffeln* or Hunting Squadrons.)

The metamorphosis of the reconnaissance plane to bomber aircraft may have been a simpler and more natural one.

---

years later a machine gun was fired at a target from an American plane, but it was peacetime and no one thought much about these experiments and they were all but forgotten.

[2] To the Frenchman Roland Garros goes the credit for first mounting a machine gun on his scout. This was a crude arrangement where the propeller was protected by a steel plate which deflected the bullets that struck it. Anthony Fokker perfected this arrangement with a gear that synchronized the gun to the prop, so that it fired only when the prop blade wasn't in front of it.

[3] There was also a type of aircraft on which the engine was mounted behind the pilot and "pushed" the aircraft rather than pulled it. One of these "pushers" was the British D.H. 2, on which the pilot had a gun mounted in front of him that fired straight ahead without fear of striking the propeller, which was to the rear of the cockpit.

What youngster hasn't found great delight in spilling a glass of water or dropping a missile of some sort from an upstairs window on an unwary parent or friend, below. This natural desire to pelt his fellow from the lofty heights carried over to those pioneer military fliers of 1914–15.

It didn't take a great deal of imagination to see the possibilities for aerial bombardment.

Some took bricks up with them to drop on opposing aircraft or to harass the enemy infantry engaged in a different kind of battle on the ground. French pilots dropped over the side bunches of a deadly little device known as a *flechette*. Resembling darts, shorter than a pencil but as thick, with fins, these devilish little "toys" played havoc with the enemy troops below.

Soon the game began in earnest and airmen carried aloft actual bombs which they aimed and dropped by hand—right over the side of the cockpit. These were small and relatively ineffective, but never underestimate the ability of man! Progress was rapid in those early days as the infant aviation industry moved ahead by leaps and bounds. The planes were being built better, stronger, and faster. They no longer resembled box-kites or the packing crates in which they came. They began to take on a more attractive, more streamlined appearance.

To be sure the techniques and skills of aerial bombardment kept pace with aircraft development. No more crude dropping of projectiles by hand. Now they were shackled under the wings or fuselage and dropped by the pilot or bombardier by means of a toggle release in the cockpit.

At this point it might be well to mention the Zeppelin—also known as a dirigible and as an airship. This lighter-than-air craft was developed by the German, Count Ferdinand von Zeppelin. During the First World War his country used these long, giant gas bags (they were inflated with hydrogen and were highly inflammable) to bomb France, Belgium, and England. Some were as much as 700 feet long and were veritable "ships of the air." The Germans, however, did not limit themselves to lighter-than-air craft. They also built giant *Gotha* bombers and *R* Planes, with a range great enough to strike at London and return. The British matched these with their Handley-Page and Vickers *Vimy* bombers. A model of the latter was piloted in a historic crossing of the Atlantic by Alcock and Brown, following the war.

The Italians, not to be outdone, came up with the mammoth Caproni bomber. Some of these were flown by American pilots under the command of Major Fiorello La Guardia, a U. S. Congressman and later the peppery Mayor of New York City.

Early proponents of strategic air power were the British General Sir Hugh M. "Boom" Trenchard, and Billy Mitchell, the American general who commanded a 350-plane Allied force of bombers, escorting fighters, and other aircraft for an assault on Saint-Mihiel. This, one of the first massive air raids in history, succeeded in dropping some 30 tons of bombs. By comparison it is interesting to note that the single atomic bomb dropped on Hiroshima, at the end of the Second World War, was the equivalent of 20,000 tons of TNT.

Following World War I, Mitchell continued to agitate for the supremacy of air power, and the potential of the bomber against naval surface vessels. His contention was that the bomber rendered the battleship obsolete. Such a brash challenge did not endear Mitchell to the Navy nor to its champions in Congress. However, with the cooperation of the Navy, he proved his point. The Navy provided the ex-German battleship, *Ostfriesland* which on July 21, 1921, Mitchell's force successfully bombed and sank.

Again, in 1923, Mitchell's neophyte bomber force sank the U.S. battleships *Virginia* and *New Jersey* which had been destined for the scrap heap as a result of the Washington Arms Limitation Treaty. Despite his successes the outspoken Mitchell did not have his way. In fact after much unpleasantness he was court-martialed and reduced in rank. But in the end, posthumously, too late for him to appreciate it, this early prophet of air power was finally vindicated. Events in World War II proved him right and many years later a grateful Congress awarded him a gold Medal of Honor.

At the same time that Mitchell was fighting his battle, an Italian, General Giulio Douhet, did a great deal of writing on air power, strategic bombing, and the independent air force. His efforts were a little better received.

It is interesting to note that the British established an independent air force in the midst of World War I. They expanded their infant Royal Flying Corps (RFC) into the Royal Air Force (RAF). The United States did not follow suit until after the Second World War when the Army Air Force (USAAF) became the independent U. S. Air Force (USAF).

The Spanish Civil War, as a forerunner of World War II, gave some idea of the devastating power of aerial bombardment on undefended cities. At the start of the Second World War the Germans also used air power effectively in crushing Poland and Holland, among others.

Probably the best proof, however, that might have been offered in defense of Billy Mitchell was the unprovoked Japanese attack on Pearl Harbor and the resultant crippling of practically the entire U. S. Pacific Fleet in one nearly decisive blow. Unfortunately it was left for the enemy to first prove Mitchell's point.

But Billy Mitchell had his day! After the Japanese had destroyed Pearl Harbor, taken the Philippines, and all of the other U.S. and Allied Pacific islands and Southeast Asian land bases within range of their homeland, sixteen American land-based, medium bombers, led by the then Lieutenant Colonel Jimmy Doolittle, attacked Tokyo and a number of the other principal Japanese cities. The bombers that accomplished this mission were twin-engine B-25s, known as *Mitchells* as a tribute to

America's champion of winged strength. The B-25 proved its namesake's thesis once more against Japanese shipping at the Battle of the Bismarck Sea, as did the B-26s, B-17s, B-25s, and B-29s, at other places, many times over. And it was verified again and again by German Junkers, Dornier, and Heinkel bombers; by British *Lancasters, Wellingtons, Sterlings,* and *Halifaxes;* by Soviet *Stormoviks;* and by others.

Bent on invading England after the conquest of France the German *Luftwaffe* day after day pounded the "island stronghold" in wave upon wave of ferocious aerial assault. Were it not for the stalwart "few" of the RAF Fighter Command who broke the back of the *Luftwaffe* in their *Spitfires* and *Hurricanes,* Nazi hordes might have goose-stepped triumphantly through Trafalgar Square as they did on the Champs Élysée.

Before not too long, however, the shoe was on the other foot as RAF bombers pounded Cologne, Dresden and other German cities. Soon it became "bombing around the clock" with the USAAF heavy B-17s and B-24s hitting the enemy by day and the British striking by night.

Aerial bombardment was refined considerably, if one can use that term, during World War II. Bombs were no longer slung under the wings or fuselage but were carried within the aircraft, in bomb bays. On the final bomb run, bomb bay doors were opened, "Bombs away!", and closed again.

Fighter-bombers like the P-47 *Thunderbolt* and dive-bombers like the *Stuka,* however, continued to carry their missiles in the underslung position as did their predecessor scouts of the First World War. The same was also true of the *Mustang, Corsair,* and *Shootingstar* fighter-bombers in the Korean War and of the *Thunderchiefs, Skyhawks,* and *Skyraiders* in the Vietnam fracas.

Accuracy, too, was improved to a fantastic degree. American bombardiers, with their Norden bomb sights, were truly able to drop their bombs "right down the pickle barrel." Bomber range was extended considerably and the weapon itself was honed and sharpened to an awesome degree—well beyond the dreams and the ken of the ordinary man of 1945, or of today, for that matter.

Scientists developed the bomb which ushered in the Atomic Age. Two of these aweful weapons were dropped on Japan— one apiece on Hiroshima and Nagasaki. Each of these bombs had the equivalent destructive power of 20,000 tons of TNT and were dropped by B-29 *Superfortresses*. Forbidding and devastating as were these "primitive" A-bombs (by today's standards) they served to end the war in the Pacific and saved the lives of countless numbers of American soldiers and Marines who would have had to invade the Japanese homeland, as well as the lives of the Japanese who would have had to defend their country to the bitter end.

Simultaneously with the development of the A-bomb, German scientists were working on another fantastic weapon—the rocket. General Walter Dornberger, Wernher von Braun, and others, following the principles laid down by the Russian Ziolkowsky, the American Goddard, and their own Oberth, developed the V-1 missile and the V-2 rocket with which they pelted London and Antwerp.

The V-1, first of Hitler's "vengeance" weapons was a pulse-jet propelled guided missile, and the V-2[4] was a pure rocket. While the A-bomb opened up the Atomic Age, the V-2 introduced the Space Age. The marriage of the two, the combination of the Atomic or Hydrogen weapon and power, and the rocket, was to become the bomber of the future—the strategic weapon of today!

Korea—the first jet war—saw the jet F-80 *Shootingstar* used as a fighter-bomber along with the prop driven *Corsair* and *Mustang* holdovers from World War II. The B-29 *Superfortress*, which had dropped the A-bombs on Japan, also acquitted itself

---

[4] The American Redstone rockets which launched the first U.S. satellite and astronaut were direct lineal descendants of the enemy V-2.

well in a stint as a "retread" heavy bomber in this conflict. But it dropped only conventional gunpowder bombs.

No true jet bombers were used in the Korean War.

It remained for the Vietnam War to see the great 8-jet B-52 bombers in action. These giant swept-wing *Stratofortresses* hit Viet Cong and other enemy targets in Vietnam after flying from Guam—and return. The entire 7000-mile round-trip bombing run was made non-stop with mid-air refueling over the Pacific. Other B-52 bombing runs were made from nearby Thailand.

But this graceful, long-range, strategic bomber was even then considered obsolete and slated for the junk heap in the near future. It was planned that it be replaced, in part, by the FB-111, a bomber version of the controversial TFX or joint Navy—Air Force fighter. But the FB-111 proved not to be effective, and a new manned bomber—the B-1—is on the drawing boards. However, a great deal of reliance will also be placed on the unmanned bomber—the strategic missile.

The bomber of the future then, may be similar to the Air Force *Minuteman* and *Titan* missiles with ranges approaching 9000 miles, and the Navy's *Polaris,* or their descendants.

Sixteen *Polaris* or second-generation *Poseidon* missiles are carried aboard each of the forty-one nuclear submarines designed to launch them. Each of the new *Poseidons* has a range greater than 2500 miles and their submarine "mobile launchers" can cruise, practically indefinitely, beneath the sea. They can roam the seas, virtually undetected, and can come within striking distance of any target in the world.

The portend for the future? Hopefully man will find a peaceful way to settle his differences. But even if the millennium should not come to pass, it is hoped that future generations will ever again hear the cry, "Bombs away!"

BOMBS AWAY!

WORLD WAR I

When the conflict that we now know as the First World War erupted following the assassination of the heir to the throne of Austria the principal belligerent powers had few aircraft. And those they had were a rather harmless handful of canvas, wood, and wire "crates." They were certainly not awesome and could hardly be called weapons or tools of war. But then the airplane had only been invented a mere ten years before, in the Wright brothers' bicycle shop in Dayton, Ohio.

In that short span of time the airplane had advanced very little. Four years of war, however, probably accelerated its growth tenfold and gave birth to the concept of strategic airpower.

An old proverb states that "It's an ill wind that blows no good." Certainly there is no compensating for the countless lives lost and the wanton destruction, but thousands of young men learned to fly and many thousands more learned to build and repair aircraft engines. This was repeated in all of the warring nations giving impetus to a newly budding aviation and air transport industry.

Even before the invention and development of the airplane, however, there existed another type of flying machine. Developed from the older balloon was the dirigible or zeppelin, named after its inventor, Count Ferdinand von Zeppelin. This aircraft had a rigid metal frame as compared to the balloon, or non-rigid type, which took its shape when inflated. (Hydrogen, which is highly inflammable, was used both in balloons and zeppelins for this purpose because of its buoyant properties. Helium, which is also lighter than air and had a far lesser propensity to ignite, came singularly from the United States and during the war was obviously denied to Germany. The zeppelin resembled a giant cigar, with its control cabin on the bottom, forward of center, and its reciprocating engine-driven propellers to the rear. Unlike the airplane it did not have wings but did have a rudder and control surfaces, aft.

These giant behemoths were used almost exclusively by the Germans in the early part of the war. They had a fairly long range and were able to strike at England, a feat beyond the capability of winged aircraft, at that time. But their very size and relatively slower speed made them prey to the smaller winged aircraft. Their vulnerability was somewhat offset by their ability to drop ballast, gain altitude rapidly, and soar beyond the reach of the attacking "gnats." Goading the airships to seek a higher altitude, however, was also an effective offensive fighter aircraft tactic because in attaining the greater height the dirigibles lost too much of their buoyant gas forcing them to lose control and make crash landings. Also, in order to drop their bombs, unlike today's B-52s which can soar 40,000 feet over a target and accurately deliver its weapons, the "zepps" actually had to see their targets. This, of course, took them into the range of heavier-than-air craft. Not many airships were brought down by airplanes (but actually, there weren't a lot of dirigibles, either). Included in this section is the actual official report of Flight Sub-Lieutenant R. A. J. Warneford of the British Royal Naval Air Service who, while flying over Belgium, was able to maneuver his French Morane above a zeppelin and drop his bombs on it. He successfully crashed the monster and was awarded the Victoria Cross, his nation's highest decoration for valor.

The zeppelin, which was also vulnerable to storms, was augmented and replaced by great Gotha, Friedrichshafen, and

R-planes which took their turns at bombing London. The Allies too, built giant Handley-Page, Vickers Vimy, and Caproni bombers to strike at the heartland of the enemy.

In addition to the giants built exclusively for bombing missions, practically all of the winged aircraft types of the First World War—whether single-seater scout or 2-seater observation plane—were rigged at one time or another to carry bombs, even from the earliest attempts of the pilot actually aiming and dropping the bomb by hand over the side of the cockpit.

It is also interesting to note that a number of that war's greatest scout or fighter pilots began their combat flying careers in bomber aircraft. The famous "Red Baron" (Rittmeister Manfred Frh. von Richthofen) the highest scoring ace of the First World War with eighty victories, and Capitaine René Fonck, the Allied "Ace of Aces" (seventy-five victories) both flew missions as bomber pilots. They describe some of their experiences in the pages that follow.

World War I also sired the concept of strategic bombing as envisioned by the RAF's chief, General Sir Hugh "Boom" Trenchard, and the American, General Billy Mitchell. This concept was to play an important role in the Spanish Civil War and an even more decisive one in the Second World War that were to follow.

ZEPPELIN

[1]ERNST A. LEHMANN, *HAUPTMANN* (CAPTAIN)
IMPERIAL GERMAN ARMY

On March 17, 1915, the weather improved, and the radio repeated, "Attack on London." When I arrived at the hangar to give the order to "Ready ship," I found my men at work. My officers reported; the chief engineer tested the engines; the helmsmen checked the rudder controls and elevators; the gas valves and water ballast bags were in order; and the sailmaker used a paintbrush to retouch the camouflaging of the cover. Hydrogen hissed through the inflation tubes, the gasoline tanks were filled, and the capless bombs were hung in the release mechanism.

As soon as the airship was reported clear, I took my place in the control car while the Watch Officer remained outside to direct the launching. The sandbags, which weight down the ship, were removed, and it rose from the wooden blocks on which the bumper bags rested. The ground crew grasped the handling lines, and at the command "Airship march" they drew it out of the hangar. The Watch Officer was the last to swing aboard, and the man who substituted for him, or rather for his weight, jumped out. The ship was set against the wind and after releasing water ballast was "weighed off." Then with thundering motors it climbed up in wide curves to gain altitude and took course over Ostende to the North Sea.

[1] In 1936 Lehmann commanded the LZ-129, the zeppelin *Hindenburg*.

The air was clear and calm and we searched in vain for a cloud behind which we could slip through the English coastal defense. Under us, on the shimmering sea, cruised enemy patrol boats; I prudently ordered the lights out. The airship became a ghostly apparition. In the control car, the only light was on the dial of the machine telegraph. The two helmsmen stood like phantoms beside the wheel. In his narrow cubicle the radio operator sat with his headset over his ears, listening to the confusion of signals and voices whispering in the infinity of space. Under our keel the end-weight of the antenna followed the airship like the spawn of a mother fish. The cold penetrated the control car through the floor and open windows. Despite two suits of underwear, and leather jackets and helmets, we were cold. The thermos bottle was passed around, and the hot coffee stimulated us.

To pass the time while waiting, von Gemmingen and I made an inspection tour. The Watch Officer and Navigation Officer remained in the control car with the helmsmen. We climbed the smooth aluminum ladder leading to the walkway inside the ship. The head-winds blew icily between the car and the body of the ship, pressing me to the ladder, and my gloved hands involuntarily clutched tighter around the rungs. It sometimes happened that a man was overcome by vertigo and slid off, falling 8500 feet into the North Sea.

Even the walkway which extended through the entire ship was no promenade. In the darkness we made our way not so much with the aid of the self-illumined plaques marking the route as by habit and instinct. On the narrow catwalk between the rigging and the tanks, we balanced ourselves as skillfully as if we were walking in broad daylight down a wide street. Like the rest, I was wearing fur-lined shoes; and this thick footwear was not solely a protection from the cold. The hobnailed army boot might have damaged the ship's metal frame, and shoes with rubber or straw soles were therefore regulation.

Near the gas-cells, which threw shadows along the walkway like giant mushrooms in a prehistoric landscape, I heard a noise. In the light of my pocket-torch I saw the sailmaker climbing about with monkey-like dexterity. In his buttonless overalls (so that he couldn't get caught on anything) he braced himself between two gas-cells like a mountain-climber in a rock chimney. He was searching for a leak in the cover. Brush and cellon pot (fabric glue) were below him, close at hand if a bullet hole in the fabric had to be temporarily repaired. The sailmaker's duties involved great responsibility and were in themselves not without danger. Under certain circumstances he could be rendered unconscious by escaping gas almost before he knew it. Consequently, he always had an assistant or a comrade to attend him during his work.

On bombing raids I had no superfluous men aboard, and there was no such thing as relief after short watches, as in peace-time service. Thus the hammocks in the crew's quarters, which were eked out between the girders, were empty now. There was only a man relieving himself of his inner feelings on the throne-seat in the background. He jumped up in fright when he recognized me; but I smilingly motioned him back. The non-com who was the cook on board, reported in the darkness; I ordered him to give all hands a plate of soup from the aluminum pot on the fireless cooker—they could use something hot as long as the enemy was not making it hot for us. We didn't carry much in the way of provisions for they would have been superfluous—either we returned in twenty hours or we did not return at all. Our food was limited to bread, butter, ham, bacon, a few eggs, some preserves, a few bars of chocolate, and tea and coffee; we permitted ourselves a swallow of cognac only when we were back on land after a fulfilled mission.

Amidships, the narrow defile of the walkway widened out. Perpendicularly below me, the sea looked like lead. In the pale glimmer coming through the hatchway, I saw the bombs hanging in the release mechanism like rows of pears; besides explosive bombs weighing from 125 to 650 pounds, there were phosphorus bombs for igniting fires in the bombarded objectives. The safety catches were not yet off, but my Bombing Officer was already lying on his stomach, staring impatiently through the open trap-door. He was a fine fellow and in peace-time wouldn't have hurt a fly, but now he was eager to spill his murderous load overboard. We were at war, and war knows only severity toward the enemy, who repays in the same coin.

While Gemmingen discussed with the Bombing Officer the cooperation between him and the control car, I continued the inspection and descended to the aft engine car, which swayed under the airship like a celestial satellite. The car was enclosed and so crowded by the two 210-horsepower Maybach motors that the two mechanics could scarcely turn around. The noise of the motors drowned out every word, and the Chief Machinist simply raised his hand, which meant that everything was O.K. The air in this nutshell was saturated with gasoline fumes and exhaust gases. I almost choked, until I opened the outlet and let the icy air stream in. To exist for hours in this roaring devil's cauldron, where glowing heat and biting cold alternated, required a stone constitution and iron nerves. Yet it was as nothing compared to the demands made upon the mechanics when, during a battle with the enemy or the elements, the lives of the entire crew depended upon the repairing in mid-air of damages to the motor or propeller.

It is self-evident that in the narrow community of the airship, where all our fates were bound together, I was intimately acquainted with my men even beyond the line of duty. The commander on board is not solely a superior officer, he is also comrade, friend, father, doctor and spiritual adviser all in one. Thus, I was familiar with the personal lives of my crew, and knew that one had a wife and child at home, another had married young, and a third was the only son and sole support of aged

parents. Emotional ties bound each one of them to life. No one
wanted to die—all wanted to return after the war. Yet this longing for home did not make them cowardly or fearful in time of
danger, but strengthened them ten-fold in their determination to
repel the overwhelming enemy forces.

Proud of being permitted to lead such gallant men into the
enemy's territory, I strolled through the marvelous structure that
was our weapon and our home. In the darkness behind me, the
stern, with its control and rudder fins, merged with the delicate
filigree of girders. I passed the shaftway which led between two
gas-cells to the back of the airship, fifty feet up. There, on the
platform beside his machine-gun, hunched up in the winds
created by the speed of the ship, the gunner acted as look-out
and reported through the speaking-tube the instant he sighted
an enemy flier. He was forbidden to shoot until he had received
the order to do so. For when the ship climbed, gas escaped upward, and there was danger that a volley of gun-fire might
ignite the mixture of gas and air. Consequently, there could be
shooting on the platform only when the ship was not releasing
gas.

It was eleven o'clock when I returned to the control car. The
ZXII had been cruising long enough, and now I set a direct
course for England. The sharp coastline, with surf foaming
against it, rose out of the dip of the horizon. And suddenly we
had a queer feeling, as if our nerves were tightening in an almost
joyous anticipation. Would we succeed in breaking through the
chain of coastal batteries and remaining unobserved or at least
undamaged? Strange that we could see so little of the mainland;
it couldn't possibly have been that dark. The mystery was solved
when we came closer, for suddenly we were in a thick fog. The
island was protecting itself from the flying invaders as it had
protected itself from the invasions of enemy seamen centuries
ago.

I brought the heavily laden ship as high as she would go. But at 10,000 feet the fog was just as thick. We cruised in all directions, constantly hoping to find the Thames, since the clouds are generally thinner over rivers. Finally I brought the ship down almost to the earth—in vain; the great metropolis was simply not to be found. We did arouse the furious fire of an anti-aircraft battery, which we were unable to find either. We had to owe it our reply.

In order not to waste the entire night in fruitless searching, we turned and steered for Calais. Much to our surprise, the weather conditions there were actually ideal for the testing of our observation basket under fire. The clouds were 4000 feet high, and the air beneath them was clear as crystal. We could see the lights of Calais from miles away, and we prepared to attack. Gemmingen and I had a friendly quarrel because both of us wanted to get into the observation basket. Then Gemmingen pointed out that he was assigned to the airship as General Staff Officer and Observer, whereas I, the commander, was obliged to remain in the control car. I had to admit that he was right.

Before we reached Calais, we throttled the motors so that they made the least possible noise while still permitting us to maneuver. The ship dove into the clouds, and Gemmingen was lowered 2500 feet in the observation car. In the infinity of space he was suspended like a disembodied ghost. But as events were to prove, he was a dangerous ghost. When we arrived over the city, the observer hung 2500 feet above it and had a clear view, whereas his tiny gondola was invisible from below. The garrison of the fort heard the sound of our motors, and all the light artillery began firing in the direction from which the noise seemed to come. But only once did a salvo come close enough for us to hear the crash of the exploding shells. When we leaned out of the car, we saw nothing but darkness and fog, but Gemmingen directed us by telephone and set the course by compass. Following his instructions, we circled over the fort for forty-five minutes, dropping small bombs here and larger ones there on the railroad station, the warehouses, the munitions dumps and other buildings. From time to time we noticed large oval spots on the clouds; they were the searchlights gleaming as through an outspread tablecloth.

Later we learned that a panic broke out in Calais not only as a result of the air attack, but because the airship remained invisible. There was a great deal of theorizing as to how we had succeeded in concealing ourselves. They suspected a system of mirrors and colors, although science had already proven that to be impossible. At any rate, the authorities arrested a few innocent inhabitants who had been outside the city limits with their bicycles on that night. They were accused of having signalled us with their bicycle lamps.

Back from our raid, I had brought the ZXII down to 400 feet and was weighing off; that is, I had stopped the motors in order to leave the ship to its own buoyancy. Our forward motion had ceased, the elevator helmsman reported that we were descending slowly, and I was just about to start the motors again when I suddenly saw a great black smokestack looming against the sky. The weather had changed, the barometer had fallen more than ten millimeters in less than twelve hours, and the altitude gauge had indicated 325 feet too many. Before we could drop ballast, the ship touched ground. It fell on a railroad track between two factories in the vicinity of our landing-field. The forward gondola came down on a foot-bridge and the rear portion of the ship squatted on the rails. Part of the steering apparatus was torn off by a telegraph pole. I jumped out, inspected the damage and sent out a man to stop all trains. After we had moored the ZXII to a number of telegraph poles, we waited for daylight and then dragged the limping giant back into its hangar, where it was hospitalized for the next fourteen days.

Apparently, we were due for a streak of bad luck during this time, for no sooner was my ship in order again than it suffered a second accident. Once more we had started for a raid on London when we struck heavy rains at night over the North Sea. The rain streamed from the hull and encumbered the ship to such an extent that the execution of our plan was out of the question. In order not to bring our bombs back home again, I took course for Dunkirk and emptied one and a half tons of explosives over the fort, which in turn plastered the air with shrapnel. Suddenly, the ship quivered, there was a crash, and immediately thereafter the crew in the aft motor gondola telephoned that the starboard propeller had disappeared. A large tear in the outer cover and a smaller one in the under side of a gas-cell betrayed the course of the propeller which had evidently been struck by a splinter. We made for home, somewhat downcast, because we had once again failed to reach our real goal.

But some of my comrades had more luck with their raid on Paris than we had with ours against London. On March 20, 1915, the commanders of the army airships ZX, LZ35, and SL2 received orders to attack the French capital on the following night. By blinking their code names, German searchlights at Douai, Cambrai, Noyon and other places served as directional beacons. The wooden SL2, built by Professor Schütte at the Lanz works, was struck on the outward journey over the trenches and therefore dropped its bombs over the French Headquarters at Compiègne and returned to its hangar. The other two airships continued their raid on the metropolis.

Paris had been warned. Its searchlights played in all directions, and a battery to the south fired furiously at a cloud which, in the gleam of the searchlight, they mistook for an airship. For reasons best known to themselves, the French left their capital brightly illuminated, in sharp contrast to London, which always lay in darkness. My comrades could clearly see the fire from the muzzles of the heavy guns in the forts. Most of their shells fell back into the city again, and some of them struck the government quarter, where they caused considerable damage. Even the "Archie" was a failure, its shells bursting far beneath the German airships. As Commander Horn of the ZX told me, he reached the French capital fighting strong head-winds and, at an altitude of only 8000 feet, cruised around for half an hour in order to drop his bombs carefully and accurately. Even the Reuter newspaper agency was obliged to acknowledge the German success, and reported that a large munitions factory had been hit. "Half of the factory operating at the time was blown to bits. The rest of it looked as if it had been struck by a cyclone. An enormous hole in the earth was filled with beams, girders and stone débris." A large power house was destroyed in the same manner.

The LZ35 likewise reached Paris, bombarded it and, upon leaving the city, was followed by motorized units of anti-aircraft guns and searchlights. Commander Masius shook off the pursuers by altering his course over the forests north of Paris. When the airship crossed the frontier it was again fired upon, but despite hundreds of holes in its outer cover, returned home safely.

The ZX was less fortunate on its homeward journey. "Dawn broke just as we were passing the front near Noyon," Captain Horn relates. "The French were waiting for us. Although we flew as high as we could, nevertheless, at an altitude of 10,000 feet, the ZX was struck by two full salvos from a battery. Shells and shrapnel burst around us, and their splinters tore through two or three cells simultaneously. A whole shell went through the ship, and two shrapnel shells missed the control car by inches.

"We escaped behind our own lines by speeding away. German planes convoyed us in case enemy fliers appeared, but the latter didn't even take off, not wanting to risk getting into the hail of shells. The Chief Engineer, who made the rounds with two mechanics, reported that no less than five cells were rapidly losing gas, and the elevator helmsman supplemented this news with the information that the ZX was losing more than five feet per second. I brought the ship down to 4000 feet in order that the buoyant gas would be forced upward, where the cells were not so full of holes. We lightened the ship by throwing machine-

guns, gasoline tanks, oil reserve tins, tools and equipment overboard. Our coats and shoes followed. And when nothing else
seemed to help, we resigned ourselves to the inevitable and
brought the leaking ship to an emergency landing in a field near
St. Quentin, without injury to the crew."

Despite his misfortune, I envied Captain Horn, for he had
been able to carry out his mission. On my third foray against
England I got only as far as Harwich, where I emptied my load of
explosives. Two days later the LZ38 was over London, thus being
the first airship to bombard the capital of the British Empire.

BOMBING THE BOMBER—
DOWNING THE FIRST ZEPPELIN
(*An Official Report*)

R. A. J. WARNEFORD, FLIGHT SUB-LIEUTENANT

RNAS

No. 1 Naval Aeroplane Squadron,
7th June, 1915.

Wing Commander Longmore.

Sir,

I have the honour to report as follows:

I left Furnes at 1:0 a.m. on June the 7th on Morane No. 3253 under orders to proceed to look for Zeppelins and attack the Berchem St. Agathe Airship Shed with six 20 lb. bombs.

On arriving at Dixmude at 1:5 a.m. I observed a Zeppelin apparently over Ostend and proceeded in chase of the same.

I arrived at close quarters a few miles past Bruges at 1:50 a.m. and the Airship opened heavy maxim fire, so I retreated to gain height and the Airship turned and followed me.

At 2:15 a.m. he seemed to stop firing and at 2:25 a.m. I came behind, but well above the Zeppelin; height then 11,000 feet, and switched off my engine to descend on top of him.

When close above him, at 7,000 feet I dropped my bombs, and, whilst releasing the last, there was an explosion which lifted my machine and turned it over. The aeroplane was out of control for a short period, but went into a nose dive, and the control was regained.

I then saw that the Zeppelin was on the ground in flames and also that there were pieces of something burning in the air all the way down.

The joint on my petrol pipe and pump from the back tank was broken, and at about 2:40 a.m. I was forced to land and repair my pump.

I landed at the back of a forest close to a farmhouse; the district is unknown on account of the fog and the continuous changing of course.

I made preparations to set the machine on fire but apparently was not observed, so was enabled to effect a repair, and continued at 3:15 a.m. in a southwesterly direction after considerable difficulty in starting my engine single-handed.

I tried several times to find my whereabouts by descending through the clouds, but was unable to do so. So eventually I landed and found out that it was at Cape Gris Nez, and took in some petrol. When the weather cleared I was able to proceed and arrived at the aerodrome about 10:30 a.m.

As far as could be seen the colour of the airship was green on top and yellow below and there was no machine or gun platform on top.

I have the honour to be, Sir,
Your obedient servant,
(Sgd.) R. A. J. Warneford,
Flt. Sub-Lieutenant.

BOMBING THE RUSSIANS

[1] MANFRED VON RICHTHOFEN, *RITTMEISTER*
IMPERIAL GERMAN AIR SERVICE

In June we were suddenly ordered to move out. We did not know where we were going, but we had a good idea. When our commander finally announced that we were going to Russia, we were not overly amazed. We traveled through the whole of Germany on a train consisting of dining and sleeping cars until we finally came to Kovel. There we stayed in our railway cars. Living in trains has many advantages, of course; one is continually ready to travel on, and one always has the same quarters. But a sleeping car is the most dreadful thing there is in the heat of the Russian summer. For that reason I agreed to go with two good friends, Gerstenberg and Scheele, into a nearby forest at Kovel, where we erected a tent and lived like gypsies. That was a lovely time.

In Russia our battle squadron dropped many bombs. We busied ourselves with angering the Russians and dropped our "eggs" on their finest railway installations. On one of these days our whole squadron set out to bomb a very important train station called Manjewicze, about thirty kilometers behind the Front. The Russians were planning an attack, so this station was filled with trains standing side by side. A whole stretch of track was

[1] The "Red Baron."

covered with engines and cars. From the air one could see troop trains at every switch. It was really a worthwhile target.

There are many things to be enthusiastic about in flying, and for a while I was much interested in bombing. It gave me a sinister pleasure to plaster our "friends"[2] down below. I often went out twice a day on such flights. This day Manjewicze was the target. Each squadron made preparations to set out against the Russians.

The machines stood ready and each pilot tested his engine, for it is a painful thing to be forced to land on the wrong side of the Front, especially in Russia. The Russians are terrible to captured fliers. If they catch one they will certainly kill him. That is the one danger in Russia, for they have no fliers of their own, or as good as none at all. If a Russian flier appeared, he was sure to have bad luck and be shot down by his own men. The anti-aircraft guns in Russia are often quite good, but their number is not sufficient. Compared to the Western Front, in any case, flying on the Eastern Front is like a holiday.

The machines rolled with difficulty to the starting line. They were filled to capacity with bombs. Many times I hauled one-hundred-fifty-kilogram bombs with a normal C-type airplane. I have even had with me heavy observers, who had apparently not suffered from the meat shortage, as well as two machine guns, although I never got to try them out in Russia. It is a shame that there is not a Russian in my collection of victories. His cockade would look very picturesque on the wall. To get back to the main point, a flight with a heavily laden, clumsy machine is not easy, especially in the afternoon heat. On the take-off run, the planes sway very uncomfortably. They do not falter, of course; the one-hundred-fifty "horses" see to that. But it is not a pleasant feeling to have so much explosive material and gasoline along. At last one is in a calm sea of air, and gradually comes to

[2] Von Richthofen referred to the enemy in this jovial way.

enjoy the bombing flight. It is beautiful to fly straight ahead, with a definite target and firm orders. After a bombing flight one has the feeling he has accomplished something, whereas many times on a pursuit flight, when one has shot down nothing, you reproach yourself with the feeling that you could have done better. I liked dropping bombs. Gradually my observer had gotten the knack of flying perpendicular to the target, and, with the help of an aiming telescope, he waited for the right moment to lay his eggs.

The flight to Manjewicze was beautiful. I made it often. We flew over gigantic complexes of forests in which elk and lynx certainly must roam. To be sure, the villages looked as if only foxes could live in them. The only large village in the whole area was Manjewicze. Around the village countless tents were pitched, and by the train station were innumerable huts. We could not make out the sign of the Red Cross. A squadron had been there before us. One could determine this solely by the smoking houses and huts. They had not done badly. The one exit of the train station was obviously blocked by a lucky hit. The locomotive was still steaming. The engineer was probably hid in a dugout somewhere. On the other side of the town a locomotive was coming out at three-quarter speed. Of course, I could not resist to temptation to attack. We flew toward the engine and dropped a bomb a hundred meters in front of it. The desired result was obtained: The locomotive had stopped and could not move. We turned and neatly dropped bomb after bomb, finely aimed through the telescope sight, on the train station. We had plenty of time and no one bothered us. An enemy airfield was in the vicinity, but its pilots were not to be seen. Antiaircraft shells burst sporadically but in a different direction than where we were flying. We saved a bomb for use on the flight home. Then we saw an enemy flier as he started from his field. Did he plan to attack us? I don't think so. More than likely he sought security in the air, for during a bombing flight over an airfield the air is certainly the most comfortable place to be to avoid personal danger.

We took a roundabout way home and looked for troop encampments. It was special fun to harass the gentlemen below with our machine guns. Such half-civilized tribes as the Asiatics are more afraid of such things than the refined Englishmen. It is especially interesting to shoot at enemy cavalry. It causes an enormous commotion among the men. They rush off to all points of the compass. I would not like to be the commander of a Cossack squadron shot up by fliers with machine guns.

Soon we saw our lines again. Now it was time to get rid of our last bomb. We decided to present a bomb to a captive balloon, the only captive balloon the Russians had. We descended smoothly to a few hundred meters from the balloon. They had begun to reel it in with great haste, but as the bomb was falling, the reeling stopped. I do not believe I hit it but, rather, that the Russians in their panic had left their officer in the lurch up in the basket and had all run away.

We finally reached our own lines and, after arriving back home, were somewhat surprised to find that one of the wings showed a hit.

Another time we were in the same area preparing to attack the Russian troops about to cross the Stokhod River. We approached the dangerous place laden with bombs and plenty of ammunition for the machine guns. On arriving, we saw to our great astonishment that the enemy cavalry was already crossing the Stokhod. One single bridge served as the crossing point. It was clear that if this was hit, it would hurt the enemy advance tremendously. There was a thick mass of troops trundling over the narrow footbridge. We went down to the lowest possible altitude and observed that the enemy cavalry was crossing with great speed. The first bomb burst not far from them; the second and third followed directly after it. There was immediate confusion and disorder below. The bridge itself had not been hit; nevertheless, traffic was completely stopped and everything that had legs used them, taking off in all directions. That was quite a successful attack, for it cost only three bombs; besides, another squadron was coming behind us. So we could proceed to other targets. My observer fired the machine gun continually at the chaps down below, and it was wild fun. How successful we were, I cannot say, of course. The Russians have not told me either. But I imagine that it was our plane alone that had repelled the Russian attack.

THE BOCHE LOST NOTHING

RENÉ FONCK, *CAPITAINE*

FRENCH *Armée de l'Air*

I soon understood that aerial warfare is not engaged in only by fliers in search of a hypothetical adversary. I learned that, in addition to trench observations and artillery range finding, there was another task that I did not like, but which I had to carry out, nevertheless.

Our enemies preferred to drop their bombs at night on our big, wide-open urban centers, where it was easy for them to massacre the harmless population. I, myself, took part in some bombardment operations. It was a kind of fight to the finish in which, in order to more accurately drop my bombs on a military objective, I usually flew very low over the ground, and the air was filled with projectiles whose concentrated trajectories aimed in my direction enveloped me like dangerous currents.

I knew the risks I ran with these tactics, but what remorse there would have been for me if one of my bombs, dropped blindly, had killed even a single one of our Alsatian brethren.

My first mission against Fribourg-en-Brisgau was interrupted by the bad weather at this time. That day the sky was covered with clouds, and it augured well for the success of my undertaking; but suddenly, over Alsatian territory, the wind freshened. In the unleashed storm my plane was tossed about like a leaf. I had to turn back. I would have been able to lighten my load by dropping my bombs at random, but I never liked to drop my "calling cards" this way on defenseless noncombatants.

The Boches, moreover, lost nothing by waiting. On August 1, I flew above the city at an altitude of 3000 meters. It was a retaliatory operation, and I tried to do as much damage as possible. Fires broke out all over, and I pictured in my mind's eye the bursting of the shells and the shouts and curses of the enemy coming up at me.

A short time later the Squadron was moved. I did not leave my native Lorraine soil and Alsace without a little heartache. As I looked down upon it from my plane, like the Hebrews contemplating the Promised Land in biblical times, I thought that I would perhaps never again see its fields of hops; its dark forests of fir trees; its summits, all of whose peaks I now knew so well; and the hamlets and cities over which I had so often flown. That thought saddened me. I still was not accustomed to these perpetual moves and displacements which, since that time, have become familiar to me.

ATTACKING THE GOTHA BOMBER

CHARLES J. BIDDLE, MAJOR

U. S. AIR SERVICE, AND FRENCH *Armée de l'Air*

Bergues, November 12th.

I am in a particularly bad humor this morning, so do not be surprised if it is to a certain extent reflected in this letter. To-day is the most beautiful one that could be desired—better than any we have had for two weeks, and just what I have been waiting for. Three-quarters of an hour ago I was all dressed sitting in my machine, about to start out, when a mechanic discovered a leak in a gasoline tank, which means that it must be changed and that the machine will not be ready until the morning, so there goes another day to pot.

A few days ago I started out on a patrol with two lieutenants and on our way to the lines we saw a number of miles to one side of us a great many of our own anti-aircraft shells bursting. We went over to investigate and what did we run into but ten Hun Gothas and a couple of chasse machines flying over them for protection. The lieutenant who was leading our patrol says he shot at a couple of them, but I could not see him do it, as I was a little behind. The cover of my radiator had cracked and the water, mixed with glycerine to keep it from freezing, had sprayed out, covering my telescope sights, the windshield and my glasses, so that I could not see well. I had gotten a little behind the others in trying to clean things up with my handkerchief. At all events, the lieutenant's machine gun went back on him, and he started back with the other lieutenant after him; seeing them both go, I thought they must be after a Hun that I had not seen, so I started to follow them, but when I could see no signs of a Boche in that direction, I turned back.

A Gotha machine, you know, is the enormous Hun machine that they use for their night bombing in the raids on England. They are almost as big as the Caproni[1] which they have been recently demonstrating in the U.S. They have two motors and as a rule carry three or four men. They are unusually well armed with movable machine guns, fore and aft, and the usual zone of safety under the tail is removed by means of a tunnel in the fuselage, which enables them to shoot under their tails. It therefore behooves you to "mind your eye" when you attack and to make sure you either get him or put his rear gunners out of business at least, for although you may be able to approach without giving him much of a shot it is impossible not to give him a shot in getting away.

These Gothas were the first that I had ever had a real look at for they are rarely seen by day; once or twice I have seen them in the distance over the lines. At all events, when I turned back, I spotted one Gotha off a little to one side of the squadron and somewhat over my head. As they were only about 9000 feet up climbing was easy and I started after him. They saw what I was up to however and the Hun drew in alongside of his companion for protection. Under these circumstances, it is foolishness to attack by yourself, for you will have at least two or three machine gunners shooting at you with their movable guns and no way of protecting yourself when you want to shoot, for then you

---

[1] An Italian bomber. Some of these were flown by Americans under the command of Major Fiorello H. La Guardia, Congressman and later Mayor of New York City.

have to hold your machine steady. You will just get riddled with practically no chance of success to compensate for it. I accordingly looked for better game and saw another Gotha behind the squadron all by himself and below me. I flew around over him for a minute to see if the coast was clear and then dove down behind his tail. When I started after him he left the others and put for home as fast as he could go. All these Huns were well within our lines, and this was just what I wanted.

About this time I looked around to see if any other Huns were coming on my tail and there were two chasse machines just behind me in the sun. This gave me a jolt for with my glasses all fogged up it took me several seconds to make sure that they were English and not Huns. All the time the "Archie" shells were bursting in every direction, for in this sector at least, they often do not stop shooting just because one of their own machines goes after a Hun. As they generally shoot behind they come closer to you than to the Huns, and it always makes me sore. They did the same trick the day before when I was trying to sneak up under a Hun's tail. That time our guns were shooting at him and their guns shooting at me, so that between the two there was quite a bit of a bombardment. It seems to me that this is bad policy for it is comparatively rare that they hit a machine with the "Archies" and why bother a man who really has a good chance of accomplishing something.

To come back to the Gotha, I got within 150 yards of him just behind his tail, so that he never fired a shot, but when I tried to aim everything was so gummed up I could not see the sights and the Gotha was nothing but a blur. Now as I have explained, these machines are regular battle ships of the air, and to get them you have got to fairly riddle them for they frequently carry two pilots in case one is killed. I had to give this one up without firing a shot and I have been wondering ever since whether I did what I should have. My mistake was, in not going in quicker, and if I had then had time to get right up close to him before he got into his own lines, I could probably have seen well enough to shoot anyhow. On the only other time that I have seen Gothas by day they have been escorted by a whole flock of fighting planes. Being by myself on this occasion and not able to see clearly I don't mind saying those Huns had me nervous. But it was such a glorious chance and would have been such a triumph if I could have bagged him, that it was worth taking much bigger risks than one would usually take. The only Frenchman I ever heard of who got one was Captain Guynemer. I shall probably not have such a chance in six months, but if I do I shall certainly try to make better use of it. I am sort of ashamed of myself for not sticking to that Hun and perhaps accomplishing something.

AN AMERICAN FIGHTS FOR FRANCE

NORMAN PRINCE, ADJUTANT

FRENCH *Armée de l'Air* (LAFAYETTE ESCADRILLE)

I sailed for Europe in the latter part of the year 1914 in order to do what I could to help the cause which I believed, and still believe, to be that of my own country, as well as that of the Allied Nations.

Reaching France I offered my services to that Government as an aviator. They were promptly accepted and I contracted an engagement to serve France until she had achieved victory. Seven other Americans enlisted with me at the same time as aviators, and we proceeded from our dépôt, where we were clothed, to the flying school at Pau in the south of France in the Pyrenees, where conditions for flying are exceptionally good, there being hardly any wind in that region. The school at Pau at the time was the largest flying school in the world. While we were there about three hundred young men were in training, and at last accounts, there were over five hundred pupils practicing in aviation, using at least two hundred modern machines. We remained there a month. As a rule it takes about forty-eight days to turn out a military aviator, qualified and fitted to obtain the civil and military licenses required. In order to obtain the latter it is necessary to make a successful flight of about four hundred miles across country. I had already acquired a fair knowledge of the science of aviation at home and had made numerous flights in different machines, so that the training at Pau came comparatively easy to me, but it was necessary for me to become thoroughly acquainted with all the rules governing the French military aviation service, as well as to make myself familiar with the French machines in order to meet the full requirements of the training. When we were through this school we received our *brevets militaires* and we had ridden every kind of air craft used in the French Army.

All licensed aviators, as it turned out, are sent to the reserve station for aviators near Paris. In our case, after spending a week or two there, we were found fit for more active service, and we were suddenly sent to the front in the north of France, arriving there in time for the May attacks near Arras and Artois. Our perilous experiences in aerial warfare were soon to begin. After one reconnoitering tour we were sent out to bombard munition dépôts, railway centers, and aviation fields in the rear of the enemy's lines, from ten to forty kilometres distant from our base. I have a vivid remembrance of my first bombarding expedition. The action took place at a point not far within the enemy's lines. I was sent with two or three members of my squadron to bombard a station where ammunition was being unloaded. It takes about forty minutes for a machine heavily loaded with bombs to get to a sufficient height to cross the lines. The minimum height at which we crossed was about seven thousand feet. I saw my comrades cross ahead of me and noted they were being heavily shelled by the enemy. Accordingly, I decided to go a little higher before crossing. When I found I had only sufficient gasoline left to make my bombardment and return to my base, I started over. I was soon to experience what I may call my baptism of fire. The impression made upon me by the terrible racket and the spectacle of shells aimed at me and exploding near by made me shiver for a moment. Though I was confident and unafraid, my limbs began to tremble. Still I kept straight on my course. I would not have changed it for the world. My legs were so wobbly from nervous excitement that I tried to hide them from my observer, who was an old hand at the game. I confess to a feeling of relief when I reached the point where our bombs were to be thrown over. Having discharged this duty I was glad to return to my starting-point with the motor running at slow speed, and knowing that I was soon to be out of range of the enemy's deadly fire.

In this bombardment my machine was made almost entirely of steel tubing with a 140-horse-power engine, capable of carrying a load of bombs weighing from four to seven hundred pounds. As an arm of defense it carried a machine gun. This is the type of machine that has made most of the long raids on the enemy. I soon became accustomed to the duty I had to perform and to flying with the spectacle of shells bursting all around me, at the same time keeping on the lookout for the 'planes of the enemy. We made seventeen bombardments during the ensuing month of June and we got to be old hands at this kind of warfare. It is never quite agreeable to be shelled up in the air or elsewhere, and those who make the boast of liking it do not tell the exact truth.

To illustrate how well the French military aviation service is organized and supplied with machines, let me tell you of my experience at the front in Lorraine, where one day I had the misfortune to break one of the wings of my machine. Instead of stopping to have it repaired, all I had to do was to turn it into a supply station near by where it was at once dismantled and sent to the rear. I was then promptly supplied with a new machine. A change of aeroplanes by an aviator in action in France is like a cavalryman changing his horse. If there is anything the matter with the animal, even if it is only a corn, a new one is at once forthcoming. There is no suggestion of parsimony or niggardliness in giving out the supplies necessary for efficient fighting.

On another occasion, when we were making a raid on the

railway station at Douai, which was about twenty-five kilometres within the enemy's lines, we started with a squadron of some twenty machines. There happened to be that day a great many German machines out. Somehow or other they knew we were coming. We had four or five brisk engagements with them. Our planes had only machine guns with which to defend themselves, while the Germans used regular fighting machines. This aerial engagement resulted in four of our machines coming back riddled with bullets, my lieutenant being hit in the leg.

I was fortunate enough that day to escape the range of the German flying machines by going farther north and passing through the clouds, though I was shelled from a long distance all the way. I succeeded in dropping my bombs on a railroad station, one of which I saw explode in a bunch of freight cars in the railroad yard. As I was returning within our lines the Englishmen, by mistake, opened a brisk fire on me which necessitated my going up into the clouds again. I proceeded due west until I ran out of gasoline and I then descended in the dark near the headquarters of the English. It was my good fortune to land safely and on my arrival at my post I was brought before the English commander, who asked me to tell my story. Mine being one of the four machines out of twenty that had reached Douai in the raid, I was awarded a citation and given the right to wear a War Cross—my first decoration.

My squadron spent a month in the east and during this time I went farther into the enemy's territory than I had been before. I think the longest distance was when we made the raid on two localities over one hundred kilometres within the enemy's lines in Bocherie, as we called it. During this month General Joffre came to review our four squadrons of bombarding machines. With him came the President of France and the King of the Belgians. These distinguished visitors witnessed the departure of a squadron of some ninety of our machines on a bombarding raid loaded with bombs and flying four abreast. They were highly complimentary in their salutations to us Americans.

During this month in Lorraine I experienced the hardest knock I had received up to that time. One day six German machines, fully equipped, bombarded Nancy and our aviation field. To retaliate, my squadron was sent out to bombard their field on the same afternoon. We started with thirty machines to a designated rendezvous and fifty minutes later, after getting grouped, we proceeded to our ultimate destination. I had a very fast machine, and reached the German flying field without being hit. When about to let go my bombs and while my observer was aiming at the hangars of the Germans my machine was attacked by them—one on the left and two on the right. I shouted to my observer to drop his bombs, which he did, and we immediately straightened out for home. While I was on the bank the Germans opened fire on me with their machine guns which were even more perilous than their shells. My motor stopped a few moments afterwards. It had given out and to make matters worse a fourth German machine came directly at us in front. My observer, who was an excellent shot, let go at him with the result that when last seen this German aeroplane was about four hundred feet below and quite beyond control. The other Germans behind kept bothering us. If they had possessed ordinary courage, they might have got us. Flying without any motive power compelled me to stand my machine on end to keep ahead of them. As we were nearing the French lines these Germans left us, but immediately batteries from another direction opened fire on us. As I was barely moving I made an excellent target. One shell burst near enough to put shrapnel in my machine. It is marvelous how hard we can be hit by shrapnel and have no vital part of our equipment injured. I knew I was now over the French lines, which I must have crossed at a height of about four hundred metres. I finally landed in a field covered with white crosses marking the graves of the French and German soldiers who had fallen the previous September at this point. This was the battle the Kaiser himself came to witness, expecting to spend that night in Nancy.

Thousands fell that day, but the Kaiser did not make his triumphal entry. Looking back on this latter experience of mine I think myself most fortunate in having been able to return to the French lines without a scratch. I got home safely because the German aviators lacked either courage or skill or both. They had me with my engine dead, four against one, and twenty kilometres within their lines.

SAFETY IN NUMBERS

W. A. McCARTHY, LIEUTENANT

U. S. AIR SERVICE

On account of the concentration of archie fire, the American day-bombing squadrons had to cross the German line at from 12,000 to 14,000 feet. Frequently, in squadrons of from ten to twelve planes, five or six planes would be unable to make this altitude and would have to drop out of the formation. But so eager were their pilots and observers to reach their objectives that many times, despite their failure to keep up with their formation, they would go on bombing expeditions by themselves, crossing the Hun lines alone without any protection whatsoever and offering battle to as many attacking German planes as wanted to fight. Some of these lone Americans reached their objectives, dropped their bombs, and got back home safely. Many of them, however, were lost.

As the offensive continued, the performance of the day-bombing planes grew better and better. The planes seemed to improve in quality. Better protection to the gas tanks was afforded by new devices. When strict orders cut out individual bombing, casualties decreased, but even in formations of eight and ten such was the weight of the attack delivered by the German single-seaters that seldom did a plane return to its hangar without being full of holes. Wounds were frequent, and the cloth-

ing of the aviators torn by German machine-gun bullets. One
pilot had his goggles shot away but escaped injury himself.

The Hun attacking squadrons, sent to meet us, had a way of
climbing from the ground between the sun and our formation.
It was difficult to see them, and we seldom did until the Fokker
biplanes were dropping down on our tails and the Fokker triplanes climbing up under us. Those triplanes had great speed
in climbing, and it was a favorite trick of some of their best
flyers to come up under the formation, get behind the leader,
and pump lead into him before the American gunners on either
side could get their guns on him. He would dive out of this
pocket as quickly as he got into it. Because of their speed, these
German single-seaters were hard to hit, and all we usually got
in a fight between six of us and twenty of them was only two
or three.

FIRST AMERICAN FIGHTER-BOMBERS

UNIDENTIFIED OFFICER

U. S. AIR SERVICE

September 16, 1918

I was with the 103d Aero-Pursuit Squadron, the old Lafayette Escadrille, one of the four squadrons forming the Third Pursuit Group, under command of Major William Thaw.

On the 11th of September, 1918, at twenty-one hours, Major Thaw called a meeting of the Squadron Commanders. Captain Rockwell, my C.O., was away at the time, and upon the Major's orders I represented the 103d. Major Huffer of the 93d, Lieutenant Hamilton of the 213th, and Lieutenant Jones of the 28th were the other Squadron Commanders present.

Major Thaw then proceeded to explain to us the details of the American attack scheduled to commence the following morning at five o'clock. It was an unforgettable meeting. The attack was to be under the personal command of General Pershing, extending over a front of some seventy-five kilometers from Verdun to the east of Pont-à-Mousson. American troops and American aviation, aided by French troops and French aviation, were to be under American leadership and direction. It was an inspiring thought.

Major Thaw, who had returned that afternoon from a conference with the Wing Commander, detailed to us the part the Pursuit Aviation and our *groupe* in particular, was to play in the attack. The shooting-up of troop trains, convoys, and the like with our machine guns, the bringing-down of enemy observation balloons and the harassing of towns by dropping bombs, was the main work assigned to us. The dropping of bombs was an entirely new operation for pilots of American pursuit squadrons. We were also expected to bring in reports of all activity observed upon the ground, and when necessary to carry out special reconnaissance missions behind the enemy's lines.

I returned about 10.30 and explained to the fellows the seriousness of the approaching operation and the part each man would be expected to play. Everything conducive to rest, sleep, and well-being was strictly adhered to, that each man might be able to give the best that was in him on the following day. My announcement of the approaching attack caused a great stir. Many of the fellows were new to the Front. I myself felt a thrill and found it difficult to keep still. After bidding them good-night and recommending early retiring I returned to my barracks and advised the two other Flight Commanders (Tobin and Dolan) of what I had learned. I had no difficulty in falling off to sleep for all my inner excitement. Outwardly I tried to give the impression of perfect self-control and calm. I think I succeeded. Just what our particular work was to be on the following day I did not know, because the orders had not come from Wing Headquarters and were not expected until later that night.

When I awakened at six, the guns were hammering faintly away off to the north. The sky was dark and overcast, with rain beating against the roof of the barracks, rain driven by a strong west wind. As I lay in bed wondering about the flying orders and the weather, I could hear the roar of the motors being tested at the hangars. I wondered if the day would prove as bad as the day before when I had made a special reconnaissance trip at low altitude some twelve kilometers back of the German lines, dodging below the clouds at 400 meters.

While I was eating lunch a telephone order came from the Group Operator's office that I was wanted at fourteen hours for a special mission. I presented myself, with curious little thrills agitating my spine; the future looked uncertain and exciting. I received orders to follow the route Mont Sec, Pannes, Beney, Thiaucourt, and return, reporting on all enemy activity on roads and railways. I decided to cross the lines at 1000 meters and then dive, to gain speed. Just before leaving, the clouds broke a little, allowing me to go to 1500 meters. I was thankful for this, as I did not relish the idea of crossing the lines at 400 meters.

As soon as I had passed them I put the nose of my plane down and went to 500 meters, striking first Pannes and then Beney and coming out along the road leading from Thiaucourt to Regiénville. A high wind was blowing from the west. The trenches and roads were practically deserted. Between Pannes and Beney I saw a *camion* train of some twenty-five trucks, and a few cars on the railroad going north from Thiaucourt. Coming out I was shot up a bit by "Archies" and machine guns from the ground. When I landed—rather pleasantly surprised because my work had proved less difficult than I anticipated—I found my propeller had been broken and a hole put in the wing by machine-gun bullets. I had the pleasure of meeting General Patrick, Chief of the Air Service in France, and Mr. Ryan, Chief of Aircraft Production. They, together with General Foulois, asked me several questions about my trip and then allowed me leave to 'phone my report in to Wing Headquarters.

The next morning at two o'clock the Americans started their preliminary bombardment. At five they went over the top and the great attack was on.

At seven o'clock flying orders for the Squadron came in. We were to be on *alerte* all day, commencing at eight o'clock. At the hour designated fifteen pilots were at the Operations tent, their planes on the line ready for anything that might turn up. At 8.40 a call came in for a special reconnaissance mission around Thiaucourt and Lachaussée to observe enemy movements on the ground. Three pilots left immediately, covering the mission at 400 meters altitude. All reported the roads greatly congested, with traffic moving in a northerly direction. One pilot got lost, but found his way out again by means of his compass. At eleven o'clock we were all called out to machine-gun and bomb the road from Pannes to Beney. Fifteen of us started. We discovered the road full of artillery, all pointing to the north, but standing still beneath the trees. I let go with my two guns. The others followed suit. I let go my two bombs on Beney and saw two houses go up in smoke and dust. The two dull booms from the exploding bombs sounded very real. I then returned to the lines and started back for the road once more. I saw American cavalry drawn up in the fields before Pannes, waiting to advance. On the other side of the town the German artillery was retreating. I gave them a long burst and saw the men scatter and break. As I turned away from the road a machine gun had a good chance at me and hit my plane in several places. At that moment my motor went bad, so I came back as rapidly as possible, with a broken tachometer and coughing motor. In the afternoon we went out again on the same sort of work.

Excitement was very great everywhere at the field. At one time three squadrons went off at the same time, sixty planes leaving together. It was a wonderful sight. At another time a formation of fifty Bréguets passed over our field, heading for Saint-Mihiel and intent upon bombing. The clouds were never more than 600 meters high, generally lower. Every half-hour squalls of wind and rain swept down from the west. Yet we kept on making our patrols and accomplishing our work. It was a ripsnorting day! In the afternoon the Americans had captured Mont Sec, the strongest position between Saint-Mihiel and the Moselle River. It was splendid news. By evening the line ran thus: Saint-

Mihiel, Mont Sec, Nonsard, Beney, Jaulny, Pont-à-Mousson. The French were to attack in the region of Dommartin-la-Montagne at ten o'clock to meet the Americans at Vigneulles. No word came from them until the following day.

Friday the 13th was a worse day than the preceding—if such a thing is possible. The clouds were at not more than 400 meters and it was very misty. Again we were on *alerte* for the day. About 9 o'clock word was received that the Germans had evacuated the salient of Saint-Mihiel, making their line Fresnes, Vigneulles, Saint-Benoit, Xammes, Jaulny, Norrey. This was thrilling news. About 9.30 the order came to *mitrailler* and bomb the road between Chambley and Arnaville. My motor was running badly over the field, but I determined to stick it out if possible. Upon reaching Chambley, it was going from bad to worse. I did not dare go close enough to the ground to use my machine guns. I dropped my bombs at a cross-roads filled with troops, then started back for the lines, fear and trembling in my heart on account of my bad motor. The five fellows with me shot up the road and then followed me out. I just did manage to make the field, with a couple more bullets in my wings. The roads were filled with re-treating Germans, wagons, artillery, etc. I could see them distinctly, walking and riding, on my way out.

After lunch we returned to the Operations tent, ready for action. At 5.30 we were ordered to shoot up and bomb the road running south from Mars-la-Tour to les Baraques, reported choked with German artillery. We started in two formations of seven each, I leading the first, Jones leading the second. As we left the field a rainstorm blew up from the west. The day before I had flown in rain so thick it was impossible to see the ground, so the present drenching did not worry me. We went by Lake La Chaussée, then headed for Mars-la-Tour, going as much with the wind as possible. Jones's formation was about a kilometer behind mine, following the same route. The roads around the lake were generally deserted except the few leading into Chambley. By this time a heavy rain had settled in from the west, covering Mars-la-Tour and all the adjacent region. I headed off for Chambley, intending to drop my bombs on the railroad yards and shoot up the roads to the south. We were flying at 500 meters. Suddenly the sharp bursting of shrapnel just behind us drew my attention. As I glanced back I saw Jones's formation gyrating around in a crazy fashion, evidently shooting up troops on the ground—so I thought. At that instant I saw a Spad burst into flames and drop straight down. I continued on dropping my bombs on the yards at Chambley. Directly they were released I looked up to see coming straight toward us above a rainstorm a formation of six Pfalz and one Albatross *biplace*. They had surprised me while I was intent upon the ground. By this time they were shooting at us from the ground with machine guns. I gave a hurried glance above and behind, figuring how best to meet the situation. My motor was running very badly all the while, causing me to feel anything but secure. My first thought was to get into the rainstorm to cut off pursuit. Accordingly I headed for it, the two planes close to me following. It was curious to feel and see these seven Huns just overhead coming for us. I knew we were in for it good and plenty. They seemed very black and imminent with their dark camouflaging and black and white tails. I thought to myself: "Now we are in for it; we are going to get it this time all right." I really didn't see how we could escape. All day I had been thinking some one would get it and asking myself who it would be. Now I wondered who the two were maneuvering around behind me.

I kept "S"-ing, to keep myself from being a steady target. No Boches appeared to be specially near me. Instinctively I kept climbing (the others told me this later) to get into the thick of the clouds and rain. In a few minutes I could discern very little of what was going on behind me. I kept wondering about my motor, whether she would continue or quit dead. I wanted to go back and help those behind, but could not do so with a motor

1) The British Avro 504 K single-seater.

2) Although nicknamed the "Flaming Coffin," the British designed DH-4 was one of the best day bombers of the war.

3) The DH-9A resembled its predecessor. It was manufactured in both the U.S. and Britain and later models were powered by the American Liberty engine.

4) The French built Salmson 2-seater was also used by the American Air Service as a day bomber.

5) An American crew of the 96th Aero Squadron returning from a bombing raid on German positions in a French Bregnet.

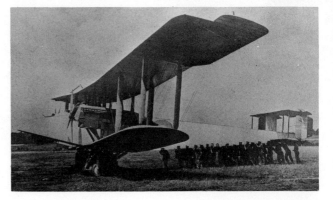

6) The Handley-Page 0/400 heavy night bomber was the largest aircraft built by the British for the war against Germany.

7) The Caproni CA 33 was an Italian bomber. This type was flown by Americans under the command of Major Fiorello H. La Guardia.

8) The U.S. Navy built HS2 seaplane releasing its bombs in a test flight.

9) German Gotha bombers together with Friedrichshafen bombers and giant R planes raided London.

10) Those German Zeppelins were mighty big, but here's one that was brought down.

11) The Kettering Aerial Torpedo, affectionately referred to as the "Bug," was the world's first "guided missile." Developed by Charles Kettering, Elmer Sperry, Orville Wright, and "Hap" Arnold for the U.S. Army Signal Corps in 1917-18, the Bug was demonstrated in actual flight on a number of occasions. However, World War I came to an end before the missile was ready for operational use in combat. This model of it is in the Air Force Museum at Wright-Patterson AFB.

which threatened to stop any second. To go on seemed almost a cowardly course, yet the only reasonable thing to do was to retreat under cover of the rain and clouds.

We were at a tremendous disadvantage, only 500 meters from the ground and surprised by a formation that outnumbered us by at least three planes. Momentarily I expected to be attacked. As I glanced back I could see a few Huns following, taking it out on the end men of my formation. I wondered if they would be able to get away. It was horrible to be running ignominiously in that fashion. But I did not dare get into a tight scrap with my motor on the point of failing altogether.

In a few minutes I saw a Spad dive steeply, zigzagging from left to right and followed closely by three Boches, all firing at the Spad. I expected the latter to land any minute, he appeared to be going so slowly. "The poor devil," I thought. "Another one done for!" I was then about 900 meters high: two other Spads following me and several Boches following us. I looked for Pont-à-Mousson. It seemed miles away. I watched the lone Spad below, skimming the low land that borders the west bank of the Moselle River. Behind him was one Hun, not gaining, but still following. The Boche did not appear to be firing, so I thought the Spad had a chance. We were still eight kilometers from our own lines and I did not dare go down to his aid. It was here that I felt the worst, for neither of the two Spads following me could go to the aid of the poor luckless fellow below—he was by this time jumping the trees in the river-bed—on account of two more Huns joining in the pursuit. Finally the single Boche following the Spad turned back and the Spad made his lines. Then two more Boches left us, leaving only one. He kept coming on. Directly I was within gliding distance of the lines, I turned about sharply to meet this following Hun. Head on I gave him about fifty shots and he went over on his back in a half-turn, going down in a *vrille*. I thought I had him. Then he seemed to right himself and fall away toward his own lines, but one of the other two Spads followed him down close to the ground, driving him into a wood.

At last we got home, three of our number missing. Later that night, however, the fellow who had been chased by the river showed up in a side car and another 'phoned in, leaving only Jones, who had gone down in flames. The one who had had such a narrow escape by the river had forty bullet holes in his fuselage alone, all passing within a foot—and at places less than that—of his body. His propeller was broken in four places by bullets, and a spark-plug had blown out, giving him only one half his power. But he had got the *biplace* in flames and was as tickled as could be, apologizing to me (he was in my flight) because his plane had been hurt so much. Imagine thinking of his plane before himself! Some nerve! We were lucky to get out of that place with the loss of only one. That night the *groupe* had brought down seven Huns.

The next day there was a little less activity, the weather clearing up and the attack stopping before the Hindenburg line, our *groupe,* however, asked for confirmation on four more enemy planes brought down. In the official reports of the First Army, the *groupe* was mentioned three times as often as anybody else. Besides, General Pershing sent a personal congratulation to the Wing for the work the pursuit planes had done in shooting up the ground. *And that was sent to us, because we did that work alone.* Pretty good, eh?

A RAID ON OSTEND

UNIDENTIFIED OFFICER

U. S. AIR SERVICE

August 13, 1918

August 11 proved to be a great day for me; one which I shall not forget for some time. We went to Ostend. I was sighting to drop bombs when I saw a German machine right under me—I was sitting right above the town and let go on a warehouse near the railroad. The bombs, however, nearly hit the German. I turned out toward the sea with the rest of the formation, to get out of the *barrage* which was bursting all around us. I looked up—the *barrage* had stopped suddenly—and four small, very fast planes were speeding down the coast toward us from Zeebrugge. At this moment my engine began to lose power very rapidly—so fast that I could not stay with the formation, which began to pull away. I stuck the nose of the machine down a little and in this way increased my speed so that I was able to stay under the formation. The four Boches came closer and closer. A slight mist, through which I could barely see, now came between the formation and myself. I kept watching my tail, and sure enough the Huns had picked me out for their meat; just as I had expected, I was to be the goat. Alone, twenty miles behind the lines, and with a bum motor, the scrap started. I began to maneuver just as soon as one was within range of my observer's gun. Three of them came at me—they were Pfalz scouts, very fast, and handled very well. George Lowry, my observer, kept up a continual fire at them, shooting each time I maneuvered him into position.

All three Germans came within one hundred yards of me, shooting continually. I maneuvered constantly, changing my direction at the moment I saw one of them getting in position to fire. It was great work sitting there, shaking the stick and foot controls back and forth while my observer emptied pan after pan of bullets into the Huns. I could not shoot or do anything but sit still, watching and wiggling the controls, while the *tac-tac* of their machine guns was going behind me and the *zip-zam* of their explosive bullets passed. I let out my wrath by yelling. I was trying to encourage George, yelling encouragement, but not knowing or remembering what I said.

The noise of the German machine gun makes you try to pull in your neck, but when an explosive bullet enters the machine, two inches from your arm, and explodes on the cartridge container right in front of you, believe me, you do some tall thinking! The bullet went through that box, making a hole as big as a silver dollar, passed through my bomb-carrying gear, pierced my gasoline-tank, and finally hit the engine, taking off one of my magnetos. I never heard before of an explosive bullet going through a gas-tank without setting the plane on fire.

In this fight, Lowry thinks he brought down one of the Germans, as he saw the machine go into a spin soon after he had fired a burst into it, but as it was 'way back in Germany and no one saw it but ourselves, we are not sure. Anyway, we saw our tracer bullets going through the Hun machine just as he was going to dive on us. The machine turned over on its back and went into a spin, disappearing below. We were not able to watch it, as the other two kept us busy, and so do not know what happened to him. At any rate, he did not come back and join the fight.

Well, to make a long story short, I maneuvered for twenty minutes, with that bad engine coughing away in front of me. By the end of that time I had arrived at the lines; I came out under the bank of mist and was seen by the formation. Two of our planes dove from above on my two persistent friends, firing as they came, and the Germans beat it back to Germany. As soon as I had support, I wanted to turn and get a few shots in on my own account, but on looking around at George I changed my mind. He had been swinging the gun turret from side to side so rapidly that he was all in. Big drops of perspiration were all over his face. He watched the Huns as they disappeared, and then turned around and patted me on the back. I hurried home, landed, and found that the machine was badly shot up by explosive bullets; a complete wreck. The Captain, who dove to help me, told me afterwards that he was afraid that it would be all up with me before he could get there. I thanked him for coming, but you should have seen his face when I told him the fight had been going on for twenty minutes!

THE GREAT ATTACK ON ST. MIHIEL

WILLIAM MITCHELL, BRIGADIER GENERAL

U. S. AIR SERVICE

August–September 1918

I estimated that within three days after we attacked, the Germans could concentrate very nearly two thousand airplanes against us. I therefore decided to assemble a force of two thousand to cover our initial attack, no matter where it might be. I immediately took up the matter with the French, through Armengaud, to find out what they could spare. General Foch approved everything in principle that we put forward, and our work went rapidly on.

I now began to get together the old staff officers whom I had trained, with Colonel T. D. Milling as Chief of Staff, the best one I have seen in any service. Different commanding officers use their Chiefs of Staff in different ways. I always had mine coordinate the various staff sections and see that the machine functioned properly.

When commanding, I always drew up my own orders for the military operations of the fighting units, and personally checked the sending and receipt by the unit commander of their special orders. When orders were not obeyed, it was usually the commanding officer who was at fault. Either the orders had not been delivered or they were so written that nobody could understand them. I always kept an officer at my headquarters, whose name I shall not mention, whom I had read all the orders. If he could understand them, anybody could. He was not particularly bright but he was one of the most valuable officers I had.

I now prepared and completed the details of our exact method of operation during the proposed attack, the summary of which I had given General Pershing on Aug. 20th, as follows:

HEADQUARTERS AIR SERVICE
FIRST ARMY

SECRET
August 20, 1918.

MEMORANDUM FOR   Commanding General, 1st Army.
    The employment of aviation in the proposed attack is divided into four phases:

> I. Preparation.
> II. Night preceding the attack.
> III. Day of the attack.
> IV. Exploitation.

I. *PREPARATION:*

    (a) In order that the attack be made by surprise, it is important that the attitude of the sector be not changed.
    (b) The general mission of aviation (in I.) is to—
        (1) Absolutely prevent access to our lines by enemy reconnaissance aviation;
        (2) Secure complete information about hostile formations by means of photo missions and night reconnaissances without arousing the suspicion of the enemy.
    (c) Mission of pursuit aviation in I.—
        (1) Constant patrol on our lines in order to produce an absolute barrage;
        (2) Usual offensive patrols in order to maintain the normal activity of the sector.
    (d) Mission of bombardment aviation:
        Normal work of the sector.
    (e) Mission of observation aviation—
        (1) Maximum photographic reconnaissances;
        (2) Night reconnaissances when enemy movements are suspected.

II. *NIGHT PRECEDING THE ATTACK:*

(a) Mission of bombardment aviation; during the whole night preceding the attack.

    (1) Attack by high-explosive bombs (English Aviation) of the strategical objectives, i.e., airdromes, stations, railroad crossings, bridges, ammunition dumps; (confirmed by photos)

    (2) General attack by bombs on personnel (French Aviation) of camps, enemy cantonments and airdrome.

III. *DAY OF THE ATTACK:*

(a) Mission of pursuit aviation—

    (1) Offensive mission—High patrols deep to the rear of the enemy lines to break up enemy aerial formations and help the bombardment aviation in its mission of bombarding enemy airdromes, and scattering enemy columns on the road.

    (2) Protective mission—If the infantry signaling is efficient, *and in this case only,* an attack may be made by machine guns on the enemy's reserves which are in formation for counterattack. To prevent enemy infantry planes from entering the battle zone. To help the advance of the tanks.

(b) Mission of bombardment aviation—

Protected by pursuit aviation to attack and destroy enemy airdromes, break up trains and convoys on the roads, and carry on the same work as that of the night bombardment aviation in destroying stations, bridges, railroad crossings, ammunition dumps, cantonments, etc.

(c) Mission of observation aviation—

Surveillance, artillery adjustment, liaison and reconnaissance.

IV. *EXPLOITATION:*

The squadrons move forward to the new advanced fields which were previously prepared, extend their zone of action and execute the same missions as the day before. However as a retreating army is in open ground, the airplanes will operate as low as possible in order to seek the obligatory points of passage of the enemy's columns and to destroy them with bombs and machine guns at such places.

The high-explosive bombardment aviation (English

Aviation) will be specially detailed to destroy railway crossings and important bridges located in the zone far from the battlefield.

WM. MITCHELL
Colonel, A.S.S.C.,
C.A.S., 1st Army.

We worked hard on every branch of our aviation and I took particular pains to have the observers in the observation flights carefully instructed as to what they should do with their ground troops.

I moved my headquarters up to Ligny-en-Barrois on August 27th. Lieutenant Miller had prepared for the movement. He had a fine mess organized for us, run by a wine merchant, his wife and daughters. We took over a public school building as our headquarters. Each staff section had its appropriate location and I had a splendid big room, on one side of which was Milling and on the other, Armengaud.

I had an amazing relief map of the whole St. Mihiel salient where we were about to attack. It had been made up by the French balloon companies operating in the area, and was the work of several years. I had procured the various pieces and put them together, and the whole thing occupied a floor space of about twelve by twelve feet. Each hill, woods, road, detached house, large building, railroad yards, ravine—in fact, every incident of the terrain—was remarkably depicted. This map, combined with my intimate knowledge of the country derived from studying it for many years and from flying over it, made me feel that I knew this part of the world as well as any man living, better probably than any Frenchman.

General Pershing was now in high spirits; we were getting our American army together and our air people, who for a long time had felt that Pershing did not know, or care to know, very much about aviation, were beginning to change their minds as he was helping us in every way possible. I guess he could not swallow the whole hog to begin with, had to take it easy, but it had put us back a good many months. One had to expect that in the organization of a new outfit, and from now on I hoped he would do better. I was sure he would if we delivered the goods.

Our old air units were now becoming well organized, and, although they had only been on the front two or three months, they were going like clockwork. The closing days of August saw my staff splendidly organized under Milling as Chief of Staff. No better working organization ever existed in the American armed services.

We were assembling the greatest army the United States had ever seen, to do battle on European soil. Thousands upon thousands of men filled every road, while all means of transport were bringing up the tremendous amount of supplies they required.

September 1918

The first of September saw my headquarters permanently organized and a force of 1,476 airplanes and twenty balloons, under my command, concentrating to join battle with the Germans.

Thirty thousand officers and men handled the airplanes. They were disposed on fourteen main flying fields and a great many substations, while three large supply points handled the material for the Americans, French, British and Italians. It was the greatest concentration of air power that had ever taken place and the first time in history in which an air force, cooperating with an army, was to act according to a broad strategical plan which contemplated not only facilitating the advance of the ground troops but spreading fear and consternation into the enemy's line of communications, his replacement system and the cities behind them which supplied our foe with the sinews of war.

In addition to the American, French and British units, I had some squadrons of Italian bombardment aviation, who did all they could in their sphere. Here we were, a force of four nations, acting together with no discord, misunderstanding, jealousy or attempt to shirk or escape the maximum duty or losses which may be required. Such a thing could not have occurred with ground troops. I say this because the game on the ground is such an old one, and the element of novelty and development has ceased to exist in it. In aviation, there is an entirely different feeling between the persons engaged in it. It is an extremely dangerous and hazardous occupation and every man who is a real pilot is looked up to and appreciated by his fellows.

Most of the officers on our general staff, with a few marked exceptions, had no appreciation of what this great air force meant. Not a single one, however, except Major Bowditch, had shown any inclination to go up in the air and see what was going on. Just think of such a thing! Here was a great military operation about to be undertaken, the success or failure of which meant everything to American arms. A tour in the air by the Commanding General or the Chief of Staff would have given them an insight into the positions and locations of the enemy and our own troops which could have been obtained in no other way. I could have taken them myself and protected them so that there would have been ninety-nine chances out of a hundred of their getting back unscathed (even if they did get killed, there were plenty of people to step into their shoes); but out of all this group only one chose to go up in the air.

There are a great many points of difference between the management of an air force and that of an army or navy. An air force operates in a new medium, the air, which offers a wider scope for action than either land or water. They must be communicated with through the air, that is, by radio or visual signals.

When air forces are committed to a combat they cannot be withdrawn and redisposed ordinarily, but must come back to the airdromes to refuel and replenish before renewing the fight. Air forces cannot dig holes in the air and get into them where the enemy will not see them, and where they may sit in safety and comfort. The premium of successful combat is shooting down the enemy and the forfeit when unsuccessful is to go hurtling to earth in a flaming coffin. Air forces are the eyes of the army, and without their accurate reports, ground forces cannot operate.

We had three tasks to accomplish: one, to provide accurate information for the infantry and adjustment of fire for the artillery of the ground troops; second, to hold off the enemy air forces from interfering with either our air or ground troops; and third, to bomb the back areas so as to stop the supplies for the enemy and hold up any movement along his roads.

The shape of the St. Mihiel salient furnished an interesting situation. It projected into our line in the shape of a horseshoe, rather a sharp one at the toe, the point of which was located at the city of St. Mihiel. The Germans pushed in here in 1915 and occupied it in an attempt to surround Verdun.

It must be remembered that the most direct line of advance from Germany into France is through Koblenz, Treves, Verdun, Nancy and then straight toward Lyons, where the centers of population and factories of France are located. Conversely, if we could advance into Germany by way of Treves and Koblenz, we would have the shortest line through this great gateway into the country of the Teutons. Now our American army, acting under its own chiefs and holding its own sector of the line, was charged with the duty of advancing into the Treves Gap, and by pushing on, to threaten this great open portal into Germany.

Our line at most places was more or less straight and the Air Service acted out from it more or less homogeneously all along the front. Now we were attacking a salient, so I intended to change the ordinary procedure and employ massed air attacks against the vital points in the enemy's rear. In this case, we could hit first from one side of the salient, then from the other, just as a boxer gives a right hook and a left hook successively to his opponent.

In the present case, I would have a preponderance in the air for at least two days before the Germans could concentrate. I had therefore issued orders to the French Air Division that they would attack entirely by brigades, nothing smaller. There were two brigades of about four hundred airplanes each in the Division. One brigade would habitually attack twice a day on the right of the salient, entering it from west of Pont-à-Mousson. The bombardment would attack Vigneulles, Conflans and Briey.

At the time their gas was beginning to run out, the second brigade of the Air Division would attack the same places from the left of the salient, crossing the lines in the vicinity of Genicourt and Fort Haudainville. In this way, while the Germans were resisting and fighting one of our brigades, I would catch them in the rear with the other brigade. I would time it so there would be sufficient gas left in the airplanes of the 1st Brigade for them to continue the combat for about thirty minutes after the second arrived.

Nothing like this had ever been tried before. It marked the beginning of the great strategical air operations away from the troops.

Our own observation squadrons were assigned definitely to the troops on the ground. For their local protection at low altitude, we had our own American 1st Pursuit Group, under Major Harold E. Hartney. I considered this group the peer of any fighting organization on the front.

Our bombardment wing, consisting of the 2nd and 3rd Pursuit Groups, with the bombardment group, would act out from the head of the salient and attack Vigneulles. We had done everything we could with this new bombardment organization but they had not yet had the experience required to make them proficient.

Our bombardment group was not in good condition. It was poorly commanded, the morale was weak and it would take some time to get it on its feet. This was largely due to the fact that when I was away in Château-Thierry, the 96th Squadron was left behind in the Toul area. The Major who was then in command of the 96th flew over into Germany with what ships he had available for duty. He lost his way in the fog and landed in Germany with every ship intact. Not one single ship was burned or destroyed and the Germans captured the whole outfit complete. This was the most glaring exhibition of worthlessness we had had on the front. The Germans sent back a humorous message which was dropped on one of our airdromes. It said, "We thank you for the fine airplanes and equipment which you have sent us, but what shall we do with the Major?"

I know of no other performance in any air force in the war that was as reprehensible as this. Needless to say, we did not reply about the Major, as he was better off in Germany at that time than he would have been with us.

The day for the attack drew near. Major I. B. Joralemon had done wonderful work in locating our great air host, preparing its airdromes and getting its supplies. Colonel DeWitt, G-4 of the General Staff, had helped us to the limit. On September 7th, the French Air Division reported and took its place.

We moved the air forces into their airdromes with the greatest secrecy possible so as not to let the Germans know how many airplanes we were assembling. We were careful not to make too great a display over the front; but on the other hand, we kept our pursuit patrols working up as high as they could go, about twenty thousand feet, so as to prevent German reconnaissance.

In our advance airdromes for the observation groups, such as at Souilly, I had camouflage or fake hangars constructed with fake airplanes in front, so that if the Germans took pictures of them, it would look as if a certain number of aircraft were there. Each day I had the position of these camouflage airplanes changed so as to make it look as if the place were active.

I issued orders to the 88th Squadron, among others, which was commanded by Major Christy, to occupy the airdrome at Souilly. They were to come up from Luxeuil, near Belfort, and arrive just before dark, so as to put their airplanes into the hangars immediately and in this way escape observation from the enemy. During the night of September 9th, I had real hangars put up exactly where the camouflage hangars had been. This same system had been followed on the other airdromes. In every other case, the organizations, flying low, arrived just before dark and immediately hid themselves. Christy, however, apparently did not get the spirit of the order. He arrived with his squadron in broad daylight, leading it himself, lined it up on the airdrome, then took his own ship with the best observer and actually made a reconnaissance away over Metz and got away with it. He was lucky not to have been killed but it disclosed our whole position at Souilly. The enemy then knew exactly what was there. It was a very brave act but absolutely the wrong thing to do. I told Christy what I thought of it. (Christy never did anything like that again; in fact, he developed into one of the best commanders that we had on the front.)

September 12th had been decided upon as the day of our grand attack. It was the greatest army ever assembled under the American flag; four hundred thousand men with over three thousand cannon were facing the enemy. Our air force consisted of nearly fifteen hundred airplanes.

Of course the Germans knew that we were going to attack them in the St. Mihiel salient. Their power of offensive and initiative passed after the battle at Soissons. St. Mihiel was a dangerous place for them to hold; in fact, they could not; all they could do was to delay our operations. They therefore had no intention of holding it and had put in, in addition to a few of their first-line organizations, a lot of second-line troops and Austrians, in which were included many *Honvéd* or Hungarian regiments.

In my personal reconnaissance with Major Armengaud over the lines on September 10th, I had noticed considerable movement to the rear which indicated that the Germans were withdrawing from the St. Mihiel salient. To my surprise and consternation I found at the meeting of General Pershing's staff on the evening before the attack that our Chief Engineer recommended that we delay the attack because there had been considerable rain. This, he said, held up our light railways used for getting up artillery ammunition. The question of adequate water for some of the troops would be difficult and a thousand and one things which could not be done were mentioned. I was surprised to see that several of the old fossils there agreed with this foolish view. You can always trust an Engineer Officer to go on the defensive whenever it is possible. I was the junior member of the staff and when it got to me for my opinion, I told them very plainly that I knew the Germans were withdrawing from the St. Mihiel salient as I had seen them personally, that our troops were now in position for the attack and were keyed up to it; furthermore, I said, there was not going to be much of a battle at St. Mihiel anyway, and our troops might be better off without artillery, as they would probably shoot a good many of our own men anyway; and all we had to do was to jump on the Germans, and the quicker we did it, the better.

General Pershing smiled, and ordered that we attack.

On September 11th I assembled the officers from every major organization of the Air Service within our great force—British, French, Italians and Americans. I read them the orders myself and asked each one individually what he could do to comply with them. Each one went back to his organization thoroughly conversant with what he was to do for each day of the attack.

The morning of September 12th dawned dark and cloudy, with intermittent rain. Clouds hung low and the visibility was very poor. Nevertheless, our Air Service with that of the Allies went over the lines, and I was much pleased with the fact that virtually no German airplanes got over our ground troops.

We forced the German airmen to fight away back of Vigneulles and Conflans, thirty miles away from our ground troops. We had many combats at these places during the day.

On the 13th, we could see that the enemy was concentrating all his available air power against us because he was losing too many prisoners. The Germans did not care whether we took the St. Mihiel salient or not, as they knew they were incapable of taking the offensive in the Verdun and Metz areas, but they did not want to lose a lot of prisoners and equipment. Our air force, however, by attacking their transportation trains, railroads and columns on the roads, piled them up with debris so that it was impossible for many of their troops to get away quickly, resulting in their capture by our infantry. We had forced them to measure strength with us in the air with their main forces, and if they did not come and attack us, we intended to destroy Metz, Conflans, Diedenhoffen and even Treves.

The British, under General Trenchard, tore into their airdromes, smashed up their hangars and forced them to fight at all points. An airman may stay on the ground if he wants to and let the other fellow go ahead, but if the other fellow starts blowing up everything, he will have to get up in the air and fight him, or allow complete destruction. We were constantly forcing them to fight in the air; of course, it was a walkover on the ground for the army.

By the 14th, the German air service began to appear in great numbers and we had a tremendous number of combats. There was one fight which I wish to mention particularly, because it illustrates the terrific destructive power of pursuit aviation when acting against bombardment aviation.

On September 14th, one of our bombardment squadrons, belonging to a French group, failed to meet the pursuit aviation detailed to protect it, on account of poor visibility in cloudy weather. Nevertheless it proceeded in the direction ordered, to bombard the objective. There were eighteen airplanes in the squadron, fifteen being two-seaters and three being three-seaters. The three-seaters were equipped with six guns each, and, as far as volume of gunfire was concerned, were the most powerful airplanes on the western front. They were unable to maneuver as rapidly as the single-seaters, however, and therefore did not fulfil the ideas of their originators who thought that through volume of fire alone they could defend themselves against small, highly maneuverable single-seaters. The three-seaters were supposed to be for the protection of the two-seaters; that is, these powerfully gunned airplanes were expected to fight off the enemy pursuit while the bombers concentrated their whole attention on dropping their bombs on the targets.

The squadron flew in a V-formation, like a flock of ducks. One of the great three-seaters was on each flank and one in the opening behind. When this squadron crossed the line on the way to its objective, it was passed by a patrol of twelve German pursuit airplanes flying one behind the other, about five hundred meters above it. The German patrol deployed in line formation behind the bombardment squadron. Four of the enemy planes attacked the three-seater which was behind and sent it down in flames. The other eight kept up a long-range fire at the squadron so as to derange its aim while dropping its bombs on the city of Conflans. At the same time, anti-aircraft artillery opened fire at the vanguard of the squadron while the German pursuit ships attacked the rear. While anti-aircraft guns failed to hit any of the airplanes, their bursting shells allowed the German pursuit organizations, which were now concentrating for an attack on the squadron, to see where they were. During this time, the Commander of the Bombardment Squadron noticed German airplanes rising from Mars-la-Tour, the airdrome close to Conflans.

All the bombs were dropped on the objective and the return flight was started to our lines. Just as the turn was made, a fresh enemy pursuit squadron joined the former, immediately deployed and attacked the rearmost plane and shot the observer through the leg. He continued to battle, however, and hit one enemy plane which fell in flames. The formation was now well on its way back when a third enemy squadron attacked ours in front and to the left. The bombing squadron was now being attacked in three dimensions, from underneath, above and on the same level.

The great lumbering bombing machines huddled together as a flight of geese might when attacked by falcons. The pursuit planes dived at them from all directions, firing their machine guns, then zooming up in the air or turning over on their backs at a speed of about two hundred miles an hour, taking an erratic course to avoid the fire of the big ships and then resuming their position for attack again.

By this time the big three-seater protection plane on the left had been shot in one of its engines and started slipping down. Immediately when it left the formation, it was jumped on by three German machines. In a moment, it was shot to pieces and disappeared in flames. The fighting had now become terrific. More German machines were constantly joining their comrades. The signals made by the artillery projectiles bursting in the air and the radio on the ground told the German aviators that our bombardment squadron had no pursuit protection and was an easy victim. The attacks of the German pursuit ships were carried on up to within fifty feet of the bombardment planes.

The next airplane to be hit was No. 13; a two-seater, which caught fire and dropped its movable gasoline tank. It dived at a sharp angle, turned over on its back about two hundred meters below the squadron, lost its left wing and then crashed to the ground.

At this same moment a German pursuit ship was shot down, on fire. No. 2 bombardment airplane was hit in the gasoline tank in the upper wing and caught fire; but the machine, flaming like a torch, kept its position in the formation. The machine gunner was magnificent in his courage, fighting the hostile airplanes while the flames slowly crept up around him. The plane continued to fly for about two hundred meters, leaving behind it a trail of fire about twice as long as the ship itself. Pilot and observer by this time were consumed and the airplane dived to its doom.

At about that time a German Fokker plane, diving vertically with its engine full on, lost both its wings. Now the whole right wing of the squadron had been shot down and a rearrangement of formation was made so as to get the remaining machines into V-formation again. Machines Nos. 9 and 14 were then both hit at the same time, No. 14 catching fire. The pilot of No. 14 stretched out his arms toward the sky, and, waving his hand and saying farewell to the remainder of the squadron, went to eternity. No. 9 machine disappeared and, as it did, an additional German pursuit machine retired from the combat crippled. No. 15 machine was now having a hard time keeping up with the formation. Its gasoline tank had been perforated by bullets, its aileron control cut and its rudder hit. However, it kept up.

By this time the squadron had come back to our lines and was joined and protected by our pursuit aviation. The combat in its intensity lasted for forty minutes, and of eighteen airplanes which had constituted the squadron, only five remained. Most of the crews were wounded and their planes perforated in all parts by bullets. They had never once broken their formation or failed to obey the orders of their leader. They furnished an example of military precision and bravery which is required of all airmen.

The battle of St. Mihiel was really over on the first day, and every objective had been accomplished. I was glad to see that our tanks did so well, because I am convinced that in the future the tank will be the only means of advancing on the ground against a well-intrenched and determined enemy. George Patton rode into St. Mihiel on the back of one of his tanks, away ahead of any other ground troops in the vicinity.

We won a great victory at St. Mihiel. But we actually advanced only two or three miles on the ground. We had not had to move any of our airdromes or to change any of our air arrangements. The army might fight for a month and not get too far away from the support of our present aircraft locations. This was not getting to the interior of Germany. What did it amount to, except killing thousands of our men and the enemy's?

General Pershing was tremendously pleased with our operations at St. Mihiel. He told me that we had been the eyes of the army and led it on to victory. He wrote me the following letter:

AMERICAN EXPEDITIONARY FORCES
Office of the Commander-in-Chief
France, Sept. 1, 1918.

Colonel William Mitchell,
    Chief of Air Service, First Army, A.E.F., France.
My dear Colonel—
    Please accept my sincere congratulations on the successful and very important part taken by the Air Force under your command in the first offensive of the First American Army. The organization and control of the tremendous concentration of Air forces, including American, French, British and Italian units, which has enabled the Air Service of the First Army to carry out so successfully its dangerous and important mission, is as fine a tribute to you personally as is the courage and nerve shown by your officers a signal proof of the high morale which permeates the service under your command.
    Please convey to your command my heartfelt appreciation of their work. I am proud of you all.
                                        Sincerely yours,
                                        JOHN J. PERSHING

THE SPANISH CIVIL WAR

The Civil War in Spain, which took on the air of a minor international fracas, bridged the gap between the two world wars. Here the Soviets, who supported the Loyalists, and the Germans and Italians, who sided with the Nationalists or Insurgents, tried out their new aircraft and military strategy and "blooded" their pilots for the greater conflagration that was yet to come.

Although German zeppelins, Gothas, and other heavy bombers had bombed England and France in the First World War, these were only piddling raids—scarcely of more than nuisance value —that dropped few bombs, very inaccurately, very spasmodically, and did very little damage. On the other hand the Spanish Civil War was the first conflict where undefended cities were pounded unmercifully, regularly and systematically from the air. The war was amply covered by correspondents on both sides of the line. The Soviet newspaper *Pravda* was well represented as were United States, German, and Italian newspapers. And, for that matter, newspapers from all over the world. With these vivid, often bloody and frightening descriptions of the awful and devastating effects of aerial bombardment on beleaguered Madrid, together with the dramatic presentation given by Hemingway in *For Whom the Bell Tolls,* it is hard to understand how the world could embark on that far greater scene of destruction we know today as World War II.

André Malraux, the well-known French novelist, was one of the leaders in the Loyalist (Republican) Air Force during the Spanish Civil War. He was instrumental in obtaining aircraft for the Spanish government and flew them in combat, as well. Some of his experiences, as he recorded them, are in the pages that follow. (During the Second World War Malraux was active in the French Resistance and later served as Minister of Culture under President Charles de Gaulle.)

Oloff de Wet, another Loyalist pilot, describes, here, a bombing mission over Barajas, a Spanish town that had just fallen to the Rebels, who were pushing on to the relief of the Alcazar.

BOMBING A FASCIST AIRFIELD

[1] ANDRÉ MALRAUX, *CAPITÁN*

SPANISH LOYALIST AIR FORCE

It is the Epiphany, the feast of the Three Kings, the great festival of the children of Spain. In the morning when I came to the War Ministry all the streets were filled with armored cars. They have been passing by all day long, while one hundred kilometers away the International Brigade and the columns of militiamen captured, lost and recaptured the Teruel cemetery. It is the first children's feast since the birth of the new Spain, and the trade unions have wanted to give them a celebration such as they have never had before. For a week the workers have been busy all night making cardboard figures taken from the animated cartoons which the children have been clamoring for, and, in addition to the traditional cake fortresses, the old bulls, the king and the playing-card characters, twelve-foot figures of Mickey Mouse and Felix the Cat have on this occasion invaded Valencia.

My car is taking me back from the War Ministry to the front. It is three o'clock in the morning. In the starlight that breaks through the clouds one senses the tall buildings around the great square, grounded in the night like the prows of old Spanish galleons. The blue wartime lights, like the blue lights of deep-

---

[1] Famous French author, veteran of Chinese Civil War (1925–27), French Minister of Information under General de Gaulle (1945–46), and Minister of State for Cultural Affairs in 1959.

sea fishes, cast a faint glow over the square and the shadows of Mickey Mouse figures are swallowed up by the asphalt that is wet from the last brief shower. When the automobile reaches the broad boulevards that encircle Valencia we are stopped by the heavy traffic. We turn on our headlights for a moment: all the characters that people the dreams of children, from the early dreams of Christianity to those of American children, from the Magi to Mickey Mouse, are there in a jumble; and between their legs some of the thousands of children who have come for the feast of the Epiphany have sought refuge from the rain that may start again any moment and have fallen asleep.

Here and there for miles we come upon these great phantoms of childish dreams abandoned in the night, as if the genii of all races were to come here to fetch them for the dreams of all the children who sleep. On each base, around their legs, the dimmed automobile lights reveal in passing a cluster of children, calmly asleep—stretched out like the wounded of Teruel a little farther on, on the same ground.

The dull explosions from the cannon of Teruel, that seem imperceptibly to shake the earth, seem at the same time to shake these frail phantoms above the serene slumber of all the motionless children, their arms relaxed in gestures of the dead.

A battalion of militiamen is leaving for the front. They are heading toward the Prado, and the loud strains of the Internationale draw nearer. When they are almost immediately below my window, at the moment when the singing should be loudest, it subsides, only to pick up again a little farther on, on a lower note, muffled. I go to the window; a blind man, holding his white cane out in front of him, is walking down the middle of the street. None of those adolescents on their way to the battle front has dared to push him aside, and he advances against the current of the marching militiamen who go around him on both sides, and stop their singing. After they have passed him and gone on a little way their song again breaks out, in a more sober strain.

The blind man continues forward, throwing back his shoulders as almost all blind men do, distressed by this crowd which he cannot see, and which is silenced by his presence—and, surrounded by an empty circle as by the respectful terror with which the blind men of old were regarded, not understanding and wanting to escape, he walks faster and faster; and the militiamen swerve aside before he touches them, as though to let Destiny pass by.

I saw him again. The Moors were in Carabanchel—at the gates of Madrid. Those of us who had fought in the infantry and were used to hearing the tom-tom of the Moors at night opened the windows to listen; but the wind was coming from Madrid, and we could hear nothing in the rainy night, not even the rattle of machine guns. After nine o'clock the patrol of the thoroughfares was extremely strict, and the streets were almost wholly deserted.

From the top of one of the big hotels, no doubt for the benefit of the police, a searchlight periodically swept the street. Suddenly before me, in the vast flood of light, appeared two enormous hands, hands fifty feet long, that vanished into the night. The police and the militiamen no doubt knew the blind beggar and had let him pass. He was without a cane and was protecting himself with his groping hands; he was barely visible in the beam from the searchlight, but his outstretched hands, trembling like those of a god of the night, seemed to be seeking the living and the dead with a frightful maternal gesture.

On the outskirts of a village between Madrid and Talavera the dynamiters were awaiting the enemy tanks.

Messengers would come and give them the warning signal. For the time being there was nothing to do but wait. They were in a deserted bar, telling each other stories:

"I took part in the retreat with Gorde and Sabranek. They are both miners in the country where they come from; they were assigned to the company at our rear back of the village. At that time there weren't any dynamiters. They had both been machine gunners in the army, and so they were put on the machine guns. The first day of the attack their company of machine gunners was detailed to hold a small wood. Hell was popping right and left, when they suddenly noticed that their two flanking companies had been pushed back and that they were surrounded by Moors. There was nothing to do but to take to their heels and try to get through; make a three-hundred-yard dash, stop, fire a roll, make another three-hundred-yard dash. So off they went, jumping like rabbits, taking their Hotchkiss with them. After the first three hundred yards they stopped and began to fire. It was Gorde who was at the gun. He shot his roll. The Moors were falling in their tracks, just like in the movies, but they were bound to catch up to them.

" 'Beat it!' shouted Sabranek. The other continued to tinker with his roll.

" 'Beat it, for God's sake!' He continued to tinker with his roll, sitting 'way back in the saddle, and then opened fire. The Moors once more began to go down. Exasperated, Sabranek let go with his booted foot and kicked him in the pants again and again. The other got up, hesitated a moment. And again Sabranek kicked him in the tail. Then with both arms Gorde grabbed his machine gun and took to his heels, running full speed right into the enemy, with Sabranek behind him still yelling at the top of his lungs. And they both disappeared over the ridge held by the Moors, like Laurel and Hardy. I can't get over seeing them again here. I thought they'd been killed."

Others, outside, are sitting or lying down with their horse blankets wrapped round them, giving the effect of a Mexican army, minus the sombreros. The flames at intervals light up the faces, as in engravings of the Napoleonic wars.

"Pedro was in the Asturias in '34 with Gonzáles Peña. We were fighting with one bullet to every five men. When the cartridges were empty the women gathered them up, put them in their salad baskets, and the baskets went off in a truck to be reloaded with bullets. The enemy planes chased the armored trains that scurried into the tunnels, waited till the planes went back to refuel, and then made a dash for another tunnel. And so on. The peasants were fighting all around Miejes. It was the last day. Nothing more could be done. But they needed three hours to prevent the outer flanks of the Moorish guard which was advancing like a crescent toward Miejes from closing together, and to evacuate all who could be evacuated.

"There was still quite a bit of dynamite that came from the mines. But nothing to make bombs with. No copper, no steel. The Moors were advancing. In a little peasant hut the committee was deliberating. The Moors were advancing. A strange rumbling was beginning to make the walls tremble. It was not an earthquake: the walls were trembling, but not the ground. And it was not cannons: it was a dull, but multitudinous sound, like thousands of muffled drums. Pedro went outside, and the moment he opened the door the noise of machine guns, like the ripping of cloth, could be distinctly heard in the room beneath the rumble that was growing louder and was as mysterious as ever. Suddenly a cow appeared in the main street, hesitated, passed in front of the central committee shack and fled down the other end of the street. A bull ran after her, with the jerky, nervous gallop of the *corrida*. And when Pedro saw a rabbit scurrying toward him, he understood.

"To encircle the town, the Moors were advancing as for a roundup. Game and cattle, thrown back on Miejes by machine-gun fire, were beginning to pour in among the peasant huts on the outskirts, toward the center, and it was the sound of thousands of hoofs that was making the ground shake. The cattle were coming down the mountain with the rumble of great herds returning from pasture. And now, seemingly rising from the ground, the sound of bells could be heard.

"The animals all carried bells—the heavy, deep-sounding bronze bells of mountain cattle, like those of the Moslem herds.

In a moment tables, chairs, boards, objects of all kinds were thrown out through the windows of the hut or brought from near-by houses. The rumble was growing louder: the cattle were coming. The materials gathered for the barricades were feverishly piled up. From all sides the peasants were converging for the building of a new barricade—the barricade against the cattle herd.

"The herds were stopped. One by one the peasants unfastened or tore off the heavy bells, which sixty dynamiters transformed into bombs. And they began to take their places in all the hollows in the rocks along the path of the Moors.

"For more than three hours they held them off by hurling cowbells from the hollows. The fighting population scattered into the interior of Spain or crossed the frontier into France. Fifty-eight dynamiters were killed."

"I was in Talavera," said another. "We were being bombarded by their planes as we had never been before. Around Saragossa there are holes like those in the valley of the moon; here there were twenty-five-pound bombs all over the place—unexploded. During the bombardment only one out of ten went off. It was an amazing sight. The Fascists were bombarding almost entirely with light bombs. No doubt they had no heavy ones left. The bombs came out of their holes like handfuls of grain, fell right on us, and here and there one of them would burst, as if by accident. It was as if the Fascists were bombarding us with enormous darts. On the embankment of the road where our trucks passed they must have bombarded us fifteen times, in small squadrons of five to nine; on both sides the bombs were piled up as if they were there ready to be carted away. They had fallen on top of each other and had not exploded.

"It was rather odd. When a few don't explode it's more or less natural; but with so many it was uncanny. Some of our men had been aviation mechanics; they had often helped with loading the bombs on their planes. They began to unscrew the percussion fuses to examine the bombs. The first one turned round, excited as a windmill, holding out a little slip of typewritten paper to show to the second one who, no less excited, was holding a similar slip. It was the message of the Portuguese workers: 'This bomb will not explode.'"

The messengers had just arrived. It was the signal for action. The dynamiters scurried off with their bombs. I thought of an Annamite I had known several years back who had been killed in his first elephant hunt: the animal was charging, and it had seemed to my friend that a man was so slight a thing before this great mass that he had dropped his gun and run; the elephant had killed him with one blow of his trunk. So slight a thing before the mass that was coming down on him. . . . The men continued to advance to the firing line, one behind the other, their bombs on their backs or under their arms. We heard what sounded like distant motors. And with our eyes fixed on the broken crest of the hill in front of us we waited for the first armored car to appear.

"There's a peasant who wants to talk to you. He's come over from the Fascist lines."

I follow him to where the peasant is standing, surrounded by aviators who are questioning him. His answers come reluctantly. As I approach I see his face in full profile—the long, dark, lean profile of the Spanish peasant: of the men who fought Napoleon; to complete the illusion one has merely to imagine the visored cap he is wearing replaced by a knotted kerchief.

"You say you want to speak to me?"

"No. I've come to speak to the commander of the air squadron."

"That's him," the aviators tell him.

The peasant is suspicious. My outfit—the planes will be leaving in half an hour—bears no insignia of rank.

"Can you give the word for the planes to take off?"

The pilots stand round him, some friendly, others suspicious;

he comes from the enemy lines. I draw him aside. He has been sent to me by the People's Front of León. The Fascist planes are in the vicinity of his village. He has just gotten through the lines and has gone to notify our people in León; they have immediately sent him to me.

I have one of the men get a phone connection through to the People's Front headquarters in León to check the story, and come back to the peasant.

"Where are the planes?"

"In the woods. The Fascists have made clearings under the trees where they can keep them out of sight."

"What's the field like?"

"Where they take off?"

"Yes."

He makes a drawing. Long and narrow.

"The soldiers have been working since yesterday to make the field wider."

"How does it run?"

He thinks for a moment.

"East and west."

"And the wood?"

"To the east."

This means that the enemy planes have to take off from east to west. The wind, which is very strong, comes from the east, and it is undoubtedly the same in Olmedo. The enemy planes would have a hard time taking off from the field which the peasant has described.

"How many planes are there?"

"There were twelve large ones and six small ones last night. We managed to find that out through some of our boys."

We have only four planes at our disposal. If the peasant is telling the truth it is worth attempting to surprise the enemy camp. If he is lying the enemy planes will be able to take to the air before we discover them, and we will not return. A telephone operator comes, bringing the answer from León. The man does, in fact, come from Olmedo, but the León people don't know those in Olmedo. It is up to us to decide what to do.

"It's near Olmedo," he repeats.

I show him a map; as I supposed, he is unable to read it.

"Take me to Olmedo," he says: "I'll show you. I can guide you right to the spot."

"Anyone in your family been killed by the Fascists?"

"No. Take me in your plane."

In such a situation spies are likely to betray themselves— in aerial warfare enemies cannot choose their victims. Olmedo is an hour and a half away. Our planes hold enough fuel to last five hours.

"Have you ever been up in a plane?"

"No."

"Aren't you nervous?"

He didn't quite understand.

"Aren't you afraid?"

"No."

"You think you will recognize the way?"

"From Olmedo, yes. I know the country better than a dog."

We have no pursuit planes, but the sky is overcast and we may be protected by the clouds.

The three other planes that follow us in triangle formation disappear from minute to minute in the clouds that grow increasingly dense as we approach the Sierra. The inverted plow-shares of the highest crests rise above the great expanse of piled-up snow; up there the enemy scouts are awaiting us with the rockets that will warn their pursuit planes. But no doubt the sea of clouds is compact on the other side and separates the scouts from their observers. We fly amid the clouds, emerging from time to time so as not to crash into the mountains—as sperm whales come to the surface to breathe. Above us and the enemy scouts, far above the subterranean agitation of war, is a wonderfully clear sky of autumn morning. An almost biting cold finds its way into the plane; these combats that were to have lasted only a few weeks settle on the invisible earth like wounded men in their beds, and in the wind that strikes our faces winter once more passes its hands over the old face of war.

The clouds draw nearer. The peasant looks at me. I know that he is thinking: "How am I going to guide you if I can't see anything?" But he asks nothing. I yell into his ear:

"We'll cross above Olmedo."

He looks at the Sierra, looks below him and waits. In each plane the crew commander, his eyes on the crest rising above the clouds, watches for the rockets.

We are now above the Sierra. On the other side the sea of clouds forms a compact mass.

We navigate by the compass, but the compass does not record the drift caused by an oblique wind. If we are carried twenty to thirty kilometers out of our course the enemy planes may have a chance to take off. I will try to reconnoiter the country without completely getting out of the clouds, rise again to pick up the other planes, rectify our course, and head for Olmedo. Then it will be up to the peasant to show the way.

We have passed the Sierra; we are over enemy territory. Now any accident to the motor is fatal. The Moors have a special predilection for wounded aviators. Beneath the radiant sky, buried under the clouds, lie torture and death. Behind us the other planes, still in triangular formation, follow us with the comradeliness of two arms of the same body.

We are approaching Olmedo. The clouds, the sky, still the same serenity. . . . We enter the clouds. As soon as the mist envelops us it seems as if the battle were beginning. The plane descends slowly, so as to stay within the clouds as much as possible; at the fighting posts the machine gunners and the bombers are now on the lookout. And the pilots and I watch the compasses and the altimeter with more intensity than we ever watch a human face.

The altimeter drops: 800—700—500—400—375—350. We have not yet pierced through the blanket of fog. If we continue to drop and we are not exactly over Olmedo (which is probable) we are going to crash—there are hills throughout this region.

We begin to take on altitude again. Before dropping I have observed that the sea of clouds was punctured here and there. We shall wait, circling over the point where we are, till a rift appears below us.

Our plane loses all contact with the earth. Until now we have been advancing, our eyes and our minds always turned to what lay before us, fascinated by what we were approaching; for the first time now we must wait. The planes circle above the bank of clouds that extends beyond the distant crests; but the clouds advance with a movement that gives the illusion of being the movement of the earth itself, and it seems as if men, earth, destiny, flow away with that immensity that is gliding beneath us, while high up, beyond the world, the planes circle with the fatality of stars.

Yet at the same time the old savage instinct of the bird of prey has taken hold of us. With the centuries-old wheeling flight of hawks we circle as we wait for a break in the clouds, the eyes of all the crew looking downward as though we were on the lookout for the entire earth and expected it presently to appear in a sudden rift. And it seems as if the whole landscape of clouds and mountain peaks is turning with the slowness of a planet round our motionless machine.

A cloud darker than the rest, and greenish in hue, approaches. It is the break. Like a worn and dirty map, the earth begins to appear.

Olmedo is not immediately below us, but a few kilometers to our right, russet because of its tiles, like an old smear of blood on

the shredded surface of the clouds. My plane beats its wings—
the combat signal—and we swoop downward.

All heads are stretched forward, parallel like those of ancient
bas-reliefs. We are above the church; below us, the houses rush
past at full speed like a herd in flight.

The peasant looks, his whole body tense, his mouth half open,
and tears zigzag down his cheeks, one by one; he does not recognize anything.

Some distance away large puffs of shell smoke appear, like
fragments of the clouds from which we have just emerged. The
enemy antiaircraft guns are beginning to fire. The battery is no
doubt close to the enemy camp, but there is no trace of smoke on
the ground. We have two minutes at the most. The peasant said
that the field was north of Olmedo. I put the signal on the command dial square north; no one in the other three planes is aware
that we don't know where we are going.

For a brief moment I bank the plane 90°. Our path is parallel
to the main street of Olmedo. I point it out to the peasant:

"There's the church. The street. The Ávila road."

He recognizes all that in passing, but can't get his bearings for
the direction we have to take. What will he be able to recognize
when we no longer have even the buildings? Below the immobile
upper half of his face from which the tears are flowing his chin
quivers convulsively.

The Fascist pursuit planes are surely getting their motors
started. The first one that takes off will show us the field; but if
its attack allows the others time to leave the ground, none of us
will return. It is now a question of seconds.

There is only one resort: give the peasant an angle of vision
that he is used to. Perpendicularly he does not recognize the
country; on the ground—horizontally—he would recognize it at
once. We must get a view as close as possible to that which one
gets from the ground. I shift the course a few points off north
and drop to thirty meters.

The machine guns rattle, but that doesn't matter. The anti-aircraft guns have ceased firing—we are too low, below their range. Soldiers and farm animals scurry off frantically below us like snow shooting sideways from a snowplow. If one could die of looking and seeking, the peasant would die. He catches hold of my arm, points with a taut, crooked finger which he does not manage to straighten at a large publicity billboard, black and pale yellow under the low sky. And he pulls me to the right, with his whole might, as though I were the plane. I put the command signal east. The peasant shouts. None of the men turns his head. The peasant yells, but does not speak, and with his finger which is still crooked points to a wood.

"Is that it?"

He answers yes with his whole head and shoulders, without relaxing his outstretched arm. And there, next to the wood, is the oblong field which he had drawn for us before our take-off. A pursuit plane and a bombing plane are out in the open. The propeller of the pursuit plane is in motion.

We are approaching in the very direction in which it must take off. In order not to be brought down by our own bombs, we take on altitude, and in a few seconds we will again become targets for the antiaircraft shells. As we pass over the field we drop a few light bombs—enough to cut the path of the pursuit plane and prevent it from taking on speed. We circle and turn back dropping a string of light bombs. It's impossible to aim, but our blind firing cuts the path of the Fascist plane. We drop bombs as we pass over the wood, where a cluster of figures is trying to push the bombing plane. We bank as we did a while ago above the clouds and come back. As the field comes into sight again, the pursuit plane is lying on its side: a heavy bomb from one of our planes must have struck close by.

At full speed the four wheeling planes in oblique formation pass again one after the other over the wood and rise toward the shells which are beginning to form a barrage—as though we were deliberately going to meet them. Our bombs fall on the wood, where we can make out nothing. Undoubtedly the pursuit planes from the nearest enemy airdrome, advised by telephone, are already in the air. Our machine gunners watch the sky, the pilot and the bombers keep their eyes on the ground; the round continues.

We are suddenly jolted as by an air pocket. Has a shell just burst close by? There is no puff of smoke near us. But down below, from the wood, a thick, black smoke begins to pour, which I immediately recognize: gasoline. Directly or indirectly, we have struck the enemy depot. Still we see nothing of what we are bombarding. The enormous smoke begins to rise as if subterranean beds were burning beneath the quiet wood that looks exactly like all the others in the late morning. A few men come running out of the wood—and, in a few seconds, hundreds of them, in the same headlong animal flight as the flocks of cattle a while ago. And the smoke, which the wind beats down as if the sky would fling every trace of war back toward the wretched world of men, begins to spread. Beside me, shivering with joy and cold, the peasant stamps his feet in the fuselage.

Madrid is being bombarded. I am following a man who lugs a manuscript as big as himself. People rarely write on paper of that size, and such a large manuscript naturally interests a writer. I stop the man:

"What is that manuscript of yours?"

The sound of airplane bombs reaches our ears.

"It isn't a manuscript," he answers gently. "I'm changing the wallpaper in my apartment."

BOMBERS OVER SPAIN

H. OLOFF DE WET, *TENIENTE*

SPANISH LOYALIST AIR FORCE

Great excitement in the Commandant's office. The rebels have
taken Barajas. They are pushing forward to the relief of the
Alcazar. The three heavy bombers, Potez's 54's, their Lorraine
engines warming, stand ready, each loaded with nearly two thousand pounds of bombs. Six Bréguets are rapidly being prepared.
Everywhere there is activity. Nobody is very gay, we do not
need to be told that we shall not all come back. This will be the
biggest show I shall have ever have been on. The Potezes are to
take off first, bomb the positions at Barajas, and on their return
the six Bréguets are to repeat the operation. I am detailed for
the second escort, with Loire No. 3-14, to fly in a mixed flight
with five other fighters. We are ready to take off at 9:40.

It seems as though the first expedition had hardly left when
they were back once more, freed of their cargo of bombs. The
escort precede the bombers by a few minutes. One, two, three,
four—surely six took off. Yes, six did take off—Smith-Pigot was
last seen by Collins about six miles north of Toledo. He had two
Heinkels close on his tail, was doing flat turns. Moullenet, a
French pilot, went down in flames after colliding with a Fiat—
it was the Loire No. 3-14 I had been supposed to take over.
They got one of the Potezes as well; it crashed close to the objective. Four of the enemy had been shot down. I could wait for

no more details. I am relegated to a Dewoitine in the next escort.

Four of the Bréguets already in the air, the other two, meandering into position for the take-off are temporarily lost in the clouds of dust. Somebody is warming his guns on the tarmac. My finger has got pinched fixing the clips of the parachute—I never fail to do that; I shall tighten those thigh straps, I think, but interrupted by some remark from the mechanic, I clamber into the machine with the webbing loose about my legs. I settle into my seat; the man, straddle-legged across the fuselage, tightens the harness until I feel the pack of the 'chute hard in my back. Now with the mechanic's body flung across the tail of the fuselage, I open the throttle, check the Gnome-Rhone revolutions, and give the two Chatellerault guns a short burst. The chocks waved away, I taxi off the tarmac. We are to take off individually and get into formation in the air. Into the wind, no other aircraft about, I pull the throttle full open (the controls on many French engines work in the reverse); the Dewoitine, with its three-bladed propeller, takes rather a longer run than most fighting aircraft.

This is my first patrol with a Dewoitine; apart from the solitary Hawker Fury it was the best machine we had. It is highly maneuverable and has a wonderful climb. At 500 feet I circle the aerodrome. Inside me I am at peace at last; it is that waiting that is the worst part. It is always the worst and the best of everything—anticipation. I like this aircraft; she has lots of guts. I wish I always flew a Dewoitine. Poor Moullenet, he was a quiet fellow, I have hardly ever spoken to him, I realize. I thought it was only in films and stories that aircraft collided in flight; I wonder how it happened. I bet this little high-winged monoplane I am flying will spin just as easily and fast as the Siskin I was once taught on by Peter May at Grantham. What a long time ago it seems!

Heading toward Toledo we fighters are flying in two flights of three machines. Our motors are throttled back to keep pace with the six Bréguets a thousand feet beneath us. I wonder how old those Bréguets can be. They must have only just missed the World War. How solid they look wallowing along under the power of their single motor, how like those pictures I have seen of the German Taubes with their swept-back wing tips, only the war time bomber looked a much cleaner job. Spaniards call the Bréguet the "Guardian Angel"; they say no one ever gets killed in them.

It is 10:20, twenty-five minutes since we left Getafe. Away to the south I can distinctly recognize the turrets of the Alcazar, and beyond them the white bridges across the Tagus. We should be over the objective at any moment now. Hardly is the thought formed in my mind, when, glancing over the side of the cockpit, I see the anti-aircraft barrage that is bursting unpleasantly near the Bréguets. From high above, the explosions are vast daisies breaking into sudden bloom. I can see no aircraft. They will not have been expecting us back so soon perhaps. On the return flight they will be there to punish us. The bombers have formed a "fairy ring" over the road junction. I suppose they know what they are dropping their stuff on. I cannot see anything; white mushrooms of smoke rise as another salvo falls wide of the crossroads. Is that a column coming up the road? I am hanging forward in the webbing of my harness, for we are diving almost vertically on to the road crowded with troops.

The bombers have finished their work and low to the ground are heading for Getafe. This is splendid. (I am holding my breath.) Down, down, down . . . red berets, lorries, trees, the khaki coats of the running men are coming to meet us. It is like blowing on a plate of sand; the grains are scattering, leaving the road naked and white. Like a live thing in ecstasy the Dewoitine shivers to the touch of my hand on the trigger release. We plunge on. The skin is tight on my forehead, my neck is cold, the strap of my helmet whips my face. I can see flecks of flame on the leading edge of my wing. Could any life be as good as death like this? Gently I ease on the stick. The world is moving round me—trees, houses, roads, villages, slip underneath the belly of my machine. The horizon falls like the edge of a blue blind suddenly drawn down, and I am climbing heavenward. The day-bleached face of the moon peeps from beneath my wing. The sweet metallic flavor of blood is on my tongue as my nose bleeds. Once again we dive alternately on the specks and dots of men scattered in the fields adjacent to the road.

Turning back for home we can see far away the sun reflected from the Bréguets. Less than twenty minutes will see us over Getafe. The scene of our attack is already many miles behind us. I wonder what can have become of the Heinkels and the Fiats.

MADRID IS BURNING

MIKHAIL KOLTZOV

WAR CORRESPONDENT, *Pravda*

November 19th

These last two days were the worst this unhappy city has ever suffered.

Madrid is burning. A light glows in the streets, heat pours out of the streets, but it is not daylight, and not summer, but a November night. As I walk through the city enormous fires from all sides, and wherever I turn, light my way.

Madrid is burning, set on fire by German airplanes. Public buildings, hotels, hospitals, schools, all are burning. The residences of the people are in flames. The firemen cannot cope with the fires. They are completely exhausted. Even if they were five times as many, they would be unable to put out the flames. With the help of volunteers they are trying to prevent further disasters —explosions and mass deaths. They have quickly cut off gas-mains, removed gasoline stores, and isolated burning buildings.

With blind fury the Fascists are determined to break the resistance of Madrid. They are determined to wipe the capital of Spain from the face of the earth, to destroy her habitations, and at the very least to compel the defenders to surrender the city so that the million people living here shall be spared. What is happening now could destroy the sanity of sane men. I cannot vouch for the psychic health of all adult Madrileños, but I know that in this city many are suffering from nervous collapse.

The suffering of Madrid has by no means come to an end. The Fascist High Command is continuing to bombard Madrid with increasing fury. They have concentrated all their aviation here. Twenty Junkers with thirty supporting fighters bombarded the city today—there were fifty planes in the air at one time. The Republican air force is numerically weaker, and their courage cannot always compensate for the numerical superiority of the enemy. However, our "snub-nosed" brought down two Junkers and two fighters today.

Every three or four hours the bombardment is renewed. After each bombing there are more and more blazing ruins, more and more heaps of bloody flesh. The prayers, screams and lamentations of the people rise from the street. Those sharp-sighted, quietly murderous men manning their dark grey, steely planes circle the city, and the rumble of death can be heard above the defenceless roofs. The victims are removed from the streets. The cold winter air pours into the houses—there are few unbroken windows left. And then everything begins again from the beginning. What seemed to be an ominous shape of the future, recorded only in books, has become fact. Before the eyes of the whole world, on the threshold of 1937, Fascist militarism is destroying an enormous European city, the capital of Spain.

A two hundred kilogram bomb can destroy a five-story building: it can even reach down into the building's cellar. Such bombs have been falling in dozens. The Fascists have dropped three hundred kilogram and even heavier bombs capable of destroying eight-story buildings. The Fascists do not have to employ these heavy bombs in order to destroy the thin, fragile walls of the workmen's dwellings. A few incendiary bombs are enough to reduce an entire working-class area to flames in ten minutes.

Late at night we wandered out into the streets. Yesterday the Fascist planes had to use flares to find their way about the city.

Today the burning city lights their way. These murderers are drunk with the spectacle of the flames as they fly about freely, dropping more and more bombs on more and more human beings.

The marketplace on the Plaza Carmen has become a blazing inferno. Suffocating smoke, the acrid smell of olive-oil, burnt fish . . . These market-products, brought here with so much labor, have all perished, and tomorrow most of the Madrileños will have to go hungry. Walls, beams and girders crash to the ground. An enormous pillar of flame lights up all the surrounding houses. Squeezing her hands together, silently weeping, the poetess María Teresa León looks out at the burning city. Glassy and motionless, like lenses, are the eyes of Rafael Alberti. Madrid burns, and it would seem likely that if she burns much longer there will be nothing left. Certainly, today, it seems that nothing will be left.

The palace of the Duke of Alba is burning. It lies on a hill in a beautiful park, and is filled to the brim with books, works of art, whole galleries of paintings. When I visited the palace towards the end of October the Workers' Militia proudly explained how they had posted guards over these relics from the ancient past, guarding everything from the most important statues, paintings and tapestries to the veriest baubles. Even the Duke's old gloves are being protected. The Duke however has fled to London, and from there he has been heard complaining of Red vandalism— this at a time when the guards are carefully wiping the dust from the backs of his books. German airmen dropped incendiary bombs on his palace—not just one, but many. Now all his treasures are shrivelling and burning to cinders in the flames, or would be burning, if the worker-guards at the risk of their lives did not rescue them from the flames and lay them out on the grass—ancient weapons, paintings, mediaeval armor, costly folios from his library. What a picture for those who want conscientiously to determine which class is defending culture and which class is destroying it! . . .

All this while the rebels have been ferociously storming the University City. They have brought up great numbers of reinforcements, artillery, mortars. They have suffered, especially among the Moroccans, huge and terrible losses. The squares in the University City are piled with corpses.

The diplomatic corps are beginning to show some signs of life. One cannot say it is out of pure affection for the Republican Government or the people of Madrid. The nerves of the diplomats are giving way. Bombs from Junkers do not choose where they will fall. They have destroyed a French Lycée in University City, though it was clearly marked with a huge and brand-new Nationalist flag. Several bombs have fallen close to the British Embassy. Representatives of France and England have been inspecting the damage in the city, especially the hospitals. They have published a note of protest against the bombing. All the acceptable words are included in the note—"humanity," "defenceless population," "the horrors of destruction," "the rights of man." Only one small detail is missing: there is no address. For some reason the note was sent only to the editors of the Madrid newspapers.

November 20th

Rain has been falling since morning. It is something of a relief —enemy planes have not come over. The Militia and the International Brigade and the Santa Christina almshouse. But the three attacks produced no result.

November 21st

It rained again all day . . .

WORLD WAR II – EUROPE

The Second World War opened up with swift German lightning or *blitz* armored attacks on the ground coupled with paralyzing air strikes against the Low Countries, Poland, Norway, Denmark, and France. Once the Nazi armored juggernaut had subjugated most of Europe and occupied France it turned its attention to that relatively small island a scant 20 miles away, across the English Channel.

With the words of *"Wir fahren gegen England"* ("We Are Sailing Against England") on their lips the *Luftwaffe* launched the greatest aerial attack the world had ever seen, up to that time. Wave upon wave of "Stuka" dive bombers, Heinkel 111s, Junkers 88s, Dorniers, and other German bombers struck at the British Isles bent upon destroying the Royal Air Force and thus opening the way for invasion. RAF fields were hit incessantly, day after day, crippling *Hurricanes* and *Spitfires,* which were already in short supply. Hangars and sorely needed supplies and spare parts were destroyed and runways torn up with bomb craters so that the fighters could not take off to strike back at the oncoming Nazi horde.

And then a miracle happened! The German High Command lifted its concentrated attacks against the RAF and began a concerted bombing effort against London and the other principal British cities. This was a serious strategic blunder, one of a few such errors that, thank God, lost the war for Nazi Germany! Were the German Military Intelligence experts asleep? Didn't they know that the poor exhausted RAF was down to a pitifully small handful of pilots and fewer aircraft?

Now the civilians, the ordinary Englishmen, caught the full brunt of the powerful Nazi air machine as night after night the *Luftwaffe* pounded Britain's population centers. But the people proved that they could take it and still come up with a smile and the finger formed "V" for Victory sign. While the civilians suffered the RAF was busy repairing its fields, its aircraft and training more pilots and British industry was turning out more fighter planes. Soon the tide of battle turned as "the few" to whom "so many owed so much" took the offensive and shot down more and more of the attacking waves of enemy bombers. They went aloft, attacked the enemy, returned for refueling, and took off again, repeatedly, seemingly inexhaustibly. Before long it became too costly for the *Luftwaffe* to fly over England. The Battle of Britain had been won by the RAF, their game little *Spitfires* and *Hurricanes,* and the indomitable British people.

The war, however, was far from over. Britain was sorely in need of matériel and supplies. The United States, which had not yet entered the war, called itself the "Arsenal of Democracy." It had given Britain fifty World War I destroyers in exchange for the use of some naval bases. The U.S. also sent bombers to Britain. These were flown across the Atlantic by ferry pilots of the Air Transport Command (ATC). They were civilian pilots employed by the U. S. Army Air Force. Many American women served as ferry pilots including Jacqueline Cochran.

The air war over Europe was a vast and complicated affair. It involved thousands of aircraft of many nations and ranged many thousands of square miles over the Atlantic to the American coast, across to the Soviet Union, north to the Arctic, and south to Africa. American *Flying Fortresses, Liberators,* and *Mitchells;* British *Wellingtons, Lancasters,* and *Hampdens;* German Dorniers, Heinkels, and Junkers; Russian *Stormoviks,* and French and Italian bombers thundered across the skies bearing their heavy burdens of death and destruction. While it is difficult to tell the entire story of such a massive operation, with all of its varied ramifications and innuendos, the selections presented here are representative. They tell the story of bombing missions over London, Berlin, Rome, Schweinfurt, Regensburg, Ploesti, Bizerte, and others. The British bombed the Germans by night, and the Americans, who had now entered the war, hit them by day. Some of the most dramatic and costly AAF raids were made over the oil refineries of Ploesti, and on Schweinfurt-Regensburg.

The Schweinfurt-Regensburg raids were in reality two distinct but coordinated, long-range AAF bombing attacks deep into Germany. A total of 376 unescorted B-17 *Flying Fortresses* took part in those two raids on August 17, 1943. The first mission against the Messerschmitt aircraft factory in Regensburg was made by 146 of the bombers. Though the raid was a success twenty-four of the *Fortresses* fell before the flak and the guns of the concentrated enemy fighters. As planned, the remaining B-17s made their way back over the Mediterranean Sea to Africa and bases in Algeria rather than fight their way across Germany again.

While this was going on the second wave of B-17s were pounding the ball-bearing complex at Schweinfurt. Bad weather had delayed their departure and they too battled massed enemy fighters all the way—from the moment they first crossed the German frontier until they reached the English Channel on the return trip. Of this force of 230 heavy bombers more than 16 percent, or a total of thirty-six, were downed by the enemy.

In their own words German and Allied commanders, pilots, co-pilots, bombardiers, navigators, and gunners recount their own dramatic experiences, from combat duty to being shot down, bailing out, being taken prisoner, and escape. In some cases the writers are authors of distinction such as Lieutenant Colonel Beirne Lay, Jr., who was later to write the best-selling novel and movie *Twelve O'Clock High* upon which the famous TV series was based; Lieutenant Bert Stiles, who wrote *Serenade to the Big Bird;* the legendary war correspondent Ernie Pyle; and Sergeant Bill Hess, author of a number of books on World War II flying and a current volume on the P-51 *Mustang* fighter. Other writers are famous (and infamous) wartime leaders such as General "Hap" Arnold, Chief of the USAAF; Lieutenant General Ira Eaker, commander of the mighty U. S. Eighth Air Force, and of the Mediterranean Allied Air Force; and *Reichsmarschal* Hermann Goering, who tells here why his much vaunted *Luftwaffe* was defeated.

"SWORDFISH" AGAINST THE "BISMARCK"

IAN CAMERON, LIEUTENANT

FLEET AIR ARM, ROYAL NAVY

> I propose a special tribute to the Fleet Air Arm, to whom the
> destruction of the *Bismarck* must really be attributed.
> —FIRST SEA LORD.

A great deal has been written about the sinking of the *Bismarck*.
Books, articles, films, radio and television scripts and even a
play have unfolded the drama of the great battleship's brief but
eventful sortie into the Atlantic. Is there anything new, it might
be wondered, to say? I think there is.

For looking back after an interval of some twenty years, the
Bismarck episode can now be seen in true historical perspective,
can be seen for the first time for what it really was: a bridge
between the old techniques of Naval warfare and the new, an
event which looked both back to Trafalgar and Jutland and
forward to Midway and Leyte Gulf. For when, that tempestuous
evening in May, the torpedoes of the *Ark Royal's Swordfish* bit
deep into the vital parts of the German warship they announced
in no uncertain manner the coming-of-age of the modern conception of Naval warfare, a conception of vessels striking at
each other by air from far beyond visual range. Yet at the same
time the chase and destruction of the *Bismarck* saw in plenty
the old techniques of Naval war, with vessels within visual range

of each other swinging broadside-on to deploy their full arcs of fire (a manœuvre already old at the time of the Armada). Thus to the drama and excitement of events were added another and inner drama: that of a young and as yet unaccepted branch of the Navy struggling to prove its worth. And how magnificently its worth was proved! For from first to last the hunt of the *Bismarck* was an indictment of the Old Navy (and its ineffective guns), and a vindication of the New Navy (and its carrier-borne strike planes). But to begin at the beginning . . .

On the 18th May, 1941, Admiral Lutjens sailed from Gdynia in the *Bismarck,* the world's largest and most formidable battle-ship. His object: to carry out a series of attacks on the Atlantic convoys which were already being sorely harried by U-boats. In company with the *Bismarck* was the heavy cruiser *Prinz Eugen,* and the two vessels together constituted about as grave a threat as the Allies ever had to face. For that spring the battle of the Atlantic (on which the whole British war effort depended) was not going well; and if two such powerful warships as the *Bismarck* and *Prinz Eugen* had been allowed to break out into and remain for long on the convoy routes, then the whole move-ment of shipping to and fro across the Atlantic would have been brought to a standstill. It was therefore essential to the prosecu-tion of the war that the two vessels were at once brought to action and sunk.

On 20th May a Norwegian Resistance agent saw and re-ported the German warships as they came up through the Skagarrak, and the following afternoon they were spotted in Kars Fjord (a few miles south of Bergen) by a reconnaissance plane of Coastal Command. The Admiralty were alerted, and they at once strengthened their watch on the northern escape routes into the Atlantic. They didn't, however, order the heavy units of the Home Fleet to sea, for the very good reason that they were unsure of the *Bismarck*'s intentions. She could have been merely escorting a troop convoy to Bergen, or she could be intending to remain for some weeks among the Norwegian fjords before trying to break out into the Atlantic. If the latter was indeed her intention, then the British Fleet must on no account put to sea prematurely, or they would find themselves short of fuel at the vital moment. The Admiralty therefore decided to maintain an air watch on the *Bismarck,* at the same time keeping the Home Fleet "on a split yarn", ready to sail at a moment's notice should their quarry leave the safety of the fjords.

Then the weather took a hand. On the morning of 22nd May fog and low cloud shrouded the Norwegian coast. Coastal Command reconnaissance planes were unable to get through to Kars Fjord. And the Admiralty, at this critical moment, had no means of telling whether the *Bismarck* was still in harbour or had already put to sea and was several hundred miles into the Atlantic. Urgent telephone calls passed between Admiralty and Air Ministry. But the latter declared themselves quite unable to help. The weather, they said, was too bad for their planes to fly in. All Coastal Command aircraft were grounded. And that was that.

And this perhaps is a good opportunity to take a look at the vexed issue of the rôle of Coastal Command: to ask why, at this vital moment, the Navy had to go cap in hand to the Air Force and ask them to perform a task which should, beyond doubt, have been an exclusively Naval commitment. The answer once again lies in the evil legacy of the years between the wars when the Fleet Air Arm was neglected by both Navy and Air Force and its development irreparably retarded. For if the Navy had not been forced to give up its air branch in 1918 it would surely have developed as one of its top priorities a long-range, long-endurance reconnaissance aircraft capable of keeping watch on enemy ports. For this was in the classic tradition of Naval duties. In the days of Drake and Nelson, it had been fast frigates which had patrolled outside the French and Spanish harbours reporting the movement of enemy ships; what more natural than that aircraft should, in time, have taken over the frigates' rôle and become the eyes of the fleet? Yet because of inter-war parsimony no aircraft capable of fulfilling this rôle was ever developed by the Navy. During the Second World War long-range reconnaissance over the sea had therefore to be left exclusively to the planes of another Service—R.A.F. *Sunderlands,* or American *Catalinas* or *Liberators.* It was R.A.F. planes, for example, which had carried out the vital reconnaissance flights over Taranto; it was R.A.F. planes again—this time based in Russia—which carried out the reconnaissance flight preceding the attack on the *Tirpitz;* it was American *Catalinas* whose photographs led to the pinpoint accuracy of the raids on Sumatra's oil refineries. For one Service to have to rely on another to perform an integral part of its duties was, to say the least, an arrangement that was not satisfactory. It led to friction, misunderstanding and inefficiency —all of which traits were exemplified, that spring, in Coastal Command's efforts to locate the *Bismarck* off Bergen.

For throughout the whole of 22nd May not a single aircraft of Coastal Command got through to Kars Fjord. In view of what happened later that evening only two conclusions are possible: either they didn't try very hard, or else their aircrew were not very efficient.

For a couple of hours before sunset an obsolete target-towing aircraft of the Fleet Air Arm, unarmed and manned by a scratch volunteer crew, made a thorough reconnaissance of Kars, Bergen and Hjelte Fjords and was able to report that the *Bismarck* had sailed.

This flight—as important as it is little known—was a minor epic of the air: and an example, if ever there was one, of the dictum that "men make the city, and not walls or ships without men in them".

It was initiated by Captain Fancourt, commanding officer of the Royal Naval Station at Hatston in the Orkneys. Throughout 22nd May Fancourt had been in frequent touch with Coastal Command—for he had a force of *Albacore* torpedo-bombers ready to take off the moment the *Bismarck* came within range—and he therefore knew all about their failure to get through to the Norwegian coast. He also knew, being a Naval officer, just how vital it was that some plane, somehow, *should* get through. As it became increasingly clear to him that the R.A.F. were unlikely to reconnoitre the critical fjord, Captain Fancourt began to wonder whether he mightn't himself be able to gain the information which was needed so urgently by the Home Fleet. For he had under his command a number of Fleet Air Arm officers with much experience of bad-weather flying over the sea; in particular his thoughts turned to a certain Commander Rotherham—whose flying days were over but whose reputation as an observer was second to none. At about three o'clock, after the failure of yet another Coastal Command plane to get through, Fancourt put the idea of a Fleet Air Arm reconnaissance to Rotherham, who at once declared himself ready to make the attempt. Fancourt then approached Goddard, C.O. of the Fleet Requirements Unit stationed at Hatston, with a view to discovering what aircraft—if any—were available. Noel Goddard was a pilot whose ability and experience matched Rotherham's: and he not only suggested a plane (one of the *Marylands* used by his squadron for target towing) but declared that he would fly it himself. A volunteer telegraphist-air-gunner completed the crew, who at 4 p.m. assembled in the Hatston control tower for briefing.

It was a pretty desperate undertaking that they were about to embark on. For twelve hours Coastal Command (with its many fast, modern and well-equipped planes) had been trying to get through to the Norwegian coast in vain. How could a single, obsolete, unarmed, Fleet Air Arm target-tower hope to succeed where so many planes so much better equipped had failed? The answer, of course, lay not in the aircraft but in the crew.

At their briefing Goddard, Rotherham and Armstrong (the telegraphist-air-gunner) paid special attention to two things: the weather and the exact conformation of the coast around Bergen. The weather was fine in the Orkneys, but a front lay low over the North Sea, and 10/10 cloud, from sea level to 7,000 feet, was wedged tight against the Norwegian shore: a barrier it would be suicide to fly through. The conformation of the coast was equally unpromising: a mosaic of islands and steep-sided fjords, many of them rising sheer from sea level to close on 1,500 feet —not a pleasant coastline to be approaching blind through cloud. For an hour Goddard and Armstrong studied the weather charts and memorised details of the coast, while Rotherham made a series of the most careful calculations. He decided to adopt the old device of aiming at a point some miles to the right or left of the real objective, with a view to knowing which way to turn if a doubtful landfall were made. In this case he selected Marsten Island about twelve miles south of Bergen, with the intention of turning north the second they sighted land—if indeed they sighted it at all before they flew into it! As soon as Rotherham had finished his calculations, the three men clambered into the *Maryland* and took off.

It was one of those rare days in the Orkneys with bright sunshine, unlimited visibility and not a cloud in the sky. They climbed to 500 feet and headed on a course of 082 degrees for Norway. For about half an hour the flight was uneventful as a summer cruise round the bay. Then a shade after 1730, Goddard noticed that the horizon ahead was beginning to take on a hazy opaqueness. And five minutes later they saw in front of them the cloud, rising like a solid wall out of the sea.

The cloud was thick: a mixture of cumulus and mist. And its base was frighteningly low. To have gone above it (and to have had later to come down blind over a mountainous coast) would have been lunacy. To have gone through it would have prevented Rotherham from seeing the sea (and hence precluded his making those frequent assessments of wind-change on which pin-point navigation depends). There was, therefore, only one course open to Goddard: to go below it.

He took the *Maryland* down to a hundred feet; but was still in cloud. He took her down to fifty feet. That was better. To start with. But the strain of flying for long at such a height and in such visibility was appalling. For the *Maryland* was soon plunging down a hazy ill-defined tunnel: above her, the solid canopy of cloud; below her, the great stillness of an almost dead-calm sea; and in between, straight in their path, the occasional drifting patches of mist-cum-cloud which came rushing at them out of the haze, building up like sudden snowballs aslide down the slope of a mountain. Goddard needed all his concentration and all his skill to keep the plane in the narrow safety margin between cloud and sea. If he had eased back, even a fraction, on the stick, they would have been in cloud, and quite unable safely to descend. If he had eased forward on the stick, again only a fraction, they and their *Maryland* would have been splintered to fragments against the sea. It was a time for strong nerves and steady hands.

Goddard hoped that once they had passed through the front, conditions might improve. But they didn't. They worsened.

Soon visibility became so restricted that flying below cloud was no longer possible. And Goddard had no alternative but to take the *Maryland* up, and fly blind through the cumulus at some 2,000 feet. They kept course on instruments for the best part of half an hour; then Rotherham insisted on having another look at the sea.

Goddard let down slowly: cautiously. At 500 feet he could see nothing. At 100 feet he could still see nothing.

"When my Kolsman registered fifty feet," he said, "and I still couldn't see the sea, I began to get worried."

They levelled off at zero feet. And even then—when they were literally skimming the water—they could only see it occasionally through gaps in the drifting patches of cloud.

From the observer's cockpit Rotherham peered at the almost

infinitesimal ripples made by the wind. He was adept at reading the language of the waves; for he belonged to that vintage generation of observers accustomed to finding their way over the oceans without the help of radio fixes, beams and complicated astral computers; and, like most of his contemporaries, he had on more than one occasion "smelt" his way back to his carrier when scientific aids were absent or had failed. He spent a long time now staring at the faintly-seen evidence of a wayward wind. Then he gave Goddard a 5 degree alteration of course and let him return to 2,000 feet.

The *Maryland* flew steadily east. Twice more in the next twenty minutes the nerve-racking procedure of dropping to sea level to find a wind was repeated. And on each occasion Goddard needed all his skill to avoid dropping those few extra feet which would have brought their reconnaissance to a sudden and most unpleasant end. Then Rotherham said quietly:

"Another five minutes and Marsten ought to be coming up. Dead ahead."

The minutes passed. One minute: two minutes: three minutes. They were nerving themselves to flying straight into the side of a cliff, when, miraculously, the cloud thinned out. And there, fine on the starboard bow and less than a mile ahead, was Marsten.

After flying blind for over three hundred miles, Rotherham had made a landfall, dead on E.T.A., which was accurate to within a couple of hundred yards. Neither war nor peace can boast a finer example of dead-reckoning navigation.

But their troubles were far from over.

The clouds had indeed lifted and thinned, but their base was still on an average less than a thousand feet above sea level, and in several of the fjords it was a great deal lower. They skirted Marsten (which was known to house a number of A-A batteries) and after flying for some minutes parallel to the shore, nosed into Kars Fjord. It was a gloomy, forbidding place: a corridor of dark water hemmed in by hills but mercifully free from mist. They flew up it at five hundred feet. There was no ack-ack. And no sign either of the *Bismarck* or *Prinz Eugen*. They passed low over a pair of fir-green islands and took a quick look into Hjelte Fjord. It too was silent and deserted. The *Bismarck,* it seemed, had sailed.

Yet they couldn't be sure. For as Rotherham now pointed out to Goddard, she might simply have put into Bergen because of the weather. They knew that Bergen was heavily defended; but they also knew that their reconnaissance wouldn't be a hundred per cent conclusive until they had taken a look at it.

They approached the harbour cautiously on the fringe of cloud. But they were spotted, and soon ack-ack heavy and accurate was straddling the *Maryland*. Again and again the blast shook them. Shrapnel thudded into their fuselage; and their intercom chose this inopportune moment to go completely dead. Rotherham (having taken a quick look at the shipping in harbour) wanted to climb for cloud. But he had no means of communicating with Goddard, who thought their best chance of escape was speed, and promptly proceeded to dive. Zigzagging at zero feet, the *Maryland* flashed over the roof-tops of Bergen. Ack-ack was heavy. A burst of tracer shattered their cockpit canopy. Another burst flashed inches below their fuel tanks, which, Goddard remembered, were not self-sealing. Then in less time than it takes to tell they were clear of the town and skimming the waters of Bergen Fjord. The ack-ack faded and died; and they climbed into the protecting canopy of cloud, astonished to find themselves still alive.

Rotherham realised the vital importance of signalling the information that the warships had sailed as quickly as possible—lest they were shot down by fighters on the way home. But he was unable to make himself heard on the intercom and the *Maryland* was so constructed that pilot, observer and wireless operator were in separate cockpits cut off from each other by bulkheads. He therefore wrote on a piece of paper "Signal C.-in-C. that

'The battleship and cruiser have left'," and pushed the message through a hole in the bulkhead to Goddard, who in turn passed it to the wireless operator.

Armstrong spent over ten minutes calling up Coastal Command, to whose frequency he was tuned; but without reply. Realising there must be maladjustment on a wavelength he was unaccustomed to using, he proceeded on his own initiative to tune into his normal target-towing frequency at Scapa and passed the message on that. At Scapa Flow target-towing was in full swing, when the telegraphist-air-gunners, to their great astonishment, suddenly picked up a most urgent operational signal. This was at 1900 hours. And the vital message was at once passed to Sir John Tovey, C.-in-C. Home Fleet.

Sir John decided that the issues involved were of such importance that he would interrogate the aircrew personally as soon as they landed. So it was that the moment the *Maryland* touched down, Rotherham was rushed to the telephone and questioned. He was able to convince the Admiral that the *Bismarck* and *Prinz Eugen* had, beyond all doubt, left the Norwegian fjords. Accordingly, Tovey ordered the Home Fleet to weigh anchor, and one of the most dramatic sea chases in British history was under way.

A good many people know that the *Bismarck* was sunk because she was first crippled and halted by planes of the Fleet Air Arm. Not so many know that the whole hunt for the German battleship was triggered off by a Fleet Air Arm reconnaissance flight carried out in weather too bad for Coastal Command to be airborne. And the significance of the *Maryland*'s reconnaissance is this. It enabled the Home Fleet to put to sea at exactly the right moment. For if Tovey had sailed six hours earlier he would, on the final day of the hunt, have run out of fuel before the *Bismarck* could have been brought to action; and if he had sailed six hours later his ships would have failed to intercept her as she passed through the Greenland gap. Such was the value of what Rotherham and Goddard called their "Cook's tour of the fjords".

It has already been remarked that during the war the Fleet Air Arm received little publicity for its work. And neither Rotherham nor Goddard was especially surprised when, a few weeks after their reconnaissance, one of London's principal evening papers contained a dramatic account of how a *Coastal Command* pilot, acting on his own initiative, had made the flight to Bergen in a *Coastal Command* training plane! As Goddard remarked, "Coastal Command never forgave us for doing something which they couldn't!"

The events of the next five days, with their sudden and dramatic changes of fortune, have all the ingredients of a carefully synthesised thriller.

At 7.22 on the morning of 23rd May the *Suffolk*'s look-out spotted the *Bismarck* and *Prinz Eugen* as they skirted the fringe of the Greenland ice-pack. There followed a piece of shadowing as skilful as it was arduous. For hour after hour the cruisers *Norfolk* and *Suffolk* clung to the German warships. The weather was appalling with heavy seas, squalls of snow, mirages thrown up from the ice blink, and drifting patches of fog. Hour after hour the four ships plunged at top speed through the ice-cold waters of the Greenland gap; the *Bismarck* struggling to throw her shadowers off, the cruisers clinging grimly by radar to their powerful adversary and sending off frequent reports of her position, course and speed. And these reports bore fruit. At dawn the two most powerful ships of the British Navy—the *Hood* and the *Prince of Wales*—steamed up at high speed to intercept the *Bismarck* as she debouched out of the Greenland channel. The action which followed was as swift as it was unexpected. For in the cold light of the sub-arctic dawn, it was not the hunted who died but the hunter. After six minutes of violent gunfire the *Hood*, symbol of British sea power, blew up and sank; and the *Prince of Wales*, badly battered, was forced to break off the engagement. The guns of the Old Navy had failed. It remained to be seen whether the aircraft of the New Navy would fare any better.

The loss of the *Hood* came as an almost unbelievable shock to the C.-in-C., the Navy and the nation as a whole. For a full generation she had been regarded as the embodiment of British Naval strength, the most powerful warship in the world. Now in the flash of one terrible explosion, she was gone, and out of her ship's company of over fourteen hundred only three had survived. To the already weighty reasons for bringing the *Bismarck* to action there was now added another: the desire for revenge, the need to reassert a supremacy threatened as it had never been threatened since Jutland. The Admiralty took a number of drastic decisions. They stripped the convoys bare. They assembled from both sides of the Atlantic and from the Mediterranean a concentration of warships of unparalleled weight: thirty-nine battleships, battlecruisers, aircraft carriers, cruisers and destroyers, all of which were ordered to devote themselves exclusively to the one task: the hunting down of the *Bismarck*.

After the *Hood* v *Bismarck* action, the cruisers *Norfolk* and *Suffolk* continued their shadowing while the C.-in-C. (with the *Victorious, King George V, Repulse* and the 2nd Cruiser Squadron) attempted to close from the south-east. Throughout the day the weather was patchy; there was a good deal of mist and visibility alternated between two and eighteen miles. The *Bismarck,* apparently undamaged, was still steaming fast and Tovey feared that with the coming of darkness she might well be able to give him the slip. He therefore ordered *Victorious* to close her and fly-off a twilight striking force in an effort to slow her down with torpedoes. The *Swordfish* strike was pressed home with great gallantry at extreme range and in very difficult conditions. But only one hit (which did little damage) was achieved. And that night what Sir John had feared took place. The shadowers lost the *Bismarck*.

The evening of 24th/25th May marked the acme of Lutjens' success. He had broken out into the Atlantic. He had brushed aside the first force to make contact with him, sinking in the process the best-known ship in the British Navy. He had survived an air attack, and he had just shaken off the shadowing cruisers which had been dogging him for the previous thirty-six hours. On the face of it the barometer of his fortunes was set firmly at fair. But in point of fact he had his troubles. The *Bismarck* had been damaged twice: once by a fourteen-inch salvo from the *Prince of Wales* (which had penetrated her oil tanks), and once by the *Swordfish*'s torpedo (which, albeit only slightly, had reduced her speed). And all the time the net around her was tightening. Singly or in little groups of three or four the thirty-nine warships alerted by the Admiralty were closing in. They had of course a vast area of ocean to encompass and search; and many of them were pitiably weak—if the *Bismarck* had come across them singly she would have blasted them off the face of the sea. But already the process of attrition which was to bring the great battleship to her Armageddon was at work, sapping her capacity to resist, grinding away at her defences as slowly but irrevocably as the mills of God.

Throughout 25th May the search for the *Bismarck* continued.

For those viewing events twenty years later, secure in the knowledge of hindsight, it is of course easy to be critical of the way the search was conducted. But even allowing for hindsight, it would seem that errors were made that day which were inexcusable and which resulted in the *Bismarck* all but slipping out of the net. For instance, in the C.-in-C.'s flagship Admiralty bearings on the *Bismarck* were plotted on a "Mercators Projector" chart instead of on a "Polar Co-ordinate"; with the result that for over four hours the main body of the Home Fleet steamed at full speed to the north-east when they should in fact have been steaming full speed to the south-west! Again, the Admiralty had come to the conclusion by 11 o'clock in the morning that the *Bismarck* was making for Brest; yet for a further four hours they allowed Tovey to go steaming away to the north-east with every revolution of his engines taking him farther from the scene of operations. The result was that by evening the *Bismarck* had all but escaped. She was steaming fast for the French coast; the main units of the British fleet were labouring far behind her (nearly a hundred miles in her wake); and in her path lay only a scattering of destroyers and the two units of Somerville's Force H. The destroyers, everyone knew, had no hope of halting her by themselves. Force H consisted of the *Renown* and the *Ark Royal*. The lightly-armoured *Renown* wouldn't have stood one chance in a million against the *Bismarck*. So there remained only the *Ark Royal* and her handful of archaic *Swordfish*. They were the last hope. Unless they could slow the *Bismarck* down and allow Tovey's warships to overhaul her, Admiral Lutjens would, in thirty-six hours, be returning to the Fatherland in triumph.

It was, for the Fleet Air Arm, the hour of destiny.

Throughout the night of 25th/26th May, Force H ploughed steadily north into a rising head sea. Somerville knew that provided he kept going he could head the *Bismarck* off. But during the night the weather—already bad—deteriorated, and Somerville was forced to reduce speed. Soon even at seventeen knots the great ships were labouring dangerously. Dawn on the 26th broke sunless, with low clouds racing over a foam-capped sea. The *Renown* was a terrifying sight; huge waves were sluicing her from stem to stern so that she appeared continually awash and about to founder; while even the *Ark* was taking it green over her flight-deck—a full sixty feet above the Plimsoll line.

Aboard the carrier conditions were so bad that many of her ship's company thought flying was impossible. Her flight-deck, sometimes awash and constantly swept by spray, was slippery as a skating-rink. Her wind-over-the-deck recorder was wavering between forty-five and fifty-five knots. And her round-down was rising and falling by fifty-six feet—the height of a four-storey house! The *Ark* had flown her *Swordfish* in bad weather before; but never in weather like this. Yet fly them she must, if the *Bismarck* was to be halted.

At 7.30 the planes were brought up from the hangar. The flight-deck handling parties, under Lieutenant-Commander Stringer, had been trebled. And it was as well they had. For ranging the *Swordfish* that morning called for the strength of Hercules and the patience of Job. Time and again, as the flight-deck tilted at fantastic angles, a plane would slide bodily towards the catwalks, dragging with it the forty to fifty ratings who were struggling to manhandle it aft. But somehow by 8.30 ten planes were ranged and ready to fly-off on a broad-fronted search to locate the *Bismarck*. At 8.35 the carrier reduced speed and swung into wind. Traill, choosing his moment carefully, dropped his flag; and aboard both *Ark Royal* and *Renown* ship's companies held their breath as the leading plane gathered way. Would she make it?

As the flight-deck tilted down, the take-off degenerated into a frantic slithering glissade. It looked, for one terrible moment, as though the aircraft were plunging straight into the maw of an approaching wave. But Traill had timed his signal well. At the last second, the deck swung up; and the plane was flung off, through the spume of a sixty-foot wave as it cascaded over the carrier's bow. And the almost unbelievable thing was this. The miracle was repeated not once but nine times, until the whole of the searching force was airborne and fanning out on their respective courses.

As the planes disappeared Traill and Stringer breathed a prayer of relief. But their troubles, they knew, were far from over. The *Swordfish* had been difficult to fly-off; they would be more difficult still to land-on.

There followed an anxious wait. Then, a shade after 10.30, the reports began to flood in. First an enemy report from a

Catalina of Coastal Command, then a sighting signal from one of the *Ark Royal's Swordfish,* then a second *Swordfish* report: all indicating that the *Bismarck,* heading east and steaming at twenty knots, was roughly seventy-five miles to the west-north-west of Force H. After an interval of thirty-six hours, contact had been re-established. And—what was even more hopeful—the *Ark Royal* was between the *Bismarck* and the French coast, *and* in the ideal position to launch a strike.

Aboard the carrier, relief shadowers (fitted with special long-range tanks) were at once ranged and flown-off: their task, to keep the *Bismarck* under constant observation.

The weather by this time was appalling: a full gale, heavy seas, 8/10 cloud from 300 to 11,000 feet, and driving squalls of sleet. Difficult conditions in which to shadow. Working in pairs the *Swordfish* circled the *Bismarck.* If they got too far away, they lost her in the poor visibility; if they got too near, they were collandered by her extremely accurate ack-ack, which, controlled by radar, even followed them into cloud when they thought they were safely hidden. Throughout that day and the following night the shadowing *Swordfish* clung to the *Bismarck* in relays, never losing contact. Their work was unspectacular. But it was also vital, dangerous (more than one plane failing to return) and demanding of no little endurance and skill. All too often when tribute is paid to the *Ark Royal's* aircrew it is only the striking forces who are remembered. Yet the shadowers are equally deserving of praise. They did quite as difficult and dangerous work, with none of the *kudos* or sweet smell of success.

And while the shadowers kept in touch with the *Bismarck* Traill and Stringer struggled to range a strike.

By 2.15 the aircrew had been briefed—the *Bismarck,* they were told, was some fifty miles to the south-west and they would find her quite by herself with no other warships anywhere near. By 2.40 the *Swordfish* had been armed, ranged and warmed up. And a few minutes before three o'clock, in weather which had if anything deteriorated still further, the fly-off began. At the end of half an hour fourteen out of fifteen planes had got airborne safely and were formed up and heading south-west for the *Bismarck*.

There followed an agonising period of suspense. Aboard the ships of the Home Fleet, as they panted east in the *Bismarck*'s wake, it was known that the *Swordfish* were airborne. It was known, too, that everything depended on them. If they failed, there would be no hope of bringing the German battleship to action.

The hours passed. Four o'clock, five o'clock, six o'clock; and still no news that the *Bismarck* had been slowed down. Then, as Sir John Tovey was anxiously pacing the bridge of his flagship, he was handed a signal. It was as brief as it was dispiriting. "1830 hours. Force H to C.-in-C. Estimate no hits."

It would be impossible to exaggerate Sir John's despair. For four days and four nights he had chased the *Bismarck* through 2,000 miles of ocean. And now, at the eleventh hour, she had escaped. For the planes of the Fleet Air Arm, it seemed, had failed him as abysmally as the guns of his battleships.

What Sir John didn't know were the special circumstances of the *Swordfish*'s failure.

The striking force had set course from the *Ark Royal* with high hopes, and after about forty minutes their A.S.V. had picked up a vessel ahead and below. It was a few miles to the west of where they had expected to find the *Bismarck*, but it was clearly her—for hadn't they been told at their briefing that no other vessel was in the vicinity. In loose formation they dived on to their target on an A.S.V. bearing. They were down to four hundred feet before they broke cloud, and saw, directly ahead, the dark ill-defined bulk of a warship plunging through heavy seas. About two-thirds of them had dropped their torpedoes before they realised, to their horror, that the vessel they were attacking was not the *Bismarck* but the *Sheffield*.[1] It could have been one of the major tragedies of the war. But it turned out to be a blessing in disguise. For fifty per cent of the *Swordfish* torpedoes exploded on impact the moment they hit the mountainous seas, and the other fifty per cent the *Sheffield* managed to avoid.

It was a crestfallen band of airmen who returned to the *Ark Royal*. They had been given the opportunity, with one blow, of sinking the *Bismarck* and at the same time of putting Naval aviation firmly on the map. And all they had done was to attack (and miss!) one of their own ships. But as, on landing, the aircrew recounted their doleful story to Maund and Traill, they all and without exception added an impassioned request to be given new torpedoes and another chance. And their request was granted.

Within an hour every available *Swordfish* had been refuelled, re-armed (this time with contact-type torpedoes) and re-ranged on the storm-lashed flight-deck. And the hazardous business of flying-off was begun all over again.

Half an hour later the planes disappeared to the southward in a flurry of driving sleet. Very soon it would be dark and the *Bismarck* inviolate. It was a case of now or never.

The attack which followed was remarkable for three things: the weather it was carried out in, the determination with which it was pressed home, and its far-reaching consequences.

It still needed a few minutes to eight o'clock when the fifteen *Swordfish* of the second striking force passed over the *Sheffield* *en route* for the German battleship. The cruiser signalled them, "The enemy is twelve miles dead ahead", and they acknowledged

---

[1] About two hours previously Somerville had signalled the *Sheffield* to locate and shadow Lutjens. His signal was repeated to the *Ark Royal*, but not addressed to her directly. It so happened that the carrier's overworked cipher staff failed to decode this signal before the striking force had left—since the signal had not been addressed to the carrier it had been assumed to be of relative unimportance to them and had therefore been accorded a low priority for decoding.

the message and started to climb into cloud—in order to gain height for their dive. But in cloud, visibility was down to a couple of dozen feet, and the *Swordfish* became split up. Two sub-flights, experiencing heavy icing at 7,000 feet, returned to the cruiser for another bearing; two more sub-flights, finding nothing when they broke cloud, started a square search: only the leader, Lieutenant-Commander Coode, made a clean interception, spotting the *Bismarck* to leeward as she steamed directly under a front in which violent rain squalls alternated with patches of low scudding cloud. Coode attacked at once, and the other *Swordfish,* drawn by the gun flashes as moths to a candle, followed him in at intervals. The attack was therefore imperfectly co-ordinated—it was in fact spun out over a period of some twenty minutes—but it was pressed home with the greatest gallantry. The flak started while the *Swordfish* were still five miles from their target. And all the way down it was heavy and extremely accurate. Almost every aircraft was hit. Some, like Sub-Lieutenant Swanton's, were hit 175 times. Wings were shredded, landing wheels shot off, and several aircrew wounded. But each of the *Swordfish* closed in to point-blank range. And the *Bismarck* was hit.

She was in fact hit twice: once amidships and once right aft (level with her steering compartment). And it was this last hit which sealed her fate. For, in the words of the official German report, "the torpedo hit astern was the decisive blow; by destroying the steering gear it made the ship incapable of holding a course for our base". As the last sub-flight of *Swordfish* completed their attack, the great battleship was seen to make two complete circles, and go limping off, very slowly, to the northwest, *away* from the French coast, *towards* the Atlantic and the eagerly waiting guns of her pursuers. At almost literally the last minute the *Swordfish* had turned defeat into victory.

But for the fifteen aircraft struggling back to their carrier, the battle was far from over. For they still had to land-on. And the way their landing-on was accomplished was, perhaps, the finest achievement of all.

For a good many of the *Swordfish* were damaged. All the air-crew were exhausted—some of them having made three exceptionally difficult operational sorties within twenty-four hours—and several were wounded. The light was fading. Wind and sea had risen to a frenetic malevolence; and the *Ark Royal* was pitching and rolling like a cork in a mill race. The landing-on of the fifteen *Swordfish*, which would normally have taken about ten minutes, took that evening just over an hour and a half.

From the *Ark Royal*'s island Maund and Traill watched anxiously as the first plane began its approach. It seemed impossible that any aircraft could land-on so wildly plunging a deck. For the carrier's round-down was now rising and falling by a full sixty feet; and one moment the approaching plane would be far too high, poised near stalling some fifty feet above the deck; and the next moment far too low, about to shatter itself against the up-flung plates of the carrier's stern. Under these conditions the task of the Deck Landing Officer was, to say the least, difficult in the extreme.

The Deck Landing Officer was Lieutenant-Commander Stringer.

Patrick Stringer had been batting aircraft on to the *Ark* for a good many months now and the pilots had come to trust his judgement. And it was as well they had. For that evening his skill and his patience saved their lives. For no matter how wildly a carrier is pitching there is always, sooner or later, a period of a few brief seconds when its deck is level and relatively steady. This period can't be judged from the cockpit of an approaching plane, but it can be judged from the batting platform. Provided therefore that pilot and batsman have confidence in each other and are possessed of sufficient patience, they can almost always engineer between them a landing of sorts. And it was this confidence and this patience, which, that evening, saved the lives of the *Swordfish* aircrew. Again and again a plane would make a perfect approach only to find itself waved off, as, at the crucial moment, the deck either fell away from it or rose too sharply. Round and round went the aircraft: again and again and again: with the light fading and their fuel running low. One plane was waved off seven consecutive times; but at the eighth attempt it got down. Another landed so heavily that it snapped off its undercarriage and squelched to the deck like an overripe plum, breaking its back; but the crew clambered out unhurt. Another flew straight into the barrier. Another ended up in the catwalk. But from every landing the crew walked away. And therein lay the value, and the reward, of Stringer's batting.

It was a trio of depleted but happy *Swordfish* squadrons who, that evening, watched the daylight ebb out of an angry sky. Of the two dozen planes which had been in their hangar when they'd left Gibraltar, only six were serviceable; the rest had been lost in the searches, had crashed on landing or been too badly shot up to be repaired. But they had done what had been asked of them. They had left the *Bismarck* crippled and impotent, her bows into wind and sea, and with the look of death already upon her.

That night the warships of the Home Fleet, in ones and twos, came silently out of the darkness and took up their positions around the crippled battleship. And at dawn they closed in and overwhelmed her. The *Bismarck* fought gallantly but without hope. Broadside after broadside poured into her at point-blank range. Her turrets were silenced, her bridge shattered, her engines wrecked, and between her decks fires were soon raging fiercely. But her colours still flew and she refused to sink. At 10.30 Tovey was forced to pass the rueful message, "Am unable to make her sink by gunfire". Overhead, by this time, was a striking force of the last of the *Ark Royal*'s *Swordfish*, longing to finish off what they had begun but whenever they tried to approach the *Bismarck* they were driven off by the guns of the Fleet! In the end it was the cruiser *Dorsetshire* which closed in and sent two salvoes of torpedoes into the *Bismarck*'s screws; and the shattered leviathan heeled silently over and disappeared beneath the widespread Atlantic rollers. Out of her ship's company of nearly two thousand only a hundred and ten were saved.

The sinking of the *Bismarck* has been described as "a glorious victory: a decisive re-assertion of British Naval supremacy". But that is so much nonsense. For the fact is that the *Bismarck* ought to have been sunk. From the moment she left Bergen Fjord the odds against her ever seeing the Fatherland again were of the sort which no self-respecting punter would look at, and the wonder is not that she failed but that she came as close as she did to success. Indeed, if the adjective "glorious" has to be used in connection with the *Bismarck* episode it would seem to suffix the German defeat more aptly than the British victory. Thirty-nine ships against one is not, after all, exactly glorious odds.

Nor does the phrase "decisive re-assertion of British Naval supremacy" bear close examination. For the *Bismarck* came too close to success for her demise to be regarded as by any means decisive—if, for example, the torpedo hit achieved by the second of the *Ark Royal*'s *Swordfish* had been fifty feet farther forward, the German warship would almost certainly have escaped and the *Bismarck* episode would have gone down in history as a humiliating British defeat. Britannia's trident in fact was proved that May to be more than a little rusty, and serious weaknesses in the Navy were brought to light. The guns of the capital ships for example were found to develop technical faults; the arrangements for refuelling at sea were proved inadequate; and on at least one occasion the tactics of senior officers were sadly at fault. Indeed both the weapons and the techniques of the Old Navy were thoroughly discredited that May; and it was left to the New Navy—the radar operators of the cruisers and the aircrew of the carriers—to pull the chestnut which had so nearly escaped out of the fire.

And in this fact lies the real significance of the sinking of the *Bismarck*. It marked the twilight of one era and the dawn of another. It proved that although the past belonged to the gun, the future—beyond all shadow of doubt—belonged to the carrier-borne aircraft. And when, that tempestuous morning in May, the guns of the *Rodney* and *King George V* thundered out into the Biscay dawn it was not only the requiem of the *Bismarck* they were sounding but their own.

FERRYING THE BOMBERS ACROSS

EDGAR J. WYNN, CAPTAIN

FERRY COMMAND

Of the forty-four transocean flights I made before stepping out of the ferry service temporarily, my third was the one that took me nearest to death.

The thrill was still new and I was a little nervous when I made that third trip over the northern route in a Lockheed-Hudson twin-engine bomber. Late in the afternoon of departure day, I called my navigator, an English youngster named Sims who had recently completed his RAF training, and my radio operator, a mellow Canadian lad named Phillips. It is good to know, as intimately as possible, the traits and characteristics of your crew members, so I had them come over to the apartment to help route our flight.

We spent several hours with maps spread on the floor, checking every detail minutely. We didn't miss a thing. I checked my navigator's knowledge of dead reckoning, conversion angles and radio bearings. Carefully I looked to see that he had marked in his notebook all beacons and radio stations from which we could obtain bearings. These rug conferences are held by most captains before every transoceanic flight. It is a healthy thing—helps morale and enables the commander of the ship to know something about his crew. I knew that my crew wanted to know something about me; crewmen must depend on their skipper as much as he depends on them.

We drank the usual toast—a coke. Alcoholic drinks were forbidden twenty-four hours before a flight. A few hours later, we met at the airdrome. On this trip we carried extra gas tanks; the bomb bays were sealed and filled with fuel. I stood there and watched every drop of gasoline go into the plane. We checked the tires ourselves and nosed around the plane as last-minute checks were made. Sabotage did exist, and even though such instances were rare, men didn't head out over the Atlantic without seeing to it personally that every precaution was taken. So precious was gasoline on those trips that even after warming the engines I refueled again. Not a drop was to be wasted. Every ounce counted.

The weather was explained to us studiously by McTaggart Cowan, a British meteorologist at our jumping-off point in Newfoundland, and one of the best weathermen in the world for my money. He pointed to the charts in his serious manner and showed us bluntly where we would encounter a "tough front," a bad storm, that night. Coolly, he predicted the spot where, as he put it, the ice would be its bloody worst.

We wandered around our hop-off point, for a bit.

Take-off time came. Seventeen planes left that night and several of them never reached the other side.

"Quite a smooth trip so far, Captain," Phil mused, after the first couple of hours. "What about your first two trips across? Were they very rough?"

"Phil, any time a pilot has a smooth flight on this route, let me know," I told him.

Three hours out and I spotted Cowan's "tough front." Black, ominous clouds bounced around us. I knew the struggle was on. No co-pilot up there on that trip, only a couple of kids, a navigator and a radioman.

"Hey, take it easy, baby," I said aloud to myself as the plane began bobbing.

"Anything wrong, sir?" Phil queried anxiously.

"Yeah, better get Sims up here in front. Strap yourselves in, both of you. Mighty nasty looking weather ahead. This is going to be ugly."

"Looks like it's closing in fast," Phil said. "Think you can climb over it?"

"We're at 11,000 now," I answered. "Hang on to your hats, boys, here it comes."

Ice, sleet and a wild wind began to beat the sides of the plane. I climbed up to 18,000 feet. We put on oxygen masks. The weather not only got no better, it was worse and the rattle of ice began to get on our nerves.

"Sounds like a machine gun, doesn't it?" Phil ventured in a husky voice.

"Yeah, and just about as dangerous, too. Turn on those prop de-icers."

The plane began staggering. Sims, making his first flight, was frightened. He was only eighteen and this initiation was a rough one.

"Phil," I shouted over the noise, "brace your feet against that instrument panel. It's bouncing so damn bad I can't read the air speed."

I knew I had to come down. We were flying as slowly as the ship would cruise, as we did on all flights, to conserve gasoline. We began to lose altitude at the rate of 800 feet per minute. I could feel the plane getting heavier. Ice was coating us everywhere. The windshield was a frozen chunk.

"Sims, stick your spotlight out the window and let me know if the ice is beginning to build up on the wing," I ordered.

Before he could tug the side window free, I knew the answer.

"Captain, ice is building up over the de-icer boots," Sims reported. "It looks bad as hell. They're not doing any good at all."

I shouted to Sims to come back and brace his feet against the bobbing instrument panel.

"Look at the air speed," I yelled. "I've got the throttles wide open and the props full forward, and still we're losing 800 feet a minute. Phil, turn on full carburetor heat, both engines!"

Those two kids were looking to me for help. I was scared as hell myself. I wondered how I had ever let myself get into such a jam, why I had gone into this fool business of ferrying planes over the ocean. I was mad at myself and I had a queer feeling around the throat when I thought of home. As the plane went on losing altitude, I even began to envision the scene when Mother would be informed of my disappearance.

It was against all common sense, but I had to push those throttles wider and shove the props in full low pitch. It was tripling my gasoline consumption and two-engine bombers carry very little excess fuel on an ocean hop, but I had no alternative.

The props were spinning at 2,000 revolutions per minute, but still they picked up ice and kept it. I closed and opened the engines, trying to snap that death load off the props. Ice chunks flew and hit the fuselage with the sound of a machine-gun barrage.

Phil screamed: "Sir, look at our altitude; we're down to two thousand. God, are we going to hit the ocean?"

"Any minute, maybe," I told him grimly. "That altimeter, you know, can be a thousand feet wrong, up or down, and we'd never know it. Sims, have you got the pressure reading?"

"No, Captain, we don't have a reading for this zone."

The ice houses on the de-icer boots of the wings had built up to a staggering size. The de-icers had lost their punch, and were puffing idly inside the ice houses. It looked like the last flight, so I decided on the last possible chance—to shut off both engines until we got as low as I dared take the plane, possibly 800 feet by our altimeter, and then blast both engines wide open suddenly. It was our only hope for getting ice off the props and out of the carburetors. The constant sucking of air and gas into those carburetors had refrigerated the motor completely.

"Maybe this is it," I told the two kids, "but it's the last chance. I'm going to throttle both engines. When we get down to 800 feet, I'll give 'em everything."

"Down to a thousand feet, sir," Sims panted.

"A little more to go yet," I almost whispered.

"Nine hundred. . . ."

"I hope those goddam engines take!"

"Eight hundred. . . ."

"O. K., boys, here goes nothing! Hang on and brace your feet against the panel."

I opened both engines wide. It was one hell of a roar. It sounded like every noise I had ever heard rolled into one thunderclap. Great chunks of ice flew off the props. The plane vibrated and staggered for fully two minutes. We prayed in a profane sort of way. Finally the airplane righted itself and began to sound normal again. We were still on instruments and I wasn't certain of the altitude. The ocean could have been fifteen feet below us, for all we knew.

Gradually, almost to a maddening degree, we gained altitude at about 100 feet a minute. It was warmer down below and the ice started ripping off. We got back to 2,000 feet after an eternity.

"Brother, she's climbing now," Phil shrieked.

"Yeah, looks pretty thin up ahead, too," I answered. "God, I thought we were going to swim that time."

"I did too," sighed young Sims. "How about a cup of coffee now, Captain?"

We could see the ocean, finally, and even that was a relief. Phil mumbled that he guessed the worst part of the trip was over. I wasn't so sure. We checked our gas and discovered that we had more than doubled our consumption during that forty-five minutes of hell. I didn't have the heart or the guts to tell those two kids, but I believed that only a miracle would get us to land.

"Phil," I said, rather apologetically, "we're lost and we've dropped a lot of gasoline. Let's not get too optimistic about this thing. Try to get master control on the radio. Get anything! Get somebody!"

But nothing was available. Phil tried for an hour, doing the best he could, but the Germans were jamming the air. They jammed us constantly with the letters "B-U-M." I never knew whether they were just calling us bums or what they were up to.

"Might as well throw the damn thing overboard," I finally shouted to Phil. The kid broke down and cried.

We had made a careful estimated-time-of-arrival into a rocky promontory on the northernmost tip of Ireland. As we approached what we thought must have been our ETA, I began silently sweating out the gas supply. I watched it constantly. Dawn came and we broke into a clear layer of flaky clouds. It would have been a lovely sight on any other day; I only cursed it that morning.

"Luck on that radio yet?" I questioned again.

"Not a thing," Phil said. "I'm trying to get a loop bearing, but I can't pick up one anywhere."

"Try again. Don't quit trying!"

"God knows I'm trying, Captain," Phil said, "but nobody answers."

Our gasoline was dangerously low. No one knew how far off course we were. Still no radio bearings—nothing but the droning of the plane and those mockingly beautiful clouds.

"Forget the radio, Phil," I said. "I'm going to try something else. It may not work, but we've got to gamble again."

I had my own pet way of letting down in Scotland. It was impossible to come down blindly over there. Balloon barrages towering thousands of yards into the skies were plain death if you smacked into them. Mountains were numerous—and we could see nothing but fleecy cloud banks.

I feared two things: running out of gasoline, and catching a tail wind in that blind wilderness that would blow us into occupied France. It was time to take a desperate chance.

"I'm going to make a 90-degree turn," I shouted to the crew. "I know we've passed our ETA. I'm taking a chance as the last hope. We'll fly straight south; at least we won't be flying into France."

Three minutes passed.

"Our petrol is almost gone," Sims said.

"O. K., hold on. We're going down!"

At that moment a rock formation jutted up ahead of us through the overcast.

"Let's get under this ceiling," I shouted.

I went down and God was with us. We found a hole in the clouds. We dived just like a fighter plane and came out over the ocean at 200 feet. I looked around and there was Malin Head, our original point of arrival, off the shoreline. Visibility was limited to a quarter of a mile and we crept along the coastline and into Prestwick.

"Don't give up now, fellows," I shouted to the two kids as the gasoline needle quit moving. It was a guessing game, from minute to minute, whether we would make the landing field.

We did make it, and came in with a good landing. I turned the plane to taxi in, the motors sputtered and she went dead on the runway. Not a drop of gasoline left! Sounds a little on the storybook side, but it was too true to suit three boys who were very tired from fighting a pretty big ocean.

And that, friends, is why my temples are gray at twenty-nine.

STUKAS DIVE-BOMB THE SOVIET FLEET

HANS ULRICH RUDEL, *HAUPTMANN*
Luftwaffe

The centre of the fighting is gravitating more and more North-wards. So, in September 1941, we are sent to Tyrkowo, South of Luga, in the Northern sector of the Eastern front. We got out daily over the Leningrad area where the army has opened an offensive from the West and from the South. Lying as it does between the Finnish Gulf and Lake Ladoga, the geographical position of Leningrad is a big advantage to the defenders since the possible ways of attacking it are strictly limited. For some time progress here has been slow. One almost has the impression that we are merely marking time.

On the 16th September Flight Lieutenant Steen summons us to a conference. He explains the military situation and tells us that the particular difficulty holding up the further advance of our armies is the presence of the Russian fleet moving up and down the coast at a certain distance from the shore and intervening in the battles with their formidable naval guns. The Russian fleet is based on Kronstadt, an island in the Gulf of Finland, the largest war harbour in the U.S.S.R. Approximately 12½ miles from Kronstadt lies the harbour of Leningrad and South of it the ports of Oranienbaum and Peterhof. Very strong enemy forces are massed round these two towns on a strip of coast some six miles long. We are told to mark all the positions precisely on our maps so as to ensure our being able to recognize our own front line. We are beginning to guess that these troop concentrations will be our objective when Flt./Lt. Steen gives another turn to the briefing. He comes back to the Russian fleet and explains that our chief concern is the two battleships *Marat* and *Oktobrescaja Revolutia*. Both are ships of about 23,000 tons. In addition, there are four or five cruisers, among them the *Maxim Gorki* and the *Kirov*, as well as a number of destroyers. The ships constantly change their positions according to which parts of the mainland require the support of their devastating and accurate gunfire.

As a rule, however, the battleships navigate only in the deep channel between Kronstadt and Leningrad. Our wing has just received orders to attack the Russian fleet in the Gulf of Finland. There is no question of using normal bomber-aircraft, any more than normal bombs, for this operation, especially as intense flak must be reckoned with. He tells us that we are awaiting the arrival of two thousand pounder bombs fitted with a special detonator for our purpose. With normal detonators the bomb would burst ineffectively on the armoured main deck and though the explosion would be sure to rip off some parts of the upper structure it would not result in the sinking of the ship. We cannot expect to succeed and finish off these two leviathans except by the use of a delayed action bomb which must first pierce the upper decks before exploding deep down in the hull of the vessel.

A few days later, in the foulest weather, we are suddenly ordered to attack the battleship *Marat;* she has just been located in action by a reconnaissance patrol. The weather is reported as bad until due South of Krasnowardeisk, 20 miles South of Leningrad. Cloud density over the Gulf of Finland 5-7/10; cloud base 2400 feet. That will mean flying through a layer of cloud which where we are is 6000 feet thick. The whole wing takes off on a Northerly course. Today we are about thirty aircraft strong; according to our establishment we should have eighty,

but numbers are not invariably the decisive factor. Unfortunately
the two thousand pounders have not yet arrived. As our single
engined Stukas are not capable of flying blind our No. 1 has
to do the next best thing and keep direction with the help of the
few instruments: ball, bank indicator and vertical speed indicator.
The rest of us keep station by flying close enough to one another
to be able to catch an occasional glimpse of our neighbour's
wing. Flying in the dense, dark clouds it is imperative never
to let the interval between the tips of our wings exceed 9-12
feet. If it is greater we risk losing our neighbour for good and
running full tilt into another aircraft. This is an awe-inspiring
thought! In such weather conditions therefore the safety of the
whole wing is in the highest degree dependent on the instrument
flying of our No. 1.

Below 6000 feet we are in a dense cloud cover; the individual
flights have slightly broken formation. Now they close up again.
There is still no ground visibility. Reckoning by the clock we
must pretty soon be over the Gulf of Finland. Now, too, the cloud
cover is thinning out a little. There is a glint of blue sky below us;
ergo water. We should be approaching our target, but where
exactly are we? It is impossible to tell because the rifts in the
clouds are only infinitesimal. The cloud density can no longer
be anything like 5-7/10; only here and there the thick soup
dissolves to reveal an isolated gap. Suddenly through one such
gap I see something and instantly contact Flt./Lt. Steen over
the radio.

"König 2 to König 1 . . . come in, please."

He immediately answers:

"König 1 to König 2 . . . over to you."

"Are you there? I can see a large ship below us . . . the battleship *Marat,* I guess."

We are still talking as Steen loses height and disappears into
the gap in the clouds. In mid-sentence I also go into a dive.
Pilot Officer Klaus behind me in the other staff aeroplane follows

suit. Now I can make out the ship. It is the *Marat* sure enough. I suppress my excitement with an iron will. To make up my mind, to grasp the situation in a flash: for this I have only seconds. It is *we* who must hit the ship, for it is scarcely likely that all the flights will get through the gap. Both gap and ship are moving. We shall not be a good target for the flak until in our dive we reach the cloud base at 2400 feet. As long as we are above the unbroken cloud base the flak can only fire by listening apparatus, they cannot open up properly. Very well then: dive, drop bombs and back into the clouds! The bombs from Steen's aircraft are already on their way down . . . near misses. I press the bomb switch . . . dead on. My bomb hits the after deck. A pity it is only a thousand pounder! All the same I see flames break out. I cannot afford to hang about to watch it, for the flak barks furiously. There, the others are still diving through the gap. The Soviet flak has by this time realized where the "filthy Stukas" are coming from and concentrate their fire on this point. We exploit the favourable cloud cover and climb back into it. Nevertheless, at a later date, we are not to escape from this area so relatively unscathed.

Once we are home again the guessing game immediately begins: what can have been the extent of the damage to the ship after the direct hit? Naval experts claim that with a bomb of this small calibre a total success must be discounted. A few optimists, on the other hand, think it possible. As if to confirm their opinion, in the course of the next few days our reconnaissance patrols, despite the most enterprising search, are quite unable to find the *Marat*.

In an ensuing operation a cruiser sinks in a matter of minutes under my bomb.

After the first sortie our luck with the weather is out. Always a brilliant blue sky and murderous flak. I never again experience anything to compare with it in any place or theatre of war. Our reconnaissance estimates that a hundred A.A. guns are concentrated in an area of six-square miles in the target zone. The flak bursts form a whole cumulus of cloud. If the explosions are more than ten or twelve feet away one cannot hear the flak from the flying aircraft. But we hear no single bursts; rather an incessant tempest of noise like the clap of doomsday. The concentrated zones of flak in the air space begin as soon as we cross the coastal strip which is still in Soviet hands. Then come Oranienbaum and Peterhof; being harbours, very strongly defended. The open water is alive with pontoons, barges, boats and tiny craft, all stiff with flak. The Russians use every possible site for their A.A. guns. For instance, the mouth of Leningrad harbour is supposed to have been closed to our U-boats by means of huge steel nets suspended from a chain of concrete blocks floating on the surface of the water. Even from these blocks A.A. guns bark at us.

After about another six miles we sight the island of Kronstadt with its great naval harbour and the town of the same name. Both harbour and town are heavily defended, and besides the whole Russian Baltic fleet is anchored in the immediate vicinity, in and outside the harbour. And it can put up a murderous barrage of flak. We in the leading staff aircraft always fly at an altitude between 9,000 and 10,000 feet; that is very low, but after all we want to hit something. When diving onto the ships we use our diving brakes in order to check our diving speed. This gives us more time to sight our target and to correct our aim. The more carefully we aim, the better the results of our attack, and everything depends on them. By reducing our diving speed we make it easier for the flak to bring us down, especially as if we do not overshoot we cannot climb so fast after the dive. But, unlike the flights behind us, we do not generally try to climb back out of the dive. We use different tactics and pull out at low level close above the water. We have then to take the widest evasive action over the enemy-occupied coastal strip. Once we have left it behind we can breathe freely again.

We return to our airfield at Tyrkowo from these sorties in a state of trance and fill our lungs with the air we have won the right to continue to breathe. These days are strenuous, very strenuous. On our evening walks Steen and I are now mostly very silent, each of us guessing the other's thoughts. It is our task to destroy the Russian fleet; so we are reluctant to discuss its difficulties. Argument would be merely a waste of breath. Those are our orders and we obey them. So in an hour we come back to the tent, inwardly relaxed and ready to go out again into this hell in the morning.

On one of these walks with Flt./Lt. Steen I break the customary silence and ask him rather hesitantly:

"How do you manage to be so cool and so collected?"

He stops for a moment, looks at me out of the corner of his eye, and says:

"My dear chap, don't imagine for a moment that I have always been so cool. I owe my indifference to hard years of bitter experience. You know something of what one is up against in the service if one doesn't see eye to eye with one's superiors . . . and if they are not big enough to leave such differences behind in the mess and refuse to forget them on duty, it can be plain hell. But the most finely tempered steel comes out of the hottest fire. And if you go your own gait alone, without necessarily losing touch with your fellows, you grow strong."

There is a long pause, and I realize why it is that he understands me so well. Although I am aware that my next remark is not very military, I say to him:

"I, too, when I was a subaltern sometimes promised myself that if I were ever given a command I wouldn't at any rate behave like some of my superiors."

Steen is silent for quite a while before he adds:

"There are other things besides which form a man. Only a few of our colleagues know that and so are able to understand my serious views on life. I was once engaged to a girl I loved very deeply. She died on the day we were to have been married. When a thing like that happens to you, you don't easily forget it."

I relapse into silence and go into the tent. For a long time afterwards the man Steen is the subject of my thoughts. Now I understand him better than I did. I realize how much virile strength and strength-giving understanding can be passed from one man to another in a quiet talk at the front. It is not the soldier's way to be communicative. He expresses himself very differently from a civilian. His talk is every bit as uncivilian and tongue-tied as it is popularly represented. And because war jerks a man out of all pretence and hypocrisy, the things a soldier says, even if they only take the form of an oath or a primitive sentimentality, are integrally sincere and genuine, and therefore finer than all the glib rhetoric of the civilian world.

War awakes primitive strength in its servants, and primitive strength is only to be found in subjectivity, never in objectivity.

On the 21st September our two thousand pounders arrive. The next morning reconnaissance reports that the *Marat* is lying in Kronstadt harbour. They are evidently repairing the damage sustained in our attack of the 16th. I just see red. Now the day has come for me to prove my ability. I get the necessary information about the wind, etc., from the reconnaissance men. Then I am deaf to all around me; I am longing to be off. If I reach the target, I am determined to hit it. I must hit it!—We take off with our minds full of the attack; beneath us, the two thousand pounders which are to do the job today.

Brilliant blue sky, without a rack of cloud. The same even over the sea. We are already attacked by Russian fighters above the narrow coastal strip; but they cannot deflect us from our objective, there is no question of that. We are flying at 9000 feet; the flak is deadly. About ten miles ahead we see Kronstadt; it seems an infinite distance away. With this intensity of flak one stands a good chance of being hit at any moment. The waiting makes the time long. Dourly, Steen and I keep on our course. We tell ourselves that Ivan is not firing at single aircraft; he is merely putting up a flak barrage at a certain altitude. The others are all over the shop, not only in the squadrons and the flights, but even in the pairs. They think that by varying height and zigzagging they can make the A.A. gunners' task more difficult. There go the two blue-nosed staff aircraft sweeping through all the formations, even the separate flights. Now one of them loses her bomb. A wild helter-skelter in the sky over Kronstadt; the danger of ramming is great. We are still a few miles from our objective; at an angle ahead of me I can already make out the *Marat* berthed in the harbour. The guns boom, the shells scream up at us, bursting in flashes of livid colours; the flak forms small fleecy clouds that frolic around us. If it was not in such deadly earnest one might use the phrase: an aerial carnival. I look down on the *Marat*. Behind her lies the cruiser *Kirov*. Or is it the *Maxim Gorki?* These ships have not yet joined in the general bombardment. But it was the same the last time. They do not open up on us until we are diving to the attack. Never has our flight through the defence seemed so slow or so uncomfortable. Will Steen use his diving brakes today or in the face of this opposition will he go in for once "without"? There he goes. He has already used his brakes. I follow suit, throwing a final glance into his cockpit. His grim face wears an expression of concentration. Now we are in a dive, close beside each other. Our diving angle must be between seventy and eighty degrees. I have already picked up the *Marat* in my sights. We race down towards her; slowly she grows to a gigantic size. All their A.A. guns are now directed at us. Now nothing matters but our target, our objective; if we achieve our task it will save our brothers in arms on the ground much bloodshed. But what is happening? Steen's aircraft suddenly leaves mine far behind. He is travelling much faster. Has he after all again retracted his diving brakes in order to get down more quickly? So I do the same. I race after his aircraft going all out. I am right on his tail, travelling much too fast and unable to check my speed. Straight ahead of me I see the horrified face of W.O. Lehmann, Steen's rear-gunner. He expects every second that I shall cut off his tail unit with my propeller and ram him.

I increase my diving angle with all the strength I have got—it must surely be 90 degrees—sit tight as if I were sitting on a powder-keg. Shall I graze Steen's aircraft which is right on me or shall I get safely past and down? I streak past him within a hair's breadth. Is this an omen of success? The ship is centered plumb in the middle of my sights. My Ju 87 keeps perfectly steady as I dive; she does not swerve an inch. I have the feeling that to miss is now impossible. Then I see the *Marat* large as life in front of me. Sailors are running across the deck, carrying ammunition. Now I press the bomb release switch on my stick and pull with all my strength. Can I still manage to pull out? I doubt it, for I am diving without brakes and the height at which I have released my bomb is not more than 900 feet. The skipper has said when briefing us that the two thousand pounder must not be dropped from lower than 3000 feet as the fragmentation effect of this bomb reaches 3000 feet and to drop it at a lower altitude is to endanger one's aircraft. But now I have forgotten that!—I am intent on hitting the *Marat*. I tug at my stick, without feeling, merely exerting all my strength. My acceleration is too great. I see nothing, my sight is blurred in a momentary blackout, a new experience for me. But if it can be managed at all I must pull out. My head has not yet cleared when I hear Scharnovski's voice:

"She is blowing up, sir!"

Now I look out. We are skimming the water at a level of ten or twelve feet and I bank round a little. Yonder lies the *Marat* below a cloud of smoke rising up to 1200 feet; apparently the magazine has exploded.

"Congratulations, sir."

Scharnovski is the first. Now there is a babel of congratulations from all the other aircraft over the radio. From all sides I catch the words: "Good show!" Hold on, surely I recognize the Wing Commander's voice? I am conscious of a pleasant glow of exhilaration such as one feels after a successful athletic feat. Then I fancy that I am looking into the eyes of thousands of grateful infantrymen. Back at low level in the direction of the coast.

"Two Russian fighters, sir," reports Scharnovski.

"Where are they?"

"Chasing us, sir.—They are circling round the fleet in their own flak.—Cripes! They will both be shot down together by their own flak."

This expletive and, above all, the excitement in Scharnovski's voice are something quite new to me. This has never happened before. We fly on a level with the concrete blocks on which A.A. guns have also been posted. We could almost knock the Russian crews off them with our wings. They are still firing at our comrades who are now attacking the other ships. Then for a moment there is nothing visible through the pall of smoke rising from the *Marat*. The din down below on the surface of the water must be terrific, for it is not until now that a few flak crews spot my aircraft as it roars close past them. Then they swivel their guns and fire after me; all have had their attention diverted by the main formation flying off high above them. So the luck is with me, an isolated aircraft. The whole neighbourhood is full of A.A. guns; the air is peppered with shrapnel. But it is a comfort to know that this weight of iron is not meant exclusively for me! I am now crossing the coast line. The narrow strip is very unpleasant. It would be impossible to gain height because I could not climb fast enough to reach a safe altitude. So I stay down. Past machine guns and flak. Panic-stricken Russians hurl themselves flat on the ground. Then again Scharnovski shouts:

"A *Rata* coming up behind us!"

I look round and see a Russian fighter about 300 yards astern.

"Let him have it, Scharnovski!"

Scharnovski does not utter a sound. Ivan is blazing away at a range of only a few inches. I take wild evasive action.

"Are you mad, Scharnovski? Fire! I'll have you put under arrest." I yell at him!

Scharnovski does not fire. Now he says deliberately:

"I am holding fire, sir, because I can see a German ME coming up behind and if I open up on the *Rata* I may damage the Messerschmitt." That closes the subject, as far as Scharnovski is concerned; but I am sweating with the suspense. The tracers are going wider on either side of me. I weave like mad.

"You can turn round now, sir. The ME has shot down the *Rata*." I bank round slightly and look back. It is as Scharnovski says; there she lies down below. Now a ME passes groggily.

"Scharnovski, it will be a pleasure to confirm our fighter's claim to have shot that one down." He does not reply. He is rather hurt that I was not content to trust his judgment before. I know him; he will sit there and sulk until we land. How many operational flights have we made together when he has not opened his lips the whole time we have been in the air.

After landing, all the crews are paraded in front of the squadron tent. We are told by Flt./Lt. Steen that the Wing Commander has already rung up to congratulate the 3rd squadron on its achievement. He had personally witnessed the very impressive explosion. Steen is instructed to report the name of the officer who was the first to dive and drop the successful two thousand pounder in order that he may be recommended for the Knight's Cross of the Iron Cross.

With a side-glance in my direction he says:

"Forgive me for telling the Kommodore that I am so proud of the whole squadron that I would prefer it if our success is attributed to the squadron as a whole."

In the tent he wrings my hand. "You no longer need a battleship for special mention in despatches," he says with a boyish laugh.

The Wing Commander rings up. "It is sinking day for the 3rd. You are to take off immediately for another attack on the *Kirov* berthed behind the *Marat*. Good hunting!" The photographs taken by our latest aircraft show that the *Marat* has split in two. This can be seen on the picture taken after the tremendous cloud of smoke from the explosion had begun to dissipate. The telephone rings again:

"I say, Steen, did you see my bomb? I didn't and neither did Pekrun."

"It fell into the sea, sir, a few minutes before the attack."

We youngsters in the tent are hard put to it to keep a straight face. A short crackling on the receiver and that is all. We are not the ones to blame our Wing Commander, who is old enough to be our father, if presumably out of nervousness he pressed the bomb release switch prematurely. He deserves all praise for flying with us himself on such a difficult mission. There is a big difference between the ages of fifty and twenty five. In dive bomber flying this is particularly true.

Out we go again on a further sortie to attack the *Kirov*. Steen had a slight accident taxying back after landing from the first sortie: one wheel ran into a large crater, his aircraft pancaked and damaged the propeller. The 7th flight provides us with a substitute aircraft, the flights are already on dispersal and we taxi off from our squadron base airfield. Flt./Lt. Steen again hits an obstacle and this aircraft is also unserviceable. There is no replacement available from the flights; they are of course already on dispersal. No one else on the staff is flying except myself. He therefore gets out of his aircraft and climbs onto my wingplane.

"I know you are going to be mad at me for taking your aircraft, but as I am in command I must fly with the squadron. I will take Scharnovski with me for this one sortie."

Vexed and disgruntled I walk over to where our aircraft are overhauled and devote myself for a time to my job as engineer officer. The squadron returns at the end of an hour and a half. No. 1, the green-nosed staff aircraft—mine—is missing. I assume the skipper has made a forced landing somewhere within our lines.

As soon as my colleagues have all come in I ask what has happened to the skipper. No one will give me a straight answer until one of them says:

"Steen dived onto the *Kirov*. He was caught by a direct hit at 5000 or 6000 feet. The flak smashed his rudder and his aircraft was out of control. I saw him try to steer straight at the cruiser by using the ailerons, but he missed her and nose-dived into the sea. The explosion of his two thousand pounder seriously damaged the *Kirov*."

The loss of our skipper and my faithful Cpl. Scharnovski is a heavy blow to the whole squadron and makes a tragic climax to our otherwise successful day. That fine lad Scharnovski gone! Steen gone! Both in their way were paragons and they can never be fully replaced. They are lucky to have died at a time when they could still hold the conviction that the end of all this misery would bring freedom to Germany and to Europe.

The senior staff captain temporarily takes over command of the squadron. I chose A.C. 1st class Henschel to be my rear-gunner. He has been sent to us by the reserve flight at Graz where he flew with me on several operational exercises. Occasionally I take some one else up with me, first the paymaster, then the intelligence officer and finally the M.O. None of them would care to insure my life. Then after I have taken on Henschel permanently and he has been transferred to the staff he is always furious if I leave him behind and some one else flies with me in his stead. He is as jealous as a little girl.

We are out again a number of times over the Gulf of Finland before the end of September, and we succeed in sending another cruiser to the bottom. We are not so lucky with the second battleship *Oktobrescaja Revolutia*. She is damaged by bombs of smaller calibre but not very seriously. When we manage on one sortie to score a hit with a two thousand pounder, on that particular day not one of these heavy bombs explodes. Despite the most searching investigation it is not possible to determine where the sabotage was done. So the Soviets keep one of their battleships.

There is a lull in the Leningrad sector and we are needed at a new key point. The relief of the infantry has been successfully accomplished, the Russian salient along the coastal strip has been pushed back with the result that Leningrad has now been narrowly invested. But Leningrad does not fall, for the defenders hold Lake Ladoga and thereby secure the supply line for the fortress.

BOMBING ENGLAND

ALBERT HUFENREUTER, *HAUPTMANN*
Luftwaffe

Nearly thirty years have passed since I was a member of the then young, ambitious and, as we thought, the technically and morally most up-to-date and unequaled ultra crews of Hermann Goering's *Luftwaffe*. (I take, in retrospect, a quite different view today.) Under these circumstances it is hard for me to fulfill the wish of the editor. Anyway, being kindly asked to give an account of some of my experiences in the bombing of England, I must really force myself to find the way back, both to the year 1941 and to that air base in Northern France from where all my actions started and ended, except that last one on May 10–11 when I was shot down over enemy territory.

How to Find Barrow in Furness

April 1941. By then I knew quite a bit of the topographic outlines of England and Scotland. Our mission tonight was to take our He 111 (Heinkel) to Barrow in Furness and to drop a load of one 1000 lb., four 250 lb. bombs, and some cannisters of light incendiaries on the shipyards, if possible to destroy a big battleship under construction and soon to be completed.

At about 4000 meters altitude we had swung in from the

North Sea toward Barrow, riding on the beam of Radio Bremen and taking bearings from time to time with the help of Rennes-Bretagne radio station. Navigation didn't seem difficult and I was experienced and self-confident. We passed over the usual barrage of anti-aircraft and searchlights in short order. Further inland a good layer of clouds below stopped all searchers from spotting us, except probably the radar fellows.

According to timetable and plan we reached the region of our target. The clouds had vanished and with the help of a clear moon I could easily make out the scenery below. With the map clearly in my mind I recognized the coastline with quite a number of inlets and smaller isles. Far out at sea the line turned back to show me that I had reached the Irish Sea.

"Be on your toes, boys," I warned through the intercom. "Keep your eyes open!"

Strange, however, no ground defense whatsoever seemed to take action. Was it a trap? Where were the other crews that were bound for the same target? Where were the fires and the smoke clouds, at least some beginnings? Nothing but a large peaceful bay extended under us, and a clear moon shining on it from the northeast. I made my pilot turn to the inner end of the bay, keeping a bit inland to effect better visibility in the moonlight. A small town, a tiny port with some fishing boats, a railway line leading across a small inlet and running on near the coast, fields, hedges, single farms, little hamlets, irregular patches of small forests, everything was quite clearly visible. But there were no signs of Barrow in Furness with the shipyards that were our target!

Three or more times I followed the outline of that bay, taking about fifteen minutes for each circle, before I decided to go south to drop my bombs on Liverpool or any other worthwhile target. However, only about ten minutes later, to my own surprise, I came upon Barrow in Furness. Lots of searchlights and plenty of anti-aircraft guns gave us a warm welcome just as they probably had given to our comrades who had already caused big fires, the smoke of which reduced visibility to a minimum. I dropped my bombs right into the center of the holocaust, hoping that in the neighborhood of fires ablaze there must be something more of the target to be set aflame or to be destroyed. Anyway, no precision work this time.

Nothing special to report about the way home that night. But back in our quarters, worried about my inefficiency as a navigator, I reconstructed the way we had gone that night and with the help of the scribbled notes and the map, learned that the peaceful bay had been the Solway Firth, some 40 miles to the north of Barrow in Furness.

Going to the Firth of Clyde

Our good old He 111, how we loved her and hated her at the same time. Doing a good 300 kilometers per hour for six or even up to nine hours, when cruising economically, she was the safest plane I ever flew except for the prewar star in safety, the three-engined Ju 52 (Junkers). But she was almost like nothing because of her low speed and poor maneuverability once you were caught by any fighter in daytime, and even in the darkness she would become a rather easy prey for the night fighters.

At any rate, we had to go to the Firth of Clyde to stop or delay the building of ships in that region, especially to attack Dumbarton shipyards. In the late evening of one of the first days in May we took off from our base near Lille, headed for the Dutch isle of Texel, and then put our Heinkel's nose out into the North Sea. Keeping respectfully a good 150 kilometers off the English east coast we made for Scotland, height 4000 meters, speed about 300 kilometers per hour. To keep fresh and alert each of our five-man crew had turned his oxygen on and from time to time we had a little talk to make us feel that everything was all right.

A message from our ground station told us about enemy night fighters intercepting some planes far out at sea in a square we had already passed. A bit earlier we had crossed quite a number of vapor trails pointing to northern Germany, to Hamburg and Bremen, telling us that this night the "others" were out, too, to drop their bombs on our homeland.

After a good hour's flight, taking the bearings of Radio Bremen and Rennes-Bretagne we turned west and crossed the Cheviot Hills toward Glasgow. Very soon many searchlights came up and heavy clouds of smoke intermittently lit up by flashes indicated that something was going ahead of us, though Glasgow, a bit right of us, was veiled by haze which seemed rather customary. To the west there ran one long line of fires with only few interruptions, marking the southern coastline of the Clyde. Immense fires and black smoke emanating from the flames showed that already great damage had been done to all the industrial places between Renfrew and Greenock and even beyond. A light northerly breeze drove the clouds southward so that there was no difficulty to make out new targets along the shoreline and all around the Clyde. Dumbarton on the north bank lay bare and open in the moonlight, and I was resolved to do a good job this time.

We made a rather long approach from the southwest, the plane was quiet in the air like a "board," as we used to say, when no drifting or thermic affected the flight. Bombs fused, bomb doors opened, slowly the target showed up in the "Lotfe," sight and then, when it crossed the line, push the button for the big "things" and some twenty seconds later the other button for the incendiaries which drop almost straight to the ground because of their light weight and blunt shape. Lighter by more than two tons the plane jumped up like a barrage balloon when the wire is cut.

"Let's go north a bit, there are no guns and searchlights," I shouted to my sergeant pilot. And a little later, "You see these hills! That's the Scottish Highlands with Ben Nevis somewhere." This additional half hour we spent over the Scottish mountains made us love the old He 111 even more. And going far out in a long bend over the German Sea we had a good time listening to music and news and eating a *Schoka-Cola* from our flight rations. Nothing to report about the rest, except perhaps, that we were by far the last to set wheels down on the runway of our air base near Lille.

Portsmouth Isn't Far Away

The nights became short, and, so we were told, there would be no more astronomic darkness north of the 51st degree of latitude. That meant no more real darkness over England.

Because of putting more emphasis on the bombing war and no doubt because of lack of crews and planes, we had on several occasions done two flights per night. And today Portsmouth was to be hit twice, too.

Just to catch the optimum of darkness over enemy territory we started in almost clear daylight, hoping it would grow dark during the approach. Yet the higher our He 111 climbed the more we realized that it meant suicide to go straight to Portsmouth. So I decided to hug the French Channel coast as far as Cherbourg on Cotentin Peninsula, just to kill time and wait for some kind of darkness. But in vain, no darkness would come up. Climbing up to 6000 meters and having reached Cherbourg, I ordered my pilot to turn right, and so we made for the Isle of Wight.

Nobody talked, but everybody felt the hardness of that first job of this night, and no need to keep my boys in high alertness. They knew what was ahead of us, and in addition I had warned them about that stronghold of the British Navy that had, so I believed, the most efficient anti-aircraft defense in Britain.

Halfway across the Channel, all of a sudden a dark point came up and before any action could have been taken, developed rapidly into another He 111 rushing right at us! I don't know how but he missed us by only a scant few meters. A real narrow escape, as we stated.

The shock, however, didn't last long, for the tough job was still to come. Meanwhile the landmarks of what was to be the Isle of Wight could be made out deep below us, and minutes later our position was right over the island. None of the otherwise so familiar searchlights tried to spot us, causing uneasiness among the crew. I kept on focusing my eyes to the ground and seconds later I spotted four flashes light up almost simultaneously and fired from the corners of an irregular square. From my knowledge and experience of how our own people worked I had no doubt: that was an anti-aircraft battery! They had spotted us by radar, and we hadn't more than a good ten seconds to dodge the shells.

"Sharp right!" I urged my pilot, and two seconds later I felt myself pressed to the left because of his quick reaction. The others didn't know the why of that maneuver, but I did. I was expecting something to happen. And after a short spell it happened: a hard and bursting "bang" cut in the roaring of the engines and gave the ship just one sharp shake, making everything, especially the pointers of the instruments, tremble. I stopped breathing for a moment. Yet our plane quieted down and roared on her way just like before. We were greatly relieved over another narrow escape that night.

The rest of the mission went according to plan. After refuelling and loading up with bombs again we set out a second time that night for the same target. Now we headed straight for Portsmouth in order to avoid that damned good radar controlled battery on the Isle of Wight. We couldn't make out the details of Portsmouth as well as the first time because low tide had taken the waters out producing quite a different and less sharp coastline.

The way back taught my pilot a little lesson which I had learnt long before. Immediately after having dropped the bombs we nosed for home. Our ship dived into a rather big cloud and was instantly caught by some thermal movements. That was quite natural. But very soon we heard our hull banging just as if scores of shotguns were sending their loads against us. My pilot, a very cautious and tender man, grew nervous. "Don't worry," I said, "that's a little bit of ice!" This hailstorm decreased very soon and stopped entirely after we had left that nasty cloud. The natural phenomenon is easily explained: our undercooled plane had put on ice in the comparatively warm and humid cloud, and because of the centrifugal effects small ice particles were broken off the propeller tips and hurled against the fuselage and the wings.

Shot Down After Bombing London

This was to be our last mission, or more precisely, our last but one, for we again had a double job that night.

"I am authorized to tell you that our squadron will move, and we are going very far." So went the words of the squadron leader at the beginning of this night's briefing. Then we learned it was London again and all available planes of the Luftwaffe West were to join-in after a meticulously worked out plan as to timing, allotting of heights and sectors to be used in going and coming. His words showed confidence and our spirits went up quite a bit knowing, or at least hoping, this concentrated effort would give London that final blow. This was what our political propaganda and even some well to be trusted military informants had prophesied already at earlier occasions and which had turned out to be false. Another psychic stimulant, at least for me, was that if so many crews assembled over London some confusion must be caused to the defense giving us a chance to slip through unmolested. On the other hand there was no doubt, according to our experiences in the last months, that the skill and the ruthlessness of the British night fighters must not be underrated. Yet all deliberations had to be subordinate to that simple duty everybody had to do for Germany.

Briefing had been short, and as always, routine took its course. Before taking-off some personal deliberations made me change the given orders and adapt them to my private tactics as I had done before with satisfactory success. Right after the start, taking off to the northeast, I told my crew we were going straight to London, no detours and no other tricks. "Gain altitude, as quick as you can," I ordered my pilot, and in a wide bend we made for the bottleneck of the Channel, Calais and Cape Gris-Nez on the one side and Dover and Folkestone on the other. After about half an hour, the speed was low because of the climbing, we approached the Channel line and soon could distinguish all contours on both sides because of dangerous but good visibility in the moonlight.

For several reasons I hoped our ground defense would by some means know we were Germans and their friends. But they didn't and sent up a bunch of searchlight beams quickly followed by some shells. Damn! So I had to flash the signal patterns to quiet them down. But once this was done, I almost certainly had aroused, at the same time, the anti-aircraft people on the British side. At about 6000 meters we crossed the Channel, suffering no molestation so far. Ahead of us, no doubt, London had to take it. The nearer we came we could see the hundreds of fires blazing on both banks of the outer Thames and glowing even farther into the heart of the capital. New fires sprang up mixing with the smoke and everything was intermittently lit up by bomb flashes. We dropped down and got a better view of what the target looked like. Dozens of flares hanging down from little parachutes were a help as well as an irritation. So we got into that infernal mess where it was hard to make out who was who. Heinkels, Dorniers, and two-engined Messerschmitts curving round, flares in between, smoke boiling up from the ground or puffed out in small balls by exploding shells, English night fighters on two or three occasions. It meant that you had to keep a cool head and to stay in, for, so I felt, outsider individualists could more easily be caught. Bombs dropped, no precise target, to be honest, but not at random either. Those big docks, sheds, factories and other large buildings crowded the riverside. Any was a good target and there was little probability of a miss.

Well lighted I ordered my pilot to turn our ship south and to climb as long as he could over London. After having reached 4000 meters we left that hell behind us making directly for the Channel, by now sacrificing height for speed.

"Look round, boys, look round! we are not through yet, night fighters!" so I warned the other four of my crew. But then it happened . . .

In the midst of the tension we all felt I suddenly noticed a burst of some twelve tracer bullets chopping past under the left wing. "Night fighters, steep down!" But before I had brought out the last word, we got another burst, and this time evidently hitting the port engine. All instrument needles trembled and none recovered except those of the starboard engine. We dived, flew evasive turns and felt a little bit of relief when at about 1500 meters the attacker seemed to have been shaken off. Driven by the current, the port propeller still moved a bit, but soon it suddenly stopped. The other engine ran perfectly, but how could it carry us home even at the risk of forcing it up beyond technical tolerance. I thought of the recently installed armored plates and other additional equipment giving us more safety yet making the plane heavy and clumsy. Little more than 1000 meters above sea level by now and the silvery waters of the Channel coming nearer.

"Go on, south!" but he didn't go. The pilot turned left to have a better chance of pancaking on the land rather than in the water. I felt extremely powerless.

Losing altitude steadily, I saw the ground getting nearer and nearer. The sergeant was desperately wrestling with the stick. It moved too easily just like the pedals. There was no pressure on the rudders, and the speedometer wasn't encouraging at all. Our reserve of height dwindled from second to second and below we almost could grasp the bushes and trees quickly coming up at us. Then there were the last words of the sergeant, *"Hauptmann, I can't hold her!"* . . .

AIR OFFENSIVE—EUROPE

HENRY H. "HAP" ARNOLD

GENERAL OF THE ARMY, USAAF

The following morning I learned that Air Chief Marshal Portal was ready to sign the agreement about the allocation of airplanes to the R.A.F. It followed with few changes the ideas I had when I left Washington. That afternoon, I packed my bag and took off for "Chequers" for a visit with the Prime Minister. Admiral Towers accompanied me, and we arrived about 5:30 in the afternoon.

Present as guests that night were Ambassador Winant, Portal, General "Pug" Ismay, the Prime Minister's Military Aide, Harriman, Towers, and myself.

I have remarked before that often, during the forty years in which I watched air power grow up, I happened, with uncanny luck, to be present at the turning points.

This night, the 30th of May, in some ways topped them all, and for me personally provided luck that was rather mixed. As we sat down to dinner I knew beforehand—even without the Prime Minister's jubilation—that the R.A.F. was taking off for the greatest bombardment operation ever launched. It was not merely, as Mr. Churchill had told Harry Hopkins on the phone to the White House a few hours earlier, that the R.A.F. was sending out twice as many bombers as had ever hit Germany at once. It was not, for those of us who knew the R.A.F.'s actual heavy bomber strength, a matter of literal belief in the powerful phrase "Thousand Raid." Of the 1047 "bombers" that took off from all over Middle and North England for Cologne that night— including even little *Oxford* trainers that could scarcely hope to reach the target—715 were twin-engine *Wellingtons,* old *Whitleys* and so on, by the R.A.F.'s own standards soon to be rated as medium bombers.

That didn't matter. The fact that Bomber Command had already carried out those impressive attacks on Rostock and Luebeck did not count. Nor did the fact that 400 actual heavy bombers of the R.A.F. would presently be causing more damage to city after German city than the first "Thousand Raid" did to Cologne. This was the real beginning, in the world's eyes and in Germany's eyes, of the campaign we later came to term officially "Air Offensive Europe"—the "round the clock" destruction of Germany from the air. That night all of England was a bomber base.

As an airman who had preached bombardment for so many years, I was as thrilled as the Prime Minister himself. But—and here is what I mean by "mixed luck"—as Commanding General of the U.S. Army Air Forces, I happened to be on the spot at an ironic time. Of all the moments in history when I might have tried to sell Mr. Churchill and his R.A.F. advisers on the future of American precision bombardment by daylight, I had picked the night when they were selling their own kind of bombardment to the world.

It was not merely the difference between night and day operations. It was a whole new conception of target values, the big beginning of "night area bombing," as opposed to an attack on a precise industrial or military objective. Although "aiming points" in Cologne were given at the briefings, the crews soon understood that their high explosives and incendiaries were really to be sown between these points, blasting and gutting the whole city. As if higher headquarters were nervous about their reaction to this new kind of task, the crews were briefed to the effect that dead workmen and civil employees or workers demoralized by the loss of homes and families were as much a blow to the German war machine as smashed factories.

The target was as much public opinion as Cologne, with a special eye on opinion in America. Actually, the slim, newsprint-rationed papers in London next morning, and the BBC, could carry only a fraction of the enthusiasm that burst into print and excited broadcasts all over America in the next few days. Mr. Churchill and the R.A.F. knew it would be that way. One of the two American intelligence officers stationed at Marham that night has told me with amusement of the way in which Air Vice-Marshal Baldwin warned the crews that the whole world would be watching this performance, especially, he added with a wink, "our friends overseas" who needed a bit of jogging up. The American officer tells me there was a moment of embarrassment as the crews started to look his way, but the Air Vice-Marshal turned it into laughter by shouting jovially: "You see! They have their spies everywhere!"

Harris and Eaker came in for dinner to tell us how it was going. While we were eating, the Prime Minister, full of the subject of air power, asked certain technical questions about some of our airplanes which I couldn't answer. I said, "My pilot is a short distance away; could I bring him over?" Churchill said, "By all means." So I telephoned and Colonel Beebe came over, sat next to the Prime Minister at the table, and answered the technical questions about the capabilities and performance of some of our airplanes.

When it came time to go to bed after the long "sit up" hours the Prime Minister always enjoys, even when Thousand Raids are not in progress, Beebe was faced with the question of whether he should go home or whether he should stay at Chequers. Churchill solved it by saying, "You stay here and spend the night." Beebe answered, "But I didn't bring my pajamas." So the Prime Minister, who is about six inches shorter than Beebe, suggested lending him his. They scarcely covered him, but Gene Beebe slept in the Prime Minister's pajamas that night.

After dinner, Churchill and I went over the memorandum I had made during my conference with Portal. The Prime Minister gave me the impression that he was almost ready to accept the agreement in full, but I was to get his final answer the following morning. It was plain that now there would be renewed pressure from the British to get our four-engine bombers for the R.A.F.

The next morning, I did not awaken until about nine o'clock. A bell cord was within reach which was supposed to be used to call the valet. I pulled and pulled and pulled until 9:30, but nobody came. I couldn't find my clothes. Finally, when I was almost desperate, the valet appeared and gave them to me. Hot water was brought in and I shaved. Then I ordered a bath. The valet told me my bath was ready. I went down the hall, found an open bathroom, climbed into the tub and started scrubbing.

I had been in there hardly a moment when the door opened, the valet stuck his head in and said, "I beg your pardon, sir, but this bath is for Lady So-and-So. Your bath is down the corridor." But it was too late then.

When I finally went downstairs, no one was about but "Pug" Ismay. The Prime Minister was dictating in bed, and Portal had returned to his job in London. Ismay, Towers, and I had breakfast together and talked about the Raid. Apparently the German radio was screaming bloody murder. Cologne was still burning fiercely. Bomber Command had lost only 39 planes. After breakfast, Admiral Towers and I both had to go to the "johnny." The door was one of those cumbersome affairs with locks dating back to Elizabethan times. I had no trouble, but Admiral Towers couldn't get out. He called to me in great consternation to come and help him. Thirty-odd years before, he had contributed to the invention of aviation's first safety belt, but it couldn't aid him now.

I called the valet. He called the plumbers, the carpenters, and the chambermaids. It was Sunday, and they were all down at the pub in the village.

A bit later, with Mrs. Churchill, I was walking in the garden when to our surprise, we saw first the feet, then the blue uniform trousers, and finally the full uniform of an American admiral climbing out of a window on the first floor of Chequers Castle. Mrs. Churchill said, "My, what an extraordinary way to leave the house!"

From 11:15 until 1:15, the Prime Minister and I sat in the garden and talked about the new program for reallocation of airplanes. Finally, he agreed to the proposal I had made to Portal. I was ready to return to Washington.

That night I had my farewell talk with Portal and we went over each other's figures again. Next morning I said good-by to him, to Freeman and Sinclair; then to Winant and General Chaney. Winant sent this final message to the President: "England is the place to win the war. Get planes and troops over here as soon as possible."

I signed the various agreements with Portal, left copies with him, and brought other copies back to the United States with me.

After a stormy Atlantic crossing, our party, including Lord Mountbatten, Air Marshal Slessor, and Mr. Harriman, landed at Goose Bay at midnight where an incredibly bad cold meal was waiting for us. The American mess sergeant said we were having trouble with the Canadians because of our superior rations. They wouldn't let us run our own mess. "In fact, General," said the mess sergeant, "they actually take our good food out and bury it in the woods." I made up my mind to do something about the setup at Goose the minute I got back to Washington.

After V-J Day, General Marshall wrote of the summer of 1942:

It was a very black hour.

In July, Admiral King and I went to London for further meetings with the British Chiefs of Staff to determine if there was not something that could be done immediately to lessen the pressure on the Soviets, whose armies were facing a crisis. Poverty of equipment, especially in landing craft, and the short period remaining when the weather would permit cross-Channel movement of small craft, ruled out the diversionary operation SLEDGEHAMMER for 1942.

After prolonged discussions, it became evident that the only operation that could be undertaken with a fair prospect of success that year was TORCH, the assault on North Africa. Landings there would be a long way from Germany, but should serve to divert at least some pressure from the Red Army, and would materially improve the critical situation in the Middle East. It was therefore decided, with the approval of the President and the Prime Minister, to mount the North African assault at the earliest possible moment, accepting the fact that this would mean not only the abandonment of the possibility for any operation in Western Europe that year, but that the necessary build-up for the cross-Channel assault could not be completed in 1943. TORCH would bleed most of our resources in the Atlantic, and would confine us in the Pacific to the holding of the Hawaii-Midway line and the preservation of communications to Australia.

General Eisenhower, who was then established with his headquarters in London, directing the planning and assembling of American resources, was, with the generous acceptance of the British Government, appointed Commander-in-Chief of the British and American Forces which were to carry out the landings in North Africa. . . . The target date was fixed for early November.

Things had moved fast after my return from England in June. The document which I had signed jointly with Portal had helped us to jump a big hurdle in our race to build a U.S. Air Force at the same time we supplied our Allies. The President and General Marshall had listened with interest to my report on Churchill's and Portal's understanding in the matter of the delivery of planes. The Prime Minister's comprehension of our own problems, I pointed out, did not diminish one of his greatest fears: that we would not get planes to England in time, whether heavy bombers or troop-support types. He realized the necessity for a U.S. Air Force. He wished to see the biggest one we could get. But he wanted it over there—at once—fighting alongside the R.A.F. He feared that reasons, and good ones, would be advanced for delaying the movement.

I told the President that we were already doing everything possible to assure that our airplanes were sent to Britain on schedule in the numbers planned by Portal and myself; that we had settled that one way to keep all adjustments up to the minute was to get together personally once every six months. The President agreed with me in everything I reported, and told me if I ran into trouble at any time to let him know.

Of course, these conversations, taking place in June, preceded by several weeks the decision to make the North African invasion the all-out priority for 1942. At the Joint Chiefs' level, the U.S. Army, the Navy, and Air Forces were equally disturbed. For the moment, at least, my own top priority was knocked on the head. Our plan for the rapid build-up of an American heavy bomber force in Britain, striking at Germany itself with a thousand *Flying Fortresses* and *Liberators* by April, must wait.

I would shortly have to tell Tooey Spaatz, in London, and Ira Eaker, whose eager little nucleus of a Bomber Command was just then welcoming the arrival of its first combat group, that not only must the original schedule be abandoned, but this very bomb group with which they were about to begin, the 97th, would soon be taken away from them and sent to Africa. So would two of the next three heavy groups that followed the 97th to England. Of the eight fighter groups that Brigadier General Monk Hunter was to have assembled in England for a few weeks that late summer, only one, the 4th, made up of pilots who had flown in the R.A.F.'s American Eagle Squadron, would remain in the Eighth Air Force. The rest were all earmarked for North Africa. At the same time, I privately resolved that wherever the exigencies of the new priority permitted, I would somehow keep our Eighth Air Force building at the most rapid pace still possible.

The direct strategic bombing of Germany by the R.A.F. and ourselves remained, as I continued to state, the central road to Germany's defeat. Apart from the over-all effect of this air assault on Hitler's war factories, cities, fuel, and communications, and on the morale of the German people, it would produce rapid bene-fits for both the Russians and the two British-American fronts in Africa. This was subsequently proved by the way in which our Britain-based bombers began to pull the *Luftwaffe* back from those theaters to the defense of France and the Reich itself. Within ten months, the daylight attacks of our still small VIII Bomber Command had completely changed the disposition of the German Fighter Arm. In January, 1943, 42 per cent of the German fighter strength was concentrated in Western Europe, 33 per cent of it in Russia, and 25 per cent in the Mediterranean area. In October of that year, the line-up was 19 per cent on the Russian Front, 12 per cent in the Mediterranean, and in Western Europe 60 per cent. How much faster the relief for the Russian and Mediterranean fronts might have been effected had my original plan of a thousand heavy bombers in Britain by April not been interrupted, is indicated by the conventional estimate that TORCH set our bomber offensive back by four months. That air offensive over Europe, as planned and as later carried out jointly with the R.A.F. night bombers, was itself, of course, a Second Front.

Marshall wrote Eisenhower that the projected invasion of North Africa had, in the opinion of top advisers in Washington, only a fifty per cent chance of success, though he qualified this pessimism by saying it was "immediate and artificial" in his own view.

As we tried to build up the enormous preparations for TORCH without letting anybody know we were doing it, the uninformed pressures became tremendous. American popular opinion looked toward the Pacific. A separate intramural war, which, as we shall see, required a personal trip on my part to try to temper things down enough to get the necessary air power for TORCH, flared up at this same time. The Navy's carrier-based air victory at Midway did not settle, but vindicated in the Press the immediate need for more planes in the Pacific. To come from where? From us! From the Army Air Forces!

The cries naturally included a plea for heavy bombers. The Press, and the American people, didn't know about TORCH. All the smaller Air Forces I was just then setting up—and which were to grow, each one vitally important in its strategic spot, as any vein in the body is important—could not answer the public demand, the international demand, for a Second Front.

Butler, in Alaska, Brereton's Ninth Air Force arriving in the Middle East, Willis Hale's Seventh Air Force in Hawaii, such far-flung and unsung U.S. air efforts as our Persian Gulf Command or the outfit in Iceland, were doing critically important work. But they were not a Second Front. Still, everything taken away from each one of these hurt the balanced air war effort, as planned up to that moment, in some degree.

For replacements in planes and crews that hard winter, VIII Bomber Command used the people and the B-17s of the 92nd Bomb Group, part of its planned operational strength but now necessarily broken up. Most of the original combat personnel of the 92nd were lost in action, mourned doubly by their own old outfit because they went down as losses of the 91st, the 303rd, the 305th, or the 306th.

My own view of TORCH was based on a larger strategic aspect than that of air power alone. It seemed to me, and I was not alone in this idea, that we were dispersing our military power, even before we really had it. The "accepted" strategy against Germany was the massing of our full strength—air, ground, and sea—at the most direct point, and an all-out assault from England as soon as possible. But, despite the President's directive, not only did the Navy and other dissident points of view continue to argue, especially as the Pacific crisis grew; it was the President himself, with the Prime Minister, who decided to make this gigantic diversion, TORCH, our first priority. And having done so, it was presently Mr. Roosevelt who unwittingly gave ammunition to the Navy in its opposition to his own established plans by insisting that Guadalcanal be held "at all costs." This is not to imply that Guadalcanal should not have been held, or that the heroism of the Marines there was in any sense wasted. I simply mean to emphasize that the interservice and inter-theater wars for priority continued as steadily as any effort against the foreign enemy, with no holds barred.

A natural word of encouragement from the President was at once seized upon as proof that he had changed his mind. As far as I know, the President, no matter what he said, never actually altered his original view that Germany must be defeated first. However, it is true that, as Mr. Stimson puts it, "the Mediterranean Basin fascinated him" more than it did the American Joint Chiefs of Staff.

A year before, in the summer of 1941, Hitler had given military students one of the most horrible examples in history of what the wasteful dispersion of forces can do. In the opinion of such members of the German High Command as Keitel, Jodl, Heusinger, and others at the end, it was just there that he lost the war, when he had only to follow through to win it.

Following the Battle of Britain, the German war machine still held Europe. Blunders and all, Germany was still in control of everything between the North Sea and the north shore of the Mediterranean, between the Channel and the Russian border. Where the Wehrmacht wasn't actually in control, it could acquire domination at will, merely by moving in, as in the Balkans. Despite the bravest resistance of the Royal Navy, Crete fell. Within three days, 25,000 German paratroopers, and other airborne troops, descended on Crete's three airfields, and captured that vital air-sea base. Wavell's fate seemed sealed. All that massed German air power, all that airborne power that had grabbed Crete, was now everywhere around him, and behind him, waiting to drop on his rear. As for Malta, even after the war the R.A.F. never estimated that even the most heroic air defense could withstand a concentrated assault by 400 bombers of the type the Germans now had within easy reach. The whole Mediterranean, Egypt, Suez, Syria, the oil fields of Iraq, the life line through to India was apparently gone.

Hitler solved it for the Allies. He suddenly pulled most of that assembled air strength back from the Mediterranean to the eastern border of the Reich to refit, and three weeks after the fall of Crete, invaded Russia.

The next year, in the spring of 1942, in the same gambler's spirit, Hitler and Goering suddenly withdrew a heavy part of their air strength from the Russian Front and again concentrated it in the Mediterranean. But now it was too late. The time Hitler had given us had enabled us to get American P-40s ("Kitty-bombers" they called the P-40s modified into fighter-bombers), A-20s ("Bostons"), and other American planes to Tedder's Middle East Command and to Coningham's Western Desert Command. The Desert War was no longer solely one of tank against tank, although it was still that too. It was no longer just British ground forces against outnumbering air superiority. It had become primarily what Tedder called: "A battle for airfields. Lose them, and you retreat. Hold them, and you advance." Tobruk had fallen at last because Rommel had captured the air bases ringing it in the Cyrenaican plains, putting Tobruk beyond the defensive range of the British fighters and attack bombers. But those R.A.F. planes were still intact, retreating with relatively small losses of their ground equipment in a masterful manner.

The numerical air superiority of the Axis notwithstanding (achieved on paper by adding in the Italian Air Force), the truth was that in the past year the R.A.F. had built up so tremendously that its air power in the Western Desert and in the Middle East strategic operations (bombing of shipping, ports, etc.) was at least equal to, if not greater than, the *Luftwaffe*'s. The German air strength in the Desert had not built up at all, though the introduction of a certain number of Me-109s had provided marked improvement in quality. By the time the plans for TORCH were being completed, just before Alamein, Brereton's fighters, fighter-bombers, and B-25s had joined the British in the battle. His few B-17s and B-24s, operating singly and in pairs, usually at night, were already affecting the delicate balance of logistics.

That balance remained so tricky in this corner of the war that the loss of a single ship could spell either temporary victory (as Lewie Brereton wrote happily when one of his bomber units wiped out a good part of Rommel's immediate oil supply by sinking a 10,000 ton tanker), or could mean disaster (as when Lewie wrote me gloomily that the sinking of one British ship had cost him all the long-awaited equipment for a new depot at Gura in Eritrea, setting that project back several months). The cooperation of the Ninth Air Force tactical planes with Coningham's Western Desert Command, provided an invaluable experience for our American crews, flying the same type of aircraft. Brereton's few strategic bombers flew under Tedder's administrative jurisdiction but under Lewie's operational command. His force, at the time of Alamein, comprised only 164 of the 1281 British-American planes engaged, but they carried a weight out of proportion to their numbers. The Axis Air strength was about 2000, but well over half of these planes were Italian.

Meanwhile, General Geissler's Sicily-based *Luftwaffe* fleet gave Hitler more or less complete air superiority in the western half of the Mediterranean. It was a main cause of gloom to the TORCH planners, who decided, after unusually detailed deliberation by the Joint and Combined Chiefs of Staff, that since Algiers was already within the *Luftwaffe's* range, it might be suicidal to try to push any part of the landings farther east than say, Philippeville and Bone, the main idea being to land as close to Tunisia, the real goal, as possible.

After the invasion, when we had got so close but were still so far away, it was argued that we should have taken the risk. Admiral Sir Andrew Browne Cunningham, R.N., Ike's Naval Commander for TORCH, was emphatic about it, and said, in effect, that we had missed the boat by not landing closer to Tunis. But at the same time he was saying it, he had to express himself as "disinclined" to send any more shipping east of Bougie, because of what Geissler had already started to do from the air.

On the eve of TORCH there was no philosophic satisfaction among American air leaders—twenty-one years after Billy Mitchell had sunk the *Ostfriesland*—that from the military point of view, *Mare Nostrum* had become mostly an air problem. There was air power on both sides of the problem now, and in Northwest Africa the Allies held the short end. From the American point of view, TORCH offered about as poor an air deal as could have been dreamed up. Practically every one of our own principles for the use of air power in amphibious landing operations on a hostile mainland had to be violated.

The factor of surprise, the political machinations, fancied solutions, uncertain notions about whether the French would fight or not, ruled out any softening-up operations with our bombers. Anyway, even if there had been any strategic bases other than the jammed-up way station of Gibraltar, with the guns of Hitler's friend Franco pointing down on it through the barbed wire a few yards away, with that vulnerable gasoline cached all over the Rock, making Governor-General Mason-MacFarland and Eisenhower look for an all-out German air attack right up to the night of the invasion, there were no strategic targets in French Northwest Africa.

There were no industries to speak of, from the military point of view; no depots, oil stores, railroad yards, supply dumps other than a few installations we hoped to find intact for our own use if we got ashore. Certainly nobody wanted to harm that single narrow road along the coast from Casablanca through Algiers to Tunis, over which Patton's Western Task Force must hurry as fast as it could get itself and its air support together. The few precious airfields were not targets for our bombs but immediate objectives on the ground. Until they were secured, our planes would not be able to operate.

There could be no land-based air support for the men hitting the beaches through the mountainous Moroccan surf. Naval carrier-based aircraft, our own over the Moroccan coast, and U.S. Navy and Royal Fleet Air Arm planes at Oran and Algiers, would be their sole protection from the air until the French fields were seized and our ground people were able to service our arriving P-40s, and Air Marshal Welch's *Spits* at Algiers. We knew that we could count on the high quality of the Navy airmen at all points, but it was still a poor setup, and their ability to knock down the faster Dewoitines and French P-36s (remnants of Pierre Côt's pathetic attempt to buy a French Air Force after Munich) would be more a matter of their personal skill and courage than of the right conditions.

The first P-40s of General Joe Cannon's Western Air Task Force would have to fly ashore from a carrier or carriers, hoping to find their air service people at Mehdia airfield when they got there, instead of hostile Frenchmen. The air service people must land with the first wave. In any case, our P-40s would be out of gas.

We knew they could make it off the carriers all right, as we had landed 68 P-40s, reinforcements for India, China and Brereton, off the *Ranger* not long before. Despite the fact that none of the pilots had ever made such a take-off, all had got into the landing field at Accra, 125 miles away, without mishap, to start their journey across Central Africa to the Middle East, South Asia, and China. Also, our carrier, *Wasp,* had twice flown R.A.F. *Spits* off to the relief of Malta earlier in the year.

The planes accompanying more than supporting the landings at Oran and Algiers must first accomplish the long hazardous flight down from England to Gibraltar. All ended their flights nesting under Franco's guns when they made it.

The only other land in sight, as they waited for TORCH's D-Day, was Spanish Morocco, just across the Straits. From there, Ike and his staff, worrying about Hitler and Franco, could remember that the *Luftwaffe*'s Ju-52s, in July, 1936, had flown the Moorish mercenaries to Northern Spain to put the Spanish dictator in business. The TORCH planes assembling at Gibraltar —until at last there were over six hundred of them on the narrow little field—would have to take off for Oran and Algiers long before the landings occurred. Arriving at Tafaraoui, Maison Blanche, and Blida airfields out of gas, they must hope that things had gone well. If not, they would be written off.

If things had gone well, then they could gas up and get quickly back into the air to meet the *Luftwaffe* counterattack that was sure to come. A long paratroop mission, coming all the way from England, was part of the plan, which eventually was carried out with all the high courage and all the high confusion I had expected. Worst of all the North African rainy season was at hand. Whichever side won the race for Tunisia would be sitting on the only air bases with adequately hard runways and dispersal points in that part of the world.

Because of the weird air aspects of the intended assault, I sat in on the detailed planning for TORCH to a far greater extent than I did on the tactical preparations for other landings. In time, however, I saw that, as usual, I must start working in some other part of the world, if the materiel for this particular operation was to be available.

I left Spaatz, who would be Eisenhower's over-all air commander, to carry out the movements from Britain to North Africa in general, and Brigadier General Jimmy Doolittle, whom I had put in command of the newly formed Twelfth Air Force, to work out the tactical details with Ike's staff in London.

Logistics were my biggest headache now. Where was the air power for TORCH to be assembled from? Like Marshall for the Army, and Ernie King for the Navy, for the Air Forces I was the end of the line in this respect. When, after long travail, sweating, and brilliant argument, the plans were at last settled upon in any given theater, its commander would turn to the Joint Chiefs and say: "Well, here it is. This is the minimum. This is what we need." Then what?

We had to get it for them. The Joint and the Combined Chiefs of Staff were entirely responsible to the President and the Prime Minister, naturally, but though the Big Two might disapprove some plan we had agreed upon and submitted—the priority of TORCH itself was a reflection of this—when they said Yes, it simply meant we had their approval to go ahead on our own. Having finally reached an agreement among ourselves, with all the international and interservice differences at stake, the Combined Chiefs were free, indeed ordered, to go out and get it. That probably meant taking it away from some other theater, from some of your own people, whether you were Air, Army, or Navy.

While all these preparations were going on in quiet chaos, and attempts from the Pacific to make that theater the top one were still strenuous, TORCH or no, the following things happened.

We carried out our first heavy bombardment mission against German-held Europe.

This was the mission by thirteen B-24s led by Colonel Harry A. Halverson, from Fayid, Egypt, on June 12, 1942, to attack the most important target in the war—the oil refineries at Ploesti. The target was not much damaged. The very improbability of this two thousand-mile round trip was its best protection, and enemy opposition was not heavy.

Though the ships had to land all over the Middle East on their return journey, four being interned in Turkey, only one was lost, in a crash landing at Habbaniya. The Russians felt this American bombardment mission on their Front with impressed surprise. The R.A.F., Tedder and his people, who had told Halverson my orders could not possibly be carried out, also felt it. The handwriting for the epic Ploesti mission of August 1, 1943, for the later attacks of the Fifteenth Air Force from Italy for the whole long-range American air offense, was on the wall. Had the headlines not been so full of the battle of Midway in the Pacific that week, this extraordinary mission—virtually into the unknown—would have been better appreciated at the time.

On July 4th, six American light bomber crews in R.A.F. *Bostons* signalized the date by flying from the English base at Swanton Morley, together with six R.A.F. crews, in a low-level attack on coastal airdromes in Holland. Two of our crews and one R.A.F. crew were lost. Captain Kegleman turned on the flak tower that had knocked out one of his two engines, bounced a wing off the ground, destroyed the flak tower with his guns, and came on home on a single prop. That night in London, Eisenhower, reading this report of the first official American encounter with the enemy in his Theater, wrote an immediate recommendation for the D.S.C. across it.

On August 17th, commanded by Brigadier General Ira C. Eaker, the first dozen B-17s of the Eighth Air Force made their famous beginning against Rouen. Next day found twenty-four helping in the Commando landings at Dieppe; two days later twelve again being used against the little Le Trait shipyards. But our heavy bomber missions were started, even if their communiqués, self-conscious about the R.A.F.'s tons, announced the number of "pounds" they had dropped.

Their fourth mission was the smallest yet, but made the most history so far. On the morning of the 21st, after a couple of aborts for mechanical failures, a formation of only nine *Forts,* on its way to bomb the docks at Rotterdam, was nearing the Dutch coast when it was recalled, ordered by radio to abandon the mission and return. As the *Forts* turned along the coast, out of the clouds suddenly appeared twenty to twenty-five of the toughest fighters in the world—all FW-190s and Me-109s. In a running battle, the unescorted *Forts* beat them off. In the B-17 of Lieutenant Starks, his copilot, Lieutenant Walter, was killed, first *Fortress* crewman of the Eighth Air Force to die in action. Starks' own hands were badly burned. Up into the cockpit climbed Lieutenant Sconiers, the bombardier—a washed-out flying cadet, as I remember—and took over at the controls. And they came on home behind the others, straggling on two engines, crash landing at an R.A.F. base, but home! The first of thousands!

What a pattern this became! In Washington our hearts soared. Starks and his crew were the first of that long gallant company who were to capture and then hold on to the daytime air over Europe for a year and a half until the long-range fighter escort came.

I had seven air forces overseas by then, as well as the four big ones at home, and a letter from Butler in Alaska summed up the mail from all of them: "I need everything!"

The success of our missions was becoming apparent to the Prime Minister. "I shall be obliged," he wired, following the great attacks on Marienburg, Anklam, and Gdynia on October 9, 1943:

> . . . if you will convey to General Eaker and his Command, the thanks of the British War Cabinet for the magnificent achievements of the Eighth Air Force in the Battle of Germany in recent days, culminating in the remarkable success of last week. In broad daylight, the crews of your Bombers have

fought their way through the strongest defenses which the enemy could bring against them, and have ranged over the length and breadth of Germany, striking with deadly accuracy many of the most important hostile and industrial installations and ports.

Your Bombers, and the Fighters which support them in these fierce engagements, have inflicted serious losses on the German Air Force, and by forcing the enemy to weaken other fronts, have contributed notably to the success of the Allied arms everywhere.

The War Cabinet extends our congratulations, also, to your ground crews of the Eighth Air Force without whose technical skill and faithful labor this feat of arms would not be possible.

I am confident that, with the ever-growing power of the Eighth Air Force striking alternate blows with the Royal Air Force Bomber Command, we shall, together, inexorably beat the life out of industrial Germany and thus hasten the day of final victory.

W. C.

Though it has become a familiar thing to read that "the first task facing the Eighth Air Force was the destruction of the *Luftwaffe*," and so on, this has often been misinterpreted as a reference only to our bombing campaign against the German aircraft factories. During that campaign itself, from April, 1943, to the spring of 1944, the fact that we had to return to the same targets and hit them again within a few months, had caused our bombing claims to be challenged.

It was not understood that the more valuable the factories were, the faster they were rebuilt, either in the same places or somewhere else. We not only had to knock them down, but keep knocking them down. As our ground forces finally entered Germany and found more airplanes parked around than Goering had ever had in 1943, and as captured production figures showed the monthly output of single-engine fighters to have been far higher *after* our campaign than before, there was another tendency to doubt. The Air Force, said certain ground officers and correspondents, had deceived itself—and the public! This bomber ballyhoo was all nonsense! Look there for yourselves! The *Luftwaffe* had not been destroyed at all!

Well, then, what did become of it?

The fact is, the bombing of the aircraft factories, while magnificently done, was only part of the picture. When I say that the Eighth Air Force's other big function was to make the German Air Force come up and fight, I mean just that. There was no analogy between this very grim attitude and that of a cocky champion calling on all comers to appear and be taken on. Our view was coldly scientific.

In our strategy for Germany's defeat, the first major step, conditioning all the others, was the elimination of the *Luftwaffe;* to eliminate the *Luftwaffe* we had to come to grips with it, not defensively, as the R.A.F. had done in the Battle of Britain, but on our own initiative. The German Air Force had to be attacked, and no airplanes existed at that phase of the war with the range, the fire-power, and the philosophy to attack it, except our daylight bombers. The decision was a grave one for the commanders. We knew what the consequences would be, the price that would have to be paid, until we could get our long-range fighter escort into action. We took our course deliberately, and in fact, however bad it was, it actually wasn't as bad as we expected.

At first the crews themselves didn't realize that their collisions with the FW-190s and Me-109s were more than the outcome of a calculated risk. The view of any combat crewman is necessarily more personal than strategic.

It has been written rather frequently that despite the twelve feet of concrete over the sub pens at Lorient, St. Nazaire, and La Pallice, we were heartened by the way the bombardiers still pin-pointed the targets. It was more than that. We knew before they left the saltflats of Lake Muroc that they could bomb precisely. But in this phase, without fighter escort, against the worst aerial opposition ever seen until that time, they proved much more about the future.

To the combat airmen of those days, to the little Eighth Air Force holding on in Britain, already beginning to force the *Luft-*

waffe back before the first reinforcements came in April, 1943, the country owes a considerable debt. The fighter escort didn't arrive until the end of that year.

Their chiefs—Spaatz, Eaker, Fred Anderson, and Doolittle—such Air Division Commanders as Bob Williams, Curt LeMay, and Bill Kepner, who had already turned the VIII Fighter Command into a going concern before he produced the same change in our Britain-based *Liberators,* deserve a rather special kind of credit, too.

"PHYLLIS" HAD THE STUFF

CHARLES W. PAINE, LIEUTENANT

USAAF

It was dark, and for a moment I didn't know quite where I was. The mission hut was so small that I could reach out on either side of me and touch the other officers in their beds. I wondered what I was doing awake. Then I remembered I had been assigned as pilot of a B-17 on a bombing operation over Occupied France.

I dressed quickly and gulped down the tea that was brought me. After that I went to the intelligence office. My navigator, Lt. John A. Thompson of St. Louis, and my bombardier, Lt. S. A. Komarek of Muskegon, Mich., were there. We learned that the objective was the Potez plant of Meulte. It was October 3, 1942.

Very shortly afterward, we got news that the operation wouldn't take off as planned, but we were to stand by. There was a good possibility that we'd get "on with it"—as the RAF says—before the day was out.

We stalled around until about noon, while I got acquainted with my crew. I didn't know them, so I went through the motions of inspecting the ship. I discovered her name was *Phyllis*. It was because of a picture on her front end. It was a picture of a swell girl, but no one in the crew could quite agree as to whose girl it was. The rear gunner, Technical Sergeant Taucher, a coal miner in normal life, said it was because *Phyllis* was the name of the girl of two of the crew members. That remark caused indignation among the rest, and the thing has never finally been settled. The ship, so far as I could see, was just called *Phyllis* because she was *Phyllis*.

I went through the usual routine of checking the ship and seeing that everything aboard—including the guns—was OK. They were. I've never seen a sweeter functioning aircraft than *Phyllis* when we took off.

One thing I found in our favor was that two of the crew— Lt. R. H. Long, the copilot, and I—were lawyers, and that Lieutenant Komarek, the bombardier, was in his last year of law before he joined the Air Force. My copilot and bombardier were damn good airmen. The rest of the boys did OK, too.

In the middle of the afternoon, the signal for our takeoff came. As is usual at these moments, I was so scared I could hardly walk.

We were in vee of vees all the way in to the target. The main formation was in vees, and we, who were in the "rear guard," were in echelon of vees, from left to right, inside the rear wings of the main formation. Our ship was "tail-end Charlie."

We hit flak on our way in, but it was slight and did no harm. We got well over our targets, in formation and unmolested, when I heard the bombardier yell through the interphone, "Bomb doors open!—Left!—Right a bit!—Right hard!—Right, damn it! Right!"

I kept trying to follow his directions. It was tough because we were in the slipstreams of the ships ahead, and it took a lot of rudder to keep *Phyllis* on the course he wanted. At last he said, "OK! Bombs away! Button her up!" which meant for me to get the bomb-bay doors closed. Then he said, *"Hit-hit-hit* on target!" It sounded fine.

The bombing part was easy. We'd got over the target and dropped them on the nose—by the grace of Lieutenant Komarek. All we had to do now was get back.

But that's when they started to pour it on. The open bomb

doors had slowed us down a lot, and we were behind the formation. The Germans' strategy was obviously to pick on the last ship and shoot it down. Most of the others got no attention at all from them.

But there we were. Behind the others, pulling between forty-seven and fifty inches of mercury—a hell of a lot at that altitude—and trying to catch up, meanwhile taking evasive action. The flak was really being poured on. Heavy flak. I saw it below me, in front, and then above me. We were bracketed, and I knew that when it came next, they'd have us. They did. We started getting hits and plenty of them.

Things were happening fast, and it's a little hard to get them in their proper order. I'm trying to tell what occurred in about five seconds, but it's going to take a lot longer than that to do it. I forgot to say that I had seen a dogfight—or what looked like one—ahead and above me. Just a flash of it. That was when we were on the target.

Then came the flak, as I've said before. And then the hits. But after that came something worse. The flak suddenly stopped cold, and I knew we were in for it. That's the toughest moment of a bombing raid—the few seconds between the time the flak stops and the enemy pursuit comes at you. I found time to be scared but not for long.

Just then all the gunners in the crew started calling through the interphone: "Enemy aircraft at three o'clock, Lieutenant! . . . At five o'clock! . . . At nine o'clock! . . ."

T/Sgt. B. D. Taucher, the rear gunner, was more specific. He yelled: "Hell, Lieutenant, they're coming in! From behind! There's a jillion of them! They look like pigeons!"

The other dodge they used was to pretend to come in on one of the other ships, and then do a twenty-degree turn and shoot hell out of us. And while Taucher said their fire came mostly from a range of about 1,200 yards, he also said that they were so close when they finished firing that he could see their faces.

Mostly they came from the rear, but at least one of them got up under us from in front, stalled, and, as it fell off, raked us the length of *Phyllis'* belly. I could feel his hits banging into her.

As a matter of fact, I could feel the effect of all their fire. It was like sitting in the boiler of a hot-water heater that was being rolled down a steep hill.

I began to realize that things were getting tough. There was an explosion behind me as a 20-mm cannon shell banged into us just behind the upper turret and exploded, and I kept thinking, what if it hit the flares? If it hit the flares and ignited them, I knew we'd go up like a rocket.

Then I looked out at the right wing and saw it was shot to hell. There were holes everywhere. A lot of them were 20-mm cannon holes. They tore a hole in the skin you could shove a sheep through. The entire wing was just a damn bunch of holes.

I looked at Lieutenant Long, the copilot. That was a treat. There he was with his wheel shoved clear over to the right in a desperate-looking right-hand-turn which seemed, at the time, very funny because my control wheel was centered. I started to laugh and then decided there wasn't anything to laugh about. The position of his wheel meant his aileron-control cables had been shot away. That wasn't funny at all.

About that time several other unpleasant things happened all at once. First, the waist gunner, Sergeant Peterson, yelled through the interphone: "Lieutenant, there's a bunch of control wires slapping me in the face," which meant that the tail-surface controls were being shot up. Second, the right-hand outboard engine "ran away" and the engine controls were messed up so we couldn't shut it off. Third, the left-hand inboard engine quit. And fourth, the ship went into a steep climb which I couldn't control.

The whole left-hand oxygen system had gone out with the first burst of flak, and I was trying to get the ship down to keep half my crew from passing out. Behind me there was a pretty nice drama going on that I couldn't see. My radio gunner, Tech Sergeant Bouthellier, passed out from lack of oxygen, and the radio operator, T/Sgt. Walter Parcells, seeing him lying by his gun, abandoned his own oxygen mask and put the emergency bottle over his face. Sergeant Bouthellier revived, just in time to see Sergeant Parcells pass out. He, in turn, took the emergency bottle off his own face, and revived Parcells. After that, on the verge of going out again, Bouthellier called through the interphone to tell me that the oxygen supply line was damaged. With Lieutenant Long's help I managed to put the ship into a steep dive and leveled out at 20,000 feet. At this altitude, everyone could keep going without oxygen.

To return to the fourth unpleasant thing that happened—when *Phyllis* went into a steep climb I simply couldn't hold her level. There was something wrong with the controls. I had my knees against the wheel and the stabilizer control was in the full-down position. The control column kept trying to push me through the back of my seat. I motioned to Lieutenant Long to help me, and between the two of us we managed to get it forward and assume normal level flight.

Then I started to think. The enemy fighters were still shooting us up, we had a long way to go to reach England and safety, we were minus two engines, and it took almost full left aileron to hold that damaged right wing up. It was clearly time to bail out of that aircraft. It seemed a funny idea, but I decided it was the only thing to do. So I yelled into the interphone: "Prepare to ditch."

I called the roll. Everyone answered "OK, Skipper!" except the top gunner, Sgt. Thomas Coburn. Sergeant Peterson was badly hurt, but he answered, "OK, Skipper," and even had time to ask me if I was wounded. He said, "How's the ship, Lieutenant?" I said, "OK." He said, "On second thought, what I really want to know is how are you?"

But to get back to what happened: I gave the order to prepare to ditch ship, with visions of a German prison camp in my mind.

But just about that time Sergeant Coburn, the top gunner, slid out of the top turret and fell to a position between me and the copilot. Coburn's face was a mess. He was coughing blood, and I thought he'd been wounded in the chest. It later proved that he wasn't, but he was clearly in no condition to bail out of an airplane.

Things were tough right then. They were still shooting at us, and the coast of France was a long way away. Our target had been about sixty miles inland, and, with our reduced speed—two engines out of action—it would take us quite a while to get back to the coast. I felt a little sick inside. I yelled through the interphone that anyone who wanted to could ditch right then and there. But no one wanted to. *Phyllis* was still "airborne," as the British say, and I guess by this time they trusted her. Meanwhile, the enemy pursuit kept pouring lead into us, and there's no evasive action worth a damn you can take when you are shot up the way we were.

Lieutenant Long left his controls and went back to give first aid to Sergeant Coburn. Immediately, I had the problem on my hands of keeping *Phyllis* from climbing through the ceiling. The damned stick just wouldn't stay forward, and I kept on gaining altitude. I called for help through the interphone, and I'm sure that everyone on that ship thought I was injured. Lieutenant Komarek tried to get up through the hatch to help me, but he couldn't make it because Lieutenant Long and Sergeant Coburn were on the door in the floor through which he'd have to come. I didn't dare throttle the engines, either, for fear we'd just quit flying. *Phyllis,* at this point, had a stalling speed of about 160 miles per hour, in spite of her ambitious climbing tendencies. So I just fought her.

Meanwhile, Coburn was doing his best to bleed to death. Throughout, however, he never lost consciousness, and he kept making funny remarks.

Finally, the radio operator, Sergeant Parcells, came forward and took over the first-aiding of Coburn, allowing Lieutenant Long to crawl back into the copilot's seat. Between us we got *Phyllis* under control.

We were over the Channel by that time, and some British Spitfires took us in tow. The Jerry pursuit stuff gave up and departed for home. We went into a dive from 20,000 feet for anywhere on the coast of England.

The runaway engine gave us a lot of trouble. The electrical system was shot to hell, and we couldn't shut it off. Long tinkered with the fuel valve but no soap. I was afraid to tinker with the fuel valves. Finally we gave it up. *Phyllis* was still flying, and I didn't want to ask her too many questions.

We made a wheels-up landing at the first airdrome we saw in England. We could only make left-hand turns because both Long and I knew that if we ever got that shot-up right wing down we could never pick it up again.

I buzzed the field once and scraped a chimney or two off some buildings at the end of the runway. I knew we were going to have to crash-land because the hydraulics were shot, and I couldn't get the wheels down. Besides, I didn't want to land *Phyllis* normally at 160 miles an hour. She'd have coasted clear across England.

So we belly-landed her—the long way of the runway, and crosswind. It was a damned fine landing—marred only by the fact that Coburn, the wounded man, kept making remarks about how tired he was of flying. Sarcastic remarks. I promised him that I'd put him on the ground and was lucky enough to do it in good shape. We all walked away from that landing.

As one of the boys said after we got back: "*Phyllis* had the stuff." God rest her soul.

HELL OVER BIZERTE

H. M. LOCKER, LIEUTENANT

USAAF

It was the day after Christmas.

We took our regular place, number three in the last element of the formation, and off to Bizerte we went. We flew east past docks south of the town just far enough to miss the flak.

Swinging north and back west for our run on the target we could see the flak hopping all around the planes in the first element. I knew it would get worse as element after element of three ships came up to the bomb-release line. And our B-24 was the last of the group.

Every plane was leaving a beautiful vapor trail to guide the flak and fighters to us. Now we were in the stuff. It was bursting all around in those greasy black puffs. Many times the ship bounced from an explosion. Someone in the rear called out, "We're hit," but we could feel no difference on the controls. It was time for the bombs to go. We were loaded with six 1,000-pounders. I watched the bomb-release light blink six times.

I turned then for a look at Tom Borders, flying number two in the *Birmingham Blitzkrieg*, letting his bombs go. I've always had a mania for watching those beautiful golden eggs come sliding out. This time I wish I had curbed my curiosity, for just as my eyes found him there was a blinding flash and the loudest explosion I've ever heard. I saw the tail of Tom's ship fly backward, then down toward the ground five miles below. It was the only visible piece of the ten-man crew and airplane. A direct flak hit in his bomb bay had set off three tons of TNT. When the flash and smoke cleared there just wasn't anything left.

But right now we were having our own troubles. I remember saying, "Poor boys, God bless them," and, in the same instant I saw our right wingtip curl up. About three feet had been broken off by the explosion. Number-three and number-four engines were just starting to burn. The rest of the formation turned north to avoid the flak, but we were too busy to turn and began to fall back fast.

Right down flak alley we flew. The constantly bursting shells and shrapnel hitting the plane reminded me of a sudden hailstorm heard from the inside of a tin shed. I managed to get the fire out of number four, but number three was stubborn and burned more fiercely. I finally feathered it. Number four still was running, but it was not much use. The vibration shook the whole ship. The blaze coming out of the trailing edge of the wing grew larger and larger. I knew it was burning around the gas tank and would soon cause an explosion.

About that time all hell popped loose. All our guns were blazing at seven FW-190s that had just attacked right through the flak. Suddenly a hole about two feet square appeared in the wing where number-three gas tank is located, and flames shot out. It must have been a hit from the bottom because the fire in number three gradually dwindled to the burning of oil. We called for the P-38s to come up and help us, but the message probably never went through. Enemy fighters kept hitting us in the rear.

Harry Lawrence, our pilot, hadn't said a word so I told the crew to put on their chutes and then go back to their guns. Just then one fighter got our instrument panel and windshields with a 20-mm shell. It exploded right in front of Harry, and for a second I thought his face was bleeding as he looked toward me. I knew I was hit too because blood was running into my eyes and oxygen mask. I jerked off my glasses and threw them to the floor. I thought my right eye had been knocked out.

The same shot had shorted the parachute bell so Fozzy bailed out.

Someone called up and said we were afire in the bomb bay, radio compartment, and in the waist. I told them to fight the fire but keep an eye on the '190s. Suddenly our aileron controls went limp, and the tail dropped abruptly. I knew we had an elevator knocked off. Harry and I were shoving forward with all our might making for the clouds still below us. Though our guns were going constantly, we were almost helpless. The fighters kept coming in raking the ship from one end to the other. But the flak had stopped. At last the clouds closed around us, and the men cheered up.

But instrument flying without instruments is no fun when you have only two engines and a rudder to help you. Somehow we came out below the clouds and were in a valley, limping on and on toward the sun.

Finally she quit flying. A mountain was coming up in front, we were losing altitude, and we didn't know our speed. Suddenly a little patch of plowed ground came into view. I grabbed for throttles and switches and let her hit. We made it.

We all got out by various means and began looking for wounds. Most everyone had a few scratches and bruises. Harry and I were shot in the legs, arms, and face. Vandergriff had a couple of holes in his arms. Everything was pretty hazy for awhile. We dressed our wounds and went to an Arab's house nearby to rest while some of the boys went for help. We didn't have to wait, however. The Arabs took us to a British station.

Later we were able to chuckle over several incidents.

After Fozzy bailed out, Buck was going to follow, but with his broad beam and seat-pack chute he couldn't quite squeeze through the escape hatch. He tried so desperately, however, that he almost couldn't get back in. I chuckled when Buck came crawling out of the nose with the seat of his breeches torn nearly out. Tapping me on the shoulder, he shouted, "You've got to land this damn thing because I'm too goddam big to get out."

Incidentally when Fozzy landed in his chute three Arabs came forward. Two wanted to take him to the Germans and one to the English. The one fortunately prevailed after Fozzy had given him his knife as a present. Fozzy learned from the British that he had landed in a "no-man's" valley—the Allies were on one ridge and the Axis on the other.

At one point Whimpy decided things were getting so hot he had better come out of the tail and put on his chute. When he got back one of his guns had been blown off, and there was a gaping hole where a seat was supposed to be. Then a FW-190 came in for a tail shot. Whimpy leaned across the opening and sprayed lead from his one gun without aiming. The '190 peeled off hurriedly.

When Gowan was trying to put out the flares which had caught fire, he exhausted his fire extinguishers with no apparent success. So he tossed burning flares into the empty ball turret and poured water on them. That did the trick.

When they were ordered to put on their chutes and return to gun positions the whole crew complied except Francis, who was firing so many rounds he figured if he left the gun to get the chute they would get him before he got back. One death looked as good as the other to him so he stayed and kept his turret going even after one gun had been shot away.

Vendy ran out of ammunition so he went to the back door and thumbed his nose at the attacking '190s. He figured this was the least he could do.

Of the seven fighters that attacked us we know that three will never attack again. We got one, maybe two, while Fay in another ship got two.

I guess we cheated death.

DIVE BOMBERS

ERNIE PYLE

U. S. WAR CORRESPONDENT

The Mediterranean Allied Air Force, under the command of
Lieutenant General Ira Eaker, covered everything in the whole
Mediterranean theater from Casablanca on the Atlantic almost
to Cairo at the edge of Asia. It was a gigantic force. Although
there were many British planes and pilots in it, and even a few
squadrons of Frenchmen, still it was predominantly an American
air theater.

The main geographical objective of our push into Italy was
to get heavy-bomber bases near enough to start pounding Germany from the south. The great plains around Foggia were capable, they said, of basing all the air forces in the world. Our
heavy-bomber force was still being built up, and had not yet
really begun on its program of blasting Germany proper, but
planes had been flowing across the South Atlantic all winter.

Meantime the 12th Air Support Command bore the burden
of the close in fighting there in Italy. The 12th was composed
of fighters, dive bombers and light bombers, which worked over
the front line, helping our ground troops, bombing supply
dumps and strafing roads just back of the enemy lines.

I had to make some psychological adjustments when I
switched from the infantry to the Air Forces. Association with
death was on a different basis.

A man approached death rather decently in the Air Forces. He died well-fed and clean-shaven, if that was any comfort. He was at the front only a few hours of the day, instead of day and night for months on end. In the evening he came back to something approximating a home and fireside. He still had some acquaintance with an orderly life, even though he might be living in a tent. But in the infantry a soldier had to become half beast in order to survive.

Here is a subtle difference between the two: When I was with the infantry I never shaved, for anyone clean-shaven was an obvious outsider and liable to be abused. But in the Air Forces if I went for three days without shaving I got to feeling self-conscious, like a bum among nice people, so I shaved in order to conform.

I spent some time with a dive-bomber squadron of the 12th Air Support Command. There were about fifty officers and two hundred fifty enlisted men in a squadron. They all lived, officers and men too, in a big apartment house built by the Italian government to house war workers and their families. It was out in the country at the edge of a small town and looked like one of our own government housing projects. The Germans had demolished the big factories nearby, but left the homes intact.

When our squadron moved into this building it was their first time under a roof in six months of combat. They had wood stoves in their rooms, slept in sleeping bags on folding cots, had shelves to put their things on, ate at tables and had an Italian boy to clear the dishes away. They had an Italian barber, and their clothes were clean and pressed. They had a small recreation room with soldier-drawn murals on the walls. They could go to a nearby town of an evening and see American movies, in theaters taken over by the Army. They could have dates with nurses. They could play cards. They could read by electric light in a warm room.

Don't get the wrong impression. Their life was not luxurious. At home it wouldn't be considered adequate. It had the security of walls and doors, but it was a dog's life at that.

The toilets didn't work, so we had to flush them with a tin hat full of water dipped out of an always-filled bathtub. The lights went out frequently and we had to use candles. It was tough getting up two hours before daylight for a dawn mission. The floors were cold, hard tile. There were no rugs. Some of the windows were still blown out.

And yet, as the airmen unblushingly admitted, their life was paradise compared with that of the infantry. They were fully appreciative of what the infantry goes through, because the 12th Command had started a program of sending pilots up to the front as liaison officers for a few days at a time. When they came back they told the others what they had learned, so that the whole squadron would understand the ground problem and know how their brothers were living up there in the mud. The result was a touching eagerness to help out those ground kids. On days when the squadron dive-bombed the Germans just ahead of our own lines it wasn't as academic to them as it used to be. The pilots were thinking of how much that special bomb might aid the American boys down below them.

It was teamwork with a soul in it, and we were fighting better than ever before.

The dive bomber has never been fully accepted by the Allied armies. The British have always been against it—they call the German *Stuka* a vastly overrated instrument of war—and America has more or less followed suit. Our Navy used the dive bomber to good effect in the Pacific. But in the Mediterranean it didn't show up until the beginning of the Sicilian operation, and it was never built up in great numbers.

In the dive-bomber groups in Italy we had several hundred pilots and mechanics who believed with fanatical enthusiasm that the dive bomber was the most wonderful machine produced in this war. I never wanted to enter into this argument, since I was in no position to know; but certainly those dive-bomber boys were a spectacular part of our Air Forces.

Their function was to work in extremely close support of our infantry. For instance, suppose there was a German gun position just over a hill which was holding us up because our troops couldn't get at it with their guns. They called on the dive bombers and gave them the location. Within an hour, and sometimes much quicker, they would come screaming out of the sky right on top of that gun and blow it up.

They could do the same thing to bunched enemy troops, bridges, tank columns, convoys, or ammunition dumps. Because of their great accuracy they could bomb much closer to our own troops than other kinds of planes would dare. Most of the time they worked less than a thousand yards ahead of our front lines —and sometimes even closer than that.

The group I was with had been in combat six months. During that time they had flown ten thousand sorties, fired more than a million rounds of 50-caliber ammunition, and dropped three million pounds of bombs. That's more than the entire Eighth Air Force in England dropped in its first year of operation.

Our dive bombers were known as A-36 *Invaders*. Actually they were nothing more than the famous P-51 *Mustang* equipped with diving brakes. For a long time they didn't have any name at all, and then one day in Sicily one of the pilots of the squadron said, "Why don't we call them Invaders, since we're invading?"

The name was carried home in newspaper dispatches, and soon even the company that made them called them *Invaders*. The pilot who originated the name was Lieutenant Robert B. Walsh, of Felt, Idaho. I didn't meet him because he had completed his allotted missions and gone back to the States. His younger brother was then a replacement pilot in the same squadron.

The P-51 *Mustang* was a wonderful fighter. But when it was transformed into an A-36 by the addition of diving brakes it became a grand dive bomber as well. The brakes were necessary because of the long straight-down dive on the target. A regular fighter would get to going too fast, the controls would become rigid, and the pilot would have to start pulling out of his dive so early that he'd have to drop his bombs from too great a height.

Those boys dived about eight thousand feet before dropping their bombs. Without brakes their speed in such a dive would ordinarily build up to around seven hundred miles an hour, but the brakes held them down to about 390. The brakes were nothing but metal flaps in the form of griddles about two feet long and eight or ten inches high. They lay flat on the wings during ordinary flying.

The dive bombers approached their target in formation. When the leader made sure he had spotted the target he wiggled his wings, raised his diving brakes, rolled on his back, nosed over, and down he went. The next man behind followed almost instantly, and then the next, and the next—not more than a hundred fifty feet apart. There was no danger of their running over each other, for the brakes held them all at the same speed. They flew so close together that as many as twenty dive bombers could be seen in a dive all at once, making a straight line up into the sky like a gigantic stream of water.

At about four thousand feet the pilot released his bombs. Then he started his pull-out. The strain was terrific, and all the pilots would "black out" a little bit. It was not a complete blackout, and lasted only four or five seconds. It was more a heaviness in the head and a darkness before the eyes, the pilots said.

Once straightened out of the dive, they went right on down to "the deck," which means flying close to the ground. For by that time everything in the vicinity that could shoot had opened up, and the safest place to be was right down close, streaking for home as fast as they could go.

If you ever heard a dive bombing by our A-36 *Invader* planes you'd never forget it. Even in normal flight that plane made a sort of screaming noise; when this was multiplied manifold by the velocity of the dive the wail could be heard for miles. From the ground it sounded as though they were coming directly down on us. It was a horrifying thing.

The German *Stuka* could never touch the A-36 for sheer frightfulness of sound. Also, the *Stuka* always dived at an angle. But those *Invaders* came literally straight down. If a man looked up and saw one a mile above him, he couldn't tell where it was headed. It could strike anywhere within a mile on any side of him. That's the reason it spread its terror so wide.

However, our pilots had to hand it to the Germans on the ground. They had steeled themselves to stand by their guns and keep shooting. Pilots said the Italians would shoot until the bombs were almost upon them, then dive for their foxholes; then they'd come out and start shooting again after the bombs had exploded. But not the Germans—they stuck to their guns.

My friend Major Edwin A. Bland, Jr., a squadron leader, told me about flying suddenly over a hilltop one day and finding a German truck right in his gunsights.

Now it's a natural human impulse, when you see a plane come upon you, to dive for the ditch. But the German gunner in that truck swung a gun around and started shooting at Bland. German and American tracer bullets were streaming back and forth in the same groove, almost hitting each other. The German never stopped firing until Bland's six machine guns suddenly chewed the truck into complete disintegration.

For several reasons our dive bombers didn't have much trouble with German fighters. First of all, the *Luftwaffe* was weak over there at that time. Then too, the dive bombers' job was to work on the infantry front lines, so they seldom got back to where the German fighters were. Also, the *Invader* itself was such a good fighter that the Jerries weren't too anxious to tangle with it.

There were pilots in this squadron who had finished their allotted missions and gone back to America without ever firing a shot at an enemy plane in the air. And that's the way it should be, for their job was to dive-bomb, not to get caught in a fight.

For several months the posting period back to America was set at a certain number of missions. Then it was suddenly upped by more than a score. When the order came, there were pilots who were within one mission of going home. So they had to stay and fly a few more months; some of them never lived to finish the new allotment.

There is an odd psychological factor in the system of being sent home after a certain number of missions. When pilots got to within three or four missions of the finish, they became so nervous they almost jumped out of their skins. A good many were killed on their last allotted mission. The squadron leaders wished there were some way they could surprise a man and send him home with six or eight missions still to go, thus sparing him the agony of those last few trips.

Nowhere in our fighting forces was co-operation closer or friendship greater than between Americans and British in the air. I never heard an American pilot make a disparaging remark about a British flier. Our pilots said the British were cooler under fire than we were. The British attitude and manner of speech amused them, but they were never contemptuous.

They liked to listen in on their radios as the RAF pilots talked to each other. For example, one day they heard one pilot call to another, "I say, old chap, there is a Jerry on your tail."

To which the imperiled pilot replied, "Quite so, quite so, thanks very much, old man."

And another time, one of our *Invaders* got shot up over the target. His engine was smoking and his pressure was down and he was losing altitude. He made for the coast all alone, easy meat for any German fighter that might come along. He was just barely staying in the air, and he was a sad and lonely boy indeed. Then suddenly he heard over his earphones a distinctly British voice saying, "Cheer up, chicken, we have you."

He looked around and two *Spitfires,* one on either side, were mothering him back to his home field.

Although our dive-bomber pilots were largely spared the worry of German fighter planes, they were plenty concerned over the antiaircraft flak and other ground fire. The German ack-ack over the front lines was smothering.

Suppose our planes made a big circle back of the German lines in order to approach the target from a new angle, which they did every day. The Germans might pick them up forty miles from their target. Our men would have to fly every inch of that through heavy flak.

It was a game of wits. By that time, the pilots in the air and the gunners on the ground knew each other's actions so well that it was almost impossible for either side to do anything new. If our pilots did think of a novel evasive maneuver one day, the Germans had it figured out by the next; and, vice versa, if the German gunners shot a different pattern, our pilots had it figured out before the next mission.

The planes had to fly in constant "evasive action," which meant going right, going left, going up, going down, all the time they were over enemy territory. If they flew in a straight line for as long as fifteen seconds, the Germans would pick them off.

A pilot sat up there and thought it out this way: "Right now

12) The fighter escort form contrails high above their Eighth Air Force B-17 charges.

13) Fifteen Air Force B-24 **Liberators** over target—the oil refineries at Ploesti, Rumania.

14) Giant B-29 **Superfortresses** bomb a Japanese supply depot. Single B-29s dropped the Atomic bomb on Hiroshima and Nagasaki.

15) The second B-25 Mitchell medium bomber leaves the deck of the **Hornet** (Shan-gri-la) bound for Tokyo with the Doolittle Raiders.

16) Douglas A-20 **Havoc** and **Boston** attack bomber.

17) Aircraft Machinist Mate First Class D. L. Mason sent the cryptic message "Sighted sub. Sank same," from a Lockheed **Hudson.**

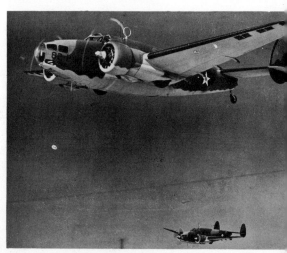

18) A Navy Grumman TBF **Avenger** unleashes a 2000-lb. torpedo.

19) A bomb drops away from a Douglas **SBD Dauntless** dive-bomber.

20) British Avro **Lancaster** heavy bombers. A number of **Lancasters,** were modified to carry bombs specially designed to destroy the Ruhr Valley dams.

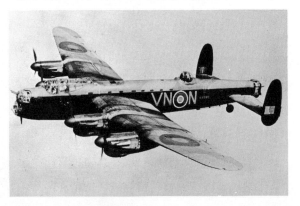

21) Vickers **Wellington** heavy bombers.

22) British **Halifax** bombers over the coast of occupied France.

23) Light **Mosquito** bombers also doubled as fighters.

24)　The Fairey **Swordfish** torpedo bomber played a big part in the seeking out and the sinking of the German battleship **Bismarck.**

25)　Best-known German bomber aircraft of World War II was the Ju 87 **Stuka** dive-bomber. They received their baptism of fire in the Spanish Civil War.

26)　The Junkers Ju 88 was one of the mainstays of the Luftwaffe bomber force.

27) The predecessor of this Do 217 bomber fought with the German "Condor Legion" for Nationalist Spain. The Do 217 played its part in the Luftwaffe bombings of England in the Second World War.

28) Hauptmann Albert Hufenreuter was shot down over England in a Heinkel He 111 bomber. Like other German aircraft, the He 111 was blooded with the "Condor Legion" in Spain.

29) So devastating was the destruction wrought to Allied shipping in the North Atlantic by the Focke-Wulf FW-200 C that Winston Churchill even made mention of it.

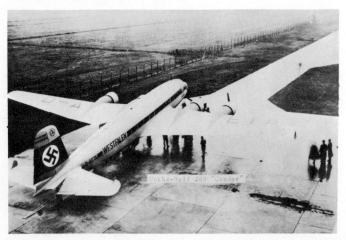

30) A whim of Hitler's decreed that the Messerschmitt Me 262 should be a bomber, over the protests of his generals. It was too late for the Luftwaffe by the time the Me 262 became a fighter.

31) The German Arado 234, the world's first operational jet bomber.

32) V-1 First of the Nazi "vengeance" weapons—the world's first guided missile. It was powered by an air breathing jet engine.

33)   The V-2 was a true rocket and like the V-1 rained down death and destruction on London. Shown here at a testing grounds in the U.S.

34)   "Betty," the Mitsubishi G4M the Japanese Navy medium bomber.

35) The Japanese Army medium bomber "Sally," the Mitsubishi Ki 21. A few moments after this photo was taken it was shot down into the jungle by a U. S. Fifth Air Force plane.

36) Japanese **Aichi** or "Val" Navy Carrier-borne dive-bombers. Some of these attacked Pearl Harbor.

37)   The famed Soviet Ilyushin Il-2 M.3 **Shturmovik.**

38)   The Savoia-Marchetti SM-79 Sparvueri was the standard Italian long range bomber, used by their **Aviacion Legionaria** in Spain and in World War II.

39)   This is a duplicate of "Little Boy," the Atomic Bomb detonated over Hiroshima.

40)   "Fat Man" the Nagasaki type Atomic bomb.

41)   Mushroom cloud at Nagasaki.

42) Some of the destruction at Nagasaki.

they've got a bearing on me. In a certain number of seconds they'll shoot and in a few more seconds the shell will be up here. It's up to me to be somewhere else then."

But he also knew that the Germans knew he would turn, and that consequently they would send up shells to one side or the other, or above or below his current position. Thus he never dared make exactly the same move two days in a row. By constantly turning, climbing, ducking, he made a calculated hit almost impossible. His worst danger was flying by chance right into a shell burst.

I asked one of the pilots, "Why wouldn't it be a good idea to fool them about once every two weeks by just flying straight ahead for a while?"

He said, "Because they've got that figured out too. They always keep the air dead ahead of you full of shells, just in case."

Pilots experienced some freakish escapes from shell blasts. Several had shells explode within a foot or two of their planes without getting hurt. They said it sounded as if somebody had fired off a dozen shotguns in the cockpit. The concussion tossed the plane around like a cork, yet often those close bursts didn't damage the plane at all. A friend of mine, Lieutenant Jimmy Griswold, of 4709 East 56 Street, Maywood, California, was thrown violently into a dive by a shell that must have exploded within a foot of the tail of his plane, but there wasn't a mark on it when he got home.

The German gunners were canny. For instance, on a bad day when there was a high layer of clouds with just a few holes through which the bombers might dive, they would fill up those holes with flak when they heard planes overhead. Or sometimes the smoke of their gunfire formed a thick layer through which the planes had to dive. If there was a hole or two in that layer they would put up a few shells and cover them up.

It wasn't the heavy flak up above or the medium flak on the way down that worried the pilots so much as the small-arms fire from the ground after they had finished their dives. If you'd ever been in a raid, you'd understand. I know that when German planes came over our line the whole valley for miles and miles around became one vast fountain of flying lead with bullets going up by the thousands. It was like a huge water spray, filling the air as far as the eye could see.

Our dive-bomber pilots had to fly through that every day. They "hit the deck" the minute they pulled out of their bombing dive, because it's harder to see a plane that is close to the ground. Also because, when they were almost down to earth, the Germans firing at them might shoot their own troops. But even that didn't stop the Jerries—they kept banging away.

The pilots said it was the accidental bullet they feared the most; nine times out of ten it was some goof—standing out in a field, shooting wildly into the air—who hit them.

When a big push was on, our dive-bomber pilots sometimes had to go through this sort of thing three times in a single day. So, although they lived well when at home base, they weren't on any picnic when they went out to work.

Before this, while I was keeping my sick record intact, I stayed at the apartment of some Air Forces friends. Pilots from the various fields dropped in there when they were in town on leave. Then it was that I met Major Bland.

It was during the summer of 1941 in Albuquerque that I decided to get a new car and as usual I wanted a convertible. The Pontiac dealer there didn't have a convertible but said that one could be sent from the district agency in Pueblo, Colorado. So three days later the shiny convertible arrived. It was a beauty and still is a beauty, even though it has spent half its life sitting in storage.

Now what does a convertible coupé in Albuquerque have to do with a dive-bomber pilot in Italy?

Well, when Major Ed Bland came to the apartment he told

me about that car. It seems that in the spring of 1941 he was a salesman for the Pontiac people in Pueblo. They had only one convertible left, and Salesman Ed had already sold it and was ready to make delivery next day. Then came word that the Albuquerque dealer wanted that car to deliver to me. So they took it away from Ed and he thereby lost his $80 commission. He was so disgusted that he joined the Army a month later.

"Well, it looks as if I owe you eighty bucks, to be real ethical about it," I said.

But Ed just laughed, and I didn't have eighty bucks with me anyhow. So despite the past, we became good friends.

Ed Bland was a tall, friendly fellow with blond hair cut in crew style. He never knew what to say when people asked where he was from. Sometimes he said Oklahoma and sometimes Colorado. He was raised in Waurika, Oklahoma, where his parents still lived. But he married a girl from Fort Morgan, Colorado, and home to almost any soldier is wherever his wife is. Ed's plane was named "Annie Jane" in her honor. He had seen their baby only once—he got home for a few hours when it was four days old, and then went right overseas.

His father was agent for the Rock Island Railway. Ed often thought how ironic it was that his father had spent a lifetime making trains run and now his son was overseas shooting up trains so they couldn't run. But he loved to fly and was torn between flying after the war or going back to Colorado and settling down to enjoy the mountains.

He almost got his'n a couple of weeks before I visited his squadron. That day Ed couldn't get his plane out of a dive. The tab on his rudder had either been shot or torn loose by the pressure of the dive. The stick vibrated so violently that it flew out of his hands and he lost control.

The only chance of saving himself was to get hold of that stick again. I asked him if it was vibrating so fast he couldn't grab it. He said, "Hell, it was going so fast I couldn't even see it."

So Ed clasped his hands, reached clear up to the dash, then lowered his hands toward the cockpit floor and drew them back toward him. He knew the stick had to be somewhere inside the circle of his arms.

As he gradually pulled back, the stick beat upon his hands and arms with killing pain, but he kept pulling until finally he had hold of it. The infernally flailing thing hit with such fury it literally pulled a big hunk of flesh out of the palm of his hand, but he finally got the plane out of the dive, just by will power and brute strength.

He was only four hundred feet above the ground when he leveled off—as narrow an escape as a man ever wants to have. "I thought it was my time," Ed said. "I figured my number had come up, and I sort of said good-bye to everybody." (After I left Italy late in the spring for England, Ed Bland, by then a lieutenant colonel, was shot down behind the German lines. Later we got word that he was a prisoner.)

The youngest pilot in the squadron was Lieutenant Robert L. Drew, who was nineteen years old and came from Fort Thomas, Kentucky. Young as he was he outranked his own father; he was a first lieutenant while his dad was only a shavetail. The father, Robert W. Drew, was in the Navy in the last war, and ran a flying-boat service on the Ohio River in recent years. Now he was a Ferry Command pilot back home. Lieutenant Drew was shot down while I was with the squadron. Nothing at all was heard from him. But the story had a happy ending. After three and a half months behind the enemy lines he escaped and returned to the squadron. Then he was sent back to America. One day he walked into his own home. His father, by now a lieutenant of equal rank, got a week's leave, and what a time the Drew family had!

One of my friends in that squadron was Corporal Adolph Seeger, who owned a farm two miles outside of Evansville, Indiana. Seeger was a driver. Although most of the other enlisted men lived in the same apartment building the pilots lived in, Seeger voluntarily slept at the motor pool in a tent in order to be near at hand in case of emergencies.

Seeger thought it was odd that he should be over there driving a car—which didn't seem to him a very important job—while at home his 64-acre farm lay idle because there was no one left to farm it. His mother lived there all alone.

Around a fighter or dive-bomber airdrome there is always talk about low-flying missions. That means jobs on which a pilot flies so low he is practically on the ground. Often the planes go so low they can hit a person standing on the ground.

On such a mission a flier went out "looking for things." He would shoot at practically anything he saw. He would go whipping up over a slight rise, then zip down the other side, and in his gunsights there might be a gun, a truck, a train, a whole line of German soldiers, a supply dump. Whatever he found he shot up.

The squadron of A-36 *Invader* dive bombers had some freakish experiences on those missions. For example, Lieutenant Miles C. Wood, of Dade City, Florida, almost shot himself down one day. He was strafing, and he flew so low that his bullets kicked up rocks and he flew into the rocks. They dented his propeller and punched holes in his wings. He was lucky to get home at all. Even a hunk of mud will dent a wing at that speed.

Another pilot flew right through an eight-strand steel cable the Germans had stretched on poles above some treetops. It was one of their many tricks, and that one almost worked. The pilot landed at his home field with the cable still trailing from his wing.

Ed Bland was so interested in his strafing one day that he didn't notice a high-tension line just ahead. When he did see it, it was too late to pull over it. So he flew under it—at about three hundred miles an hour.

Another of the pilots was diving on a truck and got so interested in what he was doing that he ran into a tree. The plane somehow stayed in the air, although the leading edge of the wing was pushed up about eight inches and crumpled like an accordion. He got the plane back over our lines, but finally it went into a spin and he had to bail out. He broke his leg getting out of the cockpit, hit his head on the tail as he went past, and then smashed his leg up some more when he hit the ground.

He was the luckiest man the squadron had. Everybody was concerned about him, and grateful that he lived. Yet when Ed went to see him in the hospital, the first thing the injured pilot did was to start apologizing for losing the plane.

Sometimes the pilots flew so low they even had German tracer bullets coming down at them from the hillsides. They flew so low that Italians behind the German lines would often come running to their doors and wave, and now and then some dirty guy who had different sentiments would run out and take a shot at them.

A man on a low-flying mission was justified in shooting at anything. One day one of our pilots, after a dull time in which he saw nothing worth destroying, decided to set a haystack afire. He came diving down on it, pouring in bullets, when suddenly he saw his tracers ricocheting off the haystack. Now you know bullets don't ricochet off ordinary haystacks, so our pilot gave it the works—and thus destroyed a brand-new pillbox.

As I have said, the Germans were full of tricks. They sent up all kinds of weird things from their ack-ack guns. They had one shell that looked, when it exploded, as if someone had emptied a wastebasket full of serpentine. They shot all kinds of wire and link "daisy chains" into the air to snag our propellers.

But the weirdest one I heard of was described by a pilot who was on the tail of a Messerschmitt one day. Just as he was pulling the trigger, the fleeing German released out of the tail of his plane a parachute with a long steel cable attached to it. By fast maneuvering, the American pilot got out of its way, but he did lose his German.

One time an artillery observer saw three big German tanks pull into a field several miles back of the German lines. The crews jumped out and began pitching straw over them, and in a few minutes they resembled a strawstack.

Not five minutes later our dive bombers came over. Their target was a gun position in an adjacent orchard. But their aim was bad, and their bombs landed directly on the three straw-covered tanks. It was just an accident, but the Germans probably wondered what the world was coming to when Americans could have planes over blowing up tanks five minutes after they had hidden them.

Another time our dive bombers couldn't find their principal target because of bad weather. They were on their way home when they picked up their alternate target, a supply dump at a crossroads.

The first plane dived in and dropped its bombs. Instantly a gigantic flame shot fifteen hundred feet into the air. Before the last plane had finished its dive—a matter of only a few seconds—the pillar of smoke was four thousand feet high. They had really hit the jackpot, but they never knew what the jackpot was. They couldn't conceive of anything that would flame that high so quickly.

Still another time a pilot went out on a reconnaissance mission. Because of hazy weather, and because two adjacent passes in the mountains looked exactly alike, he took the wrong one and got lost, although he didn't know he was lost.

He kept on flying by his map for a long time, although actually he was far north of where his map ran out. At last it began to dawn on him that something was wrong. Just as he was getting good and worried he looked down and directly under him saw an airfield with a dozen or more small German planes lined up alongside the runway. So down he went in a surprise dive, set the German planes afire, and then headed rapidly south.

He found his home field just as he ran out of gas. When the boys asked where he'd been he didn't know. It took the pilot and his squadron commander two hours of intense map study to figure out what field he had shot up so beautifully. He had been two hundred miles north of where he intended to be.

At one of our airdromes a German plane sneaked over and plastered the field with five-pronged steel spikes. Our fliers called it a "jacks raid," since the spikes resembled the jacks kids play with, only they were much bigger. Those vicious spikes would have punctured the tires when our planes taxied out.

So the field engineers got a huge magnet, attached it to the front of a truck, and swept the field free of the spikes. Then they loaded them into our planes and dropped them on German airfields. That was the end of the jacks raids.

Before the squadron moved into the big apartment house, they had flown from ten different fields in the previous six months. They had lived in tents, under trees, and in foxholes. They had lived in mud so deep the planes had to be towed to the runway, and in dust so thick they had to take off by instruments.

They had flown from fields so close to enemy lines that they could go out on a bombing mission and be back in ten minutes. So close, in fact, that ground crews could stand on the field and watch their own planes going into their bombing dives.

Once the air over one of their fields was so full of wounded planes from other stations that the squadron commander himself had to get out and act as traffic manager, deciding which planes were in greatest danger and should be allowed to come in first.

The turnover of pilots was high—partly owing to casualties but mainly because of the system of relieving pilots after a certain number of missions. It was unusual for a combat airman to be overseas more than a year.

The squadron had come into combat just six months before, yet only three of the original fifty pilots were left. Twelve had been casualties, and the rest had finished their missions and gone home. The three originals were due to be homeward bound shortly.

Those dive-bomber boys had compiled some statistics about their operations. They found that a new pilot, starting in to build up the required missions for going home, had about a seventy-five per cent chance of coming through safely, and if shot down he had almost a fifty-fifty chance of becoming a prisoner.

A dozen times during my stay, pilots voluntarily brought up the subject of how wonderful the enlisted men were. These men took a terrific personal pride in their planes, and they worked like dogs to keep them in good shape. They were a really high-class bunch. Being trained technicians, most of them were at least twenty-five years old. You could have put officers' uniforms on half of them and no one would have known the difference.

While I was on the field they pumped me about conditions and politics at home, and about the end of the war and the peace, as though I were an information bureau. They were certainly one group of soldiers who did some thinking about the war.

These mechanics were fully aware of three things about their jobs: that their life was immeasurably better than that of the infantrymen and that they should be grateful; that the pilot who flew out to battle was the one of their family who really took it; and that pilots' lives often depended on their work. The result was that they were enormously conscientious.

When a favorite pilot failed to come back the enlisted men took it as hard as the officers did. A mechanic whose plane had been shot down was like a boy who has lost his dad.

There was quite a spirit of rivalry among the ground crews. For a while there two ships were running a neck-and-neck race for the most missions flown. Then one of the ships came back so badly damaged it had to be worked on for several days, and it fell behind in the race. It almost broke the crew chief's heart.

Here are two little examples of the zeal with which the enlisted men worked. Once as the planes were taxiing out for their daily mission, it was discovered that the tire on the tail wheel of one of them was flat. Ordinarily the plane would have been just left behind. But the crew came running, other crews pitched in to help, and they had a new wheel on the plane by the time the next-to-last ship of the squadron was taking off.

Another time a plane came in full of holes, but not basically damaged. Usually it would have taken a day or two to mend the holes but, in their excitement and pride of accomplishment, the crews had that plane patched and ready to go on the next mission an hour and a half later. It was during a hot time, and the squadron was flying two and three missions a day.

Around the airdrome they joked about how one pilot won his victory over an enemy plane. It seems he caught a tiny observation plane, similar to our *Cubs,* while he was out on a low-level mission. As soon as the frightened little enemy saw our ships, he got as near to the ground as he could. One of our planes pulled up and came down at him in a dive. The little plane was so slow that our pilot misjudged its speed and completely missed him. But as he shot on past, his propeller blast caught the little ship, threw it upside down, and it dived into the ground—quite fatally.

As they say, there's more than one way to skin a cat.

You laugh at some very sad things in wartime. For instance, the pilots told with merriment about the fate of a German motorcyclist. Our planes were strafing a mountain road one day. They saw this German motorcyclist who kept looking back over his shoulder in terror at the approaching planes, and consequently rode right off the highway and over the edge of a 400-foot cliff.

In describing what it feels like to fly one of our high-powered fighting planes, one of our pilots said, "You're just sitting there with a thousand horses in your lap and a feather in your tail."

One night I went into a little Italian town with some pilots to see the movie *This Is the Army*. The Air Forces had taken over a local theater, and as long as a man was in uniform all he had to do was to walk in and sit down. About a third of the audience were pilots and the rest mechanics. I couldn't help being interested in their reaction to the picture. On the whole, they applauded, but every time the action got a little gooey or mushily patriotic, a combination boo and groan went through the audience. Soldiers at the front can't stomach flag-waving from back home.

I've already mentioned that interesting psychological thing accompanying the "rubbing out" process of the last few missions a combat airman went on before he completed that final one and returned to America. It interested not only the man himself but everybody on the field from cook to crew chief. When a pilot got within five missions of the finish everybody knew and watched his total. If one plane was missing when the group got back, the first thing on everybody's mind was the question: Was it the guy who was about finished?

For the pilot nearing the finish, most squadron leaders deliberately picked missions that were expected to be easy. There were so many ironic cases of men "getting it" on their last flight that the leaders were as nervous about it as the pilots.

When a pilot came back from his last trip he turned out of formation as he neared the field and came down wide open and screaming, to "buzz" the field just above the ground. It was a gesture of elation similar to that of a fighter pilot doing a snap roll over the home field after shooting down a Nazi plane.

While I was at the airdrome, I saw the pilots do all kinds of things after their last flights. A friend of mine—Captain Dean Schuyler of 144-55 87th Avenue, Jamaica, Long Island—felt so good the night he got down that he canceled a $300 debt another pilot owed him.

Another one who finished the same day—Lieutenant Swithin Shortlidge of West Grove, Pennsylvania—shaved off the beard he had been growing for months. The previous fall Lieutenant Shortlidge had fallen down, knocked out his upper front teeth and cut his chin. He started the beard then because he couldn't shave for a while, and he finally decided to keep it until he had finished his missions. The dentist made him a false plate to cover up the gaping hole in his mouth, but he refused to wear it. With a long beard and a big grin and no teeth he was a sight to behold.

When Lieutenant Jimmy Griswold finished his missions I asked if his last one was the hardest. He said, "No, it was all right once I got in the air, but thinking about it ahead of time almost had me in the asylum."

We were sitting around the mess-hall table, and Dean Schuyler said, "Yes, we thought this flying business was going to be very romantic. And it was, for the first few missions when everything was new and strange and we were just learning. But since then it's been a job to do, just a job of muddy, hard work." And all the others agreed.

Most dive-bomber pilots went home without any enemy planes to their credit, since attacking enemy planes wasn't their job.

Jimmy Griswold said the first thing his younger brother was going to ask him was how many planes he shot down, and when he said "None at all" the kid was going to give him an awfully funny look.

Some pilots finished and went home in as little as five months, while others were overseas more than a year before completing their missions. Occasionally sickness or wounds would keep one out of the air for weeks, and he fell behind.

There was one hard-luck pilot—an excellent one too—who was laid up a long time with a bad flak wound in the leg. Then just after he started flying again the jeep he was riding in was strafed by an enemy fighter and he went back to the hospital with another bad leg wound. As a result, he was far behind on his missions and while all his pals had gone home he was just starting to fly again.

The saddest thing about the strafing was that the pilot driving the jeep had just finished his last mission and had his orders home—and he was killed.

ROME RAID

JOHN S. TAYLOR, CAPTAIN

USAAF

I climbed out of the B-17F (cargo version of the *Fortress*). My first trip to Algiers had been wonderful. I'd seen little of North Africa, though I had been there many months.

The Intelligence Officer greeted me as I hit the ground. "Captain Taylor, report to the Group Mission Planning tent. Colonel Rainey wishes to see you."

Oh, oh . . . now, what had happened? Why this personalized request for my immediate appearance before the C.O.?

Colonel Leroy A. Rainey, better known as "Storm," was indeed a remarkable character. Having seen some twelve years' service and possessing about 9,000-odd hours, he is one of the greatest flying soldiers I have ever known. He was once the personal pilot of Lt. Gen. Barton J. Yount. From an all-around combat-pilot standpoint, the Colonel's flying ability was tops.

A look of intense seriousness was on his face as he returned my salute. I thought my days were numbered. His opening phrases eased my inward strain . . . he was speaking of the next day's mission. Why all this fuss over a mission? Then he related the details—and I damned near swallowed my tongue. The target was Rome, and who do you suppose was to be our co-pilot? *General Doolittle!* This really was an occasion! I was plenty aware of the import of the situation. Rome, the holy city, had never been bombed before. Woe to the lead Bombardier whose bombs did not hit the target area. And what a target! . . . A railroad station and yards—from 26,000 feet.

Colonel Rainey impressed upon me the significant potentialities of not concentrating our pattern on the target. Adjacent to the objective were ancient buildings and monuments known only too well to the world. The destruction of any early Roman architecture or shrines could instigate international repercussions.

That evening and the next morning, my time was spent poring over maps and photos of the target. My navigator, Capt. Wm. P. Buckley, who hails from California, worked with me. We went over the intricate details of approach, IP, etc., until the last potential, unforeseen item was covered. The maps and photos were branded into my bloodshot eyes. The target area—its relation to outstanding landmarks was fixed in my mind. Never in all my missions, had I worked so hard in briefing and poring over maps as I did for this mission. So much depended upon its success. All through the night I lay awake, going over in my mind exactly what alternatives I would follow in case of emergency. I had memorized the maps and photos so well that if I were to visit Rome, I would be a well qualified tourist guide.

Before take-off, my navigator and I checked the last few remaining details. Col. Rainey, a Texan, along with myself, had confidence in old *Ft. Alamo II,* our *Flying Fort,* to carry us through. She had been checked and rechecked. The engineers found her sound in all departments. (*Ft. Alamo I,* its predecessor, had gone down in the Mediterranean.)

I had preflighted my Sight and double checked it. Everything was O.K. I made my way back to the bomb-bays. I checked each shackle and release mechanism, even though the ship had been thoroughly inspected by the ground crew. I, as Bombardier, was responsible for the releasing of the bombs. A malfunction, no matter how small, could not be risked on this mission. I scanned all my equipment, made sure that I had brought all my computers and maps aboard with me. All was in readiness for the take-off.

When Gen. Doolittle joined us, we warmed up the engines. The thought as we took off was that this was the most important assignment that we would ever receive.

As we gradually gained altitude, I was busy taking temperatures and making tabulations. The 52 *Fortresses* that were to compose our formation gradually formed behind the *Ft. Alamo II*.

When we reached altitude, I checked the crew in on oxygen. Immediately afterwards I made my way back to take the pins out of the bombs. I looked at the bombs with respect. A lot depended upon these babies. My walk-around bottle had about petered out, so I wended my way to the greenhouse.

We were out over the sea. I called to my gunners and had them fire a practice burst. All guns were in working order. Everything was going along smoothly. The 52 ships in formation reflected the strength of air power that had been the dream of Gen. Billy Mitchell. Our mission moved forward. My navigator's voice came over the interphone, "Mainland of Italy in view. We'll be over it in ten minutes."

I had since put all my information into the Bombsight. I had checked my computations several times. No mistakes. The navigator kept me pinpointed as we progressed closer and closer to Rome.

We had decided to make the run as long as possible so that there would be no slip-ups. As we turned on to our Initial Point, we were caught by some Jerry anti-aircraft. It was pretty warm. Black puffs were all around and it seemed they would never cease.

I was busy over the Sight, looking out through the greenhouse from time to time. The black puffs seemed to get closer and closer. I kept saying to myself, "Taylor why in the hell aren't you a mess officer?" About that time, with the target in sight, I felt the ship lurch. We had been hit. I quickly checked the damage and found everything O.K. However, the flak missed the bombrack control cables by a fraction of an inch. Had the cables been hit, it would have been too bad. All the 52 ships were dropping pattern style on our ship. If the cables had been severed we would not have been able to release.

We were about eight minutes away from the release point, when I suddenly looked up. I had been so intent on checking the cables that I had not noticed our navigator. He was nearly out. On examination I found that the flak had cut his oxygen hose. This was a hell of a time for the navigator to be disabled. I needed him to help me locate the target. I quickly snapped on a spare oxygen hose to his mask. In a few seconds, he was himself once more.

Col. Rainey's voice came over the interphone, "O.K. Taylor, let's get on the ball down there and make these bombs good." I opened my bomb bay doors. There was no reason why this would not be a perfect mission. The stabilizer level I had taken while still over the sea was perfect, my bubbles were centered, even at the beginning of the run.

We were champions of the long bomb run; this was right up our alley. For six minutes I sweated and strived for perfect results. The railroad marshalling yards were resting under my crosshairs. It was no trouble at all to find the target. My memory was good, the layout and target area was the same as I had learned it from the maps and photos. I checked all my switches, then went back into the Sight once more, babying those crosshairs with the knobs as if I were handling nitro-glycerin. I glanced at my bubbles—perfect. A few seconds later, the ship gave a lurch as the bombs left the ship.

Immediately through the interphone came the voice of Gen. Doolittle. "Where are the bombs going to hit, Captain?" I answered, "Right on the target, sir." After the bombs hit, I sucked my breath in with a relieved gasp. My study and planning had paid off. The marshalling yards and station were wiped out. Nothing had been hit but the target.

HITTING THE OIL REFINERIES AT PLOESTI

[1]JOHN R. KANE, COLONEL

USAAF

Those of us who participated in the second low-level bombing of the oil refineries at Ploesti have waited a long time to survey our experience in its historical perspective.

The problem faced by General Brereton as to whether the bombers would go in at high or low level was not an easy one. Previously his staff and the operational analysts under Dr. Kaplan had made their recommendation to go in at zero altitude, based on the probability that we would do more damage and suffer fewer losses in one low-level raid than in ten high-level missions. It was realized that after the first heavy attack the Germans would increase their defenses. Yet when we were informed by General Ent that General Brereton had in actual fact decided on a single low-level attack we understood all too clearly what we faced. I knew the difficulties in low-level flying, for I had had five years of experience with the old Third Attack Group, where we turned on the oxygen as soon as we got above five hundred feet. The huge size of our planes would add to the task of such flying, for the prop-wash blasts of the four engines would interfere with other planes to the rear. Also, we would be flying right down the gun barrels of the German ground defenses.

---

[1] Colonel Kane earned the Medal of Honor for this mission.

During our practice runs on the dummy target we found that many of our high-level pilots instinctively refused to endanger their B-24s by flying on the deck in the prop-wash of the preceding planes, and consequently went over the target much too high. Since our main defense was to get down as low as possible, too much altitude would be deadly. We spent hours on lectures and demonstrations trying to drive home to the pilots that they had to fly low and stay low, only to find that on the next practice mission the pilots simply would not force their *Liberators* down into prop-wash. This phobia was not lessened when two planes were actually thrown into the ground by prop-wash, although both suffered only minor damage.

The day before the mission General Brereton explained to the combat men of each group that to knock out Ploesti oil by army methods would require a full-scale invasion; it might take at least a year before the enemy could be deprived of one drop of oil, whereas we might very likely do the job in one day, at much smaller cost in both matériel and lives, in a single low-level mission. While this reasoning was logically evident, every man realized that our losses were certain to be heavy. One of the Air Force V.I.P.s asked me if I thought my men would follow me into the target. My reply cannot be printed here verbatim, but I advised him that the men had demonstrated their courage many times, and that if he thought I was not capable of leading my men he could have me replaced and do the job himself. He declined the offer.

The hardest part was waiting for the long hours to pass before take-off. Were we afraid? To men who had been shot at through months of aerial combat, exclusive members of the Combat Club, fear was always the entrance card and courage the routine music of the dance. Yes, we dreaded this mission. And the target proved to be all that we had expected—only more so. Some pilots still failed to get sufficiently low on the way into the target, but, on the way out, all remaining planes were below treetop level and disregarding prop-wash as if it did not exist. Our losses were heavy, but we inflicted heavy losses in turn.

After the attack, the critics began their barrage. As always, those who have the advantage of hindsight fight the best battles; and to this day controversy exists over the low-level concept and execution. Later the Fifteenth Air Force pounded it from high level. The Russians contributed the final comment on the effectiveness of the entire campaign. When they pushed the Germans out of that part of Rumania they were disappointed to find that they could get no petrol without rebuilding the destroyed refineries, and a loud and eloquent complaint was made to the Western Allies.

Other missions soon crowded out the Ploesti episode in our wartime lives, but it was enough to furnish a lifetime of memories to those of us who had flown there. I have always thought that our attack was as deserving of poetic immortality as that of the *Charge of the Light Brigade.* What the historian cannot say with facts might somehow be expressed by the poet, for those men actually did fly their lumbering bombers through smoke and flame, concentrated fire from rifles, machine guns, 20- and 40- and 88-mm. cannon, exploding bombs, barrage-balloon cables, smokestacks, exploding oil tanks, and attacking fighter planes, pressing in for their turns to drop their bombs on a target a thousand miles inside of enemy territory, from altitudes as low as thirty feet. I am privileged to have accompanied those 1700 young men to Ploesti. The many who did not return died the deaths of heroes. I salute those living and dead for their consecration to our nation and to their own self-respect regardless of the physical cost. So long as America can produce this kind of men, our way of life will continue to exist. Though the price of liberty comes high, there are days when it must be paid, and in full. August 1, 1943, was one of those days.

ATTACK ON PLOESTI

JOHN S. YOUNG, CAPTAIN
USAAF

You might say that the Ploesti oil refineries in Romania were destroyed on the African desert, long before the real raid.

The actual attack on August 1 was only the continuation of a rehearsal which began six weeks earlier at our advanced bases in North Africa. A routine announcement was made that 177 B-24s would fly 2,400 miles for a low-altitude precision attack. Our target: Ploesti's cracking, distillation, and power plants.

We had already helped chase Rommel across Africa. Ours had been the first outfit to bomb Italy. We had hit Greece and Crete, and we had hunted convoys all over the Mediterranean. But this raid was going to be different.

On previous missions, we had bombed whatever we could find. We had gone out with general instructions to find Rommel and give him hell. When we hit the European mainland, we had made a lot of saturation raids. But for the Ploesti mission, every plane in every element was given a pinpoint—and we had to find it. There were no secondary targets. Col. John R. "Killer" Kane, our group CO, was not being dramatic when he said, "Either we hit Ploesti or we'll die trying."

We examined hundreds of still photographs. We saw motion pictures taken from the air before the war, showing us exactly what the area would look like from our bombers. We attended lectures given by a former manager of one of the Ploesti plants. And we had a detailed relief map of the surrounding territory, complete with roads and even trees. Finally, a miniature model of the targets, drawn and constructed to an exact scale, was laid out on the desert, and we practice bombed it for weeks.

We ran approximately twelve missions over that replica of the oil fields, approaching, attacking, and departing exactly as we intended doing on the actual raid. Each element was given a specific dummy target which had been erected to resemble the real thing, and we practiced until we could bomb it in our sleep. When we finally did get over the real Ploesti, our movements were almost automatic. In a low-altitude raid, you have to know precisely where you are going because you don't see your target until you are on top of it. And we knew we could only make one pass.

Our *Liberators* were modified considerably for the mission. An extra releasable fuel tank was added in the bomb bay. The top-turret guns in the lead planes were arranged so that they would fire forward, so the first ships could strafe the entire area, with the following planes protecting their rear. Extra .50s were mounted in the noses of the lead planes.

Five bomb groups made the raid. Colonel Kane and I were piloting the lead ship of the first element. The second group was on our right wing, a third on the left, another further to the left, and the fifth on the extreme left. We flew a flat V, wingtip to wingtip—no plane in the entire formation was more than twenty-five feet away from another plane.

We had forty-eight planes in our element, flying in sections of five. The first four sections had ten planes each, with an eight-plane section bringing up the rear. Each of the first twenty ships carried 1,000-pound bombs with sixty-minute delayed-action fuzes. The sixty-minute fuzes were a precaution against premature explosions damaging the last planes over the target. In practice bombings, we got the entire flight across the target within a minute and fifteen seconds, but we were prepared for the possibility that some ships might get lost on the way and reach the target late. Each plane in the last three elements carried 500-pounders with forty-five second delayed-action fuzes.

Weather conditions were perfect when we took off at 0710. We crossed the Mediterranean at 2,000 feet. At our initial point we ran into thick cumulus clouds at 10,000 feet and lowering. Over Yugoslavia, the clouds started settling in, and we had only about 1,000 feet of visibility over the 9,500-foot mountains. As we came into the Danube Valley, we dropped down to 2,500 feet and followed the Danube River to our target.

All the way across the Mediterranean and over part of Occupied Europe, we didn't even see an enemy plane. It was like a practice mission but, naturally, we maintained radio silence. In that long ride, I don't think anybody said a word.

About thirty-five minutes from our target, we lowered to twenty feet off the ground. And I mean twenty feet. We were coming in so low our plane actually had to pull up to avoid hitting a man on a horse. That horse probably is still running.

The fun started when we spotted a freight train sided at a railroad junction. There must have been fifty cars full of oil just inviting our personal attention. T/Sgt. Fred Leard, our right-waist gunner, and Sergeant Weckessler, top-turret gunner, were mighty eager boys. They called Colonel Kane on the interphone and asked if they could "test" their guns. They had gone through a routine test just after we left the field, and everything was in proper working order. But they wanted to make sure, and if a German oil train was sitting beneath them—well, that was just coincidental. The colonel, never a man to object to a "routine" check, gave his approval and the "test" began.

All the other gunners decided that their guns needed a check, too. It probably marked the first time in history that a routine gun inspection resulted in a Nazi train being blown right off its tracks.

About two miles from the target, the flak guns bellowed out a reception comparable to none I had seen in 330 combat hours against some heavily defended targets. Most of it was 20-mm stuff, with some 40-mm and a lot of machine guns. The fire was plenty accurate.

A mile and a half from the refineries, we opened up with our .50s aiming at the oil tanks which held about 55,000 gallons of oil. They started to explode, throwing smoke and flames about 500 feet into the air. There we were, buzzing in at twenty feet, doing 200 miles per hour, flying through intensive flak and bouncing around between oil fires. Play that on your harmonica sometime.

Our particular targets were the Orion and Astra Romana refineries. They had smokestacks about 210 feet high, so we had to climb to about 250 feet to drop our bombs. Flames were biting in through the bomb-bay doors, the heavy smoke fires made visibility difficult, and the flak fire was beating a hellish tattoo all over our ship, but with all the practice under our belt we had no difficulty picking out our targets. We laid our bombs down the middle.

Forty of the forty-eight planes in our element got over the target. One cracked up on the takeoff, and seven others turned back with mechanical troubles. The rest of us didn't miss.

After the bombs were away, we dropped back to twenty feet, and about fifty ME-109s and '110s jumped on us from the right. We were flying so low they couldn't dive on us, but they did lazy eights all over our formation and caused us plenty of trouble.

The housing around the propeller and three cylinders of our number-four engine were shot out. Two feet of the prop on the number-one engine was smashed, tearing a foot-and-a-half hole in the left aileron. The motor was vibrating like a bucking bronco. And we had a wing-cell leak in number three. We (I say "we" because Colonel Kane and I were both flying that airplane) put on ten degrees of flaps—no more. Ten degrees gives you the best lift without creating too much drag. We kept our wings straight by using the rudder, not the ailerons. Use of ailerons under those conditions is liable to drag a wing down.

We were still at twenty feet—maybe less. As a matter of fact, Lt. R. B. Hubbard, our radio operator, called Colonel Kane and suggested that we get some altitude because we were collecting a mess of branches, leaves, and cornstalks. The colonel investigated, and I'll be damned if Hubbard didn't hand him a cornstalk!

The fighters kept coming in, and we accounted for three. They attacked for about twenty minutes, and we just put the ship on the ground and ran like hell.

We muddled through the fighter attack and staggered away from the target on two and a half engines. About 200 miles south of the refineries, we realized that we couldn't return over the Mediterranean with our battered ship. We decided to hug a land route going back. The chief topic of conversation was picking a good place to set her down. Everybody was pestering our navigator, Lt. Norman Whalen. For my money he's the best in the business. He finally had to tell the colonel, "Look, if you guys will just leave me alone for a while, maybe I'll find a field." We left him alone. Whalen was navigating for two other damaged planes which were following, and the three of us were being covered by Lt. Royden LeBrecht. Nothing had happened to his ship.

We crossed an enemy airfield at 1,500 feet, and the flak batteries opened up. I don't know who was more surprised. But we got away without trouble.

In order to gain altitude to cross a mountain range, we threw out everything that was movable. We released the extra gasoline tank and tossed out oxygen bottles, gas masks, ammunition, radio equipment, and anything that a screwdriver could dismantle. I haven't yet seen the humor in LeBrecht's remark but he called and inquired: "What the hell are you doing? Redecorating?"

We finally got up to 6,600 feet, but we needed 7,000 feet to cross the mountains. By picking our way through canyons and ravines, and with some lucky updrafts, we managed to get over.

The plane was hobbling along now at 130 miles per hour, and we knew that it might stall at around 125 mph. It was still flying, however, and we kept plugging along. We had a choice of putting her down on land or flying across open water to the nearest Allied landing field. The colonel and I realized that there was a good chance the ship would flop into the water, but we had come too far to worry about that. As we crossed the coast, Whalen gave us an ETA of 2150 for the selected airfield.

Whalen was on the nose to within a minute. Exactly fourteen hours and forty minutes after we left Africa, we let her down.

We had to crash-land the plane, but nobody was hurt and the first thing I did after we got away from the ship was to kiss the navigator. Yes, I really kissed him.

A couple of days later we got back to our original base where Major Selvey had a dove and pheasant dinner waiting for us. Major Selvey is group materiel officer, and I suppose he figured that the banquet came under his department.

After the experience, I think I am in position to offer some advice to men who may go on a similar raid. The most important thing for you to do is learn formation flying to perfection. Even with a heavy bomber, you must be able to stay no more than twenty-five feet away from your wingman. You've probably been told before about flying tight formations. In combat, you do it or you don't come back.

Don't be afraid to hug the earth. A B-24 will fly ten feet off the ground, and you'll find real safety down there. Practice evasive tactics until they come out of your ears. When the enemy peashooters attack, keep in a turn, increasing and decreasing that turn, and stay on the ground. Whatever you do, don't fly in a straight line. When a fighter climbs after his first pass, he has to look for you all over again. If you are flying straight, he'll be able to pick you out very easily.

All aerial engineers should practice the *exact* procedure for transferring gasoline. That can't be overstressed. I think we lost a couple of planes on our raid due to the difficulty in making the proper transfer. Get rid of the gas in your bomb-bay tanks as quickly as possible and transfer it to the wing tanks to avoid having a chance hit in the bomb bay blow you up.

When we returned I was asked the extent of damage we did to the Ploesti refineries. Naturally, that's hard to figure, but I can speak firsthand of our particular targets, the Orion and Astra Romana refineries. The boys in our element agree that no German oil will come from them for quite some time.

THE SCHWEINFURT-REGENSBURG RAID

[1] IRA C. EAKER, LIEUTENANT GENERAL

USAAF

The first Schweinfurt-Regensburg raid by the VIII Bomber Command stands out in my mind as one of the most significant and remarkable air battles of the Second World War.

It was a bold strategic concept. It was the first shuttle bombing mission of the war. The 3rd Air Division, the force attacking the Messerschmitt fighter factory at Regensburg, took off from English bases and landed in fields in North Africa. The decisions by the VIII Bomber Commander, General Frederick L. Anderson, Jr., and the 3rd Air Division Commander, Colonel Curtis E. LeMay, to proceed to Regensburg with but part of the force, when the 1st Air Division was delayed in take-off due to weather, were two of the most dramatic and courageous command decisions of the air war in Europe. This battlefield was a thousand miles long and five miles above the earth. It was fought in sub-zero temperatures and the gladiators, friend and foe, wore oxygen masks.

Schweinfurt-Regensburg was the bloodiest and most savagely fought air battle of the war up to that time. The flight crews demonstrated a determination and courage seldom equalled and

[1] The then Major General Eaker assumed command of the Eighth Air Force at the end of 1942, and little more than a year later he was in command of the Allied Air Forces in the Mediterranean as a lieutenant general.

never surpassed in warfare. It demonstrated that enemy fighters could exact a heavy toll on unescorted bomber formations, but could not stop them. Our bombers could and did press through to their assigned targets. It set a pattern and a precedent for all the bombing missions which were to follow. It created consternation at the highest levels in the Third Reich. Speer, the German charged with over-all responsibility for weapons production, reported to Hitler after this raid that if such assaults could not be stopped by the Luftwaffe, weapons making was doomed, and the war was lost. This battle resulted in the recall of many squadrons of German fighters from the Eastern front at a critical time there, in a vain effort to meet the bomber onslaught. Even the heavy and tragic losses in this mission, nearly 20 percent of the attacking force, taught a valuable lesson. It demonstrated clearly the need for long-ranged fighter escort, stimulated production and hastened delivery of these types to the Eighth Air Force in England.

Finally, it was one of the great air battles of the pre-invasion effort to reduce the Luftwaffe to impotence, so that a seaborne land invasion of Europe could be made without prohibitive casualties. Schweinfurt-Regensburg was a dramatic symbol of the strategic air operations which destroyed Germany's Luftwaffe, and made it impossible for that force to be of any consequence against Allied landings in France on June 6, 1944. The gallant sacrifices of the Eighth Air Force bomber crews therefore saved thousands of lives of Allied sailors and soldiers crossing the beaches on D-Day.

The Allied strategic planners had determined that the most fruitful targets for daylight precision bombing were the enemy fighter factories and ball-bearing plants. Two of the most important targets in these munitions complexes were unfortunately deep inside Germany, the Messerschmitt plant at Regensburg, over 500 miles from English bases, and the ball-bearing plant at Schweinfurt, nearly 400 miles distant. Nearly half of all the critical ball-bearing production of Germany came from Schwein-furt. The planners thought these concentrated ball-bearing plants might well be the Achilles heel of Germany's weapons making potential. These targets were not practicable for the growing might of British night bombers. It was a daylight job. The Combined Chiefs of Staff assigned the task to the U. S. Eighth Air Force based in England. The plan of the attack called for the 3rd Air Division with 150 Flying Fortresses to cross the Channel at 8 A.M., fly to Regensburg, more than three hours away from English bases, attack the fighter factory there, and proceed to landing fields in Africa, fuel being insufficient for return to England.

The 1st Air Division with 150 heavy bombers would follow thirty minutes later and bomb the ball-bearing complex at Schweinfurt, returning to English bases. It was visualized the 3rd Air Division would bear the brunt of the German fighter reaction on the way in, and the 1st Air Division would have to fight its way out. Such long ranged U.S. fighters as were then available would escort the 3rd Division in and the 1st Division out.

The shorter ranged British Spitfires and U.S. medium bombers would conduct deceptive raids toward the Ruhr in order to pin down the fighters in those areas and prevent their attacking the heavy bombers moving on Schweinfurt and Regensburg.

As in all air operations, weather was a critical factor. The target area must be clear so that bombardiers flying at 25,000 to 30,000 feet could see their targets 20 miles away and aim their deadly cargoes with accuracy. Bases in England must be free of fog so that bombers and fighters could take off at first light and assemble their formations above the clouds on schedule.

On August 16, 1943, after a month of dreary waiting for suitable weather in the target area, the forecast indicated the attack could go on the following day, and orders were issued to launch the assault on the morrow. Unfortunately, English bases were fog shrouded on the morning of the 17th. The 3rd Air Division got off, due entirely to the fact that LeMay's groups had been practicing instrument take-offs for some time. LeMay displayed then the qualities of leadership which would result in his selection as Chief of Staff of the Air Force eighteen years later.

The 1st Air Division got off later, as weather lifted slightly, but was too far behind to benefit from the cover provided by the 3rd Air Division. German fighters had time to land, refuel and rearm after engaging LeMay's Regensburg force, and strike the 1st Air Division all the way to their targets at Schweinfurt and all the way home.

The long-ranged U.S. fighters were unable, due to weather, to leave their airdromes for their protective missions. The medium bombers were held to the ground by weather, and unable to carry out their deceptive missions to the north. When it became clear that the weather had defeated the well-coordinated plan of attack, Anderson, the bomber commander, or LeMay, the flight leader of the 3rd Air Division, could have canceled the mission. Both, however, knew that weather over the target area was favorable, and that the targets were of great importance. Neither hesitated, both determined to execute the hazardous mission. The 3rd Division courageously struck out alone for the long flight to Regensburg. German fighters and antiaircraft attacked with skill and fury. Fighter squadrons based in Holland, Belgium, Germany, Austria, France, and Italy, more than three hundred strong, hit the 3rd Air Division in a continual attack with guns, rockets, and bombs. Undaunted and undeterred, the embattled Flying Fortresses fought their way to Regensburg and knocked out the fighter factories, proceeding south to predesignated bases in Africa. LeMay's force lost twenty-four bombers and many more were severely damaged.

The 1st Air Division, despite its late departure, headed resolutely for the ball-bearing plants at Schweinfurt. Although under constant attack, the ball-bearing plants were hit and severely damaged. The battle was not over, for the ferocious assault on these bombers was continued during the three-hour return flight to the English Channel. The 1st Division lost thirty-six bombers. When the battered remnants of the 1st and 3rd Air Divisions limped back to their bases, they had the satisfaction of knowing they had carried out their mission against the most determined and aggressive attack the Germans could command. The Luftwaffe leaders knew that they could not stop our bombers and save their weapons making establishments. For Germany it marked the beginning of the end.

REGENSBURG MISSION

[1] BEIRNE LAY, JR., LIEUTENANT COLONEL

USAAF

When our group crossed the coast of Holland at our base altitude of 17,000 feet, I was well situated to watch the proceedings, being copilot in the lead ship of the last element of the high squadron. With all of its twenty-one B-17Fs tucked in tightly, our group was within handy supporting distance of another group, ahead of us at 18,000 feet. We were the last and lowest of the seven groups that were visible ahead on a southeast course, forming a long chain in the bright sunlight—too long, it seemed. Wide gaps separated the three combat wings.

As I sat there in the tail-end element of that many-miles-long procession, gauging the distance to the lead groups I had the lonesome foreboding that might come to the last man about to run a gantlet lined with spiked clubs. The premonition was well founded.

Near Woensdrecht, I saw the first flak blossom out in our vicinity, light and inaccurate. A few minutes later, two FW-190s appeared at one o'clock level and whizzed through the formation ahead of us in a frontal attack, nicking two B-17s in the wings and breaking away beneath us in half rolls. Smoke immediately trailed from the B-17s, but they held their stations. As the fighters passed us at a high rate of closure, the guns of our

[1] Famous writer and author of the novel *Twelve O'Clock High*.

group went into action. The pungent smell of burnt powder filled our cockpit, and the B-17 trembled to the recoil of nose- and ball-turret guns. I saw pieces fly off the wing of one of the fighters before they passed from view.

Here was early action. The members of the crew sensed trouble. There was something desperate about the way those two fighters came in fast, right out of their climb without any preliminaries. For a few seconds the interphone was busy with admonitions: "Lead 'em more . . . short bursts . . . don't throw rounds away . . . there'll be more along in a minute."

Three minutes later, the gunners reported fighters climbing up from all around the clock, singly and in pairs, both FW-190s and ME-109Gs. This was only my fourth raid, but from what I could see on my side, it looked like too many fighters for sound health. A coordinated attack followed, with the head-on fighters coming in from slightly above, the nine and three o'clock attackers approaching from about level, and the rear attackers from slightly below. Every gun from every B-17 in our group and the one ahead was firing, crisscrossing our patch of sky with tracers to match the time-fuze cannon-shell puffs that squirted from the wings of the Jerry single-seaters. I would estimate that seventy-five percent of our fire was inaccurate, falling astern of the target —particularly the fire from hand-held guns. Nevertheless, both sides got hurt in this clash with two B-17s from our low squadron and one other falling out of formation on fire with crews bailing out, and several fighters heading for the deck in flames or with their pilots lingering behind under dirty yellow parachutes. Our group leader pulled us up nearer to the group ahead for mutual support.

I knew that we were already in a lively fight. What I didn't know was that the real fight, the *anschluss* of *Luftwaffe* 20-mm cannon shells, hadn't really begun. A few minutes later, we absorbed the first wave of a hailstorm of individual fighter attacks that were to engulf us clear to the target. The ensuing action was so rapid and varied that I cannot give a chronological account of it. Instead, I will attempt a fragmentary report, salient details that even now give me a dry mouth and an unpleasant sensation in the stomach when I recall them. The sight was fantastic and surpassed fiction.

It was over Eupen that I looked out of my copilot's window after a short lull and saw two whole squadrons, twelve ME-109s and eleven FW-190s, climbing parallel to us. The first squadron had reached our level and was pulling ahead to turn into us and the second was not far behind. Several thousand feet below us were many more fighters, with their noses cocked at maximum climb. Over the interphone came reports of an equal number of enemy aircraft deploying on the other side. For the first time, I noticed an ME-110 sitting out of range on our right. He was to stay with us all the way to the target, apparently reporting our position to fresh squadrons waiting for us down the road. At the sight of all these fighters, I had the distinct feeling of being trapped—that the Hun was tipped off, or at least had guessed our destination and was waiting for us. No P-47s were visible. The life expectancy of our group suddenly seemed very short, since it had already appeared that the fighters were passing up preceding groups, with the exception of one, in order to take a cut at us.

Swinging their yellow noses around in a wide U-turn, the twelve-ship squadron of ME-109s came in from twelve to two o'clock in pairs and in fours and the main event was on.

A shining silver object sailed past over our right wing. I recognized it as a main exit door. Seconds later a dark object came hurtling through the formation, barely missing several props. It was a man, clasping his knees to his head, revolving like a diver in a triple somersault. I didn't see his chute open.

A B-17 turned gradually out of the formation to the right, maintaining altitude. In a split second, the B-17 completely disappeared in a brilliant explosion, from which the only remains were four small balls of fire, the fuel tanks, which were quickly consumed as they fell earthward.

Our airplane was endangered by hunks of debris. Emergency hatches, exit doors, prematurely opened parachutes, bodies, and assorted fragments of B-17s and Hun fighters breezed past us in the slipstream.

I watched two fighters explode not far below, disappearing in sheets of orange flame, B-17s dropping out in every stage of distress, from engines on fire to control surfaces shot away, friendly and enemy parachutes floating down and, on the green carpet far behind us, numerous funereal pyres of smoke from fallen fighters, marking our trail.

On we flew through the strewn wake of a desperate air battle, where disintegrating aircraft were commonplace and sixty chutes in the air at one time were hardly worth a second look.

I watched a B-17 turn slowly out to the right with its cockpit a mass of flames. The copilot crawled out of his window, held on with one hand, reached back for his chute, buckled it on, let go, and was whisked back into the horizontal stabilizer. I believe the impact killed him. His chute didn't open.

Ten minutes, twenty minutes, thirty minutes, and still no letup in the attacks. The fighters queued up like a breadline and let us have it. Each second of time had a cannon shell in it. The strain of being a clay duck in the wrong end of that aerial shooting gallery became almost intolerable as the minutes accumulated toward the first hour.

Our B-17 shook steadily with the fire of its .50s and the air inside was heavy with smoke. It was cold in the cockpit, but when I looked across at our pilot—and a good one—sweat was pouring off his forehead and over his oxygen mask. He turned the controls over to me for a while. It was a blessed relief to concentrate on holding station in formation instead of watching those everlasting fighters boring in. It was possible to forget the fighters. Then the top-turret gunner's twin muzzles would pound away a foot above my head, giving an imitation of cannon shells exploding in the cockpit, while I gave an even better imitation of a man jumping six inches out of his seat.

A B-17 ahead of us, with its right Tokyo tanks on fire, dropped back to about 200 feet above our right wing and stayed there while seven of the crew bailed out successfully. Four went out the bomb bay and executed delayed jumps, one bailed from the nose, opened his chute prematurely and nearly fouled the tail. Another went out the left-waist gun opening, delaying his chute opening for a safe interval. The tail gunner dropped out of his hatch, apparently pulling the ripcord before he was clear of the ship. His chute opened instantaneously, barely missing the tail, and jerked him so hard that both his shoes came off. He hung limply in the harness, whereas the others had immediately showed some signs of life after their chutes opened, shifting around in the harness. The B-17 then dropped back in a medium spiral, and I did not see the pilots leave. I saw it just before it passed from view, several thousand feet below us, with its right wing a solid sheet of yellow flame.

After we had been under constant attack for a solid hour, it appeared certain that our group was faced with annihilation. Seven had been shot down, the sky was still mottled with rising fighters and target time still thirty-five minutes away. I doubt if a man in the group visualized the possibility of our getting much farther without 100 percent loss. I know that I had long since mentally accepted the fact of death and that it was simply a question of the next second or the next minute. I learned first-hand that a man can resign himself to the certainty of death without becoming panicky. Our group firepower was reduced thirty-three percent, ammunition was running low. Our tail guns had to be replenished from another gun station. Gunners were becoming exhausted and nerve-tortured from the prolonged strain, and there was an awareness on everybody's part that something must have gone wrong. We had been the aiming point for what seemed like most of the *Luftwaffe*, and we fully expected to find the rest of it primed for us at the target.

Fighter tactics were running fairly true to form. Frontal attackers hit the low squadron and lead squadron, while rear attackers went for the high. The manner of their attacks showed that some pilots were old-timers, some amateurs, and that all knew pretty definitely where we were going and were inspired with a fanatical determination to stop us before we got there. The old-timers came in on frontal attacks with a noticeably slower rate of closure, apparently throttled back, obtaining greater accuracy than those that bolted through us wide out. They did some nice shooting at ranges of 500 or more yards, and in many cases seemed able to time their thrusts to catch the top- and ball-turret gunners engaged with rear and side attacks. Less experienced pilots were pressing attacks home to 250 yards and less to get hits, offering point-blank targets on the breakaway, firing long bursts of twenty seconds, and, in some cases, actually pulling up instead of going down and out. Several FW pilots pulled off some first-rate deflection shooting on side attacks against the high group, then raked the low group on the breakaway out of a side-slip, keeping the nose cocked up in the turn to prolong the period the formation was in their sights.

I observed what I believe was an attempt at air-to-air bombing, although I didn't see the bombs dropped. A patch of seventy-five to 100 gray-white bursts, smaller than flak bursts, appeared simultaneously at our level, off to one side.

One B-17 dropped out on fire and put its wheels down while the crew bailed. Three ME-109s circled it closely, but held their fire, apparently ensuring that no one stayed in the ship to try for home. I saw Hun fighters hold their fire even when being shot at by a B-17 from which the crew was bailing out.

Near the IP, one hour and a half after the first of at least 200 individual fighter attacks, the pressure eased off, although hostiles were nearby. We turned at the IP with fourteen B-17s left, two of which were badly crippled. They dropped out after bombing the target and headed for Switzerland. The number-four engine on one of them was afire, but the plane was not out of control. The leader of the high squadron received a cannon shell in his number-three engine just before the start of the bombing run and went in to the target with the prop feathered.

Weather over target, as on the entire trip, was ideal. Flak was negligible. The group got its bombs away promptly on the leader. As we turned and headed for the Alps, I got a grim satisfaction out of seeing a column of smoke rising straight up from the ME-109 shops, with only one burst over in the town of Regensburg.

The rest of the trip was a marked anticlimax. A few more fighters pecked at us on the way to the Alps. A town in the Brenner Pass tossed up a lone burst of futile flak. We circled the air division over Lake Garda long enough to give the cripples a chance to join the family, and we were on our way toward the Mediterranean in a gradual descent. About twenty-five fighters on the ground at Verona stayed on the ground. The prospect of ditching as we approached Bône, shortages of fuel, and the sight of other B-17s falling into the drink seemed trivial matters after the nightmare of the long trip across southern Germany. We felt the reaction of men who had not expected to see another sunset.

At dusk, with red lights showing on all of the fuel tanks in my ship, the seven B-17s of the group still in formation circled over Bertoux and landed in the dust. Our crew was unscratched. Sole damage to the airplane: a bit of ventilation around the tail from flak and 20-mm shells. We slept on the hard ground under the wings of our B-17, but the good earth felt softer than a silk pillow.

FIRST BIG DAYLIGHT RAID OVER BERLIN

JAMES W. MINCHEW, TECHNICAL SERGEANT

USAAF

709th Bomb Squadron, 447th Bomb Group
Rattlesden Air Base, England
Monday, 6 March 1944:

The CQ shook my bed and said, "Sergeant Minchew, you have thirty minutes to get dressed and get over to the mess hall."

I had not slept well at all last night, as yesterday, being Sunday, had been a lazy day except for the thirty-minute code practice class I attended before lunch. I suppose I was still shook up over the mission we had been on last Friday. The weather had been very bad and the deeper we got into enemy territory, the worse it seemed to get. We were excited about our target and were all hoping we could get through, since our target was Berlin.

On the way over we were ordered to raise our formation to a higher altitude in hopes that we would hit some better weather, but the higher we got, the colder it got and the weather seemed to be worse. We were then directed to turn back with the lead formation climbing higher to avoid accidents. This did not work too well as the group in front of us turned around too. They got mixed up with ours and we had a few disastrous mid-air collisions. One of my best buddies, Staff Sergeant Pruett from

Gadsden, Alabama, went down as a result of one of the collisions and I sincerely hope he bailed out OK. I know I will miss his guitar picking and singing.

We tried again Saturday to reach Berlin but the weather closed in once more and we bombed Bonn instead. I heard over the radio that one single formation got through to the capital.

I got out of bed, slowly, dressed in my fleece-lined flying suit and stepped out into the fresh, chilled morning air. The stars were bright and not a cloud appeared in the sky. I turned to Ted Nurre (Staff Sergeant), the tail gunner, and was about to say "This is the one," but he beat me to it with, "Well, Jim, looks like we will be able to make it today."

We walked across the barley field that separated our Nissen huts from the mess hall. There sure wasn't much conversation on the way over and the same quietness was prevalent in the mess hall. The rest of the enlisted men of crew thirty-four were already eating their breakfast. They were sitting in the far corner of the mess hall. Tech Sergeant John Hughes, the engineer; Staff Sergeant E. W. Kreps, the ball gunner; Staff Sergeant Roy B. McGraw and Staff Sergeant T. M. Christiansen, the waist gunners, were drinking their second cup of coffee and waiting until the last minute to move out and face the much-dreaded mission.

The mess sergeant reminded us that briefing would be in thirty minutes and told us to make it snappy. The GI trucks were waiting outside to carry us to the briefing room.

As the trucks approached the briefing building we could see little groups of men already assembled. The sloppiest characters imaginable were standing around just waiting until the last minute to enter the briefing room. No two of these airmen, it seems, ever dress exactly alike. They wore an amazing array of flying equipment. There were the heavy sheepskin-lined jackets, zipped up and those clumsy sheepskin-lined flying boots. Some had part flying clothes and part uniform. Others wore their own weird combinations.

We entered the brightly lighted room. At the door were the usual neat-looking guards that checked us off by name or face.

Under the bright lights, I could see a heavy blue smoke haze and bodies at every angle imaginable. Some sitting erect as if they were in a daze and some asleep. Others were engaged in conversations.

A major stepped on the platform and began the roll call. The aircraft commanders answered for their crews and I could see Lieutenant P. W. Johnson, our pilot, straining his neck to see if crew thirty-four were all present before he had to report. Just then, one of the guards on the door called "Ten hut!" and our group commander, Colonel Hunter Harris, came in and joined his crew.

The briefing officer moved to the rear of the platform and ripped aside the black curtain hanging against the wall. There was complete silence until the curtain was fully opened. We all gazed at the large-scale map of Europe and leading from our base was a red line that left England, straight across the channel to the North Sea, into Holland, over the Zuider Zee and deeper and deeper into enemy territory until it stopped at the enemy capital —Berlin.

"This, gentlemen, is your target for today. The weather is going to be partly cloudy over the city. Flak will be light to heavy most of the way in and back out and it will be especially heavy around the city itself. The city is defended with three to four hundred 88-mm. guns. And enemy fighters will be out in large numbers. You will have fighter escort most of the way in and out by P-51s, P-38s, and P-47s. Keep close formation at all times. Remember that the enemy fighters will try to break up your formations every chance they get. If the aircraft ahead of you gets out of formation, fill in his position. He may have been hit and going down and if you don't fill his position, you will be more vulnerable to enemy fighter attack."

We were then given the usual PW instructions by the briefing officer. I can still remember hearing him as he said "Be sure to wear your dog tags. Do not wear your squadron insignia. Carry your rank, name, and serial number only. After leaving this room, do not talk about the target."

The planes were lined up on the runway, waiting their turns to take off. Our *Fortress* was carrying 2800 gallons of gasoline, maximum rounds of .50-caliber ammunition and the bomb bay was loaded with ten 500-pound bombs. It was a frightening experience to try to get this much of a load into the air. The pilot and co-pilot, as usual, were checking and double checking everything that could be checked out from the cockpit. When our turn came to take off, they poured the power to the engines and we could hear them groan and then roar as we moved faster and faster down the runway. At this point, everyone was completely silent and praying that the red lights that marked the end of the runway would find us airborne. When the reverberation of the four engines against the runway turned into a steady hum, we could relax for we would be skimming over the tops of the trees and beginning to climb to our rendezvous point.

The endless climbing, circling and jockeying for position to form into a group, a combat wing, an air division continued until we built up into a great aerial armada. It seemed like hours before we were on our way to invade the enemy capital. The sun's rays began to shine into the radio compartment through the side windows and the Plexiglas dome. As far as the eye could see were B-17s and B-24s gliding through the brisk clear sky to the target for the day—Hitler's capital.

As we approached the English Channel, the pilot gave the order for all gunners to test fire their guns, and to maintain silence on the intercom. The enemy coast was in sight and suddenly the intercom silence was broken with "Pilot to crew; on your toes now. We are crossing the Zuider Zee and anything can happen. Remember, this is Germany's capital city and they will probably throw everything they have at us."

We evaded most of the flak until we reached Depole. Suddenly we were in a black cloud of it and it seemed like we could get out and walk to Berlin. The lead plane made a gradual turn to the left and no sooner had we altered our course than we were back in a heavy field of flak again. Small holes began to appear in our plane from the nose to the tail. (We learned later that the Germans had the 88-mm. guns on flat cars and would switch to spur tracks to follow the evasive action of our formation.)

We had almost a solid cloud of flak the entire 600 miles into the city. Everywhere we looked, we could see enemy fighters and our fighters in dog fights. We were constantly under attack by enemy fighters breaking through our formation using a barrel roll tactic. Machine guns and 20-mm. shells were exploding and ripping our planes apart. There were Junker JU-88s with rockets mounted under their wings flying parallel to the formation, just out of machine-gun range and at times they would turn toward the formation and lob their rockets at us. When a B-17 was hit and dropped out of formation, the Messerschmitt ME-110s with their cannons and machine guns firing a heavy stream from nose and wings would finish it off. Just before we got to Berlin, there were so many B-17s going down and parachutes opening, it looked like an airborne invasion.

After each attack, the pilot would break silence on the intercom with "Pilot to crew, report."

"Tail gunner to pilot; I have some small holes from flak and the rear tire is blown off."

"Left waist to pilot; I have some small holes in the left waist of the ship."

"Right waist to pilot; I'm still OK. I can see through the side of the plane and it must have been a big piece of flak that hit us here. Bigger than 20-mm."

"Ball gunner to pilot; I am OK. I believe I got the last plane that came through. I had him in my sights and smoke and fire were coming out of his wing."

"Radio to pilot; the left bomb bay door has been blown off.

We better get rid of these bombs before they explode. I also got a piece of flak in my radio receiver. It is completely out of whack."

After all stations reported, the pilot came back with "Pilot to navigator; Chet, how close are we to the target?" The navigator, Lieutenant L. S. Chester, answered, "We are about thirty minutes away. If we make it through this mess we'll be lucky." Then the bombardier, Lieutenant R. D. Hooker, said, "Bombardier to pilot; part of the Plexiglas nose has been blown off and the air is cold up here."

The city of Berlin was completely surrounded with a wall of flak and fighters were knocking our bombers out of the sky like flies. The ship above us got a direct hit in its bomb bay with an 88-mm. and the plane fell into a thousand pieces. Fragments of the plane and crew flew against our plane and the concussion threw our aircraft almost completely over and out of formation. We lost about 500 feet of altitude before the pilot and co-pilot could pour the power on and climb back to the safety of the formation. If we had not already dropped our bombs, we would not have been able to climb back into formation. We could see the city through broken clouds and it looked like it was 50 miles across and was burning and exploding in every block. Apparently we had accomplished our mission.

The trip back was just as bad as the one coming over. Flak and fighters all the way to the coast. When we got back to Rattlesden Air Base, we had to make an emergency landing. After landing, we examined our plane and found it was almost a total loss. The bomb bay door blown off by a 20-mm. shell, five or six 20-mm. holes in the waist and right wing. The entire ship was full of flak holes as though it had been hit by giant buckshot. The glass nose had a hole I could crawl through and the rear tire was blown off. We had no crew injuries which was a miracle. (After the plane was patched up, it was flown by another crew and was shot down on its next mission.)

There were photographers from all major news services taking pictures of the planes. The picture of our plane showed me looking at the damage from the top of the nose and Staff Sergeant Kreps was inside, examining the damage. This photo was in almost every paper in the United States and England.

We reported to the interrogation room and a sight I had never expected to see, greeted me. The flight surgeon was giving shots of bourbon and scotch to the crews, and the Red Cross was passing out good things to eat. They were all surprised to see so few of us coming back. The newspapers reported our bomber losses for the day as the highest of any raid in history.

This was my fourteenth mission and I can honestly say for me it was "The Big One."

THE PHANTOM B-17

GLENN INFIELD, CAPTAIN

USAAF

Our eighteen-plane formation of B-17s was fifteen miles north-west of Brussels, flying at 25,000 feet, when I spotted the suspicious dot on the horizon to my left. It was June 14, 1944, eight days after the D-Day forces had hit the beaches of Normandy, and the *Luftwaffe* was making its final, back-to-the-wall stand in the sky over the Continent. We could expect anything.

"Bogie nine o'clock level," I warned the crew. "Keep your eye on him."

Since I was flying the lead ship of the group, I had to watch my course to the IP closely, but every few seconds I glanced toward the speck on the horizon. Three thousand feet above our formation, I could see our P-47 and P-38 escorts circling lazily, waiting patiently for the expected onslaught by the German fighters. Apparently they had not spotted the lone plane closing from the north. Once again, I turned and stared toward the intruder. The black dot was larger now and materializing into wings and a tail, but it still was too far away to recognize. Behind me, I heard the top gunner swing his turret until his twin fifty-caliber machine guns aimed directly toward the newcomer. Looking back, I could see that both my wingmen had their guns lined up in the same direction.

"Hell, it's just another *Fort*," my left waist gunner suddenly reported over the interphone. "Must've got lost from its formation."

Immediately, the guns swiveled away from the stranger and searched the sky for enemy fighters. The new arrival was completely ignored—except by Lieutenant Harry Reed, pilot of Number 376, the "Tail-end Charlie" of our formation, and myself. Watching the *Flying Fortress* warily, I grabbed the microphone and called Reed. "Do you see it, Reed?"

The slender, drawling pilot of Number 376, a combat veteran from Detroit, Michigan, answered immediately. "Roger. What do you think?"

I made a slight correction of our heading and took another look at the intruder. It was flying parallel to our formation now, at the same altitude. There was no group, squadron or crew insignia painted on the fuselage or tail, as was usual with Eighth Air Force aircraft. Nor did the pilot indicate any intention of joining our formation. "I don't like it, Reed. The pilot is acting suspicious, but we have to be damn sure."

"Yeah. I'd hate to make a mistake."

Time was running out in more ways than one. We were approaching our initial point where we would make a sharp right turn onto our bomb run. Once the IP was reached, the strange *Flying Fortress* would have to be ignored. We came to bomb the target. And, if the intruder was actually the renegade bomber, a captured B-17 flown by a Nazi crew which had been plaguing us for weeks, the German crew was already vectoring a horde of *Luftwaffe* fighters directly to our formation. We had to make our decision.

"Do you still want to go through with your plan, Reed?"

"Roger."

"Okay, get set. We'll find out for sure whether this guy is with us or against us."

Very slowly, I eased the control wheel to the left and started a shallow turn toward the lone *Flying Fortress*. The remainder of the formation followed. As we closed the gap between the formation and the stranger-in-the-sky, I kept hoping that the pilot would give some indication that he was just another Eighth Air Force flyer in trouble. Instead, he made a move that shattered all my doubts. He banked the B-17 sharply away from us.

"It's the renegade, Reed. It's all yours!"

Behind me, I saw Reed slide his plane out of the tail slot of the formation and drift to the left. A moment later, the propeller on the number-three engine slowed and finally jerked to a stop as he feathered it to simulate trouble.

"Tail-end Charlie has dropped out of formation," my tail gunner reported.

"Roger. Keep an eye on him."

I couldn't explain why Number 376 had dropped back. Only Reed, his volunteer crew and myself were aware of the trap we were baiting in an effort to destroy the Nazi-manned *Flying Fortress*. It was an unofficial, unauthorized attempt to rid the sky of the harassing aircraft, both dangerous and daring. If it failed, Reed and his crew were dead. If it succeeded, scores of Allied airmen might well survive the aerial warfare over the Continent. It was a gamble, a big one, with the odds all on the side of Goering's élite flyers.

"Bogies. Twelve o'clock level!"

I felt every muscle in my body go tight as I spotted the swarm of enemy fighters heading directly toward the formation. The German-operated B-17 had done its work well. It had guided the oncoming ME-109s and FW-190s to us by radio.

"Pilot to gunners. Get ready for a head-on attack."

But even as I warned my own crew, I couldn't help but think about Reed. Long before the P-47s and P-38s, which were still crisscrossing high above us, could dive to the rescue, the Nazi pilot in the renegade bomber would have several *Luftwaffe* fighters swarming all over the Lieutenant's plane. Even Reed's "secret weapon" wouldn't save him now.

"My God, Reed, get back into the formation. Enemy fighters are . . ."

Reed's reply only verified what I knew. "Too late, Captain. We must go on."

I wanted to go to his aid, to lead the remainder of the group down for cover, but it was impossible. An entire mission could not be jeopardized because of one crew. It was cruel but practical.

"Good luck, buddy," I muttered as I braced myself for the first pass of the enemy fighters. It had been a daring gamble, but it was all over now. Lieutenant Reed and his crew would never see England again. The renegade bomber had fooled us once more. . . .

It is a little-known fact that the *Luftwaffe* used captured *Flying Fortresses* in a variety of combat actions during the air war in Europe and the Middle East during World War II. Initially, the air-worthy B-17s were assigned to the "Rosarius Flying Circus." This was a flight comprised of all operating captured planes which traveled through Germany and the occupied countries, to familiarize Nazi pilots with the aircraft and their capabilities. Later, a *Luftwaffe* unit, the notorious I/K G 200, used captured *Flying Fortresses* for the ferrying, parachuting, and supply by air of secret agents, especially for long-range operations.

These uses of the confiscated bombers, while having a certain nuisance value, didn't materially affect the operations of the Eighth Air Force. However, many air crewmen going to targets such as Schweinfurt, Bremen, Duren, Augsburg and Hamburg began to report suspicious actions of lone B-17s which seemed to appear out of nowhere and attach themselves to heavy bomber formations.

As a squadron leader of the Ninety-fifth Bomb Group, I saw my first Nazi-operated *Flying Fortress* while on a mission to Frankfurt on January twenty-ninth. We had just turned the IP and were on our bombing run when I noticed a single B-17 flying directly above us. It was approximately 1,000 feet higher than our formation flying at the same speed. I was just about to try to contact it, fearing that the wandering pilot might drop his bomb load on our formation, when the bomb-bay door snapped open and the eggs dropped out. But they weren't 500-pounders such as we were carrying. They were the smaller bombs the Nazi had been using. Fortunately, they fell harmlessly through the formation.

It soon became almost SOP to expect a Nazi-captured *Fortress* to harass us one way or another on a raid. Our own group was continually stalked by a renegade. Escorting fighters wouldn't get close to a straggler to give him the help he needed for fear it was a German crew waiting to shoot. Worse yet, if, during the hectic aerial battles, a B-17 even looked suspicious, the other planes in the formation turned their guns on it.

Early in June, Reed, who was on temporary duty at Bovington, came back to the Ninety-fifth with a daring idea. "Down at Bovington, we have a YB-40 sitting idle. You know, one of those B-17s which was converted for use as a long-range bomber escort before the P-51s arrived in the ETO."

The Vega-modified B-17s were actually flying gun platforms. They had a total of thirty automatic weapons of various calibers, ranging from fifty-caliber machine guns to twenty-millimeter cannons, also a forty-mm cannon in multiple hand-held installations in the waist, plus additional power-operated turrets above and below the fuselage.

"Let's you and I lay a trap for that damn Nazi *Fortress* which has been giving us such a bad time all winter," said Reed.

"How?"

"I'll fly that YB-40 on the next mission in the Tail-end Charlie slot. If we spot the renegade, I'll pretend I've lost an engine, drop out of formation and act as though I want to join up with him for mutual protection. When I get close enough, we'll open fire with every gun on that YB-40—and that's a lot of guns."

"We'd never get approval from headquarters," I muttered.
"They'd . . ."

"Who wants it? The brass won't even send the fighters after
the renegade for fear of making a mistake and shooting down a
friendly B-17. If anything is going to be done, it will have to be
done by us, unofficially. You know that."

I knew he was telling the truth. After some haggling, I agreed
to help with the daring plan. But on June fourteenth, as I led
the formation on toward our target in Brussels, leaving Reed and
his "secret weapon" YB-40 far behind, I was sorry I had listened
to him.

"Good luck, buddy . . ."

We were under constant enemy attack as we made our bomb
run on the rail yards in Brussels, but our position was not nearly
as desperate as Reed's. The lieutenant had just eased his
"disabled" YB-40 to within gun range of the renegade bomber
when he saw six FW-190s peel off from the swarm of enemy
fighters and head directly toward him.

"Here they come," he yelled to his crew. "Let 'em have it."

Knowing that even his well-armed, heavily armored YB-40
couldn't withstand the onslaught of so many fighters, the lieutenant made a quick decision. He restarted the number three
engine and slid in close on the enemy-manned bomber. Over-
lapping his wing tip with the other plane's wing tip, he hoped
that the *Luftwaffe* fighters would hesitate to fire for fear of hitting the Nazi-crewed *Fortress*.

"Hey, you're going to hit him . . ."

Even as the waist gunner screamed his warning, Reed saw the
FWs start their first pass. Watching them closely, he ruddered his
plane toward the German *Fortress*, so close that his left wing
tip threatened to go into the waist window. The enemy fighters
didn't alter course. They aimed their wing guns directly at Reed's

aircraft and dove full speed. He waited for the thump of bullets—but none came. A second later, the FW-190s roared past and started to turn right. Not a shot had been fired! They were afraid of hitting their own *Flying Fortress!*

"Good." Reed grinned. "Maybe we will . . ."

Thump . . . thump . . . thump . . . The B-17 shuddered violently from nose to tail and the control wheel nearly jerked out of his hand. Above him, he heard his own top turret guns firing steadily. Swiveling his head, he saw that the bullets hitting home were coming from the other bomber. "Get 'em. . . . Blast 'em out of the sky!"

"Number one's losing oil," the top turret gunner called. "The whole wing's black with it."

Reed stared at his instruments. The oil temperature needle was in the red, the supply needle at zero. The oil cooler had been hit.

"Feathering number one."

Every time the renegade turned, Reed banked right with it, knowing that his survival depended upon sticking close to the German. Banking right, left, diving, climbing, the two planes stayed within a few feet of each other, the gunners blasting across the narrow gap. But as the German Fortress headed back toward Berlin, Reed knew it was time to pull his last ace-in-the-hole.

"Pilot to radio," he said. "Give them the business. Now."

His radio operator was a hand-picked volunteer who not only spoke German fluently but was an expert in *Luftwaffe* communications. Now, as the FW-190s circled warily, the radio operator switched to the enemy frequency.

"Attack the *Fortress* on the left," he called to the fighters. "I will make a sharp turn right as you approach."

Reed, listening in, grinned. Contacting the fighter aircraft was not difficult or unusual, since the Eighth Air Force bombers often listened to *Luftwaffe* radio conversations. The radio operator's fluent German fooled the Nazis, and before the crew of the renegade could protest, the FW-190 nosed over for the attack.

Reed banked quickly to the right, leaving the Nazi-crewed *Fortress* all by itself to absorb the punishment. Three of the FW-190s fired on the renegade before the German pilot managed to convince them they had been tricked. Meanwhile, Reed was diving his disabled YB-40 straight toward the ground below, hoping to hedge-hop to the North Sea and safety. The furious FW-190 pilots went after him, their throttles wide open. Its heavy armor plate made the YB-40 dive like a rock, and by the time the pursuing enemy fighters were close enough to open fire, the modified bomber's air-speed needle was against the peg.

At that moment, the daring Reed pulled his final unorthodox maneuver. Seeing the renegade, alone and unprotected, a few thousand feet above him, he hauled back on the control wheel and nosed the YB-40 straight up toward it.

"Fire!" he bellowed to his crew.

Every gun on the YB-40 let go. The renegade seemed to stop in midair, wobbled erratically for a second, then fell off on the left wing. Reed dove after it.

"Here come the FWs again!"

Reed felt and heard the shells ripping into the YB-40 as the enemy fighters started their final slaughter of the trapped plane. He looked across the sky for help. There was none. All he could see were flak bursts and FW-190s.

I turned off the target sharply as soon as the bombs had dropped from the bay and threaded my way through the anti-aircraft bursts toward the North Sea. Our escorting fighters had finally cleared away the enemy attackers and I breathed more easily. It was a short respite, however. East of Ghent, I was suddenly startled to see six FW-190s below us.

I immediately contacted our escort. "Red Leader, six bogies directly below our formation."

"Roger. Red Leader going down."

The P-47s flashed past our bomber box straight for the Focke Wulfs. Once again, I concentrated on our landfall on the enemy coast. The navigator had just reported our position when a voice, faint but audible, crackled in my earphones.

"Captain, this is Number Three-seven-six. Do you receive?"

Reed! "I hear you, buddy. Where the hell are you?"

"Below you at eight thousand feet. Can you get me some fighter cover?"

"Will do."

I gave Red Leader Reed's location and three *Thunderbolts* immediately peeled off to escort the YB-40 home.

Later, talking to Reed, I learned just how lucky he had been. The six FW-190s I had spotted after turning away from Brussels were the fighters which were attacking him. He heard my radio call to Red Leader, and knew he had the help he so desperately needed. The timing could not have been more perfect.

The last Reed saw of the renegade bomber, it was burning and diving straight for the Belgian farmland. Never again were we harassed by a Nazi-manned B-17.

While the successful attack on the renegade didn't gain the official recognition for Lieutenant Reed that it should have, many flyers survived the air war over the Continent because of his willingness to risk his life. The entire Eighth Air Force benefited by his ordeal.

PORTRAIT OF A GUY LOOKING FOR AN ISLAND

BERT STILES, LIEUTENANT

USAAF

The *Fortresses* took off in the late afternoon and flew by wings to the west of England and turned south. Out of sight to the northeast there was fighting on the beaches, and many dead men lay in the surf. But the *Forts* were high above all that. Since the first day, the sixth of June, their job had been easy. Today the target was an airfield on the Brest peninsula, not so far from Lorient, where the *Forts* used to go in the old days.

He flew it when it was his turn, and watched the sun slide down through the soft blue toward the sea. When it was time to bomb, the field was already a smoky mess from the wings up ahead. The flak started shortly after bombs away. The first four puffs were just outside the window. He could see the dull flash as the shells burst. The formation leader banked steeply right. The flak tracked along easily.

There was an ugly clank underneath somewhere. He knew they were hit. Engine OK. The helpless fear of those soft black puffs tightened inside him. It was always the same. Nothing to do but sit there and pray the luck holds. And then they were out of it, turning toward home. "Ball turret to pilot," came over the interphone. "We got holes in the gut."

Once you're out of it, flak never seems quite real, till the next

time. The formations churn through the quiet sky, and the earth
is a million miles below.

The formation let down into the darkening east. He leaned
forward, waiting for England.

England. He said it in his mind, and then slowly in his mouth,
without moving his lips.

When he was eight years old he read *Robin Hood* the first
time. After that he must have read it twenty more. Sherwood
Forest and Nottingham Town in the days of Richard the Lion-
hearted. He'd dreamed of it then, waiting for the day when he
would stand at the rail of a ship, waiting for England to come
out of the haze. Almost like now.

But it wasn't the same. Because now, for a little while, England
was home, more home than Colorado. More home than the
house on York Street could ever be.

After the ride to Munich he thought that the island had sunk
into the sea and France had somehow stretched and spread on
north to the pole.

After Kiel, letting down over the North Sea, he had said a
funny knocked-out prayer. *Be there, island. Please be there.
Be there soon.* After Berlin, after the soft acres of death, above
the shattered town, nothing had ever looked so good as the dim
line of surf a half-hour ahead.

It slipped in gently, as always, clean and friendly and far
off. That would be Lands End, Cornwall, and Devon. The names
ring. He could sit with a map and say the names out loud, and
never get tired of the sound of them . . . Torquay, Nutt Corner,
Coventry, and Charing Cross.

The *Forts* hit the coast at 8,000 feet. A flight of *Spitfires* was
playing in the clouds at three o'clock low.

A guy named Mitchell lay on a cliff above the sea and watched
the gulls, and dreamed the *Spitfire*. And a guy named Leslie
Howard, who was Mitchell for a couple of hours' worth of movie,
crashed back there somewhere coming back from Lisbon, prob-

ably leaning forward, waiting for England to show through the dusk.

Strange, how any land could be so many shades of green, with the lazy netting of the lanes that wandered everywhere to nowhere. When he looked down there, war was just a word, without meaning. It looked so peacefully lovely, yet the people who lived there had fought since the beginning of time, since long before the Romans. And they were still fighting.

He flew his turn for a while, taking it easy, not trying to squeeze the lead ship any. He was glad when the pilot took over again. It was better just to look.

Airfields and towns and churches and hedges, more airfields and ponds and brooks, and cows. More airfields and roads and train tracks and radio towers.

He tried to imagine it as it must have been once, long before William the Conqueror, when King Lear was wandering mad on the heath. He couldn't bring it through. He couldn't believe it had ever been wild. Everything looked permanent, steady till the end of time.

He was so tired of sitting, he wanted to bail out. Yet he would have liked to fly on for hours, up to the lands of the Scotsmen— Stormoway, Inverness, and the Isle of Skye.

Two *Lancasters* were landing on the east-west runway. A flight of P-51s came over the top from nine o'clock. Night was slipping over the world from the east, but there was still day back at six o'clock.

Though it was not his land, and although he had only lived here a little while, he thought he knew why these quiet Englishmen raised so much hell with anyone who tried to take over.

He was tired, saggy tired, starting at the knees on up to the eyes. But he felt good, just glad to be there, just so goddam good to be there, there were no words to tell it.

It was almost dark then, and the stars were coming through.

HIT THE SILK!

WILLIAM N. HESS, SERGEANT

USAAF

"You'll either put in a mission on that plane or bust," said the operations officer.

Little did we realize the significance of this statement nor did we take the words seriously until some days later we recalled them in retrospect of the events that had happened. The craft of which he spoke was an unnamed B-17-G of the 340th Bombardment Squadron, 97th Bombardment Group, Fifteenth Air Force based at Amendola airfield in Italy. Crews didn't have any particular assigned aircraft and flew whichever *Fortress* happened to be available to them for a mission. This shiny daughter of the skies was known to us only by the last three digits of her serial number "166." I don't suppose any of us had ever noticed that these digits added up to "13" either or perhaps it would have served as an omen.

My crew, under the able leadership of our skipper, Lieutenant Bruce D. Knoblock, had joined the 340th Squadron of this veteran group in early August of 1944 and we had literally flown our pants off in the few short weeks following. There was no Italian holiday for us in view of the fact that crews were in short supply and the campaign against Axis oil was going full blast. Most of the crew had had an eye-opening mission of significance to the fabled Ploesti oil refineries only three days after arrival and its famed flak impressed upon us that we were in for no "milk run" tour even if the "glory boys" of the Eighth Air Force did deem the Fifteenth Air Force "minor leaguers."

It was with great pride that we had become members of this venerable bomb group that had flown the first heavy bomb mission over Europe from its base in England on August 17, 1942. The 97th had continued to be known as a group that racked up many "firsts" when it moved to North Africa to open up strategic bombing in that theater. Among these "firsts" from North Africa was the first mission against Sardinia on November 23, 1942, first against France on August 17, 1943, and first against Germany on October 1, 1943. By September 13, 1943, the Group had a hundred missions under its belt, another "first" for them and a lead they continued to hold until late in the war when they were finally passed after having completed over four hundred successful bombing raids.

On September 11 and again the next day we had tried to get off on a mission flying "166" only to be thwarted on both occasions. After we were airborne on the 11th the co-pilot became violently ill and we had to return to base in order to provide him with badly needed medical attention for a case of sand-flea fever. The following morning saw us up in the autumn darkness once more to go through briefing for a mission that was scrubbed at the last minute due to bad weather in the target area. The latter event brought about the fateful statement from the operations officer.

Early on the morning of September 13 we were aroused from restless slumber by the shining beam of a flashlight which groped its way through mosquito netting and into our sleepy eyes.

"Time to go, breakfast in ten minutes and trucks leave for briefing right after," growled the unwelcome, unseen voice behind the light.

Slowly we parted the netting and sat on the edge of the folding cots that graced our pyramidal tent home. That first cigarette tasted good in the chill of early morning as we delved into cardboard boxes under the cots for flying clothes and mess kits. The tempo quickened as we walked through the darkness toward the lights of our mess kitchen. If we were lucky there might be fresh eggs, but this was not the case and we had to settle for the usual "rubberized" pancakes and watery ersatz syrup to wet them down. At least the coffee was hot and warming.

With a clash of gears and clanging of tail gates the trucks pulled up in front of Operations to carry us down to the group headquarters for briefing. Grouchy and sleepy crews swung aboard for the short ride that was marked by low uttered oaths or morose silence from the airmen. Once more the time had arrived for them to put their lives on the line to deliver another load of bombs to Hitler's *Festung Europa*.

Briefing took place in a large room whose only highlight was a brightly lighted stage on which a draped large-scale map served as backdrop. Metal four-legged stools that had originally served as bomb cases now became seats for aircrews. The rasping and scraping of the legs of these conversions on the concrete floor only served to irritate the nerves and increase the air of tension as we awaited the announcement of the target.

Then it came, the cry of "Ten-hut!" as Colonel Nils Ohman, Group Commander, took the stage and feet shuffled and tin stools clanged again as the men rose to their feet. At the command "At ease" bodies dropped once more and the drapes covering the map were drawn. Eyes strained to follow the long red cord that stretched across the board. It was going to be another long haul.

"Gentlemen, your target today is the synthetic oil complex at Blechhammer, South, near Gleiwitz, Germany. This is another all important oil target and it must be destroyed."

This was the most significant fact that I can recall from Colonel Ohman's little talk and the other was the briefing that there will be "intense and accurate flak."

From the briefing room it was back on the trucks and out to the equipment shack to get parachutes, heated suits, and other sundry items of equipment. I was quite chagrined that morning over the fact that someone had taken my new chute pack that I had brought overseas with me and I was left to take a pack that was rather dirty and showed signs of abuse. Oh, well, I thought, I won't have to use it anyway. Little did I know.

On arrival at "166" there was plenty to do and not much time for thought about trifles. I had one chin turret gun, one cheek nose gun and my own waist gun to wipe down and check out. By the time these and other preflight chores were done it was almost time to go. Just time for a last quick smoke before we clambered aboard and started to taxi on the steel matting.

Amidst the screeching of brakes and the rising crescendo of engines the *Fortresses* moved slowly toward the end of the runway. Then barreling his way alongside came the operations officer sounding his jeep horn and waving for us to stop. As we complied, a gunner came running to the door and got aboard and called for our radio operator to get out and go with the "ops" officer. We had acquired the man from the standby aircraft and our operator was to fly on the lead B-17. This last-minute switch was to cost him his life.

Once we were airborne the formation began to jockey and maneuver for position. We pulled up on the wing of the group lead aircraft to fly deputy lead and the skipper tucked us in nice and easy. Nothing to do then but watch the other aircraft in the sky as we flew out over the Adriatic to begin the climb to altitude.

"Twelve thousand feet. Go on oxygen and test guns," was the order given by the bombardier as we approached the coast of Yugoslavia.

A couple of tugs on the charging handle of the .50-caliber machine gun and I cut loose a few rounds toward the coastline far below. A ripple seemed to pass through the aircraft as the

Brownings up and down the line gave forth their staccato bark. All seemed to be going well. I turned to slap the other waist gunner, Sergeant C. W. "Chuck" Collar, on the shoulder and give him the old joined thumb and forefinger circle symbol of "Roger. All OK."

We were now well into the long trip to the target and the sky was a brilliant hue of blue as the sleek and silver *Forts* cut their way through the air. Steadily I scanned the skies for black specks that could mean trouble. Suddenly specks appeared, but these weren't trouble. Fascinated, I gazed at the criss-crossing contrails of our fighter escort. The flights of four *Mustangs* seemed to be making pretzels across the sky. Here was sheer beauty; gleaming irridescent aircraft looking like Christmas tinsel streaming lines of snowy fluff on an almost sapphire background. How could such a sight be related to the gore and grime associated with war?

Then came a rude awakening from this display of grandeur. Our "Little Friends" turned to depart and I knew we were approaching the Initial Point for the bomb run.

"Target dead ahead. Gee, look at that damn flak," came over the intercom. I knew it was time to be especially alert as enemy fighters particularly liked the time when the escort left and the bombers were lining up for the bomb run.

I turned off the heated suit so all power would be available for the bombsight. It must have been 45° below outside, but my mouth was dry and beads of perspiration were beginning to pop out here and there. I picked up the heavy flak vest, snapped it on and plopped the "tin hat" down on top of my flying helmet. Now to watch the lead aircraft to see his bombs go and to observe any aircraft from formations ahead that might be hit and slide back over or under our formation.

Then the flak commenced. Ugly, black puffs that seemed to burst like ebony-colored popcorn. Really pretty on the first mission or so until you learned what they could do. Then I started to count. The bursts were coming along in clusters of four and I knew that they were tracking and not just throwing up a barrage. Still I stared intently at the lead ship just hoping that those bombs would soon be gone.

His bomb bay doors seemed to have been open for an eternity. Whoom! What the hell? Where am I? Have we blown up? What's that noise I hear? Vainly I shook my head and tried to clear it. There seemed to be a haze or smoke before my eyes and in my head at the same time. Somehow I'm lying on the floor of the waist. I look down. My flak vest is ripped and torn, but I don't feel any pain. I look around. There is my "tin hat" with a big dent in it. Damn! I look up. There is the other waist gunner trying to help me up. The waist is full of smoke and the noise comes from an oxygen line shot out over my head.

Groggy, half seeing and half not, I pull myself up by the spade grips on my gun and look out. Oh, God! The sky is full of flak, parachutes, and falling debris. There is an entire wing of a B-17 fluttering to earth like an autumn leaf. Now I look out at our wing. Number 1 engine has taken a direct hit. Its prop blades look as if it had made a crash landing. Number 2 engine has been hit and the prop is feathered and fuel streams from a big hole in the wing. Gee, what an incendiary-prone mess we are.

Someone shakes me and I look around to see him point out damage to my position. Above the window there is a hole big enough to stick a man's head through; there is no Plexiglas left in the window and two gaping holes have been torn in the armor plate below the window. Small flak holes are everywhere through the aluminum skin. They tell me that my being blown down by the explosion of our lead aircraft must have saved my life.

Now the question was what can we do. How far are we from the Russian lines or friendly territory? But, alas, we had no controls left. Apparently all the cables in the tail had been severed and the auto pilot was gone, too. We just seemed to drift over the countryside making big lazy circles. Other than some cuts and a few splinters all of my crew was OK, so at least we could be thankful for that. Three other B-17s from the squadron weren't so lucky. They all had blown up.

Then came the word: "You walk back from this one."

Staggering around like a drunk I sought out the dirty chute pack that I had brought along, but when I finally found it they tell me I sat down on it like I had been given a ten-minute break. I guess the sight of the waist door going off and away must have startled me for I got up and joined the line of men leaving the aircraft. Looking down I grabbed my ankles, but then came the sudden thought, what if this thing doesn't open!

Maybe I fell, maybe somebody pushed, but something hit me in the face like a wet towel. I was on my back and the airplane was flying away from me. Immediately I pulled the ripcord and saw the pilot chute stream out. Then, *Woof!* I was jerked, swung and then I looked up to see a beautiful white canopy over my head. Gee, this isn't too bad. But, oops, I must have hit an air pocket. The bottom dropped out for a second and I grasped the shroud lines for dear life and held on.

Now I looked around and saw other canopies drifting in the breeze. The ground was still far below, but slowly I began to make out figures running around. I wondered who these people might be and I found out when I was low enough to be in rifle range. *Twang!* Something sung through the air and I knew we were over enemy territory and they were shooting at us from the ground.

Silently I prayed that I would soon reach terra firma and suddenly I did with a rush. Trees seemed to leap up at me and crossing my legs I ripped down through limbs shearing them as I fell. Then, as softly as in a baby's swing, my heels touched the earth and I stopped; the canopy had caught in the tree. Swiftly, I got out of my harness, grabbed my GI brogans off the harness ring and made my way deeper into the woods in which I had come down.

Now, I thought, all I have to do is hide my flying suit, and Mae West, get my maps and walk back just like the man at the briefing said. Unfortunately, things don't always work out like that. I hid the life vest and heated suit, but had hardly taken two steps when that infernal *twang* sound came again, this time ripping off some twigs from a nearby tree. They had spotted me.

I found a ditch and hugged it for a while and then crawled down it for quite a distance. Getting up again I made my way to a clearing and found a road. Across the way was another clearing, but behind it there seemed to be a large forest. If I could only get over there perhaps I could evade capture. Creeping into the foliage at the edge of the road I waited and looked but saw no one. Then I cautiously stepped out onto the road. Just as I was ready to make a run for it, that sound came again. *Twang!* Looking to my right I saw three German soldiers. They had just come around a bend in the road about a hundred yards away. With rifles and a burp gun leveled at me I didn't have a chance. Stopping dead in the middle of the road, I raised my hands.

My sixteenth mission had ended. For me the war was over!

ESCAPE!

A. F. McSWEYN, FLYING OFFICER

RAAF

Would I be able to steal a Messerschmitt 110? I anxiously pondered this difficult problem as I crouched in the German wheatfield in which I was hiding on the edge of a *Luftwaffe* night-fighter airfield. As I lay there concealed, throughout the summer day, I could make out through the wheat stalks the busy forms of German mechanics working on aircraft. At about six o'clock, a Messerschmitt 110 that was only about 100 yards away from my hiding-place was refuelled, rearmed—and generally prepared for night flying. I made up my mind to try to fly that Messerschmitt back to England. However, because of roving patrols, I decided to wait till dark before I made my desperate attempt.

The date was the beginning of July, 1941. A night or two earlier, my *Wellington* 1C had been shot down after I had bombed Bremen. I was an Australian pilot who had been operating with No. 115 Squadron from Marham—and I had had to bail out on my twenty-fifth op. So far, I had managed to evade capture—and had been making towards the Dutch or Belgian borders, hoping to link up with local patriots and so get back home, when I had found myself near this *Luftwaffe* night-fighter base. Now, as darkness fell, I crept cautiously out of my hiding-place—and stealthily made my way towards the nearby Messerschmitt 110.

The cockpit canopy was open, I noticed, as I got near the dark hulk of the German night-fighter. Quickly, I glanced round to make sure that no one was watching. Then, my heart pounding, I clambered aboard the aircraft. The cockpit layout, I saw at once, was completely different from that of any other machine I had ever flown. However, I quickly got the hang of the basic controls, and, after a few minutes, I felt sufficiently at home to believe that I stood a good chance of taking off—and of getting the Messerschmitt back to England in one piece. Thinking quickly, I made a shrewd guess as to the starting procedure. Then I turned on the petrol, set my throttles, gave a short prayer—and pressed the starter button.

The initial result was not too bad—for the port engine at least started to run over. However, I was quite unable to get it to fire, no matter what I did. I did not want to waste the aircraft batteries completely, so I took another thorough look around the cockpit. Meanwhile, I hoped that no one would come over to the aircraft.

Suddenly, however, I was horrified to see one of the guards come across to the machine and look up at the cockpit. In sheer desperation, I pressed the starter button again, hoping that I would be able to get the engine to start before I was ignominiously hauled out of the cockpit. However, to my astonishment, the ground-staff man walked underneath the port engine, fiddled around under the cowling for a few seconds—then called out something. I thought he was probably helping me to start the engine and wanted me to have another go. So I pressed the starter button.

The German was obviously shattered by this action, for the propeller nearly knocked his head off. Not surprisingly, he came round to the cockpit to see what was going on. When he looked up, I do not know which of us was the more astonished: for, instead of finding a smartly turned-out young *Luftwaffe* pilot sitting in the cockpit, he was faced by a rather grubby—and certainly nervous—Australian.

The German erk was so shocked that he practically fell backwards off the wing. Immediately, he yelled loudly for help. Then he came towards the cockpit—pointing an extremely businesslike-looking rifle straight at me. A few moments later, several guards came running to the mechanic's aid. I had no alternative, of course, but to surrender—and was hauled off to the German equivalent of the guard-room.

After a series of interrogations, I was later taken to a succession of POW camps. But, from the moment I was captured, one thought constantly dominated my mind: I was determined to escape.

The most spectacular of the early escape attempts in which I was involved occurred at Oflag 6B, Warburg. This was a mass attempt to scale the wire around the camp with extension ladders. On the selected night, all the lights in the camp were fused by an electrically-minded prisoner, and a row was created elsewhere to divert the attention of the sentries. Then we escapers, in three teams of twenty each, placed our ladders, built from bed boards and sides of beds, against the fence. Afterwards, the extension part was raised to cover the eight feet or so between the inner and outer wires. We then scaled the ladders, crossed the wires, dropped to the ground, and tried to escape under cover of darkness. Quite a number of men managed to get away in the ensuing panic, and three Army officers did, in fact, get back to England as a result of this escape. However, the rest of us were fairly quickly rounded up and returned to camp.

But I was still determined to get out; and, during the fifteen months I spent at Warburg, I was personally interested in about four separate escape attempts. Three of these attempts were tunnels, in which we had little luck, since each of them was found before completion. The fourth attempt was an endeavour to escape in the back of a bread cart. I managed to get out of camp by hiding in the cart when it was on its way back to the local village after delivering our bread. But, unfortunately, I was stopped by two German soldiers who saw me crossing a paddock. I attracted their attention because I was dressed in reasonably good civilian clothes and the circumstances were obviously unusual. Since I could not speak the language very well and could not give them a satisfactory explanation as to my presence in the area, I was taken back to the camp for questioning. I received the usual seven days' solitary confinement.

When I was transferred to Oflag 21B at Schubin, escape attempts came fast and furious. With several others, I concocted a scheme to dig a tunnel out—but, unfortunately, our tunnel was discovered by the Germans. A plan to escape by mounting extension ladders against the wire, as we had done at Warburg, was also wrecked. Afterwards, I had a narrow escape when trying to cut my way through the wires surrounding the camp, to get away under cover of darkness. I teamed up with a fellow-Australian named Tom Gilderthorpe to try to pull off this attempt.

We began the attempt on two or three occasions—but always something stopped us getting to the wire. The night we finally made our bid for freedom occurred shortly after a warning had been issued that anyone caught trying to escape would be shot on sight. This threat hanging over our heads did not help to boost our morale as we wormed our way across the trip wire placed ten feet back from the main wires—and beyond which no prisoner could step without being shot at. We could work uninterrupted on cutting the wire for periods of only about two minutes before we had to knock off to lie perfectly still while the sentry passed within a few feet of where we were operating. Obviously, it was not possible to make any quick movements or noise without fear of detection.

Since I could not check accurately on the movements of the sentry patrolling outside the fence, we rigged up a warning system. Tom lay in a vegetable patch, holding a piece of string attached to my right foot—and signalled when the coast was clear for me to resume cutting. However, progress was slow; and it soon became apparent that we would not be able to cut through the full set of wires in the limited time available.

Our minds were finally made up for us when the sentry noticed my presence in the wire. Rather than wait to be arrested, Tom and I decided to risk a wild dash back to our quarters. Separating, we ran as fast as we could—zigzagging to reduce the chance of being shot. The sentry fired only one shot—and, fortunately, this came nowhere near us. When we got back to camp, we were able to hide our provisions and escape equipment before the Germans arrived to carry out a search. They found nothing.

Meanwhile we had been working on a tunnel—planning to break from it in the spring of 1943. But, just as our tunnel was ready to be broken, the Germans smelt a rat—and imposed many additional anti-escape precautions. Consequently, it was decided to put off our escape attempt for a couple of weeks. At this stage, I heard that we were to be moved yet again—this time to Stalag Luft 3 at Sagan. Taking all the circumstances into account, I decided that I would stand the best chance of escape if I made my attempt from Sagan. Puzzling over the best method to adopt, I finally decided to switch identities with one of the orderlies in Schubin, my present camp—in an endeavour to enter Sagan as an orderly.

The main reason why I decided to exchange identities was that it was much easier for an orderly to escape than an officer. Normally, an officer was not allowed out of camp. However, orderlies and NCOs attached to officers' camps for camp duties were regularly required to leave the camp boundaries to collect bread, coal and German food rations. Orderlies even had the opportunity of getting outside the camp—and, although they were always under German guard, they had far less attention paid to them than would be paid to officers. In addition, if I completed my exchange of identities successfully, I stood a chance of being able to get myself transferred to a troops' camp—from which escape would be much easier.

At this stage, I met Private John McDiarmid, of the Seaforth Highlanders. McDiarmid was an orderly in our barracks. He was roughly my own build, though a little taller; but he was not so unlike me that a rather blurred photograph could not be mistaken for either of us. To my delight, when I approached him, I found him quite happy to exchange identities before we left Schubin. However, because we were both reasonably well known to the Germans, I decided not to make any attempt at exchanging identities until the actual day of departure from Schubin.

Since any change would have to be permanent, I decided that McDiarmid and I would also have to switch identity cards. This was complicated by the fact that the Germans checked identities by fingerprints as well as by photographs. Taking a chance, I joined one of the working parties of orderlies used to carry bread from the German compound across the road to the prison camp. On my second attempt, while in the German buildings, I was able to obtain three blank German identity cards. I found them lying on a desk where one of the German clerical staff had been checking through all the camp's cards.

Taking the cards back to our own compound, I obtained the use of a typewriter by breaking into the hospital office—and typed out particulars about McDiarmid and myself on each respective new card. I also transposed our fingerprints. However, in spite of four attempts, I was unable to get hold of our photographs from the genuine German identity cards.

As luck would have it, though, I got my chance to switch the photographs on the day that the final check of all the camp was made—but I also received a nasty shock. That day, a number of orderlies were detailed to help the Germans lay out identity cards for checking. Taking a chance, I dressed up as an orderly and presented myself with the other orderlies to help the Germans. In the confusion, I was able to obtain the original cards for both McDiarmid and myself.

It was then that I got the shock. I found that the genuine German identity cards had been partly typed and partly handwritten. In addition, certain notations had been made against the originals. The point was that these unexpected variations would prevent my substituting the cards I had so carefully prepared. Following the only possible course, I took the two genuine German cards up to my hut, where I got some glue and quickly transposed the two photos of McDiarmid and myself.

Dashing back, I managed to slip the cards back into their respective boxes without any of the Germans realising that they had been removed. The big snag now, though, was that I had to depend on the altered photographs alone getting me through the German check. The fingerprint check, I realised only too well, could lead to the Germans discovering the changed identities. However, in the event, the check at Schubin went through quite satisfactorily—and, to my great joy, I proceeded to leave Schubin POW camp as Private John McDiarmid.

The date was now June, 1943. When I arrived at Sagan, I managed to survive another identity check—but I had a close shave on my second day there. It turned out that at least four people besides myself had attempted an identity change. However, these people had not bothered to switch identity cards, too. Consequently, when a complete check was made of all the newly-arrived prisoners, four people who had done nothing other than exchange identities (but had not taken the precaution of also switching identity cards) were immediately caught by the Germans. They were promptly taken off to do the normal seven days' solitary confinement as punishment. Fortunately, I managed to come through this extra check undetected—obviously due to the fact that I had changed our photos. The incorrect fingerprints were, luckily, not discovered.

I took on normal orderly duties immediately I entered Sagan—much to the amusement of my aircrew friends. I made a point of getting to know the German guards well, so that my identity as an orderly should never be questioned. I also went out of my way to volunteer for any outside jobs going—for my idea at that stage was to try to escape from one of these working parties. However, as it turned out, we were always accompanied by German guards—never once did I get an opportunity to slip away.

Finally, in desperation, I decided to get myself sent to a troops' camp—from which escape would be much easier. The tactics I adopted were to volunteer for every job the Germans called for—and then, immediately I was placed on some unpleasant duty, to refuse to work. I would throw down my tools—and tell the Germans point-blank that I had no intention of carrying out their orders.

The reaction of the Huns to my stand, after three or four times, was quite definite. A German officer told me in no un-certain manner that the next time I adopted these tactics I would be sent away from Sagan. The point was that Sagan was con-sidered to be a good camp for orderlies—whereas if I were to be transferred to Lamsdorf, as they threatened, I would be liable to be forced to work on farms, in coal mines or on any other less pleasant duties that the Germans chose. This, of course, was exactly what I wanted; and, after another couple of re-fusals, I was, in fact, sent to Lamsdorf. My chances of escape were now considerably improved.

When I was leaving Sagan, I learned of the German system of forcing privates to do whatever jobs cropped up—whereas NCOs could pick the type of work they preferred. Accordingly, when I entered Lamsdorf, I immediately promoted myself to corporal. My correct title, I told the Germans, was Corporal McDiarmid, not Private. The security check was rather vague—and my entry as a corporal was never questioned. Because of

my new rank, I was now able to volunteer for a working party—
and was immediately selected as a worker to go out to a farm
just outside Breslau. Events were now playing into my hands.

After a few days on the farm, I saw that an escape attempt
would be comparatively easy. Though we prisoners were supervised by a German guard, so few men had attempted to escape
from working parties that the average guard, after a couple of
days, was quite prepared to accept the fact that his prisoners
had no thoughts of escape. In addition, because prisoners were
employed over a fairly dispersed area, and since no check was
made between lunch-time and evening count, an escaping prisoner could get some distance before his absence was discovered.

After the lunch-hour break on my fourth day at the farm,
I waited till the guard and the other prisoners had gone down to
a paddock. Then I left the yard in which I was working—and
struck out across country. . . .

I decided that my best way to escape was to try to reach one
of the Baltic ports. So I made directly for Danzig, with the
object of obtaining a ship to Sweden. I took the precaution of
carrying with me a pitchfork, which would signify to any passing
German that I was a workman travelling to his job—and therefore
not worth querying. Stealing a bicycle, I cycled along in daytime only, since the chance of being picked up was greater at
night. On the fifth night, I entered Danzig.

My best bet, I thought, would be to locate a French working
camp. My idea was to find someone there who would shelter
me for the night and also help me to get aboard a Swedish ship.
Eventually, I spotted a party of workmen who were obviously
French. They were guarded by one German sentry who was
taking little interest in his guarding duties. I walked up to one
Frenchman as unostentatiously as possible and finally managed
to convince him that I was a British Air Force officer trying to
escape. The Frenchman told me I could go back to his camp for
the night, to hide from the Germans.

Borrowing my acquaintance's beret, and generally trying to look as much like a Frenchman as possible, I joined the party of Frenchmen. My friend told me that I should be able to enter the working party compound without difficulty, as the German guards rarely carried out checks. Sure enough, the whole party went straight into the camp—and the German guard did no more than chat to the sentry who accompanied us. Obviously, he worked on the principle that, while many people might try to escape, no one would be so foolish as to want to *enter* a prison camp. So I now found myself a guest of the Germans for the night!

Next day, the Camp Leader went out with a working party on duty on one of the wharves to try to arrange for me to get aboard a ship. Since I could not remain in the camp without fear of detection, I had to wander around the streets of Danzig all day. In the evening, I casually joined a returning party and got back into camp all right. To my joy, I then learned that the Camp Leader had contacted a Frenchman who would be working on a ship that was to leave for Sweden at seven o'clock the next night.

The following morning, I went with the working party to the wharves. I took the place of a Frenchman who had arranged to report sick; and, showing his papers, I got into the prohibited area without difficulty. About three o'clock in the afternoon, I discreetly made my way to the coal bunkers—in which I decided to stow away. I practically covered myself with coal, leaving only sufficient of the black lumps away from my head to ensure that I would be able to breathe easily.

About three hours later, following a sudden rush of activity, we sailed from the wharf and made our way out to open water. Up till this stage, I had noticed no definite search of the ship—and was beginning to congratulate myself on my good fortune in getting away undiscovered. However, my hopes were suddenly dashed. A little while after leaving the wharf, we anchored again and waited about half an hour. I soon began to realise that the reason for this stoppage was to enable Customs or police officials to search the ship—and I now became uneasily aware that the search had actually begun.

Since I was fairly near the top of the coal, I could plainly hear any sounds of activity near by. After a while, I was horrified to hear a German voice calling out in English that he knew an Englishman was concealed aboard—and that it was useless trying to hide. Worse, the German added that, unless the prisoner gave himself up immediately, he would suffer severe consequences when caught.

However, I assumed that this was probably a normal German safety precaution carried out on every search. So I remained where I was—hoping that my presence would not be discovered. But, once again, I was disappointed. To my dismay, I saw the covers removed from the bunker in which I was hiding. This fresh threat looked bad—for the Germans also had dogs on my track. A moment later, one Alsatian quickly intimated that he had scented something other than coal—*me!*

The Germans were now fairly certain that someone was, in fact, hiding on the ship. A moment later, a voice called out that, unless the person hiding in the bunkers gave himself up, the Germans would use tear-gas bombs—and so force him to come up. I was still not certain whether or not the Germans were bluffing. So I continued to remain where I was.

However, true to their threats, the Germans did use tear-gas bombs; and, because I was so close to the top of the coal, and since I was in a very confined area, I found that it was not long before I was coughing and spluttering. My eyes began to stream, and I had involuntarily to give away my hiding place. Then I had to come up.

The Germans did not handle me particularly gently. When they got me to a type of barracks near by, I admitted that I was a corporal in the Seaforth Highlanders who had escaped. The

Huns were not over-impressed with my story—and checked up with my POW camp at Lamsdorf. Fortunately, the check confirmed my story; and, since I could also substantiate my account by quoting my POW identity number (actually McDiarmid's, of course), the Germans sent me back to Lamsdorf.

Before I left Danzig, I talked to one of the Germans who had helped to capture me. He told me that a Frenchman on the wharves had given me away. The Frenchman had seen me on the dock-side and had realised that I was not a fellow-countryman. Then, when he had noticed that I was no longer present, just before the ship had sailed, he had realised that I had gone on board. So he had told the Germans that he was certain an Englishman was trying to stow away. That was why the Germans had carried out a thorough search—and had caught me so easily.

However, when I was returned to Lamsdorf, the same thought continued to dominate my mind: I was still determined to escape.

Having considered the various possibilities, I finally decided that my best chance of escaping would be to try to go right across Germany, down through France, and, with the help of the French *Maquis,* cross the Pyrenees into Spain. The big snag, however, was that languages were not my strong point. But I had a bit of luck in that I met a New Zealander, N. Geoffrey Williamson, who spoke excellent German and French, and who had himself already been out on a couple of escape attempts. Because my own escape would be seriously hampered by my lack of languages, it was agreed that Williamson and I should get out together. Our plan was to travel by train through Germany and into France, where we hoped to pick up a French Underground party who would help us to get back to England. We worked out all details carefully in advance, being given considerable help by two Canadians, Sergeant Larry Pals and Sergeant Major McLean.

On Sunday, September 19, 1943, following our carefully-

arranged plan, we secretly changed into our workmen's clothes
—and lowered ourselves into the tunnel through which we planned
to escape. We were equipped with forged identity papers to
establish our *bona fides* as French volunteer workmen returning
from a munitions factory at Blechhammer. I also carried a letter
from the Blechhammer camp doctor stating that I was suffering
from a type of laryngitis which prevented me from speaking
in anything above a hoarse whisper. This precaution was, of
course, to ensure that my lack of languages should not be detected.

Our plan necessitated us getting out of the tunnel in broad
daylight. This was tricky, because German sentries were stationed
every 50 yards along the wire. To ensure that the attention of
the German guards was distracted, McLean and Pals arranged
for a game of baseball to take place immediately in front of the
sentry box nearest the mouth of our tunnel. In addition, they
organised a football match near the next box along the wire—
with some lively scrummages going on to rivet the Germans'
attention on the game. Our main danger was the sentry box
immediately in front of the point from which we were to break
out of the tunnel. A fairly intricate system of signalling was
accordingly set up to give us the word when to attempt the
break. The danger was complicated by the fact that odd German
civilians, some of whom wandered into the camp vicinity on Sunday afternoons, might see us.

Williamson and I waited anxiously underneath the trap at
the end of the tunnel. It was not until some quarter of an hour
had passed—which seemed to us like eternity—that, at long last,
we received the signal to break. To make certain that the German
guard remained completely oblivious of the breath-taking events
going on twenty yards behind his back, the baseball game suddenly developed into a bout of fisticuffs between two of the
players. The fighting had developed into a violent scrap by the
time Williamson and myself finally, after a lot of exertion, man-

aged to push the wooden trap off the tunnel. Then we levered the trap up sufficiently to enable Williamson to crawl out. Immediately, he went into some scrub bushes some thirty yards from the camp fence.

I came out right behind him. Then I lay flat on my stomach while I gradually dropped the trap back into place. Afterwards I scraped dirt and grass over the top. I patted this camouflage in as quickly as I could—so that the tunnel location would remain reasonably concealed, ready for use again at a later date.

This was probably the most nerve-racking part of the escape. At any moment, a German might unexpectedly come along. Worse, a guard might suddenly tire of watching the game, casually look round—and see me lying on the ground in rather an awkward position, obviously attempting to escape. The snag was that the German guard would stand little chance of stopping me with a bayonet. So his immediate reaction would be to shoot. Consequently, being stuck out there in broad daylight was, to say the least, a little unnerving.

Fortunately, however, everything went according to plan— and I joined Williamson without an alarm being raised. Then we strolled slowly down the side of the camp wires. To make our presence appear quite normal, we even stopped for a few seconds to watch the fight that was still going on in the baseball match. We did not move on, in fact, until a guard told us that civilians were not allowed to loiter near the camp!

We then wandered nonchalantly on as if we were out for an afternoon stroll. Sauntering down through the German barrack quarters, we went past the main gate of the camp and on to the road leading to Lamsdorf Station. Our plan was to catch a train to Breslau, where we would pick up the Berlin Express. We hoped to reach Berlin by ten o'clock that night.

At the station, Williamson bought two tickets without difficulty. Then we boarded the train, which pulled in some ten minutes after we arrived. We stood in the midst of a large number of German soldiers on the rear platform of one of the carriages—and our presence aroused absolutely no comment. At Breslau, Williamson again simply walked up to the booking office window, asked for two tickets to Berlin—and obtained them without query.

On the way to Berlin, however, I received a nasty jolt when we passed through Sagan—the POW camp which I had left only a few weeks previously. Somewhat to my consternation, waiting on Sagan station to join the Express were three guards whom I had known quite well in Sagan prison camp. What was worse, because of my orderly duties, they knew me equally well. Fortunately, I was standing in a carriage which was very full; and, as it turned out, the guards got aboard several carriages farther down the train.

This encounter put me on my guard for the rest of the journey —for it made me realise there was a chance of my being recognised when I left the train at Berlin. So I asked Williamson also to keep a sharp look-out for the German guards. Luckily, however, by the time we reached Berlin it was dark. What with the effective black-out restrictions, and the colossal congestion on the station, we were easily swallowed up in the crowd. We walked out of the station with a sigh of relief.

Our problem now was to find accommodation for the night. However, we felt quite confident that our papers and appearance would get us by. So we went across to a hotel opposite the station, where we obtained accommodation without difficulty. When we had left camp, however, we had been warned that all hotel lists were checked by German officials each morning— and that anyone unusual was often interrogated. To safeguard ourselves against the risk of unwittingly falling into the Germans' hands again, we therefore arranged for coffee and bread and jam to be served in our room at 7 a.m. The pretext we gave was that we had an early train to catch. Next morning, we left our hotel at about 7.30 a.m., travelled across Berlin by Underground, then caught a train to Mannheim, on our way to Saarbrucken.

When we arrived at Mannheim at about 10 p.m., we were unable to obtain accommodation for the night because of damage inflicted on the city by RAF bombing. So we spent the night in an air raid shelter under the railway station. This turned out to be a particularly nasty experience—since, for some twenty minutes, we found ourselves on the receiving end of an RAF raid.

Next morning, while waiting for our train, we had a haircut and shave, and travelled round the city by tram. The reason we did this was to avoid the risk of being questioned by the police, who seemed to be keeping a pretty strict check on people moving in and out of the city. We were fortunate in making this decision, I learned later, for the Germans had a tight cordon thrown round the city to prevent people working under forced labour in Germany from escaping under cover of the confusion caused by the bombing. Later, we caught our train to Saarbrucken.

Following our pre-arranged plan, when we reached Saarbrucken we made contact with a man called Pierre. He was employed on a French working party—and was in contact with smuggling gangs who operated between the French and German areas. His contacts would get us across the frontier, under cover of darkness, without running any real risk of capture.

One of the younger Frenchmen at the working party camp once got us into what could have been quite a sticky spot. The trouble was that the Frenchmen seemed to get a real kick out of insulting Germans to their faces. On this occasion, Williamson and I were having coffee and biscuits at a local café. Suddenly, I was dismayed to see two French lads walk up to some Germans and blatantly tell them, with obvious relish, that they could hoodwink them. To my horror, they went on to say that they could probably help people to escape right under the Huns' noses! Naturally, Williamson and I beat a hasty retreat.

Next, we proceeded to Metz, which was right on the scene

of smuggling operations. Meanwhile we had picked up a companion—Georges Monclard. He was a Frenchman who wanted
to escape from German forced labour to return to his home in
Marseilles. We decided to cross into France together. Later,
we met the guide who was to take us across the border. He was
an 18-years-old Frenchman who went over the border two or
three times a week to visit his family and girl friend.

On the night on which we decided to cross the frontier, we
caught a train up to the station immediately before the border.
Then we set out to walk along the main road towards the frontier
itself. Following the road to within about three-quarters of a
mile of the patrol point, we cut across paddocks at right angles
to the border until we came to a point where our guide maintained that the crossing could easily be made.

At this point, the border was patrolled by a German guard
who covered an area of about one mile along the wire. Each
guard was equipped with a rifle, and, in certain cases, an Alsatian
dog. In addition, normal searchlight posts were situated along the
wire at about one-mile intervals. The border, I now discovered,
consisted of two barbed wire fences. These fences were about
four feet high and about fifty yards apart. We decided to go
across individually. Our guide went first—taking with him his
ten-years-old brother, who was returning home. Then came
Williamson, followed by Georges. I brought up the rear.

Everything went according to plan until Williamson slipped
as he attempted to get through the far wire. Since the wires were
fairly loose, Williamson's sudden movement caused a certain
amount of noise. The slight sound, carried through the still air,
immediately attracted the attention of the German sentry some
distance away. Though the night was fairly dark, the sentry
could obviously see that something was happening in the wire.
Immediately, he rushed up to Williamson, who was still inside
the wire—and held him up at rifle point. What was I to do?

The Hun had my friend completely at his mercy—for he had

just caught him red-handed, in the middle of the night, trying to cross the frontier. However, for some unknown reason, the sentry did not raise an alarm to attract the other guards. Nor, fortunately, in the darkness, did he see either Georges or myself. At once, jabbing his rifle threateningly towards my fellow-escaper, he began to question Williamson in German as to what he was doing in the forbidden zone.

We were obviously in a pretty tough spot; for, I realised, no matter how good a story Williamson told, he was now quite certain to be arrested. Taking all the factors into consideration, I made up my mind to liquidate the guard. Fortunately, the Hun was so excited as he interrogated Williamson that he was totally unaware of my presence as I crawled silently up behind him. I moved so quietly, in fact, that even Williamson did not know I was in the vicinity.

Suddenly, I made a wild leap at the guard; I got a good hold around his throat. My fingers closed around his windpipe before he had a chance to yell out. My object was to choke him into insensibility to prevent his raising the alarm.

When Williamson and the others saw what was happening, they all rushed to my assistance. Georges took the rifle from the German, who had, in any case, dropped it when I had attacked him. Because of the stranglehold I had on him, the guard was still unable to utter a word.

In the circumstances, I had no alternative but to go on increasing the pressure until I felt the guard lose consciousness. As soon as I was absolutely certain that he was unconscious, I dropped him to the ground. Then we picked up our packs, clambered through the wire—and raced off at top speed. Shortly afterwards we reached the small village of Aubouie, where we hid in a loft.

However, we now wanted to get out of this area as quickly as possible; for, if the Germans should link us with the incident of the unconscious sentry, the consequences for us would not be pleasant. Our task now was to leave the area before the Germans organised a search. Fortunately, a few hours later, Georges Monclard found out that we could get a bus out of the village. Accordingly, at about six o'clock in the morning we dashed down to the village square—and climbed aboard the bus.

The trouble, however, was that Georges tended to be a little bit irrational on some occasions. In this instance, to our dismay, we found that the bus on which we were travelling was taking us back across the border into German territory!

The difficulty was that it operated *non-stop* to Briey, a minor rail junction straddled right across the new border line. Since we could not leave the bus without arousing suspicion, we just had to stay where we were until the vehicle took us back into the German area. The abuse that I hurled at Georges when we finally left the bus was sufficient to stop many a man in his tracks.

However, Georges made up for his sins later on by getting us back across into French territory. He made contact with the driver of a train about to leave for Lunéville—and the driver kindly arranged to get us through. Leading the way down to the marshalling yards, Georges went up to an engine that was taking on water. Sure enough, Georges's engine-driver friend invited us up into his cab. Then he covered us with a couple of old great coats and some sacks, so that we would not be seen by the German guards.

When his engine had taken on water, he shunted up on a track immediately alongside the carriages he was waiting to pick up. Then, leaning out, he opened the door of a second-class compartment. When the driver got the "all-clear" from a guard on the platform, the three of us jumped across into the compartment. A couple of minutes later, we were handed our tickets by the guard.

On our journey to Lunéville we again encountered the desire of certain Frenchmen to share their secrets with everyone. As our train rattled along, Georges calmly informed a French farmer and his wife sharing our compartment that Williamson and I were Allied soldiers on the last part of our escape from Germany to England. When the French couple got out after a comparatively short journey, I began to fear that possibly they might give us away to the German authorities. However, evidently they did not do so, for we eventually arrived in Lunéville quite safely.

Through Georges, we now made contact with a leading citizen in Lunéville, in whose house we stayed. While there, we were introduced to the Chief Gendarme. This official told us that he hoped to arrange for us to be taken down to the Spanish border. The Chief of Police also issued us with authentic French identity cards and put all our other papers in order.

Later, on his orders, we were taken to Nancy. We were handcuffed and escorted on the journey by two gendarmes—since, ostensibly, we were being taken there to be imprisoned for stealing. The ruse worked excellently. Then, when we arrived in Nancy, we had our photographs taken—and these pictures were affixed to our identity cards, so that our papers were now 100 per cent genuine.

By devious means, arranged by the French Underground, we subsequently went on to Ruffec, in the Franco-Spanish border region. In Ruffec, we met the Comtesse de Melville, who was known as "Marie". She was an Englishwoman who was running an escape organisation. She told us that the best way home was to cross the Pyrenees into Spain, then to go to a British Consulate, or else press on to Gibraltar. The Chief of Police in Ruffec also saw that our papers were all right—so we were now all set to cross into Spain.

While we waited at Ruffec, Williamson and I were joined by two Polish escapers, both RAF sergeants. The four of us were to cross the Pyrenees from Foix, not far from the border. A hitch developed on our first trip to Foix, so we returned to Ruffec.

To my dismay, when a new route was fixed up shortly afterwards, I had to stay behind. The reason was that a danger of interrogation existed on this new route—and I was the only member of the party who could not speak fluent French. When I saw Williamson and the two Poles set off without me, I felt a lot of regret and a certain amount of envy since they were taking the first opportunity of making the final escape. I did not realise at the time that this change in plan probably helped to save my life; for, within 36 hours, Williamson was to lose his life in a Pyrenees blizzard that developed during his crossing.

Two days after Williamson's departure, I was joined at Ruffec by four more escapers. They were Captain R. B. ("Buck") Palm, of the South African Air Force; an RAF Flying Officer, Michael Cooper, who came from Kenya; and two Canadians from the same crew, Flying Officer Harry Smith, a navigator, and Sergeant Len Martin, a wireless operator. These were the men with whom I was to make my desperate attempt to escape.

A few days after their arrival, however, an unexpected complication arose. We suddenly found ourselves in the midst of a violent quarrel for the leadership of our escape organisation. The quarrel arose when a French woman who had helped us to escape from Nancy, and who I believe was a Countess, arrived in Ruffec. She immediately began to assert to Marie that only she was capable of getting us back to England. It soon became evident that the struggle for power was going to be most bitter. Weighing up the pros and cons, we settled the issue by unanimously deciding to stay with Marie.

After another hitch, we eventually set out to cross the Pyrenees. We began our journey in a truck. But, as we were going round a mountain road, suddenly we heard a loud crack at the back—and quickly came to rest on the roadside with a broken back axle. However, we eventually reached Tardets, from which we were to start out on foot on our tough trek across the mountains.

Our idea, of course, was to reach Spain. But I had already

heard many stories of escapers who had been given rough treatment in Spanish prison camps. So I took an important precaution: I carried with me letters addressed to the British Consuls at San Sebastian and Barcelona and to the British Ambassador at Madrid. These letters advised the British authorities that we had crossed the frontier and would be in a certain area. The envelopes were already addressed in Spanish and franked with Spanish stamps. So, after adding in the name of the place in which we were likely to be imprisoned, all I had to do was to post them. These letters, I was fairly sure, would probably help to hasten our rescue by the British authorities.

About one o'clock in the morning, we set out by moonlight on the last phase of our journey. Two Basque guides led us. After about an hour's walking, rain started to fall. Later, this developed into a steady drizzle, which saturated us all. Harry Smith felt the strain of our tough trek fairly badly; and, by about four o'clock in the morning, he had reached the stage where he found it virtually impossible to go any farther without rest.

We now had to cross a main road actively patrolled by Germans. We also had to go over a bridge which was normally guarded by German sentries. Because of Harry's illness, we left him in an old cattle barn for a few minutes while we reconnoitred the immediate area to find out the best way of avoiding the patrols. However, when we came to the bridge, we saw a dark shape standing by the side. Fearing the worst, we assumed that the Germans kept the bridge guarded all the time.

Crossing the mountain stream without using the bridge involved a long detour, which would disrupt the guides' plans. So we decided to wait until daybreak to find out definitely what chance we had of getting over the bridge. When morning came, we were much relieved to find that what we had thought was a German guard was, in fact, nothing more than an old post leaning up against the side of the railings with a bag flapping from its top. In the darkness, this post had looked from the distance like someone standing with a rifle slung over his shoulder.

By the time we had had a meal at an inn on the other side of the bridge, Harry had improved so much that he felt capable of carrying on for the rest of the trip. However, as we trudged up a steep slope on the next part of the route, the incessant drizzle got worse. First, it changed to sleet, then it became a solid snow storm. Shortly afterwards, the snow storm gradually assumed the proportions of a blizzard. The wind blew great gusts of snow all over us. Our shoes and clothes became sopping wet. Then, as the snow got deeper, walking became more difficult. Eventually, conditions got so bad that it became almost impossible to maintain any decent foothold.

On one occasion, we had to cross a razor-like ridge connecting two peaks. The width of the track was not more than about two feet six inches—with a sheer drop of 200 to 300 feet on either side. Because the wind was constantly plucking at us, and since it was almost impossible to retain a firm foothold, we had to cross this ridge practically on hands and knees. Desperately, we hoped that nothing unexpected would happen— for even a small slip would send us hurtling over the edge to instant death. The crossing seemed to take ages. However, we eventually accomplished it safely.

By evening, we found a type of mountain shack. We decided to spend the night there, in an attempt to regain some warmth and strength. However, the cold was so bitter that we could not get any decent rest. So, after a few hours, we were forced to push on again. It soon became obvious, however, that our guides were completely lost. All we could do was to keep heading south-west, so that at least we were making slow progress in the right direction.

Half-way through the day, our guides wanted to turn back. They had had enough, they said. However, we were determined to carry on—and told the guides so in no uncertain fashion. But both guides were feeling the strain badly. Their exertions were telling on them so much that, as we progressed, they became extremely vehement in their desire to turn back. But the guides had been paid something like 15,000 francs each to take us across; and, since, in any case, we could not make our way back with any degree of certainty, we were more or less forced to insist that they carry on.

Now Mike Cooper began to crack up. He was so weary, he said, that he was just going to sit down and rest. On one occasion, I found Mike missing. Retracing our steps, Buck Palm and myself discovered him a quarter of a mile back, lying in the snow in a low state. Obviously, if he had lain there any length of time, he would gradually have lost consciousness and would actually have died in the blizzard. Between the two of us, we managed to get Mike back on his feet. Then we pummelled him back into some sense of consciousness—and he forced himself to keep going.

Now, once more, Harry Smith did not feel terribly fit. And, of course, we also had to help Mike. To add to our difficulties, the elder guide soon showed signs of cracking up. His feet were so badly frost-bitten that he could barely walk. To make matters worse, we were all so tired that we found difficulty in continuing to help our guide and Mike.

The guide was in such a bad state that he eventually found it impossible to continue any longer. We massaged his hands and feet in an endeavour to restore his circulation. But, in a very short time, he completely lost consciousness. Now we had a difficult decision to make. If we all remained with the guide, in the open, with the blizzard still raging, the rest of us would succumb in a matter of an hour or so. However, if we left the guide where he was, he would certainly never regain consciousness—and would die. Taking into account all the factors, we eventually decided that to press on, leaving the guide behind, was the only possible course we could adopt.

While we were trying to make the guide comfortable, we were astonished to see another traveller coming towards us. He turned out to be a Spaniard—and he kindly gave us all a drink of a light wine he was carrying in a skin water bag. He also tried to force some of the wine down the throat of our Basque guide. Five minutes later, the Spaniard continued on his way.

We could still do nothing for our guide. So, covering him with a ground sheet, and making him as comfortable as possible, we left him where he was. Then we straggled off on our bitter journey.

After going about a mile, I was dismayed to see that Mike Cooper had entirely disappeared. Rather than leave him to the same fate as our guide, I went back—and again found him lying in the snow about a quarter of a mile behind us. He was so close to unconsciousness that he could not speak. I doubt if he even recognised me when I shook him. Then Len Martin came back to tell me that a small hut had been spotted by the rest of our party. It was, he said, down by a creek bank, about a mile and a half farther on.

My idea now was to get the guide and Mike down to the shelter of the hut right away. Leaving Mike for a few minutes, I went back to the guide. I found him practically covered in snow— and obviously dead.

I got back to Mike as quickly as possible, and was able to half-drag and half-carry him down the hill on to the banks of the creek. The others helped me to take him the rest of the way. We forced an entry into the hut, lit a fire to dry out our clothes, and got some much-needed rest.

We set off again at about nine o'clock next morning. Our remaining guide led us off down a river, which we hoped would eventually bring us out to some Spanish village. To my amazement, when we came to a junction of two streams, our guide insisted that we follow the *other* stream. We argued with him over this decision. But our guide maintained that he could quickly lead us to a village.

However, after following him for about five or ten minutes, we decided his directions were wrong. So, checking our bearings with the compass, we turned back and followed the original stream. Eventually, we came out on a main road, which led us to a type of frontier outpost manned by Spanish police. Since we were all in such a bad state, we handed ourselves over to the Spaniards, who, after giving us a meal, accompanied us to the nearest village.

We were taken to the local police station. But, before we got there, I found out where letters could be posted. On the way, I dropped my letters addressed to various British representatives into the box. Later, we were collected by a British representative from the Embassy in Madrid; and, safe again in British care, we were eventually taken to Gibraltar, from where we were flown back to England.

When our *Dakota* came into land at its English airfield, a strong crosswind was blowing. The pilot, it seemed to me, was not making a particularly good job of his landing. My judgement was, in fact, borne out a moment later. Immediately after touching down, our aircraft swung right off the runway, skidded across the grass and bowled over a parked *Anson*. Eventually, the *Dak* came to a rather ignominious stop—with one wing badly damaged and the undercarriage messed up. All of us eighteen passengers heaved a sigh of relief at having got down safely.

However, though I had made a somewhat shaky arrival, my escape was now, thank goodness, all over. I was a free man at last.

D-DAY — MOSQUITOS FOIL THE GESTAPO

SIR BASIL EMBRY

G.C.B., K.B.E., D.S.O., D.F.C., A.F.C., AIR CHIEF MARSHAL, RAF

Early in February 1944, I was asked by Coningham, the Commander-in-Chief of 2nd T.A.F., if I thought our *Mosquitos* were capable of carrying out an operation to release about seven hundred French Resistance Movement patriots awaiting trial and death in Amiens prison. I said I thought it would be possible but I would want to examine the full implications of such an operation before giving a definite answer. Later I told him I thought it could be successful but that it would be with the loss of some of the prisoners' lives.

The story of this operation, which went by the code name of "Jericho", has been told in full by Colonel Remy in his book *The Gates Burst Open,* and it has also been the subject of a film, so it is too well known for me to go into details. But as I was responsible for planning it and but for the intervention of Leigh-Mallory would have led it, there are a few additional points of interest I can add to the story.

The first step I took was to have the prison photographed and modelled by our modelling section. Next I called for advice from someone who could give me detailed particulars about the internal and external construction of the prison and its surrounding wall, and also the internal lay-out with all possible information about the cells, the locks to the doors, and the prison routine.

The prison was in the form of a cross surrounded by a brick wall twenty feet high and three feet thick, and was guarded by specially selected troops who lived in accommodation adjoining it. The building was outside the town on the road to Albert, a long straight highway with no obstructions near it and providing a well-defined lead on to the target for a low attack.

I got technical advice on the amount of explosive force needed to breach the thick prison wall and force the locks on cells and prison doors. I decided to breach the outer wall in two places to give an exit at either end, lest the Germans had placed obstructions across the prison yard, and that an attempt must also be made to eliminate as many of the guards as possible by destroying the part of the buildings where they were housed. We learned that the majority of the prisoners usually assembled in a central hall shortly before noon for their midday meal, so we decided to attack then, in case we failed to break the locks on the cells, which was obviously difficult to manage without doing too much damage. The point was to use enough high explosive to break the locks without killing the prisoners. Our idea was to place a number of bombs at the base of the prison so that their explosion would throw the doors out of alignment, making the locks ineffective, and at the same time damage the walls of the prison building enough to allow the prisoners to escape into the yard.

I warned those members of the French Resistance Movement with whom I was dealing that we were bound to cause casualties amongst the prisoners, because even if all went according to plan and our calculations were absolutely correct, falling debris and proximity to the explosions were bound to take their toll. In reply I was assured that the prisoners would sooner be killed by our bombs than by the Germans, and that even if we succeeded in saving only a few of them the sacrifice would be worth while.

The idea of killing our own friends weighed heavily on my mind; it was a hateful responsibility I had to carry alone both then and on several further occasions before the war ended. Those who have not borne such responsibility can never fully appreciate the mental torment of the commander who says, "Yes, we will do it, and this is how it will be done." And my burden was made no easier by having to sit on the ground and watch others put my plan into execution.

Eighteen *Mosquitos* from 140 Wing were to operate in three formations of six aircraft each, under cover of fighter escort. The first six were to break the prison walls and destroy the German guardhouse. The second formation was to place the bombs against the walls of the prison, and the third was to be in reserve and only go into action if the outside walls were not properly breached or if no one was seen to be escaping, which would indicate that the cell locks had not been forced.

The prisoners had been warned about the attack, and the Resistance Forces were to be in support of any escapers outside the prison.

Our plans were complete by the 8th February and that afternoon I flew to Hunsden where 140 Wing was located to brief Charles Pickard, the Commanding Officer, and his wing leader. I was to lead the operation myself and Pickard was to fly as deputy leader. We learned that some of the prisoners were to be shot on the morning of the 19th February, so we selected the first day after the 10th when the weather was favourable. Meanwhile Pickard would choose his crews, and brief them with the help of the model which I left with him. The next day I had to meet Leigh-Mallory when he was inspecting 137 Wing at Hartford Bridge, and before he left he asked about operation "Jericho", which I explained to him in some detail. He then turned to me and said,

"Basil, who is leading it?"

When I told him that I was, he made no reply, but the same

evening I received an order from Coningham that in no circumstances was I to fly on it. I protested, saying that the briefing had already been done and everything was set for the next morning, but he said,

"I am sorry, but those are Leigh-Mallory's orders, and he was most emphatic about it, so I am afraid you have got to accept it."

Operation "Jericho" did not take place until the 18th February because of a spell of bad weather, and even on that day conditions were very bad over England and the Channel.

Charles Pickard led instead of me and I shall always regret that decision because, although he was an exceptionally experienced operational pilot at night, he had carried out only a few missions by day, and I believe this may well have been the reason he was shot down by enemy fighters. It is impossible to measure Charles Pickard's loss to the R.A.F. and Britain, but in courage, devotion to duty, fighting spirit and powers of real leadership, he stood out as one of the great airmen of the war and as a shining example of British manhood. His navigator, J. J. Broadley, who died with him, had shared many of his dangers and triumphs since the early days of the war.

The operation resulted in two hundred and fifty-eight prisoners escaping, including most of the key members of the Resistance organisation under sentence of death, though some were subsequently recaptured. One hundred and two prisoners were killed during the action, but many of these were shot by the German guards manning a machine-gun post which unfortunately had escaped the first wave of attacking *Mosquitos*. Members of the French Resistance declared that the operation had been successful beyond their highest hopes, and still commemorate its anniversary as an historic event, linking it with the name of Charles Pickard.

A few weeks later the group was called upon to assist the Resistance Movement in Holland. After months of work the

Gestapo had collected sufficient information to identify the majority of its leaders, and many arrests were expected which would have brought the work of organised resistance in Holland to a standstill. It was known that the Gestapo records and the register of population which they used in their investigations were kept in a five-storey building opposite the Peace Palace in the centre of the Hague. The problem was to destroy the building and all the records before the Gestapo completed their investigations and acted against the Resistance Movement, without causing widespread damage to the Hague and killing large numbers of the civilian population. After having the building and approaches to it photographed and modelled, I reported that the mission was perfectly feasible.

I allotted the task to 138 Wing and R. H. Bateson,[1] the commander of 613 Squadron, was selected to carry it out. On the 11th April he attacked from fifty feet with six *Mosquitos,* and not a single bomb missed its mark. Bombs were actually seen going through the front door where two Gestapo men were on guard. In order to ensure that the records were burnt, I instructed that incendiary bombs in addition to high explosive were to be used, and this proved very effective. All that remained of the building was a pile of smouldering rubble. Two days later the Germans were still searching the debris, but all the records were destroyed together with many of the Gestapo staff.

When visiting the Hague after the war, I was told that not a civilian outside the building had been killed, and that the only external damage done was the breaking of a small glass window over the main entrance door to the Peace Palace. The aircraft completed this attack without a single gun opening fire on them, another example of the advantages of surprise and careful routeing. After the bombing Flight Lieutenant Cohen, a native of the Hague, remained behind to photograph the target, and he

[1] Now Group Captain R. H. Bateson, D.S.O., D.F.C.

made two complete circuits of the town to see, he said, if any alterations had been carried out since he had left it, before the anti-aircraft defences went into action.

Early in the New Year, as part of the general preparation for the invasion of the Continent, 2 Group Headquarters moved to Mongewell Park in Berkshire, and our wings occupied the airfields they would operate from on "D" day. To accustom personnel to field conditions and make them realise they were now part of a tactical organisation which would not have the advantage of permanent airfield facilities, I made them live under canvas and work under mobile conditions.

His Majesty King George VI always took a great personal interest in the 2nd T.A.F. and early in May 1944 he held an inspection at Northolt. Each group was allotted a section of the airfield and allowed to make its own detailed arrangements. Besides assembling representatives from all the units, No. 2 Group organised a static display in which we tried to show a cross section of our ancillary equipment, such as bomb-sights, navigational radar, signal sets, cameras and gun turrets working in slow motion. We also displayed some of the model targets we had used for planning certain operations and alongside them photographs of the results of the bombing enlarged to a big scale. Both the King and the Queen spent a long time in our exhibition and were keenly interested in all we had to show them. They gave us all great encouragement.

We had lined up a number of each of the three types of aircraft in the Group, all fully armed to show the bomb loads and guns, and with the flying and maintenance crews paraded in front. Among the *Mosquitos* was my own with my very excellent Australian Air Force sergeant, who before the war had been on a sheep station in the back of beyond, and who had been detached from No. 464 (Australian) Squadron for the purpose of taking charge of my aeroplane. I had instructed commanding officers to brief their airmen how to reply to their Majesties should they be spoken to. When the Australian was told he should use the word "Sir" if addressed by the King, he objected.

"Oh no I don't, sir! I shall call him 'Your Majesty'."

When told this was not correct in the Service, he replied,

"Well, he's always been His Majesty to me, and he always b . . . . y well will be!"

I told the King this tale and he asked me to point the man out and at once spoke to him. The words "Your Majesty" were used all right! As the King moved on he smiled at me, but I noticed that the sergeant was almost in tears with emotion, and I was delighted that I was perhaps responsible for the King speaking to him.

The King also held an Investiture on one of 2 Group's airfields in July 1944, and it was warmly appreciated by those privileged to be present. Among those to be decorated was David Atcherley, who was receiving a D.S.O. David had his arm in plaster, and the King when talking to him said,

"You must be careful, Atcherley, or you will be breaking your neck next time."

"I have already broken it three times, sir."

"You have broken your neck three times—good heavens, how did you do that?"

"The first time I fell off a piano at a guest night, sir; the second time I fell off a horse; and the third time I flew an aeroplane into a tree at night, sir," David grinned.

On May 15th I was fortunate to attend a final pre-"D" day conference held in St. Paul's School. His Majesty the King, the Prime Minister, Mr. Winston Churchill, Field Marshal Smuts, the British Chiefs of Staff, the Supreme Commander, General Eisenhower, and all the "stars" were there, with a number of commanders and some of the principal staff officers.

It opened with an address by Eisenhower, after which the three Commanders-in-Chief for the assault, Air Chief Marshal Leigh-Mallory (Air Forces), Admiral Ramsay (Naval Forces)

and General Montgomery (Land Forces), and certain others explained the plan step by step with the help of a large model of the Normandy beaches which had been erected in the centre of the room. Towards the end of the conference, to the delight of everyone present, the Prime Minister climbed on to the model and spoke of his confidence in the plan. Finally His Majesty the King gave a short address.

It was a great occasion and I am certain we all left the conference with absolute confidence in the plan, the Supreme Commander, his three Commanders-in-Chief, and the ability of the Allies to carry through this great undertaking to a victorious conclusion.

In May 1944, the Group ceased operating against V.1 sites and was turned on to attack targets directly connected with the invasion of the Continent. Our objectives were mainly gun sites, communication centres and airfields, but as "D" day drew nearer a number of bridges and heavily defended coastal batteries were added to our list of targets. The successful bombing of such small pinpoint objectives now put to the test our long training in precision bombing. The experience we had gained in our offensive against V.1 sites proved invaluable and enabled the Group to play a worthy part for its size in the vast scheme of demolition which was part of the pre-invasion plan.

On the morning of "D" day itself, our *Mitchell* squadron attacked with great accuracy gun positions directly threatening the approach of the great armada to the Normandy beach-head, and our *Bostons* flying at sea level laid the smoke screen over the invasion craft.

From now on the task of the Group was to work more closely in unison with the armies which the air forces had helped to land. In the grim battle for Caen, the Group was asked to destroy a factory which had been heavily fortified and was being used as an observation point. The thirty-six aircraft allotted the task put down such an exact pattern of bombs that not one fell outside the target area and the factory was completely demolished.

On June 22nd we were asked to bomb concentrations of enemy armour within a thousand yards of our own troops, and once again the bombing was completely accurate. This action greatly helped our armoured attack, which went in as soon as the bombing was completed.

Shortly after joining 2 Group, my staff and I had started to work out a technique for using our squadrons in a tactical role at night. The majority of our crews had done little night flying, and by day they were operating against the V.1 sites, so their training meant both days and nights of hard work. They persevered and by the time "D" day arrived they were competent to operate on the darkest of nights.

The role of the *Mitchells* and *Bostons* was to attack selected targets such as communication centres, derailing points, and villages known to be used as billeting areas for German troops, while the *Mosquitos* would search for and harass all movement on roads, railways and waterways. In the early days after the landings, some first-rate results were obtained by the combined efforts of *Mitchells* and *Mosquitos*. At ten-minute intervals one or two *Mitchells* flying at about 8,000 feet would illuminate an area with flares, allowing the *Mosquitos* to search for targets and make low visual attacks. This demanded the finest precision in timing and routeing, but for its effectiveness we had the best of testimony, that of the enemy. Many German prisoners told of their detestation of this form of attack at night, and some complained bitterly that it was unfair for troops, after fighting all day, to be bombed and shot up at night. One disadvantage of these tactics was that the flares attracted the attention of enemy night fighters, and we found that our *Mitchell* and *Boston* losses increased by nearly six per cent. The daylight commitments of these aircraft, heavy before "D" day, were growing fast with frequent calls for direct army support, so I was anxious to rest them at night, and we therefore turned our attention to developing a new technique for our *Mosquito* night operations. This involved the *Mosquitos* in carrying their own flares, flying low over the area and searching visually for any movement, and it was amazing how expert the crews became even on the darkest night. When movement was seen or suspected the crew fixed the position by the use of radar or dead reckoning navigation and then climbed to release a flare. Positioning themselves, they dived down to search for or attack the target which might be illuminated by the flare. This new method of night interdiction worked splendidly and I was able to free the *Mitchells* and *Bostons* from night operations.

Early in the campaign 2 Group carried out night interdiction on the fronts of both the British and United States armies, as at that time there were no American crews specially trained in this role nor had they the type of aircraft best suited for it.

To carry out operations in support of armies, particularly at night when identification of land forces is more difficult, it is important for the air force planners to know the exact alignment of the front, the layout of any anti-aircraft gun-defended areas,[2] and the routes by which friendly aircraft are to fly to cross the front.

In a moving battle it is sometimes difficult to get up-to-date information on all this, unless all parties concerned realise its vital importance to the air forces carrying out support.

On the night of August 4th, Peter Clapham, who was flying regularly as my navigator, and I had a lucky escape when flying in support of American forces through failure on their part to tell us they had formed a gun-defended area in a zone astride the corridor they had previously told us to follow when we flew over their section of the front to reach our patrol area. We had been in the corridor about five minutes, flying at about a thousand feet, when light anti-aircraft guns opened up on us

[2] A gun-defended area is one in which the guns are free to fire at any aircraft.

simultaneously from several directions and we were caught in a criss-cross of fire. We were hit immediately and one shell ploughed its way through the mass of pipes and electrical connections behind the dashboard, making all our instruments useless and filling the cockpit with smoke and fumes. Thinking at first we were on fire, I shouted to Peter to put on his parachute pack and prepare to jump, but I soon realised it was only smoke from the broken electrical connections and burning rubber. As we were still being bracketed by bursting shells, I dived towards the ground and we managed to get clear by flying low. I expect some gunner claimed me as destroyed. I was worried about the extent to which my aeroplane was damaged. *Mosquitos* were lightly constructed and I thought it might have been so weakened that it would disintegrate in flight. These horrid doubts crowd in on the mind once the immediate crisis is passed, and they are the cause of operational fatigue and nervous strain. However, the engines were running sweetly, which was very comforting, and we eventually gained the French coast on our homeward journey. I climbed so that we would have a better chance of getting clear of the *Mosquito* if it should start to fall to pieces. Eventually we reached base and I came in to land, congratulating myself on having brought my aircraft safely home, but when I applied the brakes after touching down it ground-looped and with a sickening rending of the undercarriage we came to rest in a cloud of dust just clear of the runway. Later inspection showed that the pipeline to one of the hydraulic brakes had been severed by a shell splinter, and so when I tried to brake they only operated on one wheel.

By the end of 1944, 2 Group was using eight *Mosquito* squadrons on night interdiction and they were taking a heavy toll of enemy road and rail transport. We had an excellent liaison with 83 and 84 Groups, whose fighters operated against the enemy by day. They informed us of movements they had observed on their evening patrols so that we could take up the offensive where they left off, and we in turn let them know the areas where we had had success at night. The enemy was attacked relentlessly and continuously day and night until eventually the paralysis started by the destruction of bridges and our heavy bomber attacks on his railway repair facilities and marshalling yards was complete. In a single night, 2 Group attacked forty-six trains and nearly a hundred road transport vehicles.

During the counter-offensive of Rundstedt through the Ardennes in December 1944 our *Mosquitos* again proved their worth. Adverse weather over our airfields had made it impossible for our fighters to operate for several days and so Rundstedt was able to assemble his forces and launch his attack. Luckily for us weather over the battle area at night was just possible for limited operations, in the course of which we attacked amongst other targets a number of heavy petrol tankers which burned gloriously. Although no one would claim that this had more than a limited effect on the enemy's mobility, the fact remains that when our land forces advanced they captured large numbers of heavy "Tiger" tanks intact but out of fuel.

Our bases were all fog-bound throughout this period and we were only able to operate at night because we had a transportable fog-clearing apparatus known as "Fido" installed at Epinoy, where 138 Wing was based. I had asked for this apparatus to be specially made before "D" day, and thanks to the good offices of my friend Clifford Hartley, who was the inventor of "Fido", it had been possible to provide it.

From "D" day until the end of the war 2 Group carried out many successful operations, but quite understandably some were more spectacular than others. Most of these involved *Mosquitos* because they were specially suited to precision bombing of small targets at low altitude and their crews were specially trained for this task. Nevertheless, the work of the *Mitchells* and *Bostons* was equally valuable to the operations of the 2nd T.A.F., and they also on occasions took part in particularly outstanding missions. One of these was when sixty-nine of our *Mitchells,* together with a *Typhoon* wing, attacked the headquarters of a Panzer Group housed in the Château of La Caine. While the *Typhoons* were tackling the parked transport, the *Mitchells* dropped over a hundred tons of bombs on the château, causing great damage and loss of life, including the death of the German Chief of Staff, Von Dawans.

The following month we made a precision attack on a large château at Châteauneuf du Fadu, not far from Brest and used as a rest centre for German submarine crews. It was known that the Germans were having difficulty providing crews for their submarines and that in the face of our intensive and successful counter-measures the strain was beginning to tell on them, so it was thought that an attack on a rest centre would be useful. We were told that the rest centre was used mainly at week-ends, so we decided to attack shortly after dawn on a Sunday morning. We calculated that it was a task for six *Mosquitos,* of which mine was one. We took off before light but the whole French coast was obscured by lifted fog, and although we tried for some time to fly underneath or find a way round it, this proved impossible and we had to abandon the raid. The following Sunday the weather forecast was marginal but we decided to make the attempt and took off about an hour before dawn. We had agreed to rendezvous and form up in formation over a point on the English coast to overcome the difficulty of getting into formation in the dark over base. Actually I narrowly missed a collision just after I took off, another aeroplane passing only a few feet over the top of mine. Peter saw it first and warned me just in time.

Although the Channel was clear, over the French coast cloud was down to two hundred feet. The formation was led by Leslie Bower.[3] By skilful navigation we managed to thread our way

[3] Group Captain L. W. Bower, commanding 138 Wing; now Air Vice-Marshal L. W. Bower, C.B., D.S.O., D.F.C.

through valleys to our target. The château was surrounded by an ornamental garden and had good approaches for a low attack. There was no smoke coming from any of the chimneys, no one was seen moving about and it appeared completely deserted. I must admit that I had a horrid feeling that the Germans had heard about our abortive mission the previous Sunday, and had abandoned the château as a rest centre. All the aircraft attacked and placed their bombs on the target, but I think we all had doubts about the usefulness of the operation. However, a few hours after landing at home we heard through the French Resistance that the raid had been an outstanding success, as there were over four hundred German sailors there, sleeping off the effects of an orgy of wine and women.

Another special mission we carried out was in support of the French maquis at Egletons, about fifty miles from Limoges. Our target on this occasion was a school being used as barracks by a strong detachment of German troops. We were to attack the building shortly before the maquis went in themselves. We flew the whole way at fifty feet and caught the Germans completely unprepared. As we attacked, arms drill was being practised and our photographs showed soldiers on the steps of the house quite unaware of their danger. This action was typical of many we undertook over a wide area of occupied Europe in support of various "forces of the interior".

On the same day as our operation against the barracks at Egletons, we carried out one of the most devastating bombing attacks of the campaign. The *Mitchells* were primarily concerned. They were on their way to another target when we learned that the Germans, who were in full retreat, were trying to cross the Seine at Rouen in very large numbers, and as the bridges were destroyed, the quays were piled up with masses of vehicles and all the approach roads to the river were jammed.

This was an opportunity target of first importance so, against all our accepted principles of careful briefing before take-off,

I gave orders that they were to be diverted to Rouen and were to bomb on a map reference which we passed to them in the air. By the time the *Mitchells* arrived, there must have been several thousand vehicles packed together. The bombs soon found their mark, and a conflagration raged throughout the area. When I received the first reports I threw in every available bomber in 2 Group, keeping up the attack with our *Mosquitos* all night. Operational scientists who went to this area a few days later reported that they had visited a scene of almost complete destruction.

Between the end of October 1944 and April 1945, we made three attacks on Gestapo headquarters in Denmark. In each instance the primary object was to destroy Gestapo records and evidence against patriots who were under arrest or about to be arrested for their activities against the Germans, with the secondary object of trying to release the prisoners held in the headquarters and killing as many Gestapo men as possible.

The first raid was directed against the Gestapo headquarters for Jutland, which was in a building in Aarhus University.

We used eighteen *Mosquitos* of 140 Wing, now commanded by Wykeham-Barnes, flying in three echelons of six aircraft and escorted by eight *Mustangs* of No. 12 Group. Peter Clapham and I flew in the first formation, and Wykeham-Barnes in the third. That day the weather was ideal for a low attack, cloud base being twelve hundred feet and in the target area visibility about a mile and a half, making interception by enemy fighters unlikely. We flew the whole way at about fifty feet, as was usual for this type of mission. As we approached Aarhus I noticed a German transport aeroplane flying on a reciprocal course to ours and about two hundred yards to one side. If the occupants saw us, they must have had quite a shock.

We approached the target so low that we were well below the level of the roof and had to pull up to clear it as we released our bombs. All eighteen aircraft bombed accurately and, looking back, Peter told me the building was wrecked. We continued flying as low as possible and at a high cruising speed until well out to sea on the way home. The aeroplane on my right had actually touched the roof of the university, knocked off half its elevator and tail wheel, and ripped a gash in the bottom of the fuselage in which was lodged a lump of masonry. The pilot had spotted a German shooting at us and, trying to silence him with return fire, had misjudged his height.

Reports from the Danish patriots were awaiting us when we reached home; they were delighted with the complete success of the raid. It transpired that the Gestapo chief for Jutland had called a conference of his subordinates from all over the province and that they numbered two hundred and forty, all of whom perished in the attack. Yet miraculously certain prisoners who were in the building survived the ordeal, and an account given by Pastor Sandbaek is interesting. He writes:

"Though many of the things which have happened to me in recent weeks stand indelibly written in my memory, many details have already become blurred. One day's terror was greater than anything I would have thought possible a few days before and yet some days later I was to be exposed to yet worse things. The bestiality of the Gestapo exceeds all description. After being arrested we were taken to Aarhus and received orders to stand against a wall till further notice. The fact that one or other of us was hit by German policemen was perhaps humiliating at the time but now appears unimportant. After being registered we were taken to our cells; the next day we were interrogated for six hours. All we had to complain of were the handcuffs which we always had to have on except when we received visitors. Day after day the interrogation became more unpleasant. They kept to threats to start with, but gradually their threats became more and more concrete. The interrogation lasted from early morning till late evening, and when it was on I received neither bread nor water. The Gestapo men relieved each other, but it was the deputy commander of the Gestapo in Aarhus, Werner, who led the proceedings. The longest interrogation, eight days after my arrest, lasted for thirty-nine hours without any rest and throughout this time I was handcuffed and given no food or drink.

I was told I had lied to the Gestapo and that I was a representative of the clergy hostile to the Germans. The interrogation
continued and every three hours new Gestapo men took over.
Finally I was taken back to the cells and I had just lain down on
the bed when two young men came in and fetched me. I was
taken to an office where the Gestapo Chief Schwitzgebel and
his deputy Werner were, and they told me that this would be
my last chance to tell the truth. I declared that I had no more
to say, after which those devils handed me over to the torturers.
They half dragged and half carried me up to the attic of the
college, took off all my clothes and put on new handcuffs. To
these a string was attached which could be tightened and caused
insufferable pain. I was thrown on a bed and whipped with a
leather dog whip. I was then taken down to the office again for
further interrogation by Werner and his two assistants. Suddenly
we heard a whine of the first bombs, while the planes thundered
across the University. Werner's face was as pale as death from
fright, and he and his assistants ran out of the room. I saw them
disappear down a passage to the right and instinctively I went
to the left. This saved my life because shortly afterwards the
whole building collapsed and Werner and his assistants were
killed. I was later rescued by Danish Patriots."

The second raid was against the Gestapo headquarters in
Copenhagen. The Gestapo had occupied the offices of the Shell
Oil Company in the centre of the town, and the building was
known as the Shell House. As usual we had the target and the
approaches to it modelled, and planned the operation with the
greatest care because the slightest error in navigation or bombing
would cause heavy casualties among the Danes.

Shortly before the operation took place, I was worried to learn
that a large number of the Resistance Movement were imprisoned in one wing of the building and it seemed certain they
would perish in the attack. I discussed this with Major Truelson,[4]
temporarily attached to my headquarters while we were planning
the operation, and he assured me that they would sooner die
from our bombing than at the hands of the Germans, adding,

"Who knows—some might not be killed and succeed in escap-

[4] The Danish officer in London in charge of Danish Resistance intelligence,
who had himself played an important part in Denmark until for his own safety
he was flown to London.

ing, as happened at Aarhus, and anyhow their death will save many more Danish lives, so don't worry."

I asked him about a house near the target which I thought was almost certain to be damaged, and he replied with a grin,

"The Germans use it for immoral purposes and so if one bomb hits it by accident, it would be excellent!"

About this time we were experiencing a spell of bad weather and for over a fortnight waited to get the right conditions over Denmark and the route from England. Meanwhile the Danish Resistance members were anxiously awaiting the attack. Many of their leaders had been arrested and we were told that unless we could destroy the Gestapo records soon, the work of the patriots in Denmark would be suppressed and most of the leaders put to death. In spite of the urgency I refused to attempt the raid until I was satisfied that the weather would be favourable, otherwise failure was certain and the patriots would be worse off than before.

We had to move *Mosquitos* from the Continent to England for this operation, so we needed a favourable forecast over a fairly wide area for forty-eight hours ahead. As I could not afford to take eighteen *Mosquitos* off night interdiction for too long a period, I was anxious not to move them to England more than one day in advance of the operation. I was in constant touch with the Central Meteorological Forecasting Establishment and at last got the news for which we had been waiting.

Shortly before the operation took place we learned that several units of the German Fleet had anchored in Copenhagen harbour. This meant a very considerable increase in the anti-aircraft defences, but we worked out by the help of our target model that if we succeeded in gaining initial surprise in our approach to the Shell House and withdrew by following a main thoroughfare through the town, flying below the rooftops, the flak from the ships could not hit us. And this was to be our plan.

As at Aarhus, we used eighteen *Mosquitos* with a *Mustang*

escort. The first section of fighters was detailed to silence some light anti-aircraft guns sited on the roof of a building near the Shell House which would have been very deadly if allowed to fire on the *Mosquitos* unchallenged. In actual fact we surprised the defences and these particular guns were not manned when our attack went in.

Bateson, who had led the raid on the Hague, led the attack, and Peter Clapham and I flew as No. 3 in his formation. We had a rough and boisterous flight across the North Sea, and flying at fifty feet above the waves called for great concentration and physical endurance under these conditions. Our windscreens were soon covered with an oily salt spray, making flying even more difficult. Near the Danish coast I opened a side window and managed with difficulty to clear a small portion of the windscreen through which I could get a limited view ahead.

As we streaked across the beautifully green Danish country-side we noticed that many Danes waved, some saluting us, and we also saw that many of the houses were flying the Danish flag.

I have rarely flown behind a better leader than Bob Bateson, who had with him that very able navigator, Sismore,[5] to help him steer a perfect course to the target. We had now worked up to our maximum cruising speed and were flying just above the ground in perfect formation, preparing for our final run up to the target. At times we had to pull up to avoid high-tension cables, trees and other obstructions, but our mean height was below tree-top level. It was an invigorating and satisfying sensation, especially as we were on our way to strike another blow at the evil Gestapo.

First one check point and then another flashed past us, and I knew we were steering an absolutely true course for the target. Peter, in his usual imperturbable and entertaining manner, was giving me a running commentary on what was going on outside,

[5] Flight Lieutenant, now Squadron Leader E. B. Sismore, D.S.O., D.F.C.

warning me of our approach to high-tension cables, chimneys and so on, an invaluable help to the pilot on such occasions. We had flown together on so many operations and understood each other's temperaments so well that it was like dancing with the perfect partner.

Copenhagen was in view and buildings began to flash past. Peter said,

"That's the target. Straight ahead of us over those small lakes."

We were now tensed for the moment of bomb release. Suddenly a bridge appeared ahead of us and I saw some poles, possibly light standards, sticking up. I eased the aeroplane up a little and then down again a few feet. By this time Peter had the bomb doors open, and the target seemed to be approaching us very fast. I pressed the bomb release and pulled up just over the top of the Shell House, and then down again almost to street level. Glancing up, I could see flak bursting just above the roof-tops. Next instant a *Mosquito* passed over us, certainly not more than ten feet above. Below us I saw people in the street throwing themselves flat and others dashing for doorways. Soon these hectic moments were over, and we were clear of Copenhagen and on our way back to Norfolk.

Unhappily Kleboe,[6] who was flying just behind me, hit one of the uprights on the bridge to which I referred, and crashed into a convent school. The second wave of aircraft, thinking this was the target, bombed the wreckage, causing loss of life to many innocent children. Naturally this unfortunate incident caused great sorrow and distress in the Group, but the Danes accepted it with brave and stoic hearts, and acclaimed the attack as a blow for freedom.

We lost three *Mosquitos* and one *Mustang* on this occasion, but succeeded in completely demolishing the Shell House, destroying all Gestapo records, liberating all the prisoners without the loss of a single life, and killing twenty-six Gestapo. It will

[6] Wing Commander P. A. Kleboe, D.S.O., D.F.C., commanding 21 Squadron.

always remain a miracle to me that anyone inside the building survived to tell the tale.

The third and last attack on the Gestapo in Denmark was on the 17th April when we raided their headquarters at Odense. Bob Bateson with Sismore his navigator again led, Peter and I flying as his No. 2. We had great difficulty in finding the target, a house in a thickly populated area and well camouflaged with netting. We must have been in the target area at least half an hour searching and of course just inviting trouble from German fighters. Happily they never appeared and eventually we found and destroyed our objective. The difficulty we had turned out to be fortunate, for it gave the people in the area time to disperse and not a single Danish life was lost.

Although I did not know it at the time, this operation was to be my last mission of the war, because not many days later the Germans capitulated.

Shortly before the war ended I won a long drawn-out war of my own with the Air Ministry over Peter Clapham. He had joined the Administrative and Special Duties Branch of the Volunteer Reserve at the beginning of the war because he was medically unfit for aircrew, but he had carried out close on seventy operational missions in the war as a member of aircrew and had won the D.F.C. and bar. It seemed grossly unfair that he should not enjoy the prestige of belonging to the General Duties Branch and be paid the same as other officers of his rank in that branch, many of whom had not seen a shot fired in anger.

To win that battle on his behalf was the only way I knew of repaying him a debt of gratitude the Service owed him for the part he had played in building up the radar capacity and efficiency of 2 Group. I could not repay him for what I owed him personally for bringing me safely through many operational trips.

In reflecting back over the work of 2 Group during my two years in command, I do not think that any commander could

have been better served by his staff and units than I was during
that period. I realise that the great achievements of the Group
were due to their devotion and sacrifice. Many deeds of courage
went unseen, many stories of gallantry untold, and many names
are forgotten, but I would like to record this account of the last
low-altitude daylight attack in the war to be carried out against
a ship target by an aircraft of 2 Group.

It happened on 1st December 1943. In response to a special
request, 2 Group was asked to intercept the blockade runner
M/V24, which had been sighted off Brest. Three *Mosquitos* took
off and landed at Predannack in Cornwall to refuel; they were
too late to attack the same night and so it was planned for the
following morning. The three aircraft were to fly at minimum
altitude escorted by a fighter squadron flying at medium height.
Owing to technical failures only one aircraft was able to carry
out the attack. In perfect visibility the pilot, Squadron Leader
Cossins, set course, located the ship and went in to the attack. He
was met by flak and set on fire before he released his bombs.
Quite regardless of his own safety, he pressed home his attack,
hit the ship and plunged into the sea. The ship was brought to a
standstill and later finished off by surface craft.

And so ended the saga of 2 Group's offensive against shipping.

Many people have asked me what my reactions were when I
heard the war was over. It is curious, but I really do not know.
What I actually *did* was to go to bed and sleep nearly twelve
hours. It had been a long war.

THE LAST MISSION

ALLAN H. GILLIS, LIEUTENANT

USAAF

Crew 29 was in a high good humor this gray, cold English morning in late September. Before take-off, we gathered under the broad expanse of one wing of our Fortress, *Lecherous Lou,* and discussed the jubilant occasion.

"The thirty-third and last straight pass at the *Herrenvolk!* Detroit I hear you calling!" Staff Sergeant Tom Travis, ball gunner, combined a Lindy hop with an Apache war dance.

Our top-turret gunner, Technical Sergeant Bill Crabtree, in his slow Texas drawl, characteristically squelched him: "Stop knocking yourself out, Tom. We'll probably just about get off the ground and blow up at the end of the runway."

Travis heaved a "Mae West" at him. First Lieutenant Joe Ross and I grinned at each other. For six months, we had been listening to this sort of high-geared kidding, and, though no one indulged in any maudlin histrionics, we both felt a twinge or two of sentiment, realizing that this was the last time the gang would be together.

Both of us were qualified first pilots. We had been assigned to the same crew after arriving in England early in the spring of 1944. The ensuing months had been full of fun, excitement, hard work, and grueling hours. On the whole, they had comprised a long and rocky road that sometimes, especially in the chilled dampness of 2 A.M. briefings, seemed to stretch endlessly before me. It would be a downright untruth to say that we were sorry to reach the end of that road. It was a good deal like graduating from school; you were glad to be through, and, at the same time, you felt somewhat reluctant to leave it all behind you.

Despite the heavy bomb and gun load, *Lecherous Lou* took off easily, gracefully, like the eager old war horse she was, with none of the earth-hugging tendencies of other ships. The two hours following take-off had always been boring to me, climbing to altitude and assembling into formation over England. But today there was no boredom. We could have assembled for five hours, and I'd not have objected. This last flight was pure enjoyment.

We had a target that would be a pleasure to smash—a factory in Germany putting out Tiger Tanks and, bane of our lives, flak guns. First Lieutenant Bob O'Connell, our well-upholstered bombardier, was particularly gleeful at the prospect, for, ever since the day a hefty hunk of flak had ripped off his oxygen mask, failing to cave in his unshaven face by a scant single inch, he had sworn a solemn personal vendetta against all German flak gunners and flak guns.

The trip across the Channel and the liberated area of Belgium was uneventful. We passed over Brussels, until just a few weeks ago one of the hottest flak areas in occupied territory. Ross and I alternated in flying the necessary close formation, wrestled through prop wash, and cursed the day we'd been assigned to four-engine ships. It was an accepted routine, after a few hours of eye- back- and arm-straining work, to moan and wait over the sad fate that had failed to place us in P-38s. The crew had become so accustomed to it they would have thought something wrong if we had omitted it.

Just before crossing into Germany, I called Technical Sergeant Ed Leitelt over the interphone and asked him to pull the valves on the Tokyo tanks so the gas could drain into the main tanks. Ed, one of the best radio operators in the group and without a doubt the most popular, was in high spirits. Married for ten years and the father of a lovely four-year-old girl, Ed was planning a joyful and long-postponed reunion with his family. Staff Sergeant Jaxon Booker, tail gunner and another Texan, interrupted us to report two ME-109s above and behind us. He kept tracking them, but before they came within range, two of our escort P-51s were hot on their tails. Booker described one Jerry going down in smoke while the other disappeared in a near-vertical dive.

We had been briefed on the possibility of enemy fighter attacks and, of course, on the inevitable flak. We soon spotted the flak, but it was off to our right and slightly below us. The lazy, black, harmless-looking puffs had always fascinated me, giving me the same sort of scared thrill that a ride on a roller coaster had when I was a kid. Today I told myself we were invulnerable. After all, it was our last mission, and being shot down on our last was hardly cricket, was it? But I wasn't kidding myself. More than once I'd seen a single burst of flak turn a powerful, throbbing four-engine plane into an enormous ball of orange flame.

For the next hour over Germany, we continued to dodge meager bursts of flak. We turned on course toward the target, and Staff Sergeant Kenneth Jorgensen, waist gunner, called over the interphone:

"There's a ship in the group behind us in flames; it's spinning in!"

"Flak off our right wing," called Sergeant Crabtree.

The interphone became crowded with reports now. Two more planes behind us had been blown to bits. Both Sergeant Booker and Sergeant Jorgensen reported that the flak was "climbing" up to our altitude. Ahead of us and uncomfortably close, flak was bursting at our level. The bursts were large, and I knew we were getting it from the 155s. Suddenly, the flak that had been ahead of us was on all sides. The whole ship shuddered and bounced as shrapnel tore into the wings, the fuselage, and the engine. I saw smoke streaming out of No. 1 engine and flames shooting out of No. 3. The oil pressure on the latter was dropping, and I had just chopped back on the throttle and hit the feathering button, when hell broke loose.

Two loud reports, like a couple of .45s being shot an inch from my ear, resounded throughout the plane. Simultaneously, the Fortress was thrown up vertically on her left wing. With all our combined strength, Ross and I struggled with the controls, narrowly avoiding crashing into the ship on our left. We were losing altitude fast, trying to escape the flak that was so persistently following us. No. 2 engine's oil pressure was almost gone, and it had to be feathered. A loud hissing sounded in our ears; it was the oxygen escaping from several broken points, and we were still at 20,000 feet.

The interphone had been clear during the past three minutes, but the silence was broken abruptly by Ed Leitelt. His voice was steady, as if by great effort, but there were undertones of strained agony.

"Al, Joe, I've been hit in the leg—bad."

Sergeants Jorgensen and Travis both rushed from the waist to administer first aid. They found the radio room full of holes and blood. Though they didn't know it at the time, Ed's leg from his knee to his ankle had been shattered to a pulp by two hundred pieces of shrapnel. Without any previous practical experience, these two men controlled the natural panicky sense of horror they felt and efficiently applied a tourniquet, gave him morphine, and administered oxygen from an emergency bottle. They did this while the flak was still hammering us. One piece of German metal tore through the radio room while Sergeant Travis was applying the tourniquet and creased the side of his head, stunning him and ripping off his helmet.

Meanwhile we had dived to 15,000 feet as quickly as we dared and were doing our best to maintain it, but this was impossible with only two engines and a full bomb load. No. 1 engine was still smoking badly, but much as we dreaded an oil fire, we didn't dare feather it—not while we were still over Germany. First Lieutenant Chuck Mundorff, our navigator, had given me an approximate heading to the nearest point in Belgium and was just about to make a correction, when a burst of flak tore through the nose, smashing Bob O'Connell's hand and entering his left leg. The nose compartment was splattered by blood. Chuck had to administer first aid to Bob, decipher the map through the blood, and figure our course at the same time.

We opened the bomb-bay doors and salvoed the bombs, letting the devil take care of the Huns they killed. With this lightening of the plane, we were able to maintain a safe air speed with a lower rate of descent. We were still over Germany, but with a strong tail wind favoring us, we knew we could make it into Belgium, if we could avoid further flak areas. All of us realized that a couple more well-placed shots would finish the job of tearing the plane apart.

The next fifteen minutes we spent praying and cursing, praying for the sight of Belgium and cursing the Huns who made us lose precious altitude in evasive action to dodge their unexpected bursts of flak. We were at a lowly 7000 feet, heading for Brussels, when we finally crossed the bomb line.

Brussels was our objective, mainly because we knew that the best medical treatment available for Leitelt and O'Connell would be there. However, No. 1 engine, in addition to smoking, had begun to shoot forth flames, and it was obvious that we could never hope to make Brussels on the one remaining engine. Chuck Mundorff spotted an airfield about five miles directly ahead of us. It was only a short landing strip from which Spitfires were taking off. I could see that one end was blocked off by bomb craters, but it was here or nowhere; so we let down over the field, shooting red flares and calling the tower.

On the final approach, Chuck called over the interphone that this was the "same damn field we bombed about two months ago when the Germans held it!" Ross and I were both struck by the irony of having to sweat out crashing into our own bomb craters, and we laughed—in a rather high-pitched way. We set the wheels down on the very edge of the runway and brought *Lou* to a brake-burning screaming halt about fifteen feet from the nearest crater. There was an ambulance waiting, and by the time we had cut the two engines the medics were inside getting Ed out of the ship.

Bob came out under his own locomotion, protesting that he had nothing but a scratch. He almost collapsed under the strain of trying to convince us, and the medics bustled him into the ambulance.

We were all pretty glum during the interrogation. Ed had been unconscious for a half-hour before landing, and no one knew just how close to death he might be. As soon as the formalities were over, we raced to the field hospital, where he had been given emergency treatment. The medical officer assured us that, though Ed's condition was serious, he would live. The wave of relief that ran through us was almost tangible.

Lecherous Lou was a sad-looking sight; she'd given her all that day. As we hauled our equipment out of her guts, we knew from now on she would be a ground-stomping spare-parts depot. It was sad, but she had brought us home from our toughest mission, and our last.

"NO ALLIED PLANE WILL EVER FLY
OVER GERMANY!"

HERMANN GOERING, *REICHSMARSCHALL*
Luftwaffe

Hermann Goering, long-time chief of the *Luftwaffe,* made the following remarks during the course of several interrogations:

"I knew first that the *Luftwaffe* was losing control of the air when the American long-range fighters were able to escort the bombers as far as Hannover. It was not long before they were getting to Berlin. We then knew we must develop the jet planes. Our plan for their early development was unsuccessful only because of your bombing attacks.

"Allied attacks greatly affected our training program, too. For instance, the attacks on oil retarded the training because our new pilots couldn't get sufficient training before they were put into the air.

"I am convinced that the jet planes would have won the war for us if we had had only four or five months' more time. Our underground installations were all ready. The factory at Kahla had a capacity of 1,000 to 1,200 jet airplanes a month. Now with 5,000 to 6,000 jets, the outcome would have been quite different.

"We could have trained sufficient pilots for the jet planes despite oil shortage, because we would have had underground factories for oil, producing a sufficient quantity for the jets. The transition to jets was very easy in training. The jet-pilot output was always ahead of the jet-aircraft production.

"Germany could not have been defeated by air power alone, using England as a base, without invasion—because German industry was going underground, and our countermeasures would have kept pace with your bombing. But the point is, that if Germany were attacked in her weakened condition as now, then the air could do it alone. That is, the land invasion meant that so many workers had to be withdrawn from factory production and even from the *Luftwaffe*.

"We bombed cities in England instead of concentrating on aircraft and engine factories despite my original intention to attack only military targets and factories, because after the British attacked Hamburg our people were angry and I was ordered to attack indiscriminately.

"Allied precision bombing had a greater effect on the defeat of Germany than area bombing, because destroyed cities could be evacuated but destroyed industry was difficult to replace.

"Allied selection of targets was good, particularly in regard to oil. As soon as we started to repair an oil installation, you always bombed it again before we could produce one ton.

"We didn't concentrate on four-engined Focke-Wulf planes as heavy bombers after the Battle of Britain, because we were developing the He-177 and trying to develop the Me-264, which was designed to go to America and return. Because our production capacity was not so great as America's, we could not produce quickly everything we needed. Moreover, our plants were subject to constant bombing.

"If I had to design the *Luftwaffe* again, the first airplane I would develop would be the jet fighter—then the jet bomber. It is now a question of fuel. The jet fighter takes too much. The Me-264 awaited only the final solution of the fuel-consumption problem. According to my view the future airplane is one without fuselage (flying wing) equipped with turbine in combination with the jet and propeller.

"Before D-Day, the Allied attacks in Northern France hurt us the most because we were not able to rebuild in France as quickly as at home. The attacks on marshaling yards were most effective, next came low-level attacks on troops, then attacks on bridges. The low-flying planes had a terror effect and caused great damage to our communications. Also demoralizing were the umbrella fighters, which after escorting the bombers would swoop down and hit everything, including the jet planes in the process of landing.

"The Allies owe the success of the invasion to the air forces. They prepared the invasion; they made it possible; they carried it through.

"Without the U. S. Air Force the war would still be going on elsewhere, but certainly not on German soil."

WORLD WAR II—PACIFIC

The war, for the United States, began early that Sunday morning of December 7, 1941, as Japanese torpedo planes, bombers, and fighters swept in over the calm Pacific to strike at Pearl Harbor, the great American naval base in the Hawaiian Islands. That devastating surprise attack was led by Taisa (Captain) Mitsuo Fuchida of the Imperial Japanese Naval Air Service. Captain Fuchida's personal, firsthand account of that attack "that shall live in infamy" is the lead story of "World War II—Pacific" and it is followed by the official report of Rear Admiral William R. Furlong, USN, who was on the receiving end of that attack aboard his flagship at Pearl Harbor.

While the U.S. was still clearing away debris from the debacle that was Pearl Harbor, the British and our other Allies were also fighting for their lives in the Pacific. Three days after that disastrous attack on the American fleet the Japanese continued to reinforce the philosophy put forth by our own "Billy" Mitchell. Japanese torpedo bombers sank the pride of the British navy, the 35,000 ton battleship HMS *Prince of Wales* and the heavy cruiser *Repulse*. On board the *Repulse* during the battle was CBS correspondent Cecil Brown. Immediately after being rescued from the South China Sea he wired the eyewitness account, that appears here, to his New York office.

The Japanese were on the offensive all over the Pacific attacking and invading U.S. territory in the Philippines, Guam, and Wake; British Malaya and Burma; Dutch Indonesia; and

French Indochina. It was going to be a long time before the United States would be able to launch an offensive against the Japanese homeland. The damage to our Pacific fleet had been extensive. Our air force was at a low ebb and General Douglas MacArthur was forced to abandon his troops in the Philippines to "return" another day. And the U.S. was heavily committed to the war in Europe against Japan's Axis partners—Germany and Italy.

The news from the Far East was all bad. America needed a psychological boost and a blow, even a token one, directly against Tokyo would certainly shake the Japanese.

In the early afternoon of April 18, 1942, Japan was rocked by an unprecedented bombing attack from a group of sixteen U.S. twin-engine, land-based bombers flying over Tokyo. The world was amazed! Where did they come from? The Japanese had overrun all of the U.S. and Allied island and mainland bases within bomber striking range of the Japanese homeland. President Franklin D. Roosevelt, in a "fireside chat," announced to the world that the bombers had come from *Shangri-la*—the mythical land in James Hilton's novel, *Lost Horizon*. But where did they come from these B-25 *Mitchell* bombers so aptly named after General "Billy" Mitchell, America's visionary of air power? Brigadier General Jimmy Doolittle, a lieutenant colonel at the time of the raid, and commander of the bomber force, gives the answer in his official report in this chapter.

One of the B-25s in Doolittle's "Tokyo Raid" force was commanded by Lieutenant Ted Lawson. Badly injured in the crash landing off the China coast, Lawson was unable to write the official report of his part of the mission. After recuperating, however, he did write the best seller, *Thirty Seconds Over Tokyo*, which was also made into a movie.

Following the crash Corporal David J. Thatcher, the engineer and gunner, became the hero of Aircraft No. 40-2261. Thatcher, least injured of the crew, wrote the official report, printed here, which is the true chronicle of that historic flight and its dramatic aftermath. The "Tokyo Raid" was the first step on the long road back. The striking victories at Coral Sea and at Midway were the next two.

When the Japanese bombs and torpedoes rained down on Pearl Harbor and destroyed a large part of our Pacific naval force in their berths, three stalwarts, by the grace of God, were at sea. One—the carrier *Lexington*—together with the *Yorktown*, their aircraft and the rest of Task Forces 11 and 17 evened up the score at the Battle of the Coral Sea. Another, the *Enterprise* together with *Hornet* and *Yorktown* rubbed it in at Midway. With the help of USAAF land-based *Flying Fortresses* they sank four Japanese aircraft carriers, and sent the rest of the enemy fleet "packing" with its heavy battleships. Lieutenant General Walter C. Sweeney, who was a lieutenant colonel at the time, commanded three flights of B-17s at Midway. Another observer of this action was a Navy pilot, Ensign George H. Gay, who had an unusual ringside seat at the battle.

Few are privileged, if one can use that term, to stand by and watch a major naval-air battle in progress. Ensign Gay, a survivor of the ill-fated U. S. Naval Air Torpedo Squadron 8, was floating in the sea, off Midway, while the battle raged around him. He participated in it, witnessed it and, like General Sweeney, reported it.

While there was a great deal of naval air action in the Pacific, strategically the air war there was no different from the air war in Europe. The enemy's industrial might that supplied his "war machine" had to be destroyed. Just as it was vital to destroy the oil refineries at Ploesti, Rumania, to deprive the Nazis of fuel, in the European Theater, so too was it necessary to knock out the Japanese oil refineries at Balikpapan in Borneo. Stretching their endurance to the limit, USAAF New Guinea based B-24 *Libera-*

tors flew the more than 1,600 statute miles, one way, to strike at Balikpapan. Lieutenant Richard S. Reynolds, a bombardier, gives his account of this raid.

The war in the Pacific, however, did differ in two ways from its counterpart in Europe. The Pacific Theater of Operations saw the use of the world's largest bomber and the mightiest weapon, by a long shot, that the world had ever known.

On August 6, 1945, Colonel Paul W. Tibbets, Jr., piloting the *Enola Gay,* a B-29 of the Twentieth Air Force, dropped the world's first atomic bomb on the Japanese city of Hiroshima. That single bomb, 8 or 9 feet long, unleashed the equivalent destructive power of 20,000 tons of TNT. It totally destroyed the city.

The Boeing B-29 *Superfort* and Atomic bomb team were to be the decisive factor that won the war against Japan.

I LED THE ATTACK ON PEARL HARBOR

MITSUO FUCHIDA, *TAISA* (CAPTAIN)

IMPERIAL JAPANESE NAVAL AIR SERVICE

In September, 1941, I was transferred from the staff of the Third Carrier Division to aircraft carrier *Akagi,* a position I had left just one year earlier. Shortly after joining my old comrades in *Akagi,* I was given additional duty as commander of all air groups of the First Air Fleet. This was an assignment beyond all my dreams. I felt that some thing big must be afoot.

It was at Kagoshima on the southern tip of Kyushu that I first learned the magnitude of events in store for me. My good friend Commander Genda, air operations officer on the staff of the First Air Fleet, came to see me at the air base and said, "Now don't be alarmed, Fuchida, but we want you to lead our air force in the event that we attack Pearl Harbor!"

Don't be alarmed? It was all I could do to catch my breath, and almost before I had done so we were on our way out to board *Akagi,* then anchored in Ariake Bay, for a conference with First Air Fleet commander, Vice Admiral Chuichi Nagumo, and his staff, including Chief of Staff, Rear Admiral Ryunosuke Kusaka.

The more I heard about the plan the more astonishing it seemed. Genda kept urging that torpedoes be used against ships in Pearl Harbor; a feat that seemed next to impossible in view of the water depth of only twelve meters, and the harbor being not more than five hundred meters in width. When I pointed this out, Genda merely grew more aggressive, insisting that if we could launch torpedoes, they would not be expected, it would add to the surprise of the attack and multiply their effectiveness. This line of argument won me over, and, despite the technical difficulties that would have to be overcome, I agreed to include torpedoes in our attack plans.

Shallow-water torpedo launching was not the only difficult problem I had to cope with. From ordinary fleet practice we had to shift our energies to specific training for this all-important mission calling for vast and intensive preparations; and, what is more, everything had to be done in haste. It was already late September, and the attack plan called for execution in December!

There was no time to lose. Our fliers had to work at the hardest kind of training. An added handicap to our efforts lay in the fact that, for security reasons, the pilots could not be told about the plans. Our progress was slow, especially with the problem of launching torpedoes in shallow water. Against my will I had to demand more and more of every man, yet none complained. They seemed to sense the intensification of the international situation and gave of themselves unquestioningly.

It was not until early November that the torpedo problem was finally solved by fixing additional fins to the torpedoes, and then my greatest worry was over. I was indeed proud of my men and felt honored to be their commander and participate in this great attack.

In mid-November First Air Fleet planes were taken on board their respective carriers which then headed for the Kuriles, traveling singly and taking separate courses to avoid attention. By the 22nd the entire force had assembled in isolated Tankan Bay on Etorofu, second island from the southern end of the chain extending northeast from Hokkaido. This force consisted of carriers *Akagi, Kaga, Soryu, Hiryu, Shokaku, Zuikaku;* battleships *Hiei, Kirishima;* heavy cruisers *Tone, Chikuma;* light cruiser *Abukuma;* destroyers *Urakaze, Isokaze, Tanikaze, Hamakaze, Kazumi, Arare, Kagero, Shiranuhi, Akigumo;* submarines *I-19, I-21, I-23;* and tankers *Kyokuto Maru, Kenyo Maru, Kokuyo Maru, Shinkoku Maru, Akebono Maru, Toho Maru, Toei Maru,* and *Nihon Maru.*

The following order was issued from Tokyo on the day that *Akagi* sailed into Tankan Bay:

Imperial General Headquarters
Navy Order No. 5

21 November 1941

To: Commander in Chief Combined Fleet Isoroku Yamamoto
Via: Chief of Naval General Staff Osami Nagano
By Imperial Order

1. Commander in Chief Combined Fleet will, at an appropriate time, dispatch to stand-by points necessary forces for execution of operations.

2. Commander in Chief Combined Fleet is empowered to use force in self defense in case his fleet is challenged by American, British or Dutch forces during the process of carrying out military preparations.

3. Detailed instructions will be given by the Chief of the Naval General Staff.

Four days later Admiral Yamamoto accordingly issued an operation order from his flagship *Nagato* at Hiroshima to Vice Admiral Nagumo, in command of the Pearl Harbor Attack Force:

The Task Force will leave Tankan Bay on 26 November and, making every effort to conceal its movement, advance to the stand-by point, where fueling will be quickly completed.

The designated stand-by point was 42°N 170°W, over a thousand miles to the north of the Hawaiian Island chain.

At 0600[1] on the dark and cloudy morning of 26 November

---

[1] East Longitude dates, Tokyo time (Zone minus 9) used primarily here; with West Longitude dates, Hawaiian time (Zone plus 10½) given in parentheses, where helpful.

our 28-ship task force weighed anchor and sailed out into the waters of the North Pacific Ocean. The sortie was cloaked in complete secrecy. A patrol boat guarding the bay entrance flashed a message, "Good luck on your mission." But even that boat was unaware of our assignment. *Akagi* signalled, "Thanks," and passed by, her ensign fluttering in the morning breeze. It would not be long before this ensign was replaced by a combat flag.

But this did not mean that the arrow had already gone from the bow. "In case negotiations with the U. S. reach a successful conclusion," Magumo had been instructed, "the task force will put about immediately and return to the homeland." Unaware of this, however, the crews shouted "Banzai!" as they took what might be their last look at Japan.

On *Akagi's* bridge Commander Gishiro Miura, the navigation officer, was concentrating all his energies on control of the ship. Whether we reached the scheduled launching point successfully rested entirely upon his shoulders. So tense was his appearance that it made us feel he was a completely different man. His usual jovial attitude had disappeared. He now wore shoes instead of his usual slippers, and he was neatly dressed, a decided change from his customary dirty, worn-out uniform. Captain Hasegawa, the skipper of the ship, stood beside him. Sitting at the flight desk control post under the bridge, I watched the gradually receding mountains of the Kuriles.

Young boys of the flying crews were boiling over with fighting spirit. Hard nights and days of training had been followed by hasty preparations, and now the sortie, which meant that they were going to war.

I felt their keen enthusiasm and was reassured. Still I could not help doubting whether Japan had the proper confidence for carrying out a war. At the same time, however, I fully realized my duty as a warrior to fight and win victory for my country.

Personally I was opposed to the operational policy. The idea of an attack on Pearl Harbor was a good one, but I thought the plan should have called for complete destruction of the United States Pacific Fleet at the outset, followed by an invasion of the Hawaiian Islands to push America entirely out of the Central Pacific. The plan covered expansion to the south—the Philippines, Malaya, Hongkong, Guam, and other such vulnerable positions. It was my opinion that if Pacific operations to the east proved successful, there would be no need for military operations in the south.

Since the United States was the main foe, I could not understand why operations were not aimed directly toward the east. Admiral Yamamoto was quoted as having said that he had no confidence in the outcome of war after the first year. Why then, did he not press and press the enemy in the first year to force an early conclusion to the war? Anyway, the immediate mission was to strike a telling blow, and my assignment carried a grave responsibility. At the time I thought, "Who could be luckier than I?"

My thoughts continued: What if the Fleet is not in Pearl Harbor? In such a case we would seek out the enemy en route to the attack. If we should meet the enemy tomorrow would Nagumo withdraw? No, we should attack and destroy him, I thought, and if the Admiral showed any hesitation, I would volunteer my views on these matters.

Such thoughts came one after another, but one remained uppermost. I was determined to do my utmost for victory.

In the meantime, the fleet had assumed formation. The carriers sailed in parallel columns of three followed by the tankers. On the outside two battleships and two heavy cruisers took positions, the whole group encircled by a screen of the light cruiser and destroyers. The submarines patrolled about 200 miles ahead of our force. The course was direct to the stand-by point, speed was fourteen knots. The first fueling at sea was carried out five days after our sortie, on 30 November.

Since our departure from Tankan Bay, a strict alert had been kept against U. S. submarines. Our course was chosen to pass between the Aleutians and Midway Island so as to keep out of range of air patrols, some of which were supposed to extend 600 miles. Another concern during the cruise was how to avoid a chance meeting with foreign merchant ships. The three submarines sent ahead of the fleet were to report any ships sighted to the fleet, which would then alter course to avoid them.

If an enemy fleet was sighted before X-2 day, our force was to reverse course immediately and abandon the operation. On the other hand, if it was one day before X day, whether to reverse course or launch the attack was left to the discretion of the task force commander.

Meanwhile, deceptive measures were being taken elsewhere to cover up our movements. On 5, 6, and 7 December sailors of the Yokosuka Naval Barracks were sent to Tokyo on a sightseeing tour. In early December *Tatsuta Maru* of the N.Y.K. Line had even left Yokohama heading for Honolulu, and she reversed course only upon receipt of the news that hostilities had begun.

Since leaving Tankan Bay we had maintained our eastward course in complete secrecy, thanks to thick, low-hanging clouds. Moreover, on 30 November, 6 and 7 December, the sea, which we feared might be rough, was calm enough for easy fueling. The not-too-rough sea also made it easy to maintain and prepare planes, and gave the men, especially the flying crews, a much needed chance to relax.

The fleet observed strict radio silence, but concentrated on listening for broadcasts from Tokyo or Honolulu. Our predominant concern was to catch any word about the outbreak of war.

In Tokyo a liaison conference between the Government and the High Command was held every day from 27 to 30 November to discuss the U. S. proposal of the 26th. It was concluded that the proposal was an ultimatum tending to subjugate Japan and making war inevitable. At the liaison conference of the 30th the decision was made to go to war. This conference also concluded that a message declaring the end of negotiations be sent to the U. S., but that efforts be continued to the last moment. The final decision for war was made at an Imperial Conference on 1 December.

Next day the General Staff issued the long-awaited order and our task force received the Combined Fleet dispatch of 1730 which said, "X Day will be 8 December."

Now the die was cast and our duty was clear. The fleet drove headlong to the east.

Why was 8 December chosen as X day? That was 7 December and Sunday, a day of rest, in Hawaii. Was this merely a bright idea to hit the U. S. Fleet off duty? No, it was not so simple as that. This day for the opening of hostilities had been coordinated with the time of the Malayan operations, where air raids and landings were scheduled for dawn. Favorable moonlight was a major consideration, three or four days after the full moon being the most desirable time, and on 8 December the moon was 19 days old.

There was another reason for choosing 8 December. Our information indicated that the fleet returned to harbor on weekends after training periods at sea, so there was great likelihood that it would be in Pearl Harbor on Sunday morning. All things considered, 8 December was the logical day for the attack.

Long before the planning of the Pearl Harbor attack we had been interested in fleet activities in the Hawaiian area. Our information showed:

1. The fleet either went out on Tuesday and returned on Friday, or went out on Friday and returned on Saturday of the next week. In either case, it stayed in harbor about a week. When it went out for two weeks, it would usually return by Sunday.

2. The fleet trained to the southeast of Pearl Harbor. Intercepted radio messages from planes flying between this training area and Pearl Harbor showed that these planes were in flight for forty to sixty minutes. Accordingly, the training area was

estimated to be near Maui, and probably north of 19°N latitude.

3. It was hard to determine whether the fleet put in to any other port during training periods, and if so, where. There were some indications that it might go to Lahaina or Marlaea for a short while.

After Japan's decision to go to war had been sent to the Attack Force, intelligence reports on U. S. Fleet activities continued to be relayed to us from Tokyo. The information was thorough, but the news was often delayed two or three days in reaching Tokyo. These reports from Imperial General Staff were generally as follows:

Issued 2200, 2 December; received 0017,
3 December

Activities in Pearl Harbor as of 0800/28 November:
Departed: 2 BB (*Oklahoma* and *Nevada*), 1 CV (*Enterprise*), 2 CA, 12 DD.
Arrived: 5 BB, 3 CA, 3 CL, 12 DD, 1 tanker.
Ships making port today are those which departed 22 November.
Ships in port on afternoon of 28 November estimated as follows:
6 BB (2 *Maryland* class, 2 *California* class, 2 *Pennsylvania* class)
1 CV (*Lexington*)
9 CA (5 *San Francisco* class, 3 *Chicago* class, and *Salt Lake City*)
5 CL (4 *Honolulu* class and *Omaha*)

Issued 2300, 3 December; received 0035,
4 December

Ships present Pearl Harbor on afternoon of 29 November:
District A (between Naval Yard and Ford Island)
KT (docks northwest of Naval Yard): *Pennsylvania* and *Arizona*
FV (mooring pillars): *California, Tennessee, Maryland,* and *West Virginia*
KS (naval yard repair dock): *Portland*
In docks: 2 CA, 1 DD
Elsewhere: 4 SS, 1 DD tender, 2 patrol ships, 2 tankers, 2 repair ships, 1 minesweeper

District B (sea area northwest of Ford Island)
    FV (mooring pillars): *Lexington*
    Elsewhere: *Utah,* 1 CA (*San Francisco* class), 2 CL
      (*Omaha* class), 3 gunboats
District C (East Loch)
    3 CA, 2 CL (*Honolulu* class), 17 DD, 2 DD tenders
District D (Middle Loch)
    12 minesweepers
District E (West Loch)
    No ships
No changes observed by afternoon of 2 December. So far
they do not seem to have been alerted. Shore leaves as usual.

Issued 2030, 4 December; received 0420,
5 December

So far no indications of sea patrol flights being conducted.
It seems that occasional patrols are being made to Palmyra,
Johnston and Midway Islands. Pearl Harbor patrols unknown.

Issued 2200, 6 December; received 1036,
7 December

Activities in Pearl Harbor on the morning of 5 December:
    Arrived: *Oklahoma* and *Nevada* (having been out for eight
      days)
    Departed: *Lexington* and five heavy cruisers
Ships in harbor as of 1800, 5 December:
    8 BB, 3 CL, 16 DD
    In docks: 4 CL (*Honolulu* class), 5 DD

Issued 1700, 7 December; received 1900,
7 December

No balloons, no torpedo-defense nets deployed around battleships. No indications observed from enemy radio activity that
ocean patrol flights are being made in Hawaiian area. *Lexington* left harbor yesterday (5 December, local time) and recovered planes. *Enterprise* is also thought to be operating at sea
with her planes on board.

Issued 1800, 7 December; received 2050,
7 December

Utah and a seaplane tender entered harbor in the evening of
5 December. (They had left harbor on 4 December.)
Ships in harbor as of 6 December:

9 BB, 3 CL, 3 seaplane tenders, 17 DD
In docks: 4 CL, 3 DD
All carriers and heavy cruisers are at sea. No special reports
on the fleet. Oahu is quiet and Imperial General Staff is fully
convinced of success.

These reports presumably had been sent from Honolulu, but
I do not know the details.

On 6 December after fueling Cardiv 2 and the Screening
Force, the 2nd Tanker Train broke off from the task force. On
the next day the 1st Tanker Train fueled the Screen again and
departed. Our force then increased speed to 24 knots and raced
toward Pearl Harbor. On the carrier decks planes were lined up
wing to wing for their final check. Maintenance crews and flying
crews worked assiduously to complete final preparation of their
planes.

About this time we received Admiral Yamamoto's message
for going to war: "The rise or fall of the Empire depends upon
this battle; everyone will do his duty with utmost efforts." The
message was immediately relayed to all hands, and the "Z" flag
was hoisted on *Akagi's* mast. This was the same signal flag that
was run up in *Mikasa* almost thirty years before in the Straits of
Tsushima.

At 1225 on the 7th (1725, 6 December in Honolulu) a message came in from submarine *I-72:* "American Fleet is not in
Lahaina Anchorage."

This anchorage was used for training because it was open
and deep. If the Pacific Fleet was there, it would have offered
our best chance for success, and we had hoped accordingly.
Receipt of the negative information, however, blasted our hopes
for such an opportunity.

It was now obvious that the warships were either in Pearl
Harbor or at sea. Admiral Nagumo was thumbing through the
message log to check on battleships reported to be in Pearl
Harbor. Completing the count, he looked up and said to the staff

members, "All of their battleships are now in. Will any of them leave today?"

The Intelligence Officer, Lieutenant Commander Ono, was first to reply: "Since five of their eight battleships reached port on the 29th, and two others left that day returning on the 6th, there is one more which has remained in harbor all this time, supposedly under repair, or perhaps in dry dock. The five ships which arrived on the 29th have been there eight days, and it is time for them to leave. I suspect they may go out today."

"Today is Saturday, 6 December," said Chief of Staff Kusaka. "Their general practice is to leave on Tuesday, which would be the 9th."

"It is most regrettable," said Genda, the Operations Officer, "that no carriers are in."

"On 29 November," Ono explained, *"Enterprise* left harbor accompanied by two battleships, two heavy cruisers and twelve destroyers. The two battleships returned on the 6th, but the rest have not yet come back. *Lexington* came in on the 29th and left with five heavy cruisers on the 6th. Thus, *Enterprise* ought to return today. *Saratoga* is under repair at San Diego, and *Wasp* is in the Atlantic. But *Yorktown* and *Hornet* belonging to the Pacific Fleet must be out here. They may have arrived with *Enterprise* today."

"If that happens," said Genda, "I don't care if all eight of the battleships are away."

"As an air man," remarked Oishi, "you naturally place much importance on carriers. Of course it would be good if we could get three of them, but I think it would be better if we get all eight of the battleships."

Chief of Staff Kusaka, who had always been strong for statistical studies of the U. S. Pacific Fleet, now spoke, "There is only a slight chance that carriers may enter the harbor on Saturday, and it seems unlikely that the battleships would leave on Saturday or Sunday. We may take it for granted that all eight battleships will be in the harbor tomorrow. We can't do anything about carriers that are not there. I think we should attack Pearl Harbor tomorrow."

Thus he set the stage for the decision of the task force commander, which was made known in the evening of the 7th when Admiral Nagumo gave his appraisal of the enemy situation:

> 1. Enemy strength in the Hawaiian area consists of eight battleships, two carriers, about ten heavy and six light cruisers. The carriers and heavy cruisers seem to be at sea, but the others are in the harbor. Those operating at sea are most likely in the training area south of Maui; they are not in Lahaina.
> 2. Unless an unforeseen situation develops tonight, our attack will be launched upon Pearl Harbor.
> 3. So far there is no indication that the enemy has been alerted, but that is no reason to relax our security.

At 0530, 7 December,[2] *Chikuma* and *Tone* each catapulted a *Zero* float plane for a pre-attack reconnaissance of Pearl Harbor. On carrier flight decks readied fighter and attack planes were lined up. The flying crews, also primed for the operation, were gathered in the briefing room. The ships pitched and rolled in the rough sea, kicking up white surf from the pre-dawn blackness of the water. At times wave spray came over the flight deck, and crews clung desperately to their planes to keep them from going into the sea.

In my flying togs I entered the operation room and reported to the Commander in Chief, "I am ready for the mission." Nagumo stood up, grasped my hand firmly and said, "I have confidence in you." He followed me to the dimly lit briefing room where *Akagi's* Captain was waiting with the pilots. The room was not large enough for all of the men, some of whom had to stand out in the passageway. On a blackboard were written the positions of ships in Pearl Harbor as of 0600, 7 December. We were 230 miles due north of Oahu.

2 West Longitude date and Hawaiian (Zone plus 10½) time used hereinafter.

Calling the men to attention, I saluted Captain Hasegawa, who spoke a brief final order, "Take off according to plan."

The crews went out hurriedly to their waiting planes. Last to leave, I climbed to the flight deck command post where Genda put his hand on my shoulder. We smiled without speaking, knowing well each other's thoughts.

Turning to me, Air Officer Masuda said, "There is a heavy pitch and roll. What do you think about taking off in the dark?" The sea was rough, and there was a strong wind blowing. The sky was completely dark, and as yet the horizon was not visible.

"The pitch is greater than the roll," I replied. "Were this a training flight, the take-off would be delayed until dawn. But if we coordinate the take-offs with the pitching we can launch successfully." I saluted the officers and went to my plane, the tail of which was striped with red and yellow to distinguish it as the commander's.

The senior petty officer of the maintenance gang handed me a white *hachimaki* (cloth headband) saying, "This is a present from the maintenance crews. May I ask that you take it along to Pearl Harbor?" I nodded and fastened the gift to my flying cap.

The carrier turned to port and headed into the northerly wind. The battle flag was now added to the "Z" flag flying at the masthead. Lighted flying lamps shivered with the vibration of engines as planes completed their warm-up.

On the flight deck a green lamp was waved in a circle to signal "Take off!" The engine of the foremost fighter plane began to roar. With the ship still pitching and rolling, the plane started its run, slowly at first but with steadily increasing speed. Men lining the flight deck held their breath as the first plane took off successfully just before the ship took a downward pitch. The next plane was already moving forward. There were loud cheers as each plane rose into the air.

Thus did the first wave of 183 fighters, bombers, and torpedo planes take off from the six carriers. Within fifteen minutes they had all been launched and were forming up in the still-dark sky, guided only by signal lights of the lead planes. After one great circling over the fleet formation, the planes set course due south for Oahu Island and Pearl Harbor. It was 0615.

Under my direct command were 49 level bombers. About 500 meters to my right and slightly below me were 40 torpedo planes. The same distance to my left, but about 200 meters above me, were 51 dive bombers, and flying cover for the formation there were 43 fighters. These other three groups were led by Lieutenant Commanders Murata, Takahashi, and Itaya, respectively.

We flew through and over the thick clouds which were at 2000 meters, up to where day was ready to dawn. And the clouds began gradually to brighten below us after the brilliant sun burst into the eastern sky. I opened the cockpit canopy and looked back at the large formation of planes. The wings glittered in the bright morning sunlight.

The speedometer indicated 125 knots and we were favored by a tail wind. At 0700 I figured that we should reach Oahu in less than an hour. But flying over the clouds we could not see the surface of the water, and, consequently, had no check on our drift. I switched on the radio-direction finder to tune in the Honolulu radio station and soon picked up some light music. By turning the antenna I found the exact direction from which the broadcast was coming and corrected our course, which had been five degrees off.

Continuing to listen to the program, I was wondering how to get below the clouds after reaching Oahu. If the island was covered by thick clouds like those below us, the level bombing would be difficult; and we had not yet had reports from the reconnaissance planes.

In tuning the radio a little finer I heard, along with the music, what seemed to be a weather report. Holding my breath, I adjusted the dial and listened intently. Then I heard it come through a second time, slowly and distinctly: "Averaging partly cloudy, with clouds mostly over the mountains. Cloud base at 3500 feet. Visibility good. Wind north, 10 knots."

What a windfall for us! No matter how careful the planning, a more favorable situation could not have been imagined. Weather conditions over Pearl Harbor had been worrying me greatly, but now with this information I could turn my attention to other problems. Since Honolulu was only partly cloudy, there must be breaks in the clouds over the island. But since the clouds over the mountains were at 1000 meters altitude, it would not be wise to attack from the northeast, flying over the eastern mountains, as previously planned. The wind was north and visibility good. It would be better to pass to the west of the island and make our approach from the south.

At 1030 we had been in the air for about an hour and a half. It was time that we were seeing land, but there was only a solid layer of clouds below. All of a sudden the clouds broke, and a long white line of coast appeared. We were over Kahuku Point, the northern tip of the island, and now it was time for our deployment.

There were alternate plans for the attack: If we had surprise, the torpedo planes were to strike first, followed by the level bombers and then the dive bombers, which were to attack the air bases including Hickam and Ford Island near the anchorage. If these bases were first hit by the dive bombers, it was feared that the resultant smoke might hinder torpedo and level-bombing attacks on the ships.

On the other hand, if enemy resistance was expected, the dive bombers would attack first to cause confusion and attract enemy fire. Level bombers, coming next, were to bomb and destroy enemy anti-aircraft guns, followed by the torpedo planes which would attack the ships.

The selection of attack method was for my decision, to be indicated by signal pistol: one "black dragon" for a surprise attack, two "black dragons" if it appeared that surprise was lost. Upon either order the fighters were immediately to dash in as cover.

There was still no news from the reconnaissance planes, but I had made up my mind that we could make a surprise attack, and thereupon ordered the deployment by raising my signal pistol outside the canopy and firing one "black dragon." The time was 0740.

With this order dive bombers rose to 4000 meters, torpedo bombers went down almost to sea level, and level bombers came down just under the clouds. The only group that failed to deploy was the fighters. Flying above the rest of the formation, they seemed to have missed the signal because of the clouds. Realizing this I fired another shot toward the fighter group. This time they noticed the signal immediately and sped toward Oahu.

This second shot, however, was taken by the commander of the dive bomber group as the second of two "black dragons," signifying a non-surprise attack which would mean that his group should attack first, and this error served to confuse some of the pilots who had understood the original signal.

Meanwhile a reconnaissance report came in from *Chikuma's* plane giving the locations of ten battleships, one heavy cruiser, and ten light cruisers in the harbor. It also reported a 14-meter wind from bearing 080, and clouds over the U. S. Fleet at 1700 meters with a scale 7 density. The *Tone* plane also reported that "the enemy fleet is not in Lahaina Anchorage." Now I knew for sure that there were no carriers in the harbor. The sky cleared as we moved in on the target and Pearl Harbor was plainly visible from the northwest valley of the island. I studied our objective through binoculars. They were there all right, all eight of them.

43) B-29 **Superforts** served as retreads from the Second World War in the Korean conflict.

44) Like the B-29 the Douglas B-26 **Invader** light bomber had served in World War II conflict, as the A-26.

45) The North American F-51 **Mustang,** one of the top fighters of the Second World War served as a fighter bomber in the world's first jet air war.

46) Carrier based U. S. Navy fighter-bombers make direct hit on Korean bridge.

47) U.S. Fifth Air Force fighter-bombers penetrated deep into North Korea to cut enemy supply lines.

48) A U. S. Strategic Air Command B-52 **Stratofortress,** loaded with conventional 750-lb. bombs, is refueled in flight by a command KC-135 tanker aircraft while en route on a mission against the Viet Cong (VC) in Vietnam. The Guam-based B-52s carry fifty-one/750-lb. bombs, twenty-four externally and twenty-seven in the bomb bay, for a total of 38,250 pounds of destructive power.

49) A B-52 drops its load of conventional 750-lb. bombs on a mission against the VC in Vietnam.

0) USAF B-57 **Canberra** tactical jet bombers airborne over the Vietnamese Mekong Delta.

51) The Douglas B-66 **Destroyer.**

52) One of the most versatile and able aircraft of the war is the tiny carrier launched Douglas A4D **Skyhawk** attack bomber.

53)   Since very few North Vietnamese fighters come aloft to do battle, all American fighters "double in brass" as fighter-bombers. Here is the 2-seater Navy carrier based **Phantom II** which has been victorious over the best the enemy had to offer—the MIG-21.

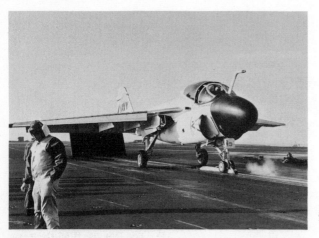

54)   An A6A **Intruder** about to be launched by catapult.

55)   En route to Vietnam for a strike against the Viet Cong, A U. S. Air Force F-105 **Thunderchief** is refueled by a SAC KC-135.

) Republic of Vietnam and USAF Douglas A-1 **Skyraiders** in action against
e VC. This retread propeller driven craft was found to be extremely effective
tactical support of ground troops.

) Closeup of the Xom Ca Trang highway in Vietnam.

ONE SPAN DROPPED

58)   Bomb craters from B-52 strikes against VC positions.

59)   The General Dynamics-Grumman F-111 B is also produced in a bomber version, the FB-111.

60) Brigadier General William "Billy" Mitchell, the "stormy petrel" of air power.

61) One of the battleships damaged by Mitchell's bombers in the controversial trials in 1921.

62)   General of the Army Henry H. "Hap" Arnold who headed
the victorious U. S. Army Air Force (USAAF) in World War II.

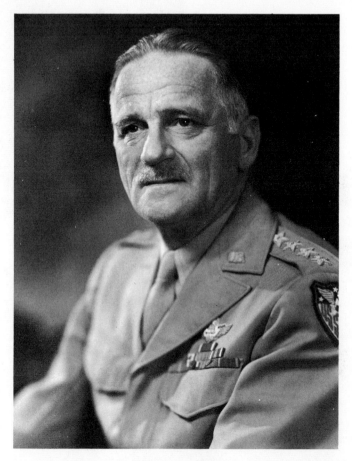

63)   Four-star General Carl Spaatz. Together with Generals Arnold, Eaker, and Doolittle, he led the world's mightiest air force.

64) The then Lieutenant Colonel "Jimmy" Doolittle ties a Japanese medal on to one of the bombs dropped by his "Tokyo Raiders."

65) World War II bomber leader and post war commander of SAC and USAF Chief of Staff, General Curtis E. LeMay.

"Notify all planes to launch attacks," I ordered my radio man who immediately began tapping the key. The order went in plain code: "*To, to, to, to. . . .*" The time was 0749.

When Lieutenant Commander Takahashi and his dive-bombing group mistook my signal, and thought we were making a non-surprise attack, his 53 planes lost no time in dashing forward. His command was divided into two groups: one led by himself which headed for Ford Island and Hickam Field, the other, led by Lieutenant Sakamoto, headed for Wheeler Field.

The dive bombers over Hickam Field saw heavy bombers lined up on the apron. Takahashi rolled his plane sharply and went into a dive, followed immediately by the rest of his planes, and the first bombs fell at Hickam. The next places hit were Ford Island and Wheeler Field. In a very short time huge billows of black smoke were rising from these bases. The lead torpedo planes were to have started their run to the Navy Yard from over Hickam, coming from south of the bay entrance. But the sudden burst of bombs at Hickam surprised Lieutenant Commander Murata who had understood that his torpedo planes were to have attacked first. Hence he took a short cut lest the smoke from those bases cover up his targets. Thus the first torpedo was actually launched some five minutes ahead of the scheduled 0800. The time of each attack was as follows:

> 0755 Dive bombers at Hickam and Wheeler
> 0757 Torpedo planes at battleships
> 0800 Fighters strafing air bases
> 0805 Level bombers at battleships

After issuance of the attack order, my level bomber group kept east of Oahu going past the southern tip of the island. On our left was the Barbers Point airfield, but, as we had been informed, there were no planes. Our information indicated that a powerful anti-aircraft battery was stationed there, but we saw no evidence of it.

I continued to watch the sky over the harbor and activities on the ground. None but Japanese planes were in the air, and there were no indications of air combat. Ships in the harbor still appeared to be asleep, and the Honolulu radio broadcast continued normally. I felt that surprise was now assured, and that my men would succeed in their missions.

Knowing that Admirals Nagumo, Yamamoto, and the General Staff were anxious about the attack, I decided that they should be informed. I ordered the following message sent to the fleet: "We have succeeded in making a surprise attack. Request you relay this report to Tokyo." The radio man reported shortly that the message had been received by *Akagi*.

The code for a successful surprise attack was *"Tora, tora, tora. . . ."* Before *Akagi's* relay of this message reached Japan, it was received by *Nagato* in Hiroshima Bay and the General Staff in Tokyo, directly from my plane! This was surely a long-distance record for such a low-powered transmission from an airplane, and might be attributed to the use of the word *"Tora"* as our code. There is a Japanese saying, "A tiger (*tora*) goes out 1000 *ri* (2000 miles) and returns without fail."

I saw clouds of black smoke rising from Hickam and soon thereafter from Ford Island. This bothered me and I wondered what had happened. It was not long before I saw waterspouts rising alongside the battleships, followed by more and more waterspouts. It was time to launch our level bombing attacks so I ordered my pilot to bank sharply, which was the attack signal for the planes following us. All ten of my squadrons then formed into a single column with intervals of 200 meters. It was indeed a gorgeous formation.

The lead plane in each squadron was manned by a specially trained pilot and bombardier. The pilot and bombardier of my squadron had won numerous fleet contests and were considered the best in the Japanese Navy. I approved when Lieutenant Matsuzaki asked if the lead plane should trade positions with us, and he lifted our plane a little as a signal. The new leader came forward quickly, and I could see the smiling round face of the bombardier when he saluted. In returning the salute I entrusted the command to them for the bombing mission.

As my group made its bomb run, enemy anti-aircraft suddenly came to life. Dark gray bursts blossomed here and there until the sky was clouded with shattering near misses which made our plane tremble. Shipboard guns seemed to open fire before the shore batteries. I was startled by the rapidity of the counterattack which came less than five minutes after the first bomb had fallen. Were it the Japanese Fleet, the reaction would not have been so quick, because although the Japanese character is suitable for offensives, it does not readily adjust to the defensive.

Suddenly the plane bounced as if struck by a huge club. "The fuselage is holed to port," reported the radio man behind me, "and a steering-control wire is damaged." I asked hurriedly if the plane was under control, and the pilot assured me that it was.

No sooner were we feeling relieved than another burst shook the plane. My squadron was headed for *Nevada's* mooring at the northern end of battleship row on the east side of Ford Island. We were just passing over the bay entrance and it was almost time to release our bombs. It was not easy to pass through the concentrated anti-aircraft fire. Flying at only 3000 meters, it seemed that this might well be a date with eternity.

I further saw that it was not wise to have deployed in this long single-column formation. The whole level bomber group could be destroyed like ducks in a shooting gallery. It would also have been better if we had approached the targets from the direction of Diamond Head. But here we were at our targets and there was a job to be done.

It was now a matter of utmost importance to stay on course, and the lead plane kept to its line of flight like a homing pigeon.

Ignoring the barrage of shells bursting around us, I concentrated on the bomb loaded under the lead plane, pulled the safety bolt from the bomb release lever and grasped the handle. It seemed as if time was standing still.

Again we were shaken terrifically and our planes were buffeted about. When I looked out the third plane of my group was abeam of us and I saw its bomb fall! That pilot had a reputation for being careless. In training his bomb releases were poorly timed, and he had often been cautioned.

I thought, "That damn fellow has done it again!" and shook my fist in his direction. But I soon realized that there was something wrong with his plane and he was losing gasoline. I wrote on a small blackboard, "What happened?" and held it toward his plane. He explained, "Underside of fuselage hit."

Now I saw his bomb cinch lines fluttering wildly, and sorry for having scolded him, I ordered that he return to the carrier. He answered, "Fuel tank destroyed, will follow you," asking permission to stay with the group. Knowing the feelings of the pilot and crew, I gave the permission, although I knew it was useless to try taking that crippled and bombless plane through the enemy fire. It was nearly time for bomb release when we ran into clouds which obscured the target, and I made out the round face of the lead bombardier who was waving his hands back and forth to indicate that we had passed the release point. Banking slightly we turned right toward Honolulu, and I studied the anti-aircraft fire, knowing that we would have to run through it again. It was now concentrated on the second squadron.

While circling for another try, I looked toward the area in which the bomb from the third plane had fallen. Just outside the bay entrance I saw a large water ring close by what looked like a destroyer. The ship seemed to be standing in a floating dock, attached to both sides of the entrance like a gate boat. I was suddenly reminded of the midget submarines which were to have entered the bay for a special attack.

At the time of our sortie I was aware of these midget submarines, but knew nothing of their characteristics, operational objectives, force organization, or the reason for their participation in the attack. In *Akagi,* Commander Shibuya, a staff officer in charge of submarine operations, had explained that they were to penetrate the harbor the night before our attack; but, no matter how good an opportunity might arise, they were not to strike until after the planes had done so.

Even now the submarines were probably concealed in the bay, awaiting the air attack. Had the entrance been left open, there would have been some opportunity for them to get out of the harbor. But in light of what I had just seen there seemed little chance of that, and, feeling now the bitterness of war, I vowed to do my best in the assigned mission.

While my group was circling over Honolulu for another bombing attempt, other groups made their runs, some making three tries before succeeding. Suddenly a colossal explosion occurred in battleship row. A huge column of dark red smoke rose to 1000 feet and a stiff shock wave reached our plane. I called the pilot's attention to the spectacle, and he observed, "Yes, Commander, the powder magazine must have exploded. Terrible indeed!" The attack was in full swing, and smoke from fires and explosions filled most of the sky over Pearl Harbor.

My group now entered on a bombing course again. Studying battleship row through binoculars, I saw that the big explosion had been on *Arizona.* She was still flaming fiercely and her smoke was covering *Nevada,* the target of my group. Since the heavy smoke would hinder our bomber accuracy, I looked for some other ship to attack. *Tennessee,* third in the left row, was already on fire; but next in row was *Maryland,* which had not yet been attacked. I gave an order changing our target to this ship, and once again we headed into the anti-aircraft fire. Then came the "ready" signal and I took a firm grip on the bomb release handle, holding my breath and staring at the bomb of the lead plane.

Pilots, observers, and radio men all shouted, "Release!" on seeing the bomb drop from the lead plane, and all the others let go their bombs. I immediately lay flat on the floor to watch the fall of bombs through a peephole. Four bombs in perfect pattern plummeted like devils of doom. The target was so far away that I wondered for a moment if they would reach it. The bombs grew smaller and smaller until I was holding my breath for fear of losing them. I forgot everything in the thrill of watching the fall toward the target. They become small as poppy seeds and finally disappeared just as tiny white flashes of smoke appeared on and near the ship.

From a great altitude near misses are much more obvious than direct hits because they create wave rings in the water which are plain to see. Observing only two such rings plus two tiny flashes I shouted, "Two hits!" and rose from the floor of the plane. These minute flashes were the only evidence we had of hits at that time, but I felt sure that they had done considerable damage. I ordered the bombers which had completed their runs to return to the carriers, but my own plane remained over Pearl Harbor to observe our successes and conduct operations still in progress.

After our bomb run I ordered my pilot to fly over each of the air bases, where our fighters were strafing, before returning over Pearl Harbor to observe the result of our attacks on the warships. Pearl Harbor and vicinity had been turned into complete chaos in a very short time.

Target ship *Utah*, on the western side of Ford Island, had already capsized. On the other side of the island *West Virginia* and *Oklahoma* had received concentrated torpedo attacks as a result of their exposed positions in the outer row. Their sides were almost blasted off and they listed steeply in a flood of heavy oil. *Arizona* was in miserable shape, her magazine apparently having blown up, she was listing badly and burning furiously.

Two other battleships, *Maryland* and *Tennessee,* were on fire; especially the latter whose smoke emerged in a heavy black column which towered into the sky. *Pennsylvania,* unscathed in the drydock, seemed to be the only battleship that had not been attacked.

Most of our torpedo planes, under Lieutenant Commander Murata, flew around the Navy Yard area and concentrated their attacks on the ships moored east of Ford Island. A summary of their reports, made upon return to our carriers, indicated the following hits: one on *Nevada,* nine on *West Virginia,* twelve on *Oklahoma,* and three on *California.*

Elements of the torpedo bombers attacked ships west of the island, but they found only *Utah* and attacked her claiming six hits. Other torpedo planes headed for *Pennsylvania,* but seeing that she was in drydock they shifted their attack to a cruiser and destroyer tied up at Pier 1010. Five torpedo hits were claimed on these targets, which were *Helena* and *Oglala.*

As I observed the damage done by the first attack wave, the effectiveness of the torpedoes seemed remarkable, and I was struck with the shortsightedness of the United States in being so generally unprepared and in not using torpedo nets. I also thought of our long hard training in Kagoshima Bay and the efforts of those who had labored to accomplish a seemingly impossible task. A warm feeling came with the realization that the reward of those efforts was unfolded here before my eyes.

During the attack many of our pilots noted the brave efforts of the American flyers able to take off who, though greatly outnumbered, flew straight in to engage our planes. Their effect was negligible, but their courage commanded the admiration and respect of our pilots.

It took the planes of the first attack wave about one hour to complete their mission. By the time they were headed back to our carriers, having lost three fighters, one dive bomber, and five torpedo planes, the second wave of 171 planes commanded by Lieutenant Commander Shimazaki was over the target area. Arriving off Kahuku Point at 0840, the attack run was ordered 14 minutes later and they swept in, making every effort to avoid the billowing clouds of smoke as well as the now-intensified anti-aircraft fire.

In this second wave there were 36 fighters to control the air over Pearl Harbor, 54 high-level bombers led by Shimazaki to attack Hickam Field and the Naval Air Stations at Kaneohe, while 81 dive bombers led by Lieutenant Commander Egusa flew over the mountains to the east and dashed in to hit the warships.

By the time these last arrived, the sky was so covered with clouds and smoke that planes had difficulty in locating their targets. To further complicate the problems of this attack, the ship and ground anti-aircraft fire was now very heavy. But Egusa was undaunted in leading his dive bombers through the fierce barrage. The planes chose as their targets the ships which were putting up the stiffest repelling fire. This choice proved effective since these ships had suffered least from the first attack. Thus the second attack achieved a nice spread, hitting the least damaged battleships as well as previously undamaged cruisers and destroyers. This attack also lasted about one hour, but due to the increased return fire, it suffered higher casualties: six fighters and fourteen dive bombers being lost.

After the second wave was headed back to the carriers, I circled Pearl Harbor once more to observe and photograph the results. I counted four battleships definitely sunk and three severely damaged. Still another battleship appeared to be slightly damaged and extensive damage had also been inflicted upon other types of ships. The seaplane base at Ford Island was all in flames, as were the airfields, especially Wheeler Field.

A detailed survey of damage was impossible because of the dense pall of black smoke. Damage to the airfields was not determinable, but it was readily apparent that no planes on the fields were operational. In the three hours that my plane was in the area we did not encounter a single enemy plane. It seemed that at least half the island's air strength must have been destroyed. Several hangars remained untouched, however, and it was possible that some of them held planes which were still operational.

Such were my conclusions as I prepared to return to our carrier. I was startled from these thoughts by the sudden approach of a fighter plane banking from side to side. We were greatly relieved to see the Rising Sun on its wings. As it came closer we saw that it was a *Zuikaku* fighter which must have been here since the first attack wave. I wondered if any other fighters had been left behind, and ordered my pilot to go to the rendezvous point for a final check. Sure enough, there we found a second fighter plane who also followed joyfully after us.

It was extremely difficult for fighter planes to fly long distances at sea. They were not equipped with homing devices and radar as were the larger planes. It was therefore planned to have the bombers, upon completion of their missions, rendezvous with the fighters at a designated point and lead them back to the carriers. Some of the fighters, however, such as these two, must have missed the time of rendezvous, and they were indeed fortunate to find our plane which could lead them safely back to the task force and their carriers.

My plane was just about the last one to get back to *Akagi* where refueled and rearmed planes were being lined up on the busy flight deck in preparation for yet another attack. I was called to the bridge as soon as the plane stopped, and could tell on arriving there that Admiral Nagumo's staff had been engaged in heated discussions about the advisability of launching the next attack. They were waiting for my account of the battle.

"Four battleships definitely sunk," I reported. "One sank instantly, another capsized, the other two settled to the bottom of the bay and may have capsized." This seemed to please Admiral Nagumo who observed, "We may then conclude that anticipated results have been achieved."

Discussion next centered upon the extent of damage inflicted at airfields and air bases, and I expressed my views saying, "All things considered we have achieved a great amount of destruction, but it would be unwise to assume that we have destroyed everything. There are still many targets remaining which should be hit. Therefore I recommend that another attack be launched."

The factors which influenced Admiral Nagumo's decision—the target of much criticism by naval experts, and an interesting subject for naval historians—have long been unknown, since the man who made it died in the summer of 1944 when United States forces invaded the Marianas. I know of only one document in which Admiral Nagumo's reasons are set forth, and there they are given as follows:

> 1. The first attack had inflicted all the damage we had hoped for, and another attack could not be expected to greatly increase the extent of that damage.
> 2. Enemy return fire had been surprisingly prompt even though we took them by surprise; another attack would meet stronger opposition and our losses would certainly be disproportionate to the additional destruction which might be inflicted.
> 3. Intercepted enemy messages indicated at least 50 large planes still operational; and we did not know the whereabouts of the enemy's carriers, cruisers, and submarines.
> 4. To remain within range of enemy land-based planes was distinctly to our disadvantage, especially since the effectiveness of our air reconnaissance was extremely limited.

I had done all I could to urge another attack, but the decision rested entirely with Admiral Nagumo, and he chose to retire without launching the next attack. Immediately flag signals were hoisted ordering the course change, and our ships headed northward at high speed.

UNDER ATTACK AT PEARL HARBOR

WILLIAM R. FURLONG, REAR ADMIRAL

USN

At about 0800 this morning, Sunday, December 7, 1941, I was on the deck of my flagship and saw the first enemy bomb fall on the seaward end of Ford Island close to the water. This one did not hit the planes parked there. Another fell immediately afterwards in the same vicinity and caused fires near the water. U. S. planes were on the ground nearby and later flames flared up from the structures at the south end of the island. The next bombs fell alongside or on board the seven battleships moored on the east side of Ford Island.

Japanese planes flew within fifty and one hundred feet of the water and dropped three torpedoes or mines in the channel on a line between *Oglala* and the seaward end of Ford Island. A torpedo hit *Oglala* and *Helena*, which were moored abreast at Ten Ten Dock with *Oglala* outboard of *Helena*. Fire was opened by *Oglala* and *Helena* anti-aircraft battery.

I at once signalled Commander-in-Chief that these three objects mentioned above which had just been dropped might be mines because they were dropped in the middle of channel. They could have been torpedoes or mines because no plume went up from them; whereas plumes over one hundred feet high went up from bombs that hit close alongside of battleships.

I then hailed two small contractor tugs, which were working

with dredges across the channel from *Oglala*, to give assistance to haul *Oglala* aft of the *Helena* in order that *Helena* could sortie. I obtained submersible pumps from the *Helena* but then discovered that there was no power in the *Oglala* because of the hit which flooded the fireroom, and she could not use her pumps.

One Japanese plane was shot down over the harbor and came down in flames to seaward of Ford Island but probably on land. There was no trouble distinguishing Japanese planes because the red Sun painted on the side showed plainly.

Meanwhile planes were strafing as well as bombing. Planes kept coming for quite some time, making it difficult to estimate numbers. I saw four battleships hit with bombs and fires broke out. I saw one battleship turn over. There were six to ten enemy planes visible at any one time over the harbor.

The *Nevada* got under way and passed out of channel near where I had seen the three mines or torpedoes fall. When she arrived in this vicinity her bow apparently hove up as if she had passed over a mine and about a minute later two bombs fell, one of which hit her starboard topside throwing up flame and smoke, and the other missed close along the port side, throwing up a plume of water.

During all of this, as these dive bombs flew within five hundred to a thousand feet of the *Oglala*, we were given an excellent opportunity to fire our anti-aircraft battery and did so for over an hour, the *Helena* firing over us.

The *Oglala* was got astern of the *Helena* with help of tugs mentioned, and was hauled and pushed in to the pier and secured with many wires and manila lines. As all compartments were closed below she settled slowly.

At this time I ordered the two tugs which were assisting the *Oglala* to go to the assistance of the *Nevada*, which was then in the channel between the floating dry-dock and seaward end of Ford Island.

On the second attack I saw a bomb drop which hit the forward part of the *Pennsylvania* or in the dry-dock ahead of the *Pennsylvania*. Two destroyers of Destroyer Division Five were in the dock ahead of the *Pennsylvania,* and flames went up from them.

Another Japanese plane was hit and fell in flames seaward of 1010 dock, possibly falling near the entrance of the channel. It went down in a streak of flame as did the first one mentioned. Of the two planes that I saw shot down in this part of the harbor one was in flames after passing over the battleships from north to south about 2,000 feet altitude; the other plane shot down flew over the harbor at about 2,000 feet in the same general direction but closer to 1010 dock and pier, and was engaged by vessels on this side of the harbor. Guns operable by hand proved particularly advantageous, especially where power was knocked out of the steaming firerooms by torpedoes.

Following the bombing of the *Pennsylvania,* I saw a bomb fall near or on the destroyer *Shaw* in the floating dry-dock. This destroyer was later in flames.

Meanwhile the *Oglala* had taken a list of about 40 degrees. The wire lines to the deck parted and her port upper deck rail was so far under that she might sink suddenly at any moment. I ordered all hands to abandon the ship shortly after 9:00 A.M., the only ones remaining being the guns' crews and myself. The *Oglala* kept up the anti-aircraft fire until the ship's list was at such an angle that the men on the machine guns were sliding off the deck and the angle was too steep to longer stick on the deck and serve the 3″ gun. During this last period the Japanese planes were strafing us, not bombing. As the ship was about to turn over, I ordered the guns' crews to leave the ship, and left with them. The machine guns were slid off the top of deckhouse to the pier as the ship went over and were set up on the pier.

The guns' crews manned their battle stations promptly and stood to their guns during bombing and strafing as if at target practice, keeping up a continuous fire at enemy planes during the bombing and strafing. The signal force manned their bridge stations and sent signals during the action; one to sortie and one to the *Nevada* warning her of mines, during which time the bridge was struck by machine gun bullets. The men on the fires when the fireroom was flooding very promptly turned off the oil fires and no one suffered oil burns. . . .

Above dictated at 11:00 A.M.

TORPEDO BOMBERS SINK THE "REPULSE"

CECIL BROWN, WAR CORRESPONDENT

COLUMBIA BROADCASTING SYSTEM

I was standing on the flag deck slightly forward amidships when nine Jap bombers approached at ten thousand feet strung in a line, clearly visible in the brilliant sunlit sky. They flew directly over our ship and our antiaircraft guns were screaming constantly.

Just when the planes were passing over, one bomb hit the water beside where I was standing, so close to the ship that we were drenched from the waterspout. Simultaneously another struck the *Repulse* on the catapult deck, penetrating the ship and exploding below in a marine's mess and hangar. Our planes were subsequently unable to take off. At 11:27 fire is raging below, and most strenuous efforts are under way to control it. All gun crews are replenishing their ammunition and are very cool and cracking jokes. There are a couple of jagged holes in the funnel near where I am standing.

It's obvious the Japs flew over the length of the ship, each dropping three bombs, so that twenty-seven bombs fell around us at first in their attack. Brilliant red flashes are spouting from our guns' wells. The *Prince of Wales* is half a mile away. Destroyers are at various distances throwing everything they have into the air. A splash about two miles off our port beam may be anti-aircraft but we are uncertain. At 11:40 the *Prince of*

Wales seems to be hit. She's reduced her speed. Now they're coming to attack us. The communication system shouts "stand by for barrage." All our guns are going. We are twisting and snaking violently to avoid torpedoes. The Japs are coming in low, one by one in single waves. They're easy to spot. Amid the roar from the guns aboard the *Repulse* and the pom-poms of antiaircraft fire, we are signaled, "We've a man overboard."

Two Jap aircraft are approaching us. I see more of them coming with the naked eye. I again count nine. They're torpedo bombers and are circling us about a mile and a half or two miles away. 11:45—now there seems to me more bombers but they are circling like vultures at about one thousand feet altitude. The guns are deafening. The smell of cordite is almost suffocating and explosions are ear-shattering and the flashes blinding. The officer beside me yells, "Here comes a tin fish."

A Jap torpedo bomber is heading directly for us, two hundred yards above the water. At 11:48 he's less than five hundred distant, plowing onward. A torpedo drops and he banks sharply and his whole side is exposed to our guns but instead of driving away he's making a graceful dive toward the water. He hits and immediately bursts into flame in a gigantic splash of orange against the deep blue sky and the robin's-egg blue water. Other planes are coming, sweeping low in an amazing suicide effort to sink the *Repulse*.

Their daring is astonishing, coming so close you can make out the pilot's outline. One coming in at 11:48 to our starboard just dropped a torpedo. A moment later I hear shouts of joy indicating that he was brought down but I didn't see that. We also claim we brought down two high-level bombers previously but I didn't see these crash. At least at the moment I have no recollection of seeing them.

At 12:01 another wave of torpedo bombers is approaching. They are being met with everything we've got except our 14-inchers. Beside me the signal officer flashes word from Captain Tennant to the *Prince of Wales*. "We eluded all torpedoes this second attack." It's fascinating to watch our tracer bullets speeding toward the Jap bombers. 12:03: we've just shot down another torpedo bomber who is about four hundred yards away and we shot it out. All of its motors are afire and disintegrating pieces of the fuselage are flying about. Now it disappears over the surface of the water into scrap. The brilliant orange from the fire against this blue sky is so close it's startling. All the men are cheering at the sight. It's so close it seems you could almost reach out and touch the remains of this Jap bomber.

At 12:15 the *Wales* seems to be stopped definitely. I've been too busy to watch the attacks against her but she seems in utmost difficulty. Her guns are firing constantly and we are both twisting. One moment the *Wales* is at our starboard, the next it's at our port. I'm not watching the destroyers but they have not been subjected to air attacks. The Japs are throwing everything recklessly against the two capital ships.

There's fire aboard us, it's not out. I just saw some firemen and fire-control parties. The calmness of the crews is amazing. I have constantly roved from one side of the flag deck to the other during the heavy firing and attacks and the cool precision of all hands has seemed unreal and unnatural. Even when they are handing up shells for the service guns, each shell is handed over with a joke. I never saw such happiness on men's faces. This is the first time these gun crews have been in action in this war and they are having the time of their lives. 12:20: I see ten bombers approaching us from a distance. It's impossible to determine whether this will be a high-level attack or another torpedo-bomber attack. "Stand by for barrage" comes over the ship's communication system.

One plane is circling around, it's now at three or four hundred yards approaching us from the port side. It's coming closer, head on, and I see a torpedo drop. It's streaking for us. A watcher shouts, "Stand by for torpedo" and the tin fish is streaking directly for us. Someone says: "This one got us." The torpedo struck the side on which I was standing about twenty yards astern of my position. It felt like the ship had crashed into a well-rooted dock. It threw me four feet across the deck but I did not fall and I did not feel any explosion. Just a very great jar. Almost immediately it seemed we began to list and less than a minute later there was another jar of the same kind and the same force, except that it was almost precisely the same spot on the starboard side.

After the first torpedo, the communication system coolly announced: "Blow up your life belts." I was in this process when the second torpedo struck and the settling ship and the crazy angle were so apparent I didn't continue blowing my belt.

That the *Repulse* was doomed was immediately apparent. The communication system announced, "Prepare to abandon ship. May God be with you." Without undue rush we all started streaming down ladders, hurrying but not pushing. It was most difficult to realize I must leave the ship. It seemed so incredible that the *Repulse* could or should go down. But the *Repulse* was fast heeling over to port and walking ceased to become a mode of locomotion. I was forced to clamber and scramble in order to reach the side. Men were lying dead around the guns. Some were half-hidden by empty shell cases. There was considerable damage all around the ship. Some of the men had been machine-gunned. That had been unquestioned fact.

All around me men were stripping off their clothes and their shoes and tossing aside their steel helmets. Some are running alongside the three-quarters exposed hull of the ship to reach a spot where they can slide down the side without injuring themselves in the jagged hole in the ship's side. Others are running to reach a point where they have a shorter dive to the water. I am reluctant to leave my new portable typewriter down in my cabin and unwilling to discard my shoes which I had made just a week before. As I go over the side the *Prince of Wales* half a mile away seems to be afire but her guns are still firing the heaviest. It's most obvious she's stopped dead and out of control due to her previous damage.

The air attack against the *Prince of Wales* carried out the same scheme directed against the *Repulse*. The Japs were able to send two British capital ships to the bottom because of, first, a determined air-torpedo attack and, second, the skill and the efficiency of the Japanese operations. It's apparent that the best guns and crews in the world will be unable to stem a torpedo-bombing attack if the attackers are sufficiently determined.

According to the best estimate obtainable, the Japs used in their operations against both the *Wales* and the *Repulse* eighty-six bombers; eighteen high-level bombers and approximately twenty-five torpedo bombers against the *Repulse* and probably an equal number against the *Prince of Wales.* In the case of the *Wales,* however, the Japs started with torpedo bombing instead of initial high-level bombing. In the first attack, one torpedo hit the *Wales* in the afterpart. Some survivors believe the *Wales* was hit twice in the initial attack, then followed two more torpedo attacks, both successful. The final attack on the *Wales* was made by high-level bombers around ten thousand feet. When that attack came, the *Wales* was sinking fast and everyone threw himself down on deck.

Most of the guns were unmanageable as a result of the list and the damage. I jumped into the water from the *Repulse* at 12:35. While I was in the water, the *Wales* continued firing for some time. The *Wales* suffered two direct hits by bombs on the deck. Like the attack on the *Repulse,* the Japs flew across the length of the *Wales* in a single line, each bomber dropping a stick. One officer said a child of six could see some of them were going to hit us. During the entire action Admiral Tom Phillips, Commander in Chief of the Far East Fleet, and Captain Leech, skipper of the *Prince of Wales,* were on the bridge.

While the torpedo bombers were rushing in toward the *Wales,* dropping tin fish and machine-gunning the decks, Phillips clambered up on the roof of the bridge and also atop the gun turrets to see better and to direct all phases of the action.

When it was apparent that the *Wales* was badly hit, the Admiral issued an order to the flag officer for the destroyer then lying alongside close by. "Signal to Singapore to send tugs to tow us." Evidently up to that moment, Phillips was not convinced that the *Wales* was sinking. The last order issued by Phillips came at approximately 1:15. It said, "Blow up your life belts."

Later the ship was under water. Phillips and Leech were the last from the *Wales* to go over the side and they slid into the water together. It's probable that their reluctance to leave the ship until all possible men had left meant their death, since it's most likely they were drawn down by the suction when the *Wales* was on her side and then settled at her stern with her bow rising into the air.

Swimming about a mile away, lying on top of a small stool, I saw the bow of the *Wales*. When Phillips signaled to ask Singapore to send tugs, the *Wales* already had four torpedoes in her. Like the *Repulse,* the *Wales* gun crews were very cool and although many guns were no longer effective the crew stood beside them. When the final high-level bombing attack came, only three guns were capable of firing, except the 14-inchers, which naturally did not go into action. I did not meet Phillips, but last week when I visited the *Wales* at the naval base, I had a long talk with Captain Leech. He's a jovial, convivial, smiling officer who gave me the impression of the greatest kindliness and ability. The *Wales* carried a complement of seventeen hundred; the *Repulse* twelve hundred and fifty officers and ratings. When the *Wales* sank, the suction was so great it ripped off the life belt of one officer more than fifty feet away. A fortunate feature of the sinking of both the *Repulse* and the *Wales* was that neither blew up.

Since the tide was strong and there was an extremely powerful suction from both ships, it was extremely difficult to make any progress away from the ship in the thick oil. The gentle, quiet manner in which these shell-belching dreadnoughts went to their last resting place without exploding was a tribute of gratitude from two fine ships for their fine sailors.

THE TOKYO RAIDERS FROM SHANGRI-LA
(*An Official Report*)

[1] JAMES H. DOOLITTLE, LIEUTENANT COLONEL

USAAF

WAR DEPARTMENT

Washington
June 5, 1942

To: The Commanding General of the Army Air Forces

Subject: Report on the Aerial Bombing of Japan

The joint Army-Navy bombing project was conceived, in its final form, in January and accomplished in April, about three months later. The object of the project was to bomb the industrial centers of Japan. It was hoped that the damage done would be both material and psychological. Material damage was to be the destruction of specific targets with ensuing confusion and retardation of production. The psychological results, it was hoped, would be the recalling of combat equipment from other theaters

---

[1] At the time of the Tokyo Raid, Doolittle was a lieutenant colonel. He later commanded the Eighth Air Force in Europe as a major general and was subsequently promoted to lieutenant general.

for home defense thus effecting relief in those theaters, the development of a fear complex in Japan, improved relationships with our Allies, and a favorable reaction on the American people.

The original plan was to take off from and return to an aircraft carrier. Take off and landing tests conducted with three B-25's at and off Norfolk, Virginia, indicated that take off from the carrier would be comparatively easy but landing back on again extremely difficult. It was then decided that a carrier take-off would be made some place East of Tokyo and the flight would proceed in a generally Westerly direction from there. Fields near the East Coast of China and at Vladivostok were considered as termini. The principal advantage of Vladivostok as a terminus was that it was only about 600 miles from Tokyo against some 1200 miles to the China Coast and range was critical. Satisfactory negotiation could not, however, be consummated with the Russian Government and the idea of going to Vladivostok was therefore abandoned.

A cruising range of 2400 miles with a bomb load of 2000 lbs. was set as the airplane requirement. A study of the various airplanes available for this project indicated that the B-25 was best suited to the purpose. The B-26 could have done the job as far as range and load carrying capacity was concerned but it was felt that the carrier take-off characteristics were questionable. The B-23 could have done the job but due to the larger wing span fewer of them could be taken and clearance between the right wing tip and the carrier island would be extremely close.

Twenty-four airplanes were prepared for the mission. Preparation consisted of installing additional tankage and removing certain unnecessary equipment. Three additional gasoline tanks were installed. First a steel gasoline tank of about 265 gallon capacity was manufactured by the McQuary Company and installed by the Mid-Continent Airlines at Minneapolis. This tank was later removed and replaced by a 225 gallon leak-proof tank manufactured by the United States Rubber Company at Mishawaka, Indiana. Considerable difficulty was experienced with this rubber leak-proof tank due to leaks in the connections and due to the fact that after having made one fairly satisfactory tank the outer case was reduced in size, in order to facilitate installation, without reducing the size of the inner rubber container and consequently wrinkles developed reducing the capacity and increasing the tendency to failure and leakage. Putting air pressure on the tank increased the capacity about ten to fifteen gallons and new outer covers alleviated the trouble. It was, however, not possible for the manufacturer to provide new covers for all of the tanks before we were obliged to take off. One serious tank failure occurred the day before we were to take off. The leak was caused by a failure of the inner liner resulting from sharp wrinkles which in turn were caused by the inner liner being too large and the outer case too small.

Room remained, in the bomb bay, underneath this tank to permit carrying four 500 lb. demolition bombs or four 500 lb. incendiary clusters. It was necessary, in order to carry the bomb load, to utilize extension shackles which were also provided by the McQuary Company.

The crawl-way above the bomb bay was lined and a rubber bag tank, manufactured by the U. S. Rubber Company, and holding about 160 gallons was installed. The vent for this tank, when turned forward provided pressure and forced the gasoline out of the tank. When turned aft the vent sucked the air and vapor out of the tank and permitted it to be collapsed (after the gasoline was used) and pushed to one side. After this was done the ship was again completely operational as crew members could move forward or aft through the crawl-way. Collapsing the tank, sucking out the vapor, and pushing it over to one side minimized the fire hazard. A very considerable amount of trouble was encountered with this tank due to leaks developing in the seams. This trouble was reduced through the use of a heavier material and more careful handling of the tank.

The third tank was a 60 gallon leak-proof tank installed in the place from which the lower turret was removed. This tank was a regular 2′ x 2′ x 2′ test cell with a filler neck, outlet and vent provided. The filler neck of this rear tank was readily available in flight. Ten 5-gallon cans of gasoline were carried in the rear compartment, where the radio operator ordinarily sat, and were poured into this rear tank as the gasoline level went down. These cans later had holes punched in them so that they would sink and were thrown overboard. This gave a total gallonage of 646 gallons in the main tank, 225 gallons in the bomb bay tank, 160 gallons in the crawl-way tank, 60 gallons in the rear turret tank, and 50 gallons in 5-gallon tins, or 1141 gallons, some 1100 gallons of which were available. It might be pointed out here that all of the gasoline could not be drained from the tanks and that in filling them extreme care had to be taken in order to assure that all air was out and they were completely full. This could only be accomplished by filling, shaking down the ship and topping off again.

The extra tanks and tank supports were designed by and installed under the supervision of the Materiel Division of the Army Air Forces.

Two wooden 50 caliber guns were stuck out of the extreme tip of the tail. The effectiveness of this subterfuge was indicated by the fact that no airplane, on the flight, was attacked from directly behind. The lateral attacks were more difficult for the attacker and gave our machine gunners a better target.

De-icers and anti-icers were installed on all airplanes. Although these had the effect of slightly reducing the cruising speed they were necessary for insurance and also because it was not decided until shortly before leaving on the mission whether Vladivostok or East China was to be the terminus. Should East China be the terminus no ice was to be expected at lower altitudes but icing conditions did still prevail along the Northern route to Vladivostok.

Inasmuch as it was decided that all bombing would be done from low altitudes and the Norden bomb sight did not particularly lend itself to extremely low altitude bombing, the bomb sight was removed and a simplified sight designed by Captain C. R. Greening was installed in its place. Actual low altitude bombing tests carried out at 1500 feet showed a greater degree of accuracy with this simplified sight than we were able to obtain with the Norden. This not only permitted greater bombing accuracy but obviated the possibility of the Norden sight falling into enemy hands. Captain Greening deserves special commendation for the design of this sight.

Difficulty was experienced in getting the lower turret to function properly. Trouble was encountered with the turret activating mechanism and with the retracting and extending mechanism. These troubles were finally overcome in large part. It was then found that the attitude of the gunner and the operation of the sight were so difficult that it would not be possible in the time available to train gunners to efficiently operate the turret. As a consequence of this, and also in order to save weight and permit the installation of the additional gas tanks, the lower turret was removed and a plate put over the hole where it stuck through the bottom of the fuselage.

We feel very strongly that in the present race to provide airplanes and crews in the greatest possible number in the shortest length of time that only equipment that is *natural* to use is satisfactory. Time does not permit the training of personnel to operate unnatural equipment or equipment that requires a high degree of skill in its operation. This thought should be kept in mind in the design, construction and operation of our new fire control apparatus.

Due to a shortage of 50 caliber ammunition the machine guns had not been fired and when we started training we immediately found that they did not operate properly. Some did not fire at all and the best of them would only fire short bursts before jamming.

Mr. W. C. Olson from Wright Field was largely responsible for overcoming this difficulty. He supervised the replacement of faulty parts, the smoothing down of others, the proper adjustment of clearances and the training of gun maintenance crews. When we left on our mission all guns were operating satisfactorily.

When the turret guns were fired aft with the muzzle close to the fuselage it was observed that the blast popped rivets and tore the skin loose. As a result of this it was necessary to install steel blast plates.

Pyrotechnics were removed from the airplane in order to reduce the fire hazard and also for the slight saving in weight. Two conventional landing flares were installed immediately forward of the rear armored bulkhead. This gave a maximum of protection against enemy fire. There was no dropping mechanism for the landing flares. It was planned, if it became necessary to use them, that they be thrown out by the rear gunner. A lanyard attached to the parachute flare and the fuselage would ordinarily remove the case some 6 feet from the airplane. It is suggested that pyrotechnics be installed against the armored bulkhead instead of along the sides of the fuselage.

Inasmuch as it was planned, in the interest of security, to maintain radio silence throughout the flight and weight was of the essence, the 230 lb. liaison radio set was removed.

The lead ship and each of the flight leaders' ships were equipped with small electrically operated automatic cameras which took 60 pictures at one-half second intervals. The cameras could be turned on at any time by the pilot and were automatically started when the first bomb dropped. Cameras were located in the extreme tip of the tail between the two wooden 50 caliber guns. Lens angle was 35°. As they were pointed down 15° the rearward field, in level attitude, covered 2½° above the horizon and 32½° below. In tests they operated perfectly.

The other ten airplanes carried 16 m.m. movie cameras similarly mounted.

All special equipment such as emergency rations, canteens, hatchets, knives, pistols, etc. were made secure before take-off.

Special 500 lb. demolition bombs were provided, through the cooperation of Colonel Max F. Schneider of A-4, by the Ordnance Department. These bombs were loaded with an explosive mixture containing 50 per cent TNT and 50 per cent Amatol. They were all armed with a $\frac{1}{10}$ of a second nose fuses and a $\frac{1}{40}$ of a second specially prepared tail fuses. The $\frac{1}{10}$ of a second nose fuse was provided in case the tail fuse failed. 11 second delay tail fuses were available to replace the $\frac{1}{40}$ of a second tail fuse in case weather conditions made extremely low bombing necessary. In this case the tail fuse was to be changed just before take-off and the nose fuse in that case would not be armed.

The Chemical Warfare Service provided special 500 incendiary clusters each containing 128 incendiary bombs. These clusters were developed at the Edgewood Arsenal and test dropped by the Air Corps test group at Aberdeen. Several tests were carried on to assure their proper functioning and to determine the dropping angle and dispersion. Experimental work on and production of these clusters was carried on most efficiently.

A special load of 50 caliber ammunition was employed. This load carried groups of one tracer, two armor piercing and three explosive bullets.

The twenty-four airplanes for the Tokyo project were obtained from the 17th Bombardment Group. Inasmuch as the airplanes had been obtained from this group and there were, therefore, crews available without airplanes, together with the fact that these crews were experienced in the use of these particular airplanes, the crews were also obtained from this source. It was explained to the Commanding Officer of the 17th Bombardment Group, Lieutenant Colonel W. C. Mills, that this was to be a mission that would be extremely hazardous, would require a high degree of skill and would be of great value to our defense effort. Volunteers for this mission were requested. More people than we could possibly use immediately volunteered. Twenty-four crews were ordered to Eglin Field for a final course of training. These crews together with the ground maintenance men, armorers, etc., proceeded to Eglin Field, Valparaiso, Florida, as rapidly as the airplanes could be converted and made available. The first of them arrived just before the first of March and the rest just after.

Concentrated courses of instruction were given at Eglin Field. The instruction included carrier take-off practice under the supervision of Lieutenant Henry Miller of the U. S. Navy. This practice was carried out on one of the auxiliary fields near Eglin. White lines were drawn on two of the runways of this field. Take-off practice was carried out with light load, normal load, and overload up to 31,000 lbs. In all cases the shortest possible take-off was obtained with flaps full down, stabilizer set three-fourths, tail heavy, full power against the brakes and releasing the brakes simultaneously as the engine came up to revs. The control column was pulled back gradually and the airplane left the ground with the tail skid about one foot from the runway. This appeared to be a most unnatural attitude and the airplane took off almost in a stall. In spite of the high wing loading and unnatural attitude, the comparatively low power loading and good low-speed control characteristics of the airplane made it possible to handle the airplane without undue difficulty in this attitude. Only one pilot had difficulty during the take-off training. Taking off into a moderately gusty wind with full load, he permitted the airplane to side slip back into the ground just after take-off. No one was hurt but the airplane was badly damaged. While we do not recommend carrier take-off procedure for normal take-offs, it does permit of a much shorter take-off, and may be employed in taking off from extremely short or soft fields. With about a ten-mile wind take-offs with light load were effected with as short a run as 300 feet. With a normal load of 29,000 lbs. in 600 feet, and with 31,000 lbs. in less than 800 feet. The tact, skill and devotion to duty of Lieutenant Miller, of the U. S. Navy, who instructed our people in carrier take-offs procedure deserves special commendation.

Special training was given in cross country flying, night flying and navigation. Flights were made over the Gulf of Mexico in order to permit pilots and navigators to become accustomed to flying without visual or radio references or land marks.

Low altitude approaches to bombing targets, rapid bombing and evasive action were practiced. Bombing of land and sea targets was practiced at 1500, 5000 and 10,000 feet. Low altitude bombing practice was specialized in. One hundred pound sand loaded bombs were used in the main but each crew was given an opportunity to drop live bombs as well.

Machine gun practice was carried on on the ground and in the air. Ground targets were attacked and it was intended to practice on tow targets as well but time did not permit. In order to get practice in operating the turret, pursuit planes simulated attack on our bombers and the gunners followed them with their empty guns.

The first pilots were all excellent. The co-pilots were all good for co-pilots. The bombardiers were fair but needed brushing up. The navigators had had good training but very little practical experience. The gunners, almost without exception, had never fired a machine gun from an airplane at either a moving or stationary target.

In spite of a large amount of fog and bad weather which made flying impossible for days at a time and the considerable amount of time required to complete installations and make the airplanes operational at Eglin Field the training proceeded rapidly under the direction of Captain Edward York. In three weeks ships and crews were safely operational although additional training of the crews and work on the ships would have improved their efficiency.

On March 25, the first of 22 ships (one airplane, as previously mentioned was wrecked during take-off practice and another airplane was damaged due to the failure of the front wheel shimmy damper. While taxiing normally the front wheel shimmied so violently that a strut fitting carried away and let the airplane down on its nose. Although the damage was slight there was not time to repair it) took off from Eglin Field for Sacramento Air Depot where the airplanes were to have a final check and the remaining installations were to be made. On March 27, all airplanes had arrived.

On March 31 and April 1, 16 planes were loaded on the U. S. S. *Hornet* alongside of the dock at the Alameda Air Depot. Although 22 planes were available for loading there was room on deck for only 15. Sixteen planes were actually loaded but it was intended that the 16th plane would take off the first day out in order that the other pilots might have an opportunity to at least see a carrier take-off. A request had previously been made of Admiral William F. Halsey, who was in charge of the task force, to permit each one of the pilots a carrier take-off prior to leaving on the mission or to permit at least one pilot to take off in order that he might pass the information obtained on to the others. Admiral Halsey did not agree to this due to the delay it would entail. He did, however, agree to take one extra plane along and let it take off the first day out or the first favorable weather thereafter. It was later agreed to keep this plane aboard and increase our component from 15 to 16.

Training was continued on the carrier. This training consisted of a series of lectures on Japan given by Lieutenant Stephen Jurika, Jr. of the Navy, lectures on first aid and sanitation by Lieutenant T. R. White, M.C. our flight surgeon, lectures on gunnery, navigation and meteorology by members of our own party and officers from the *Hornet*, and a series of lectures on procedure by the writer.

Actual gunnery and turret practice was carried on using kites flown from the *Hornet* for targets.

Celestial navigation practice for our navigators was supervised by the *Hornet* navigating officer. Star sights were taken from the deck and from the navigating compartment in the airplanes. In this way a high degree of proficiency was developed and satisfactory optical characteristics of the navigating compartment window were assured.

A great deal of thought was given to the best method of attack. It was felt that a take-off about 3 hours before daylight arriving over Tokyo at the crack of dawn would give the greatest security, provide ideal bombing conditions, assure the element of surprise and permit arrival at destination before dark. This plan was abandoned because of the anticipated difficulty of a night take-off from the carrier and also because the Navy was unwilling to light up the carrier deck for take-off and provide a check light ahead in these dangerous waters.

Another plan was to take off at crack of dawn, bomb in the early morning and proceed to destination arriving before dark. This plan had the disadvantage of daylight bombing, presumably after the Japanese were aware of our coming and the hazards incident to such a daylight attack. The third plan, the plan finally decided on, was to take off just before dark, bomb at night and proceed to destination arriving after daylight in the early morning. In order to make this plan practical one plane was to take off ahead of the others, arrive over Tokyo at dusk and fire the most inflammable part of the city with incendiary bombs. This minimized the overall hazard and assured that the target would be lighted up for following airplanes.

Despite an agreement with the Navy that we would take off the moment contact was made with the enemy and the considerable hazard of contact being made during the run in on the last day we still decided to gamble in order to get the greater security of a night attack. As a matter of fact, contact was made in the early morning and we took off several hours after daylight.

The first enemy patrol vessel was detected and avoided at 3:10 A.M. on the morning of April 18. The Navy task force was endeavoring to avoid a second one some time after daylight when they were picked up by a third. Although this patrol was sunk it is understood that it got at least one radio message off to shore and it was consequently necessary for us to take off immediately. The take-off was made at Latitude 35° 43′N Longitude 153° 25′E approximately 824 statute miles East of the center of Tokyo. The Navy task force immediately retreated and in the afternoon was obliged to sink two more Japanese surface craft. It is of interest to note that even at this distance from Japan the ocean was apparently studded with Japanese craft.

Final instructions were to avoid non-military targets, particularly the Temple of Heaven, and even though we were put off so far at sea that it would be impossible to reach the China Coast, not to go to Siberia but to proceed as far West as possible, land on the water, launch the rubber boat and sail in.

Upon take-off each airplane circled to the right and flew over the *Hornet* lining the axis of the ship up with the drift sight. The course of the *Hornet* was displayed in large figures from the gun turret abaft the island.[2] This, through the use of the airplane compass and directional gyro permitted the establishment of one accurate navigational course and enabled us to swing off on to the proper course for Tokyo. This was considered necessary and desirable due to the possibility of change in compass calibration, particularly on those ships that were located close to the island.

All pilots were given selected objectives, consisting of steel

[2] Editor's note. This is the "island" on the carrier's deck, the superstructure, funnel, etc.

works, oil refineries, oil tank farms, ammunition dumps, dock yards, munitions plants, airplane factories, etc. They were also given secondary targets in case it was impossible to reach the primary target. In almost every case primary targets were bombed. The damage done far exceeded our most optimistic expectations. The high degree of damage resulted from the highly inflammable nature of Japanese construction, the low altitude from which the bombing was carried out, and the perfectly clear weather over Tokyo, and the careful and continuous study of charts and target areas.

In addition to each airplane having selected targets assigned to it, each flight was assigned a specific course and coverage. The first flight of three airplanes, led by Lieutenant Hoover, covered the Northern part of Tokyo. The second flight, led by Captain Jones, covered the central part of Tokyo. The third flight, led by Captain York, covered the Southern part of Tokyo and the North Central part of the Tokyo bay area. The fourth flight, led by Captain Greening, covered the Southern part of Kanagawa, the city of Yokohama and the Yokosuka Navy Yard. The flight was spread over a 50 mile front in order to provide the greatest possible coverage, to create the impression that there was a larger number of airplanes than were actually used, and to dilute enemy ground and air fire. It also prohibited the possibility of more than one plane passing any given spot on the ground and assured the element of surprise.

The fifth flight went around to the South of Tokyo and proceeded to the vicinity of Nagoya where it broke up, one plane bombing Nagoya, one Osaka and one Kobe.

The best information available from Army and Navy intelligence sources indicates that there were some 500 combat planes in Japan and that most of them were concentrated in the Tokyo bay area. The comparatively few fighters encountered indicated that home defense had been reduced in the interest of making the maximum of planes available in active theaters. The pilots of such planes as remained, appeared inexperienced. In some cases they actually did not attack, and in many cases failed to drive the attack home to the maximum extent possible. In no case was there any indication that a Japanese pilot might run into one of our planes even though the economics of such a course would appear sound. It would entail trading a $40,000 fighter for a $200,000 bomber and one man, who could probably arrange to collide in such a way as to save himself, against 5 who even though they escaped would be interned and thus lose their military utility. The fire of the pilots that actually attacked was very inaccurate. In some cases the machine gun bullets bounced off the wings without penetrating them. This same effect was observed when a train, upon which some of our crew members were riding in China, was machine gunned by a Japanese attack plane. One of the projectiles which had bounced off the top of the train without penetrating was recovered. It was a steel pellet about one inch long, pointed on one end and boat tailed on the other. It had no rifling marks and was apparently fired from a smooth bore gun.

The anti-aircraft defense was active but inaccurate. All anti-aircraft bursts were black and apparently from small guns of about 37 or 40 mm. size. It is presumed that the high speed and low altitude at which we were flying made it impossible for them to train their larger caliber guns on us if such existed. Several of the airplanes were struck by anti-aircraft fragments but none of them was damaged to an extent that impaired their utility or impeded their progress. Although it was to be presumed that machine gun fire from the ground was active, none of the crew members interviewed to date saw any such action nor was there evidence of machine gun fire holes in the bottom of any of the airplanes. A few barrage balloons were seen. One cluster of five or six was observed just north of the Northernmost part of Tokyo Bay and what appeared to be another cluster was observed near the Bay to the Southeast. These barrage balloons were flying at about 3000 feet and were not in sufficient numbers to impede our bombing. Japanese anti-aircraft fire was so inaccurate that

when shooting at one of our airplanes in the vicinity of the barrage balloons they actually shot down some of their own
balloons.

We anticipated that some difficulty might be experienced due
to our targets being camouflaged. Little or no effective camouflage was observed in the Tokyo area.

We can only infer that as the result of an unwarranted feeling
of security and an over-all shortage of aircraft and pilots, home
defense had been made secondary to efficient operation in other
theaters. It is felt that the indicated low morale of the Japanese
pilots around Tokyo compared to the efficiency and aggressive-
ness of pilots encountered on the active front was the result of a
knowledge on their part of the inadequacy of their equipment
and their own personal inefficiency.

In spite of the fact that at least one radio message was gotten
off prior to our take-off by the Japanese patrol boat that was
later sunk—that we passed a Japanese light cruiser (thought by
one of the pilots to be a tanker) about 700 miles East of Tokyo
—a Japanese patrol plane or bomber headed directly for our
task force about 600 miles from Tokyo (this plane turned around
and followed one of our airplanes so we know we were observed
by it) and innumerable Japanese patrol and fishing boats from
some 300 miles off-shore until crossing the Japanese Coast,
the Japanese were apparently entirely unprepared for our arrival. Inasmuch as messages must have been received at some
message center, we can only presume poor dissemination of
information or the complete failure of their communication
system.

As previously mentioned, the take-off occurred almost ten
hours early due to contact being made with enemy surface craft.
In addition to this, the take-off was made on the 18th instead of
the 19th as originally planned and agreed, due to the Navy getting one day ahead of schedule and the undesirability of remaining longer than necessary in dangerous waters.

We had requested a fast run-in at night and slow day progress in order that we might be within safe distance of Tokyo at any time during the take-off day. This was not expedient from a Navy viewpoint due to their poor maneuverability at slow speeds and the undesirability of running in any closer than was absolutely necessary.

We appreciated the desirability of advising Chungking of our premature take-off but due to the necessity for strict radio silence, this could not be done prior to our actual take-off. We requested that Chungking be advised immediately after we took off and felt that even though they were not advised by the Navy radio that the Japanese radio would give them the desired information. As a matter of actual fact, Chungking did know that we were coming but official information was not sent to Chuchow, presumably due to the extremely bad weather and the communication difficulties resulting therefrom. As a result of this, no radio homing facilities were provided for us at Chuchow, nor were light beacons or landing flares provided. To the contrary, when our planes were heard overhead an air raid warning alarm was sounded and all lights were turned off. This, together with the very unfavorable flight weather over the China coast, made safe landing at destination impossible. As a result all planes either landed in the water near the coast or the crews bailed out with their parachutes.

The individual airplanes took off as follows:

Airplane No. AC 40-2344—Took off at 8:20 A.M. ship time

Pilot	Lt. Col. J. H. Doolittle	0-271855
Co-Pilot	Lt. R. E. Cole	0-421602
Navigator	Lt. H. A. Potter	0-419614
Bombardier	S/Sgt. F. A. Braemer	6875923
Engineer-Gunner	S/Sgt. P. J. Leonard	6248728

Proceeded to Tokyo and bombed the North Central industrial area with 4 incendiary clusters. Proceeded on to the China coast

where very unfavorable weather made it necessary for crew to
abandon ship. Put plane on A.F.C.E. and turned off gasoline
valves. Pilot jumped last at 9:20 P.M. ship time, from 8,000
feet. Landed near Tien Mu Shen, about 70 miles north of
Chuchow. After landing, contacted General Ho, Director of the
Western Branch of Chekiang Province who agreed to take the
necessary steps to collect missing crew members, locate the ship
and establish a look-out for other planes in China, on the stretch
of beach between Hung Chow Bay and Wen Chow Bay and by
the sampans and junks that might be putting out to sea. All
crew members O.K. Detailed report attached hereto.[3]

Airplane No. AC 40-2292—Took off at 8:25 A.M. ship time

Pilot	Lt. T. Hoover	0-393133
Co-Pilot	Lt. Wm. N. Fitzhugh	0-421067
Navigator	Lt. Carl N. Wildner	0-352857
Bombardier	Lt. Richard E. Miller	0-432337
Engineer-Gunner	S/Sgt. Douglas V. Radney	6266909

This is the only airplane that experienced any difficulty in
taking off. The sea was so rough that water was being taken on
over the bow of the carrier, and the take-off was made on the
upbeat. The airplane was thrown into the air and the pilot pulled
back on the stick too abruptly. For a moment it looked as though
the plane might fall off on a wing but through good piloting
Lt. Hoover was able to correct the condition and proceed without further difficulty. This together with the Navy crew member
who was struck in the arm by a propeller while assisting in
maneuvering an airplane on the deck, was the only eventuality
during take-off. Both were due to the rough sea. (After this take-
off Lieutenant Miller recommended a more normal take-off to
the other pilots.) Proceeded to Tokyo and bombed powder
factories and magazines near the river north of the main railroad
station and Imperial Palace with 3 demolition bombs and one

[3] Editor's note. Report follows.

incendiary cluster. This bombing was done from 900 feet, and the debris flew to a height higher than that of the airplane. Proceeded to a point on the China coast near Ningpo.

Airplane No. AC 40-2270—Took off at 8:30 A.M. ship time

Pilot	Lt. Robert M. Gray	0-403862
Co-Pilot	Lt. Jacob E. Manch	0-389941
Navigator-Gunner	Lt. Chas. J. Ozuk	0-419618
Bombardier	Sgt. A. E. Jones	6580258
Engineer-Gunner	Cpl. Leland D. Faktor	17003211

Proceeded to Tokyo. Bombed steel works, Gas Company and Chemical works with demolition bombs and a factory district with incendiary bombs. Proceeded on to China bailing out at 6200 feet in the mountains near and Southeast of Chuchow. Lieutenant Gray, Lieutenant Manch and Sergeant Jones were uninjured. Lieutenant Ozuk suffered a severe cut on his leg due to landing on a sharp rock. Corporal L. D. Faktor was found dead. The cause of Corporal Faktor's death was unknown as his parachute apparently functioned properly. It is suspected that he landed on extremely rough terrain and was killed in the secondary fall. A detailed report prepared by Lieutenant Gray is attached hereto.

Airplane No. AC 40-2282[4]—Took off at 8:33 A.M. ship time

Pilot	Lt. Everett W. Holstrom	0-397395
Co-Pilot	Lt. Lucian N. Youngblood	0-421153
Navigator-Gunner	Lt. Harry C. McCool	0-419329
Bombardier	Sgt. Robert J. Stephens	6936650
Engineer-Gunner	Cpl. Bert M. Jordan	6952993

Proceeded in the direction of Tokyo but encountered severe fighter opposition. Endeavored to get around the fighters and passed beyond Tokyo. They then decided to bomb a secondary target but were again attacked and driven off. Eventually dropped their bombs in the water and proceeded to a point near

[4] Their machine-gun turret failed just before take-off and they were therefore unable to protect themselves against enemy fighters.

and Southeast of Shangjao where all crew members bailed out safely.

Airplane No. AC 40-2283—Took off at 8:37 A.M. ship time

Pilot	Capt. David M. Jones	0-22482
Co-Pilot	Lt. Rodney R. Wilder	0-421149
Navigator-Gunner	Lt. Eugene F. McGurl	0-431648
Bombardier	Lt. Denver N. Truelove	0-427637
Engineer-Gunner	Sgt. Joseph W. Manske	6914440

Proceeded to Tokyo where bombing from 1200 feet, they made direct hits with three demolition bombs and one incendiary cluster on power stations, oil tanks, a large manufacturing plant and the congested area Southeast of the Imperial Palace. One factory bombed was a new building which covered approximately two city blocks. They then proceeded to China, bailing out near and just Southeast of Chuchow. All crew members are safe.

Airplane No. AC 40-2298—Took off at 8:40 A.M. ship time

Pilot	Lt. Dean E. Hallmark	0-421081
Co-Pilot	Lt. Robert J. Meder	0-421280
Navigator-Gunner	Lt. Chas. J. Neilson	0-419938
Bombardier	Sgt. Wm. J. Dieter	6565763
Engineer-Gunner	Cpl. Donald E. Fitzmaurice	17004360

This airplane landed in the Nangchang Area near Poyang Lake. From the best reports available (which are not to be relied upon) two crew members, presumably Sergeant Dieter and Corporal Fitzmaurice are missing and three crew members, presumably Lieutenants Hallmark, Meder, and Neilson were captured by the Japanese. It was reported that one of these was bayoneted resisting capture but was not killed.

Airplane No. AC 40-2261[5]—Took off at 8:43 A.M. ship time

Pilot	Lt. Ted W. Lawson	0-399549
Co-Pilot	Lt. Dean Davenport	0-427310
Navigator-Gunner	Lt. Chas. L. McClure	0-431647
Bombardier	Lt. Robt. S. Clever	0-432336
Engineer-Gunner	Sgt. David J. Thatcher	19019573

[5] "The Ordeal of Lt. Lawson's Crew" follows.

Bombed the industrial section of Tokyo with 3 demolition bombs and one incendiary bomb. This airplane landed in the water off the coast of China, west of Shangchow. One crew member was badly injured, three injured, and one slightly injured. The badly injured crew member is thought to be Lieutenant Lawson but we do not have definite confirmation of this. It is understood that he had a head and leg injury and it was necessary to give him several transfusions. Sergeant Thatcher was only slightly injured and it was due to his heroism that the lives of the other crew members were saved. Although badly cut on the head and knocked unconscious when the plane hit the sea and turned over he nevertheless waded and swam out into the perilous sea to secure the medical kit from the crashed plane. He was the only crew member physically able to carry on. After it became obvious that any further wait would result in capture by Japanese forces only 3 miles away, Chinese fishermen were persuaded by him to carry his injured crew mates to temporary safety around Japanese outposts. Then for three days Chinese fishermen were forced or persuaded by him to carry the injured crew members over difficult mountainous terrain until medical aid was reached. All of this plane's crew were saved from either capture or death as a result of Sergeant Thatcher's initiative and courage in assuming responsibility and tending the wounded day and night. As of the last report the 4 injured crew members, less Sergeant Thatcher who had proceeded on, had left the dangerous area with a Chinese escort and with Lieutenant T. R. White, of the Medical Corps from Airplane No. 40-2267 in attendance.

Airplane No. AC 40-2242[6]—Took off at 8:46 A.M. ship time

Pilot	Capt. Edward J. York	0-21151
Co-Pilot	Lt. Robert G. Emmens	0-24104
Navigator-Bombardier	Lt. Nolan A. Herndon	0-419328
Engineer-Gunner	S/Sgt. T. H. Laban	6559855
Gunner	Sgt. David W. Pohl	6152141

This airplane bombed Tokyo with 3 demolition bombs and 1 incendiary bomb. Due to extremely high gasoline consumption they proceeded to Siberia landing at a point about 40 miles north of Vladivostok. All crew members O.K. and plane apparently saved. All were interned by the Russian Government and are now at Penza about 350 miles Southeast of Moscow. Airplane No. AC 40-2303[6]—Took off at 8:50 A.M. ship time

Pilot	Lt. Harold F. Watson	0-397797
Co-Pilot	Lt. James M. Parker, Jr.	0-421128
Navigator-Gunner	Lt. Thos. C. Griffin	0-377848
Bombardier	Sgt. Wayne M. Bissell	6579237
Engineer-Gunner	T/Sgt. Eldred V. Scott	6530453

Bombed Tokyo with 3 demolition bombs and one incendiary cluster, scored hit at Kawasji truck and tank plant, on another factory building and the congested industrial districts near the railroad station south of the Imperial Palace. The crew bailed out about 100 miles south of Poyang Lake. All landed safely except Lieutenant Watson whose arm was caught in a parachute riser and dislocated at the shoulder. He suffered severe discomfort for a week until a doctor was encountered who put the arm back in place. When last seen about May 1 the arm was healing rapidly and Lieutenant Watson was experiencing no discomfort. Airplane No. AC 40-2250—Took off at 8:53 A.M. ship time

Pilot	Lt. Richard O. Joyce	0-401770
Co-Pilot	Lt. J. Royden Stork	0-421345
Navigator-Bombardier	Lt. H. E. Crouch	0-395839
Engineer-Gunner	Sgt. Geo. E. Larkin, Jr.	6984298
Gunner	S/Sgt. Ed. W. Horton, Jr.	6139178

Proceeded to Tokyo and bombed the Japanese Spelial Steel Company plants and warehouses in South Tokyo in the Shiba Ward 1½ miles north of Tana River with 3 demolition bombs

[6] Their machine-gun turrets were inoperative on take-off, and they were therefore unable to defend against enemy fighters.

and 1 incendiary cluster from 2500 feet. Proceeded to China and all crew members bailed out about 30 miles north of Chuchow. All O.K. (Jumped from 8000 feet) Detailed report prepared by Lieutenant Joyce attached hereto.

Airplane No. AC 40-2249—Took off at 8:56 A.M. ship time

Pilot	Capt. Chas. R. Greening	0-22443
Co-Pilot	Lt. Kenneth E. Reddy	0-421131
Navigator-Gunner	Lt. Frank A. Kappeler	0-419579
Bombardier	S/Sgt. Wm. L. Birch	6561172
Engineer-Gunner	Sgt. Melvin J. Gardner	6296448

Proceeded to Yokohama and bombed oil refineries, docks, warehouses and industrial area of Yokohama with 4 incendiary clusters from 600 feet. After bombing proceeded to China abandoning ship at 10,000 feet at a point about 50 miles northwest of Chuchow. All crew members O.K. Detailed report attached hereto.

Airplane No. AC 40-2278—Took off at 8:59 A.M. ship time

Pilot	Lt. Wm. M. Bower	0-398557
Co-Pilot	Lt. Thadd Blanton	0-421030
Navigator-Gunner	Lt. Wm. R. Pound	0-419333
Bombardier	T/Sgt. Waldo J. Bither	6101457
Engineer-Gunner	S/Sgt. Omer A. Duquette	6143447

Proceeded to Yokohama and bombed oil refineries, tank farms and warehouses with 3 demolition bombs and 1 incendiary cluster from 1100 feet. Proceeded to China and all hands abandoned ship at a point about 50 miles northwest of Chuchow. All O.K. Detailed report attached hereto.

Airplane No. AC 40-2247—Took off at 9:01 A.M. ship time

Pilot	Lt. Edgar E. McElroy	0-421122
Co-Pilot	Lt. Richard A. Knobloch	0-421816
Navigator-Gunner	Lt. Clayton J. Campbell	0-419327
Bombardier	Sgt. Robert C. Rourgeois	7000417
Engineer-Gunner	Sgt. Adam R. Williams	6969211

Proceeded to the Yokosuka Navy Yard and bombed the dock area and one partially completed boat from 1500 feet with 3 demolition and one incendiary cluster. Bombs apparently had maximum effect, destroying everything on the dock and enveloping the boat in flames. Proceeded to China and landed near Poyang. Bailed out at 6000 feet. All O.K. Detailed report attached hereto.

Airplane No. AC 40-2297—Took off at 9:07 A.M. ship time

Pilot	Major John A. Hilger	0-20437
Co-Pilot	Lt. Jack A. Sims	0-421340
Navigator-Bombardier	Lt. James H. Macia, Jr.	0-419330
Engineer-Gunner	S/Sgt. Jacob Eierman	6883947
Radio-Gunner	S/Sgt. Edwin V. Bain	6561290

Proceeded to Nagoya and bombed military barracks at Nagoya Castle, oil storage warehouses northwest of the business district, military arsenal in the center of city and the Mitsubishi aircraft factory on the water front with 4 incendiary clusters from 1500 feet. Proceeded to China and all crew members bailed out, landing southeast of and near Shangjoa. All members O.K. Detailed report attached hereto.

Airplane No. AC 40-2267—Took off at 9:15 A.M. ship time

Pilot	Lt. Donald G. Smith	0-389010
Co-Pilot	Lt. Griffith P. Williams	0-421356
Navigator-Bombardier	Lt. Howard A. Sessler	0-431650
Flight Surgeon	Lt. Thomas R. White, M.C.	0-420191
Engineer-Gunner	Sgt. Edward J. Saylor	6569707

Proceeded to Kobe and bombed the main industrial area, a large aircraft factory, dock yards and yards in the north part of the Bay with 4 incendiary clusters, proceeded to China and landed in the water west of Sangchow. All crew members O.K. Lieutenant T. R. White, Medical Corps, a member of the crew, at great risk to his life and with exemplary courage remained inside the sinking ship with water rising dangerously until his surgical instruments and medical kit could be salvaged. The plane plunged down into 100 feet of water just after he had completed his effort and escaped. This action, together with his unselfish devotion to duty and attendance on the injured crew of airplane #AC 40-2261[7] in spite of a Japanese advance into that area, indicated exemplary courage and deserves special commendation.

Airplane No. AC 40-2268—Took off at 9:19 A.M. ship time

Pilot	Lt. Wm. G. Farrow	0-421731
Co-Pilot	Lt. Robert L. Hite	0-417960
Navigator-Gunner	Lt. Geo. Barr	0-431644
Bombardier	Cpl. Jacob DeShazer	6584514
Engineer-Gunner	Cpl. C. Spatz	6936659

Landed on the Coast at Shiu south of Ningpo and crew was captured by soldiers of the puppet government. The best information available indicates that two crewmen are missing and three captured. Inasmuch as the two captured crews were in Airplanes No. AC 40-2268 and 2298, it is possible that some confusion exists in the identification of these two airplanes and their locations.

Before leaving China, arrangements were made with General Koo Chow Tung and Madame Chiang Kai-shek to endeavor to ransom the prisoners who had fallen into the hands of the puppet government. Some consideration was given to attempting the rescue of the prisoners that had fallen into Japanese hands in the vicinity of Payang Lake but it was indicated, due to the strong Japanese position, that at least two regiments would be required and the chance of the prisoners being killed during the action was so great that the idea was abandoned. Negotiations were being carried on, when the writer left China, to the end of offering small guerilla bands a certain amount of money for each prisoner that they could bring out of Japanese occupied territory alive.

[7] Editor's note. Lieutenant Ted Lawson's plane.

Several outstanding lessons may be learned from the flight. First, sufficient modern airplanes and competent pilots should be retained within the territorial limits of the United States to assure her adequate defense. Second, an absolutely infallible detection and communication system must be provided. Third, efficient utilization of small surface craft, such as fishing boats equipped with an extremely simple radio could, through the use of a simplified code, send messages to a message center indicating the type, position, direction of approach, speed and altitude of any enemy attacking force. Fourth, the necessity for suitable camouflage and adequate dissimulation. Fifth, the highest possible degree of dispersal in order that a bomb attack, if successful, will do the minimum amount of damage.

The desirability of stopping an enemy bombing raid *before* arrival over target is obvious. This can be accomplished only with a preponderance of fighters.

The successful bombing of Tokyo indicated that, provided the element of surprise is possible, an extremely successful raid can be carried out at low altitudes with great damage and high security to equipment and personnel.

PERSONAL REPORT—GEN. DOOLITTLE

Took off at 8:18 AM ship time.

Take-off was easy. Night take-off would have been possible and practicable.

Circled carrier to get exact heading and check compass. Wind was from 300° plus-minus.

About a half hour later joined by AC 40-2292, Lt. Hoover, pilot, the second plane to take off.

About an hour out passed a Japanese camouflaged naval surface vessel of about 6,000 tons. Took it to be a light cruiser.

About two hours out passed a multi-motored land plane headed directly for our flotilla and flying at about 3,000 ft.—2 miles away —multi-motored bomber-gunner.

Passed and endeavored to avoid various civil and naval craft until land fall was made north of Grubo Shama(?).

Was somewhat north of desired course but decided to take advantage of error and approach from a northerly direction, thus avoiding anticipated strong opposition to the west.

Many flying fields and the air full of planes north of Tokyo. Mostly small biplanes apparently primary or basic trainers.

Encountered nine fighters in three flights of three. This was about ten miles north of the outskirts of Tokyo proper.

All this time had been flying as low as the terrain would permit.

Continued low flying due south over the outskirts of and toward the east center of Tokyo.

Pulled up to 1,200 ft., changed course to the southwest and incendiary-bombed highly inflammable section. Dropped first bomb at 1:30.

Anti-aircraft very active but only one near hit.

Lowered away to housetops and slid over western outskirts into low haze and smoke.

Turned south and out to sea.

Fewer airports on west side but many army posts.

Passed over small aircraft factory with a dozen or more newly completed planes on the line. No bombs left. Decided not to machine gun for reasons of personal security.

Had seen five barrage balloons over east central Tokyo and more in distance.

Passed on out to sea flying low.

Was soon joined again by Hoover who followed us to the Chinese coast.

Navigator plotted perfect course to pass north of Yoki Shima.

Saw three large naval vessels just before passing west end of Japan. One was flatter than the others and may have been a converted carrier.

Passed innumerable fishing and small patrol boats.

Made land fall somewhat north of course on China coast.

Tried to reach Chuchow on 4495 but couldn't raise.

It had been clear over Tokyo but became overcast before reaching Yoki Shima.

Ceiling lowered on coast until low islands and hills were in it. Just getting dark and couldn't live under overcast so pulled up to 6,000 and then 8,000 ft. in it. On instruments from then on though occasionally saw dim lights on ground through almost solid overcast. These lights seemed more often on our right and pulled us still farther off course.

Directed rear gunner to go aft and secure films from camera

(unfortunately they were jerked out of his shirt front where he had put them, when his chute opened).

Decided to abandon ship. Sgt. Braemer, Lt. Potter, Sgt. Leonard and Lt. Cole in order. Left ship on A.F.C.E., shut off both gas cocks and I left. *Should have put flaps down*. This would have slowed down landing speed, reduced impact and shortened glide.

All hands collected and ship located by late afternoon of 19th.

Requested General Ho Yang Ling, Director of the Branch Government of Western Chekiang Province to have a lookout kept along the seacoast from Hang Chow bay to Wen Chow bay and also have all sampans and junks along the coast keep a lookout for planes that went down at sea, or just reached shore.

Early morning of 20th four planes and crews, in addition to ours, had been located and I wired General Arnold, through the Embassy at Chungking, "Tokyo successfully bombed. Due bad weather on China Coast believe all airplanes wrecked. Five crews found safe in China so far."

Wired again on the 27th giving more details.

Discussed possibility of purchasing three prisoners on the seacoast from Puppet Government and endeavoring to take out the three in the lake area by force. Believe this desire was made clear to General Ku Cho-tung (who spoke little English) and know it was made clear to English-speaking members of his staff. This was at Shangjao. They agreed to try purchase of three but recommended against force due to large Japanese concentration.

Left airplane about 9:20 (ship time) after about 13 hours in the air. Still had enough gas for half hour flight but right front tank was showing empty. Had transferred once as right engine used more fuel. Had covered about 2,250 miles. Mostly at low speed, cruising but about an hour at moderate high speed which more than doubled the consumption for this time.

Bad luck:

(1) Early take-off due to naval contact with surface and air craft.

(2) Clear over Tokyo.

(3) Foul over China.

Good luck:

(1) A 25 m/h tail wind over most of the last 1,200 miles.

Take-off should have been made three hours before daylight, but we didn't know how easy it would be and the Navy didn't want to light up.

Dawn take-off, closer in, would have been better as things turned out. However, due to the bad weather it is questionable if even daylight landing could have been made at Chuchow without radio aid.

Still feel that original plan of having one plane take off three hours before dusk and others just at dusk was best all-round plan for average conditions.

Other ideas and impressions were discussed personally with Col. Cooper.

Should have kept accurate chronological record.

Should have all crew members instructed in *exact* method of leaving ship under various conditions.

JAMES H. DOOLITTLE
Airplane AC 40-2344—B-25-B

THE ORDEAL OF LT. LAWSON'S CREW
(*An Official Report*)

DAVID J. THATCHER, CORPORAL

USAAF

May 15, 1942.

Airplane A.C. No. 40-2261
Pilot—Ted W. Lawson
Co-pilot—Dean Davenport
Navigator—McClure
Bombardier—Robert S. Clever
Eng. & Gunner—David J. Thatcher

Our approximate time of takeoff was 0900. From the time we left the ship until we got to Tokyo there were two of our planes ahead of us. We weren't flying very close together at any time. We saw a freighter off to our right before we reached the coast. We were flying very close to the water. We saw a lot of small boats and people on the beach. About halfway between the coast and Tokyo, while zig-zagging among the mountains, we saw six pursuits flying approximately 5000 feet above us and going in the exact direction from which we had come. Two of them broke formation for a short time but I don't think they saw us. I could only operate the turret off the emergency switch in the pilot's compartment, which operates off the battery; the

24 volt generator being out of order before we took off. I found out later that we did not have the flaps down when we took off. While flying over the bay just before reaching Tokyo we saw four or five barrage balloons off to our left but they weren't in our way. Just before we reached the target, which was a large factory near the waterfront, we climbed to 1,500 ft. When we reached this altitude AA began bursting around us. We dropped the bombs which consisted of three demolition and one incendiary. One of the demolitions had the Japanese medals on the tail of it. By the time we had finished bombing the AA bursts were very close. One bursting just off the tip of the right wing. The smoke from these bursts was black. I could see the AA battery off to our right and a little ahead of us. We went into a slanting dive and left Tokyo at 300 mph. After leaving Tokyo there was one of our planes ahead of us until we passed the southern tip of Japan, when it went out of sight. Before we reached the southern tip of Japan I saw an aircraft carrier to the right of us but there were no planes in the air. I also saw a lot of small boats and a couple of freighters before we reached the coast. When we reached the China coast at approximately 2100 o'clock it was getting dark. We found a bay and circled it about three times trying to find a place to land. During this time Lawson told us to remove our parachutes. He also said we were going to land on the water so I was sitting beside the turret tank ready to release the life raft. We hit the water with an extremely hard jolt. When I came to about five minutes later I saw the water gushing in thru the top of the turret which I thought was the rear escape hatch. Still dazed I pulled the strings on my life vest and tried to go out thru there. When I couldn't go out there I finally figured that the plane was upside down. So then I went back and raised the rear escape hatch and got out there. I went up on the belly of the plane toward the nose and saw that it was badly smashed. At that time Lt. McClure called to me from the beach. I could see that the plane was in about six feet of water. Later I learned from the pilot that he had tried to make a forced landing on the

beach. Due to rain hitting the windshield and it being nearly dark he had misjudged his distance. When we hit the water we were going 140 mph. The other four members of the crew were all thrown out of the plane when it crashed and were quite seriously injured. By the time I reached the beach there were some Chinese fishermen who had come down from a small village to where the others were. We could tell almost immediately that they were friendly. The first thing they wanted to know by sign language was whether there were any more than five in the plane. When they found out there were no more they helped us to one of their huts which was about a half mile away. When we reached the hut I bandaged the wounds as best I could. I was the only one to get out of the plane with a gun belt on so I used the bandage in my first aid packet for the large wound on Lawson's knee. I used my handkerchief on the cut on his arm. For his other wounds and the wounds on Davenport and Clever I had to use old dirty rags that the fishermen gave us. Later that night I took a lantern and went out to try and get the large first aid kit out of the tail of the plane, but it was impossible to reach the plane because the tide had come in since we crashed. Early the next morning I went out to the plane to try and get the first aid kit and morphine but couldn't find either. During the night at high tide the plane had been washed up on the beach. The engines, which had been torn loose when we crashed, were still out in the water. This was Sunday, April 19. I got a good look at the plane. The nose was just a mangled mass clear back to the bomb bay. If the four in the nose hadn't been thrown out they'd never have gotten out alive. If I'd been sitting in the turret I'd never have gotten out alive either. From the experience of that crash I've decided that the safest place for the gunner to be during a forced landing is in the radio operator's seat with the safety belt secured. Also that if a plane had, while taking off from the carrier, hit the water with its landing gear down it would have nosed over just as we did; and sank very quickly with a full load. The place where we crashed was Nantien. There we met

a guerilla who could talk a little English. We told him we wanted
to get to a hospital as soon as possible. We left there that afternoon with the four wounded wrapped in blankets and being
carried on stretchers by coolies. All the time Lawson was in terrific pain from the wound in his leg. We had to go over a high
pass to the other side of the island. By late afternoon we got to a
river boat and headed for the mainland. We were on the boat all
that night and the next day, April 20. Late in the afternoon we
reached Hai Yu. At Hai Yu were two Chinese doctors and a
Chinese nurse who gave us our first medical aid, two days after
we crashed. The next day, April 21, we traveled 40 miles by
chair to Linhai where there was a hospital. On April 23 I got a
telephone call from Hoover saying that his crew was all O.K. On
the morning of April 24 Smith and his crew arrived at Linhai.
He had White with him so White took charge of the wounded
then. I left Linhai with Smith and his crew on the morning of
April 27, leaving Dr. White there with the wounded. We arrived
at Chushien the night of April 30. From Linhai we had traveled by chair, ricksha, automobile, and train. During the time
we were at Chushien we had several air raids and went to an
air raid shelter in a hill near there, Sunday night, May 3, we
left Chushien by train. The next morning we got on a bus and
traveled by bus the remainder of the distance to Hengyang. We
arrived there the evening of May 6. We stayed there until May
14. During our stay there we had an air raid nearly every day and
would go down the river. We left Hengyang by plane and went
to Chungking.

May 18, 1942.
CPL. THATCHER'S REPORT (*Continued*)
(To be added to the other report)

We were the 6th or 7th plane to take off from the carrier, being
in Capt. Jones' formation. We didn't get close enough to the

two planes that were ahead of us to see who they were. As we passed over the coast of Japan before reaching Tokyo the people would look up and wave at us. I saw quite a few good highways in Japan but no cars, only bicycles. As we passed over the roof-tops the people in the fields and on the roads would stop whatever they were doing and look up at us. From the way they acted it seemed as though no Japanese planes ever flew that low. Before we reached the Japanese coast I tested out the guns by firing several rounds of ammunition.

When we dropped the bombs on the factory in Tokyo I think I saw the first one explode. It was a large puff or cloud of black smoke and debris coming up from the thickly congested building area. The reason I didn't see more was because I had to keep a sharp lookout for pursuit planes at all times. I didn't see any planes over Tokyo.

After leaving the southern tip of Japan I crawled up over the bomb bay to the navigator's compartment and we talked over the experience we'd just had in actual combat. We decided we had enough gas to reach the China coast. An hour before reaching the China coast I crawled back to the turret again in case we should meet some Jap planes over occupied territory.

When the plane crashed, from what I heard later, the pilot, co-pilot and navigator were thrown up thru the top of the cockpit and not straight forward. The bombardier, Lt. Clever, was in the nose of the plane when we crashed. He was thrown thru the nose of the plane head first. The injuries he received were a cut above one eye and a cut below the other eye so that by the time we reached Hai Yu both eyes were nearly swollen shut; the top of his head was so badly skinned that half his hair was gone, but there were no deep cuts in his head. These injuries I believe were gotten when he went thru the glass in the nose of the plane. His hips and back were sprained in some way so that he was unable to stand up and walk. All he was able to do was to crawl on hands and knees. I believe that was all the very bad injuries he had. Up until the time we reached Hai Yu his head was so badly covered with blood that he couldn't see. I thought it would be better to leave it thus than to try and wash it for the danger there was of getting infection in the cuts immediately from using water that was not clean. Infection would set in soon enough anyway and besides that I had my hands full with the other members of the crew. Clever was the only one that was able to sleep very well that first night and the time that we were on the river boat, although he couldn't sit up at any time, just had to be laying down all the time. He was very good about the whole matter and didn't complain very much about the pain he was in. Only after getting tired of laying in one position for awhile would he ask me to help him move into a different position; for instance if he was laying on his back he would want me to help him move over on one side. His being able to sleep and get some rest helped a lot.

Lawson, the pilot, was by far the most seriously injured. The plane landed with such force that the pilot's and co-pilot's seats and armor plate were thrown out with them. The worst injury Lawson received was a long deep gash just above his knee on his left leg. He no doubt lost a lot of blood through the injury at first but by the time we reached the fisherman's hut it had nearly stopped bleeding so I did not put a tourniquet on it. It did not stop bleeding but kept running a little all the time. He had a short deep cut in his left leg between knee and ankle. This cut was deep enough so I could see the bone. Then his foot below the ankle was so badly bruised that it started turning black in a couple of days. All these injuries were in his left leg, no cuts or even a scratch on his right leg. On his left arm between elbow and shoulder was another deep gash but not quite as bad or large as the one on his knee. It had no doubt bled a lot too but by the time we reached the fisherman's hut it wasn't bleeding very much so I did not put a tourniquet on his arm either. On the top of his head were a few minor cuts. He had two deep scratches on his chin. Eight or nine front teeth were knocked out so he was unable to bite or chew anything. He had a few minor scratches on his left hand and I think that was all. If he'd only had one of these injuries it wouldn't have been so bad, but with the four serious ones he lost so much blood it made him very weak. And then not being able to eat anything made it that much worse. I was afraid he would die or that gangrene would start in his leg before we reached a hospital. If gangrene had set in I wouldn't have known what it was because I don't know what it's like. He tried to sleep but it was almost impossible, he was in such intense pain all the time. He was very good about it tho and didn't complain very much. After I'd bandaged his injuries that first night I left them as they were and did not try to wash them out or anything.

Davenport, the co-pilot, received several severe cuts on his right leg between his knee and ankle. These were all the cuts he had so he was able to help by talking in sign language to the guerrillas and trying to make them understand that we wanted to get to a hospital. He was not able to walk after we left the fisherman's hut. The guerrilla who could talk a little English helped us to get started to the hospital. His name was Charlie, I don't know what the rest of it was. Davenport certainly didn't complain very much, even tho he wasn't able to get any sleep. I don't think he lost nearly as much blood as Lawson.

McClure, the navigator, only received a few scratches on his right foot in the way of cuts, these later being infected. The serious injury that he did get was in his shoulders. He said when we crashed that he was crouching between the pilot's and co-pilot's seats. He hit the armor plating with his shoulders. His shoulders were swollen so bad clear down to his elbows that he could hardly move his hands. By a week later his right arm from elbow to shoulder had completely turned black. With this injury of his shoulders he was unable to lay down, had to be sitting up all the time. He could not get any sleep either. He didn't complain very much considering the pain he was in.

Lawson and Davenport both said they were still fastened to their seats and armor plate when they came to on the bottom. They said they unfastened their safety belts and floated to the top, then swam or were washed ashore. It was only by the hand of God that any of us got out of there alive, let alone all of us.

The injuries I received were just minor ones. I had a slight gash cut on the top of my head. This was what knocked me out. If I hadn't had my flying helmet on it would have been much worse. My back was badly bruised and I had a few small cuts which later became infected, so I was in good shape to take care of the others.

Luckily enough, out of all these injuries, there were no bones broken as far as I know; except for Lawson losing those teeth.

Most of the wounds became infected in a short time. There was nothing I could do for them so I left them as they were. I didn't dare to wash them out with the dirty diseased water along the way.

When we left the fisherman's hut at Nantien we took four blankets, one for each one of the injured and gave the owner ten dollars for them.

We were on the river boat from about six o'clock in the evening of April 19 until three o'clock in the afternoon of April 20. There was a covering over the middle of the boat which kept us dry when it was raining. While we were on the boat they all tried to sleep but couldn't very well. I was kept busy going from one to the other trying to make them as comfortable as possible. But they'd soon get tired laying in one position so I would help them move in a different position. I helped them as much as possible but there wasn't much I could do for them. About midnight we stopped at one of the guerrilla's hideouts to get something to eat. I went up with them to the house and got a bowl of stuff, something like noodles. I was pretty darned hungry but couldn't eat very much of the stuff. Then they gave me a bowl full for each of the others to take down to the boat with me.

Luckily enough they had a few spoons so we didn't have to use chopsticks. Also when we were on the boat we didn't have much drinking water so I set my canteen cup and a couple small saucers we had in one end of the boat to catch the rain water. Lawson was wanting water all the time because his throat was dry from the blood in his mouth where his teeth had been knocked out. I didn't think that terrible night would ever end. During the time we were on the boat we went from the island that we'd crashed on to the mainland. We went thru there at night so the Jap boats wouldn't see us. The most disheartening part of the trip was that we understood the guerrillas to say it would only take two hours but it took two days.

Early that morning of April 19 when I went out to the plane to see if I could find the first aid kit I saw a Jap gunboat way out in the bay. Possibly I could have burned what was left of the plane because there was a little gasoline running out of one of the tanks, but I didn't think of that; all I was thinking about was trying to find the first aid kit or morphine for the others and get out of there before the Japs came.

After we got out of the river boat we had about five miles to go on land before we got to Hai Yu. At Hai Yu I sent a telegram to Col. Doolittle at Chungking telling him of our condition. The interpreter there was Y. C. Chang and he said I was the first American to come to Hai Yu. When we left there the next morning we were given a royal send-off with a band and everything. We all traveled by chair that day, April 21, to Linhai. It was forty miles and took us twelve hours. I can't see how Lawson was ever able to stand it.

The missionary that helped us a lot at Linhai was Frank England and his wife of the China Inland Mission. Also there was a missionary, his wife, and two small children came forty miles from another town to help us. They were Mr. and Mrs. Smith. I don't know what town they were from. Mrs. Smith was a graduate nurse and is from Walla Walla, Washington. Also there at Linhai were a Mrs. Andrews, and a Miss Marion who helped us. They all deserve a lot of thanks for helping us, especially the nurse for coming so far over such roads with two small children. The Englands would come up to the hospital every day to visit us. They had our clothes washed and mended for us.

After Doc. White got to Linhai I helped him give Lawson a blood transfusion. He got the blood from Lt. Williams and had to use syringes to do it. The doctor there at the hospital also did a wonderful job with the wounded before Doc. White got there. I don't remember his name. Also the magistrate at Linhai helped us a lot by giving each of us some clothes and hiring a cook who could cook American food like we wanted it.

When I last saw Lawson the morning of April 27 it was still doubtful whether he would pull through O.K. It still looked as if his leg would have to be amputated. As for the others I was sure they would be O.K. in at least a month or six weeks.

When we left Linhai Doc. White said he was going to try and move them out of there before the rainy season started, which he thought would be the middle of May.

After we left Linhai we traveled three days by chair. The third day going over a mountain six thousand feet high. We walked over this so it would be easier on the coolies.

The fourth day we started out in rickshas and at eleven in the morning we came to a highway where there were a 1938 Dodge sedan and a 1939 Ford sedan waiting for us. We were certainly surprised, didn't think they had such things in China after traveling so slow all the way from the coast. We went to Kinuka in these cars and from there to Chushien by train. A Mr. Liu from Linhai had come all the way to Chushien with us as an interpreter and helped us a great deal.

At Chushien were Hoover's crew, Jones, Holstrom and Ozuk. There I learned of Faktor being killed. Rev. Birch, a missionary there, gave a funeral service in the air raid shelter the Sunday we were there for Faktor, although the grave was not ready yet.

Faktor was a good friend of mine and I certainly thought it was considerate of Rev. Birch to give that funeral service. I gave Birch as much information as I could about Faktor but I didn't know his exact age or where in Iowa his home was.

I got to look at the field at Chushien while I was there and it's certainly a good one. It's a very large field with lots of space to take off in all directions and plenty of space to disperse large bombers all over the field.

At Heng Yang Mr. Liu, the interpreter, helped us a great deal; especially in the city when we wanted to buy clothes, etc. Also Mr. Yang, the owner of the Hostel where we stayed, helped us a great deal. When we left Heng Yang we were sorry we could not bring Mr. Liu and "Butch", as we called him, with us on the plane.

Corp. DAVID J. THATCHER—19019573
95th Bomb. Sqdn.,
Airplane A.C. No. 40-2261.

NAVAL ACTION IN THE CORAL SEA
(*An Official Report*)[1]

CHESTER W. NIMITZ, FLEET ADMIRAL

USN

17 June 1942.

From: Commander in Chief, United States Pacific Fleet.
To: Commander in Chief, United States Fleet.

Subject: Naval Action in Coral Sea Area, 4–8 May 1942.

1.   Forwarded with pleasure. The reports by unit and force commanders on the Coral Sea engagement from 4–8 May not only give a good picture, albeit befogged in places, of the action itself; but they bring out strongly the splendid spirit and resolution of officers and men that contributed so markedly to the succession of smashing victories.

PRELIMINARY OPERATIONS

2.   The actions reported upon in the basic letter climaxed an extremely long period of operations for Task Force SEVEN-TEEN as originally composed under Rear Admiral Fletcher, i.e. YORKTOWN, ASTORIA, (flag of Rear Admiral Smith), PORTLAND, CHESTER, MORRIS, ANDERSON, HAM-MANN, RUSSELL, HUGHES, SIMS, and WALKE. This force had departed from Pearl Harbor on February 14 and, except for one week's upkeep in the undeveloped harbor at

[1] This report was classified SECRET but was declassified for publication.

Tongatabu, had remained at sea continuously prior to this battle. The YORKTOWN air group had taken part in the very successful attacks on shipping at Lae and Salamoa on 10 March when Vice Admiral Brown of Task Force ELEVEN commanded the combined forces.

3. Task Force ELEVEN, commanded by Rear Admiral Fitch in LEXINGTON, MINNEAPOLIS (flag of Rear Admiral Kinkaid), NEW ORLEANS, PHELPS, DEWEY, WORDEN, FARRAGUT, DALE, AYLWIN and MONAGHAN departed from Pearl Harbor 16 April, initially to join Task Force ONE near Christmas Island, but before completing this rendezvous was diverted to the Coral Sea to join Task Force SEVENTEEN. Task Force SEVENTEEN, in the meantime, had been directed to return to the Coral Sea area from Tongatabu because there were excellent indications that the Japanese intended to make a sea-borne attack on Port Moresby the first week in May. These forces arrived in the area on 1 May, so it can be seen that the timing was very close. Task Force SIXTEEN, which contained two carriers, had also been despatched to the area but, due to the Tokyo operation, could not reach there in time. Fleet oilers NEOSHO, PLATTE, and TIPPECANOE serviced Task Forces SEVENTEEN and ELEVEN.

4. Before and between engagements these Forces in the Coral Sea cruised out of range of enemy shore-based aircraft, in readiness to seize such opportunities to attack as offered on 10 March and in the battle reported herein.

5. Such extended periods at sea, as have been the rule in this war, were not visualized prior to its outbreak, but training in fueling at sea was well advanced. That Task Force SEVENTEEN was able to endure this prolonged period and then give such an excellent account of itself in combat is a tribute to its personnel from the highest to the lowest, and is a remarkable record of seamanship, airmanship and operation of material. In this the personnel of the fleet tankers employed should come in for their full share of appreciation.

6. The operations of the task forces were in coordination with aircraft of the Southwest Pacific Area based in Australia, Port Moresby and Tulagi, and with fleet patrol planes at Noumea. (Australian forces evacuated Tulagi two days before Task Force SEVENTEEN struck the enemy there on 4 May). It is true, as Commander Task Force ELEVEN has stated in his report, that this coordination may be called strategical rather than tactical. In other words, the information as to enemy

concentrations obtained by shore-based aircraft was of much value, and the almost daily attacks on shipping were undoubtedly of cumulative assistance, but the furnishing of air support in tactical situations is a problem which for various reasons has not been solved for that area. Two evident drawbacks are the inadequate numbers of planes and the remoteness of the Australian bases. Difficulties as to communications are in the process of being cleared up. There is still much to be done in providing for the readiness and training of shore-based aircraft to coordinate their operations tactically with fleet units. Such coordination is essential in order that carrier based planes may be relieved of long range scouting and be ready to attack, with full groups, any targets located by shore-based craft.

THE BATTLE—PHASE ONE

7.   As noted in the basic letter the operations in the Coral Sea area were divided into three phases. On 4 May the YORKTOWN Air Group made three attacks on enemy vessels at Tulagi Harbor. In this attack a total of 22 torpedoes and 76 1000-lb bombs were released, resulting in 5 and 11 hits, respectively. Considering that there was practically no air opposition and very little anti-aircraft fire, the ammunition expenditure required to disable the number of enemy ships involved is disappointing. This is particularly true in the instance where 11 torpedoes were fired against a maneuvering aircraft tender without any hits. Although fogging of sights and windshields affected accuracy of the first attack, this condition did not apply in subsequent ones begun from lower altitudes.

8.   The Tulagi performance emphasizes how much proficiency drops off in wartime and the necessity for target practices at every opportunity in order to keep pilots completely trained in all phases of aerial warfare. Despite their lack of training the YORKTOWN Air Group demonstrated very creditable willingness and effort to keep after their enemy objective until it was destroyed. It is gratifying that heavy losses were inflicted on the enemy with very small loss to our forces.

PHASE TWO

9.   In the second phase on May 7, the combined LEXINGTON and YORKTOWN Groups attacked enemy forces whose composition is not entirely clear. The YORKTOWN reports

the enemy as consisting of 1 carrier, 1 very large heavy cruiser, 3 heavy cruisers and 1 light cruiser, whereas the LEXINGTON Group reports the enemy as 1 carrier. Reports also conflict as to damage caused, probably because without realizing it both air groups attacked the same carrier simultaneously. This seems a logical explanation of why the LEXINGTON, which attacked first, reports 7 bomb and 9 torpedo hits, while the YORKTOWN Group, which followed in the attack, reports the carrier with only one small fire aft standing into the wind to launch planes after the LEXINGTON Group had completed its attack. The YORKTOWN Group then reports 14 bomb and 10 torpedo hits on the same carrier. The YORKTOWN Group also reports sinking the light cruiser in company with the enemy carrier.

10. It seems from these two reports, which correspond quite closely in times as 1145, that the attack was made simultaneously by both air groups and that probably in the excitement neither one appreciated that the other was involved in the same attack. One thing is certain, however: *the carrier was sunk,* and there is substantiating evidence that the light cruiser was also destroyed. No mention is made of the other enemy ships which the YORKTOWN Group reported. As at Tulagi, the enemy losses were enormous in comparison with our own.

PHASE THREE

11. The final action occurred on 8 May and involved not only a simultaneous attack by enemy planes on our own carriers but also an attack by our planes on enemy carriers at about the same time. It is significant that there is no mention of attack groups engaging each other in the air enroute. The enemy group reported by the YORKTOWN scouts consisted of 2 carriers, 4 cruisers and 3 destroyers. The reports of the attacks by the two air groups do not clearly prove that both carriers were attacked and damaged. It is possible that only one enemy carrier was hit on 8 May and that the air groups from the LEXINGTON and YORKTOWN attacked the same carrier. The second carrier may have taken advantage of cloud concealment and thereby escaped. If the number of hits made is approximately as claimed (8 torpedoes and 8 heavy case 1000 pound bombs fused with Mark 21 and Mark 23 one-hundredth second fuse), both bomb and warhead must be improved.

12. In the attack on our carriers the hostile planes were picked up by radar at a distance of about 70 miles. In spite of

this warning and of the fighter protection over the carrier, only one group of our fighters was "vectored" to a successful interception before the enemy planes reached their attack point. Considering the tremendous odds against them, the performance of the SBD's in the anti-torpedo plane patrol was highly creditable.

13. It is of interest that either due to intensive anti-aircraft fire, or to a change in procedure, the Japanese torpedo plane approach on our carriers differed greatly from the approach used in the attack on the PRINCE OF WALES and RE-PULSE. The approach against the British ships was made in squadron formation. In the Coral Sea action, however, squadrons broke up into small groups which attacked from various directions. Some came in at a constant low level and dropped torpedoes 150 to 200 feet from the water at a relatively high speed; others approached in a high speed glide and dropped from heights of as much as 500 feet.

GENERAL COMMENTS

14. On the evening of 7 May enemy planes attempted to land on our carriers, indicating that enemy carriers may have been in close proximity to our own. The Task Force Commander in his remarks on this matter shows that he gave full consideration to the desirability of making a surface force night search and attack on these enemy forces. It is probable, in view of the NEOSHO-SIMS sinking to the southwest of our carriers, that another carrier was in that area. The unknown position, however, made it difficult for the Task Force Commander to institute a search with any reasonable chance of success. It is considered that his decision not to attempt such an attack was sound and that he was correct in not dispersing his forces at that particular time when he did not know the composition of the enemy force.

15. The Commander-in-Chief, Pacific Fleet, concurs in the opinion expressed by the Executive Officer and Commanding Officer, USS LEXINGTON, regarding the cause for the sudden and terrific destruction of that ship. The presence of such large quantities of high octane gasoline on board a carrier is a menace which must be accepted but it is imperative that means be provided to prevent a repetition of the LEXINGTON condition. That so few members of the crew of that ship were lost is a credit to the assistance of accompanying ships, the spirit of the

crew and the organization of the ship. The seamanlike performance of the destroyers of Task Unit 17.5.4 and the cruisers of 17.2.1 is in keeping with the highest traditions of the Service.

16. The outstanding material defect of the three day action is the fogging of bomb sights in dives from altitudes of 17,000 feet or more. Efforts now underway to solve this problem should be urgently pressed. It is gratifying that otherwise there were few material failures. Bomb release mechanisms operated well and there was practically no jamming of machine guns in the fighters. The 5″ anti-aircraft batteries performed excellently. Casualties to anti-aircraft automatic weapons were fewer than in the past. Most of those that did occur were loading-stoppages which can be reduced only by frequent firing practices. Task Force Commanders are stressing such practices in their daily training underway.

17. Experience strongly supports the recommendations of Commander Task Group 17.5 that the number of fighters on carriers be immediately increased to 27 and that the present torpedo planes be replaced by the ones of greater speed and longer range. Both of these recommendations are now being accomplished.

18. Both the report and recommendations of the Commanding Officer, USS YORKTOWN, are superior. The Commander-in-Chief, Pacific Fleet, considers these recommendations to be basically sound and concurs wholeheartedly in them.

19. It is recommended in several reports that the "V" dispositions be a tighter one, cruisers and destroyers taking station on a 1500 to 2500 yard circle around the carrier. The outboard guns thus protect against low approaching torpedo planes, while at the same time the inboard guns lay an anti-aircraft umbrella over the carrier and the disposition as a whole. This seems an excellent plan. The tighter screen has been recommended by despatch to Task Force Commanders. It will be noted that this anti-aircraft disposition is at complete variance with observed Japanese tactics. Their cruisers and destroyers screening a carrier dispersed widely, with no coordinated anti-aircraft fire for themselves or the carrier.

20. The improvement in anti-aircraft gunnery in ships of these task forces is gratifying. Important gunnery lessons of the engagement have been issued in a special bulletin to the fleet.

SUMMARY OF BATTLE LESSONS

21. The more important lessons from the engagement and comments concerning them are summarized in this paragraph for ready reference:

(a) Proficiency of both aviation and gunnery personnel drops off badly in war because of training difficulty. Not only must Task Force Commanders increase training but shore training must be broadly expanded.

(b) Fogging of sights and windshields seriously affects accuracy of dive bombing. Early correction of this defect is urgent.

(c) Insufficient fighters prevent suitable protection of either our attacking squadrons or ships of the Task Force. Carrier allowance is being increased from 18 to 27 VF.

(d) Obsolescent torpedo planes reduce effectiveness of our VT squadrons. These are being replaced by a later type.

(e) Torpedo plane attacks are most effective when closely coordinated with dive bombing attacks. Much of the success in the Coral Sea lay in this coordination.

(f) Automatic weapons urgently require the directors and lead computing sights under manufacture in order to be able to shoot down planes *before* they release their missiles.

(g) All carriers must have 2 long range radars equal in effectiveness to the CXAM.

(h) Operations of land based aircraft and fleet units must be better coordinated by intensive combined training.

(i) Aircraft bombs and torpedoes must be made more effective. Too many hits are required to destroy an enemy carrier. Larger aircraft torpedo warheads should be given priority in shipment to this area. A more suitable bomb than the present 1000 pound type is necessary for our dive bombers.

(j) The brunt of our offensive effort is now being carried by our aviation personnel in a courageous and devoted manner. Full provision must be made for replacement units in order that plane crews may not be pushed beyond reasonable endurance.

(k) Means must be provided for reducing the menace to carriers of the large quantities of gasoline carried.

(l) Screening ships provide best protection for carriers against torpedo planes when stationed on a 1500 to 2500 yard circle. Such a disposition is now being used in this fleet.

22. The Commander in Chief, U. S. Pacific Fleet, considers that Rear Admiral Fletcher utilized with consummate skill the information supplied him and, by these engagements in the Coral Sea between 4 and 8 May, won a victory with decisive and far reaching consequences for the Allied cause. Recommendations as to awards will be made in separate correspondence.

C. W. NIMITZ.

LONE SURVIVOR OF TORPEDO SQUADRON 8
(*An Official Report*)

GEORGE H. GAY, ENSIGN

USNR

UNITED STATES PACIFIC FLEET

FLAGSHIP OF THE COMMANDER-IN-CHIEF

From: Commander-in-Chief, United States Pacific Fleet.
To: Commander-in-Chief, United States Fleet.

Subject: Personal Account of Attacks on Japanese Carriers
          June 4, 1942.

Enclosure: (A) Memorandum of Statement of Ensign G. H.
           Gay, USNR, VT Squadron 8, U.S.S. HORNET.

1. The enclosure covers the most unusual experience of an
aviation officer who, after being shot down during attack, was
thereafter able to witness a major attack by our own forces on
the enemy carriers. A personal interest story based on this episode has been released to the press.

2. This statement should be given careful study with particular reference to lessons learned in the employment of torpedo-
carrying aircraft.

3. The case of Ensign Gay will be presented to the Board
of Awards, Pacific Fleet, together with those of many other
officers and men whose gallantry made possible our success in
the Midway actions.

UNITED STATES PACIFIC FLEET
FLAGSHIP OF THE COMMANDER-IN-CHIEF

June 7, 1942

MEMORANDUM FOR THE COMMANDER-IN-CHIEF:

Subject: Report of Action 4 June 1942, by Ensign G. H. Gay, USNR.

1. In accordance with your instructions, I interviewed Ensign Gay at the Naval Hospital, Pearl, today. There follows the substance of his statement regarding events previously reported in Midway despatch 060405.

2. VT8, with 15 TBD's, took off from HORNET for torpedo attack on Jap carriers. Weather was good, excellent visibility, few broken clouds at about 1500 feet, wind N.E., about 5-8 knots.

3. The entire approach on target area was made at low altitude. The Squadron was formed in two divisions: the first, of four two-plane sections; the second, of two two-plane and one three-plane sections. Ensign Gay flew in the last position in the second division.

4. On approaching target area, the enemy disposition was seen to be approximately as shown on accompanying sketch. Squadron Commander headed directly for the southernmost carrier (marked "C" on sketch) until he observed AA fire bursting some distance directly ahead. The Squadron then altered course for the central carrier (marked "B") and while on this course, and at about 16,000 yards range, attacks commenced by Jap Zero fighters. Attacks were made by a succession of dives from overhead aft, starting in on the leading planes of the flight. The Squadron Commander (Lt. Comdr. Waldron) was shot down early in this approach and others followed in quick succession. On nearing the target Gay's gunner reported himself shot.

5. Actual approach had been from the east on beam of carrier "B". Gay noticed that this ship was now turning toward him and he therefore pulled around to the north and back in on the opposite bow, and dropped his torpedo at about 800 yards. He then pulled up over the bow of the carrier and turned

sharply aft in her track. Heavy AA fire did not hit him. He was
shot down by a Zero fighter shortly after passing astern the carrier. An explosive shell (probably 20 mm.) carried away his left
rudder control, flash-burning his left leg, and he receiving one
bullet wound (probably .28 caliber) in the upper left arm and
fragment imbedded in left hand. He was able to stall the plane
in a reasonably good crash landing, although the right wing
carried away on hitting the water. This occurred about 1100
local time.

6.   The plane submerged quickly after crashing, leaving only
the tail surfaces exposed. Gay was unable to rescue the radioman before the plane finally disappeared.

7.   The rubber boat in its bag floated clear, together with
the black cushion from the bomber compartment. The pilot
inflated his life-jacket, held on to the boat-bag, and covered his
head with the cushion to avoid detection by the Japs. Several
enemy ships subsequently passed close at hand, during which
periods he took particular care not to be seen.

8.   Gay first observed that carriers "A" and "C" were of
the KAGA class, and carrier "B" somewhat smaller. Carrier
"A" was on fire. Carrier "C", guarded by one cruiser and one
destroyer, was landing Zero fighters. He noticed that landing
approaches were made from far and high, straight astern, with
long intervals.

9.   A short time after landing, possibly 10-20 minutes, our
dive bombers arrived and layed into carriers "B" and "C". Gay
had the impression that a number of our pilots were not using
their dive flaps as evidenced by their very high speed in the dive
and subsequent fast low altitude get-away. The carriers immediately began manuevering in all directions to avoid. Hits on
ships "B" and "C" started tremendous fires, with heavy smoke
billowing high overhead the vessels with flames at the top, and
periodically interspersed with additional blasts of smoke and fire
as from internal explosions. On completion of attack, carrier
"C" continued to burn fiercely, fires gradually extending
throughout the length of the vessel except for a small space aft.

10.   Later in the afternoon a cruiser apparently tried to go
alongside the carrier "C" but seemed unable to do so. She then
stood off at a short distance and commenced firing, presumably
at the CV. Later, before dark, a DD did get alongside, probably
to take off personnel.

11. During much of this period planes were flying about, obviously waiting to land. They would disappear for a short time and come back. No indication of what happened to them.

12. Just before dark, still in fairly close proximity, Ensign Gay inflated his rubber boat. During the night he observed several glowing areas to the north which he thought might be search-lights of accompanying vessels engaged in rescue work. Shortly before dawn he felt a succession of three tremendous explosions (planted demolition charges?).

13. During the next forenoon one of our patrol planes passed by on search, saw his rubber boat, acknowledged seeing him, and proceeded on mission. He later returned, landed and picked up Gay. The VP pilot stated that he had seen no ships on his patrol route, nor had he seen any yellow rubber boats except that of Gay. The surface was littered, however, with black Japanese life rafts, presumably used by the Japs in abandoning their ships. There was much debris and heavy oil on the surface.

14. Conclusions by Ensign Gay:

(a) The Japs have apparently developed a highly effective defense against daylight torpedo attack, this defense being based on the marked manueverability and speed of the Zero fighters. It appeared to him that these machines, on completion of each firing dive, simply pulled into a tight loop and were set for the next attack.

(b) The daylight torpedo attack has little chance without greatly increased speed, and ability to drop torpedoes at higher speeds (they had the reinforced Mark 13 torpedoes).

(c) This Squadron was furnished with chest holdback harness. He attributes to this the fact that he was not injured (hitting his head forward) on crash landing.

(d) Protective seat armor in the TBD's is effective against the Jap .28 caliber. Gay could feel the impacts against his seat but only one bullet penetrated, and that was almost spent when it hit his arm.

(e) Finally, although he did not see any ship actually sink, Gay is positive that the one KAGA "C" sank, with the other two as "Probables".

15. *COMMENTS* by the Originator. There is a good deal of meat in this amazing episode of a pilot having a ringside seat in the enemy's camp during an attack. I think the following major points are particularly worthy of further investigation:

(a) The use of extremely light fighters for defense of surface vessels from air attack. This probably would mean the elimination of all armor and fuel tank protection, but it would provide a plane with maximum climb and manueverability (short turning circle). There seems to be no question but that the Jap Zero is beautifully adapted to attack on torpedo planes which are committed to a fixed course and altitude during their approach.

(b) The attack of VT8, as described by Gay, was surprising in that they apparently retained a close squadron formation. Best modern practice is to make a split attack of small units, both to divide AA fire and to insure providing for any target manuevers.

(c) The torpedo plane has always been considered the weapon of opportunity and certainly is not intended for unsupported attack in high visibility. In the case in point, the VT attack should have followed slightly that of the dive bombers, and this was probably intended (failed to materialize due to the conditions of action). In any case, we must investigate less expensive employment of the aerial torpedo. Aside from bad weather and "mopping up" use, we may find an ideal condition in night attack, using the ASV equipment for the approach.

(d) In my own mind, based on Gay's account and other information, I am positive of the destruction here of one "KAGA." This is fully supported by the fires, debris, explosions, and abandon-ship life rafts. The other two CV's, damaged and burning, I believe were those later pursued by TF 16. A fourth carrier definitely sunk was that polished off with three torpedoes from one of our submarines.

16. Ensign Gay obviously displayed courage of the highest degree in carrying through his attack in the face of the prohibitive earlier losses and the almost certain destruction of himself. He also showed marked presence of mind in devising means of avoiding detection by the enemy after his crash, and great coolness in making the valuable observations which his unusual situation permitted. He is worthy of the highest decoration that can be bestowed.

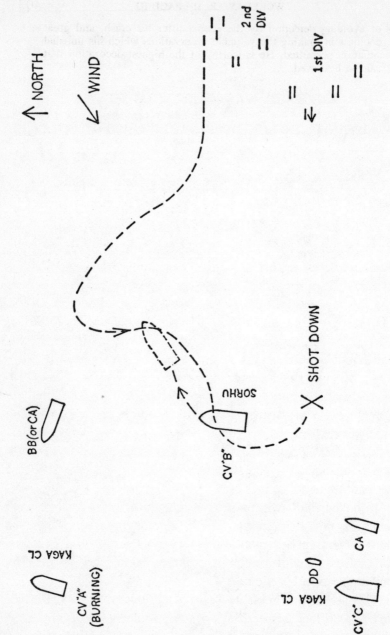

REVENGE WAS SWEET OFF MIDWAY

WALTER C. SWEENEY, JR., LIEUTENANT COLONEL

USAAF

Early in June it was my good fortune to be in command of three bombing flights against the Japanese fleet off Midway Island in two days. Every man in my command brought credit to himself and to the Army Air Forces. We acted jointly with Naval and Marine personnel, and all of us have only the most profound admiration for the coolness, courage, and bravery of such competent officers and men.

At Midway the morning of June 3 Navy patrol planes reported that a strong enemy surface force was approaching the island from a bearing of 265 degrees true.

Positive information came in about noon, and our flight of nine B-17Es took off immediately. After flying about three and a half hours we found the Jap ships, some 600 miles out, just where we had expected them.

It looked like an awful lot of ships down below. There were cruisers, transports, cargo vessels, and other escort ships. We must have surprised them, and we felt so at the time, because they started maneuvering at once. The maneuvering was orderly, but unquestionably violent.

This attack was made in flights at altitudes of 8,000, 10,000, and 12,000 feet, respectively. My flight picked out a large ship and bombed it. At the bomb-release line we encountered very heavy antiaircraft fire. It continued throughout the attack, and, as in the attacks that followed, was plenty heavy. My flight didn't claim any hits on this run. We hit all around the enemy, but we didn't see any evidence of damage.

Our second element, under the command of Captain Clement P. Tokarz, attacked a cruiser or battleship—we weren't worried about identification at the time—and left it burning.

The third element, led by Captain Cecil Faulkner, went after a cruiser and is believed to have hit it at the stern. One pilot in the second flight, Captain Paul Payne, couldn't get his bombs away on the first trip in so he returned through the ack-ack and got hits on a transport, setting it afire.

Then we headed for home in high spirits, our only regret being that we had no more bombs. On the way back, from about thirty miles away, we could see the heavy ship and the transport burning. They were both out of column and appeared motionless, with huge clouds of dark smoke mushrooming above them.

We returned to Midway in the dark, got a little sleep, and were up before daylight the next morning (June 4) to continue the attack.

This time we had more B-17s, seven having come in overnight. We assembled in the vicinity of a small island and proceeded out to attack the same main body we had bombed the previous afternoon. En route to the target we got word that another enemy task force, complete with carriers, was approaching Midway from 325 degrees true and was now at a distance of only about 145 miles from that base.

We turned to intercept and climbed to 20,000 feet. Cloud conditions were lower broken, bottoms at 1,000 feet, tops at 6,000 feet with high thin-scattered at 18,000 feet. The carriers were circling under the clouds, and we had to search for them. There isn't much doubt that they had seen us and were trying to avoid our planes.

All elements of the main body of the fleet could be observed except the carriers; then, after a search, three carriers were seen to break cloud coverage. Again it was Captain Payne who spotted the first carrier. He directed us over his radio, and we went in to attack.

The enemy started firing as soon as we opened our bomb bays. The fire wasn't effective but was a bit disturbing. The fighters came up to attack, maneuvering beautifully, but they failed to follow through. It appeared that their heart was not in their work, and in no case was their attack pressed home.

We divided our ships into three groups. Each group was instructed to take a carrier, and we bombed away. We are fairly certain we hit the first carrier, but we didn't claim it. The second group, under command of Captain Cecil Faulkner, hit its carrier amidships. Lieutenant Colonel Brooke Allen, commanding the last flight, secured hits on the third carrier. We didn't have time to wait and see them sink, but we left knowing they were badly crippled.

Captain Faulkner's tail gunner sustained the only injury—a cut finger. There was some damage to our planes from machine guns and antiaircraft fire, but we all returned to Midway successfully. We found the island had been attacked in our absence. During this attack we lost a crew chief and an officer who remained on the ground.

That same afternoon we went out again to attack a troop-ship convoy, reported to be approaching from 265 degrees true and estimated to be about 260 miles from Midway. En route we got orders to attack a carrier bearing 334 degrees true and about 180 miles from Midway. We searched that vicinity, but although a burning carrier and a burning capital ship were sighted, no commissioned carrier was located. We learned later that the others we had hit sank or were scuttled by the Japanese.

As sunset was approaching we decided to attack a heavy cruiser. All remaining units of the enemy fleet were now deployed and weaving. We attacked from 25,000 feet. Visibility was perfect and the bombing run excellent. At the bomb-release line an antiaircraft shell burst at our altitude off the wing of the number-three plane, followed by fairly heavy fire. As soon as our bombs were dropped we adopted evasive tactics.

We scored hits on the cruiser and left it burning, a heavy cloud of smoke issuing amidship. Numbers two and four planes were unable to release their bombs on the first run so they returned and attacked another ship. They did not remain to determine the results of their attack as the Japs had gotten a bracket on them, and the fire was extremely intense and all around them. About twenty-five enemy fighters were sighted below on a northerly heading as we put out for Midway, but none reached our altitude.

This same afternoon Major George Blakey led another flight of B-17s in and attacked the burning carrier. Attacking at very low altitude, they succeeded in scoring many hits.

All told, on the afternoon of June 4 our B-17s are credited with scoring three hits on a damaged carrier (probably the *Akagi*); one hit on a large ship; one hit on a cruiser which was left burning; and to have damaged one destroyer, believed to have sunk.

Other B-17s carried on the attack the next day (June 5), contacting an enemy contingent of battleships and cruisers to the westward of Midway despite unfavorable flying weather. Quoting the Navy's official report on that action by our Army bombers:

"They attacked, and scored a direct hit on the damaged cruiser. Another bomb damaged the same cruiser's steering gear. She was last observed listing badly and turning in tight circles. This attack was followed quickly by a second Army Air Force attack which scored a hit on the stern of a heavy cruiser. Meanwhile, at about noon (June 5) US Marine Corps aircraft located the damaged enemy cruiser and delivered one direct hit.

"In the afternoon of June 5, Army Flying Fortresses attacked enemy cruisers again and scored three direct hits upon one heavy cruiser. On the return trip, one of these planes was lost; a second was forced down at sea fifteen miles from Midway. All except one of the crew of the second plane were rescued."

Our morale was high throughout, but after it was over we were as tired a bunch of flyers as you ever wish to see.

A RAID ON BALIKPAPAN

RICHARD S. REYNOLDS, LIEUTENANT

USAAF

A kind of shiver runs through me when I hear that the target is Balikpapan, and I can feel it again when the briefing officer says we will be on our own. The distance is too great for fighters.

On the way to the line, I'm thinking about the target, Balikpapan. They told us in the operations tent that this will be a big one. It supplies fifteen percent of Japan's total aviation gasoline and oil. We are in for some fun; the Japs are sure to have plenty of stuff around a target like that.

We reach our B-24—*Burma*—we call her for that lovely comic-strip character—and check over our equipment and supplies. M/Sgt. Kurt Patzlaff, our crew chief, stands by, ready to defend his baby should we find some little thing wrong. We don't.

A brilliant October moon shines down, and I sit on the wing and write our load list by moonlight. Everything's set, and on signal from the tower we taxi out on the runway.

Tonight it's the number-one position in our squadron for us. Three other squadrons already have taken off. We are one of seventy-six tonight. A lot of bombs are on their way to Borneo.

I take my position in the well, forward of the bomb bays, to salvo our 250-pounders in case we lose an engine on takeoff. I stand there feeling a little miserable. I have had only two hours' sleep, and that's precious little when you are facing a sixteen-hour nonstop mission with an interlude over a rough target.

But now, *Burma* is roaring down the runway, and she lifts her heavy load of gasoline and bombs into the air. As we gain altitude, I look down on our runway lights. They will go off and then on again before we return.

I stand with my head in the transparent bubble on the roof of the plane, breathing oxygen through a mask. The cloud banks give me a sense of loneliness, as if *Burma* and the ten men inside her are flying this mission to Balikpapan alone. Yet I know if some giant searchlight were to sweep across the sky, other planes would be around us. Now and then, we can see the outline of one off our wingtip, and there is an occasional lurch caused by the slipstream of the Liberator ahead of us.

Eight hours have passed and now it is daylight. We are still over water, but land—enemy-held land—is in sight. We are nearing the target.

"Enemy interceptors ahead," our radio crackles, and we can see some of our planes already exchanging fire with them. A flaming thing curves across the sky and falls sharply away. One less Jap fighter.

We reach our initial point and turn for the bomb run. "It's your ship," the pilot calls over the interphone, and I know for ninety seconds I'll be in command, and our squadron will follow the course I set over the target.

Things are happening all around now. We expected about twenty-five enemy interceptors but there are fifty to sixty bearing down on us. I can hear our copilot and gunners calling out their positions.

"One high at twelve o'clock, two low at three."

"Watch those guys above us in the sun, Hass."

"Look out—here they come."

I can feel the vibration as our gunners fire round after round, and now we are over the target. Their ack-ack is opening up. It is very accurate, deadly. It has us bracketed. There goes one Lib, then another. Down they go, flaming a farewell to us. I split a beer with one of those guys last night.

But I've got to watch this mechanical brain. It is solving a problem from the information I put into it. Altitude, airspeed, drift. Now the pointers are closing. Bombs away! I try to get in on the interphone, but our copilot is screaming to our ball-turret gunner.

"Black, Black, two level at ten o'clock."

Black's vision is restricted, but he swings his turret around, and two Jap fighters close in together in trail to less than 100 yards. Black catches them in his sight and fires a long burst.

"I got one," he yells. "I saw the bastard explode."

"You did like hell," Romo at the right-waist gun shouts back. "You got both of them. I saw the pilot of the other ship bail out over here."

We have turned off the target now, and on the ground lights and explosions tumble on one another so rapidly I can't follow them. Weird pools of flame form in black clouds of smoke. Balikpapan's huge storage tanks of aviation gasoline are burning in a stew of fire and brimstone. I have seen fantastic sights in this war—a blue sky full of confetti that turned out to be paratroops, a big naval action at night, a dogfight between a P-38 and two Zeros—but I can roll all of them into one and still get no spectacle as eerie, as incredible, as this sea of flame beneath us. Even now, the black columns of smoke are at our flight level—18,000 feet.

The tempo of battle increases. They failed to stop us on our run, and now they are enraged and desperate. They come in even closer than before, flying recklessly in and out of our formation, always firing. One gets too reckless. He tries hard to pull up, but he is too late. He crashes into one of our bombers. Both planes explode and fall, twisting and burning. The pilot of that Lib was a buddy of mine; I feel slightly sick.

Now we are well away from the target, and most of our attackers have turned back. Their losses have been heavy—but our group paid dearly, too. Our pilot calls the crew, one by one, asking each in turn if he's all right and if he knows of damage to our plane. Jackson in the nose turret says, "I'm OK." I tell him I'm all right, and so on back to the tail turret. No answer. The waist gunners are ordered back for a look, and soon they tell us, "Mac has a slug in his leg and his interphone is shot out. There's a hell of a big hole in the horizontal stabilizer too." Seconds later, one of them adds, "Mac's OK. We can fix him up."

Our home field comes into sight just as the sun is dipping behind the horizon. We are very tired, very glad, very thankful. *Burma* seems to be, too, and she comes in for a perfect landing. She's very graceful for such a big girl. As we pull off the taxi strip and cut our engines, our crew chief walks slowly out of the twilight from the bunker's edge. He looks relieved. His name wasn't on our load list last night, but his heart was aboard, every minute of the mission.

One by one, others of our squadron come home.

"OLD 26" COMES HOME

ROBERT V. GUELICH, CAPTAIN

USAAF

WILLIAM G. MORS, SERGEANT

USAAF

Old 26 took off from her India base with the Flying Cobra Squadron on Armistice Day morning. Target for the day was He-ho airdrome, deep in Jap-held Burma. Photo-reconnaissance pictures showed *Zeros* at He-ho, lots of them; the crews had looked at the pictures the night before and knew the bombers would be intercepted.

Takeoff was routine. Because they were to fly number-three position in the first element of the squadron, pilot Lt. Ben Graves and copilot Lt. Cy Kurth swapped seats as they headed toward Burma through scattered clouds, flying in a formation that tightened up as the planes neared their target several hours later. On the flight deck behind the pilot was T/Sgt. Doug Labat, flight engineer of this B-24, who also held down the top-gun position.

At 16,000 feet *Old 26* went into its bomb run, hindered only by cloud fluffs below. At 1137 the bombardier sang out, "Bombs away!"—and the Japs struck. Sixteen *Zeros* dove out of a blinding sun.

Sergeant Labat, in the top turret, was tracking one of the Nips as the *Zero* swung out for its attack, when Graves called out a *Zero* coming in at one o'clock. But it was too late. Cannon shells ripped through the bomber, one exploding in the auxiliary wing tank with a burst of flaming gasoline. S/Sgt. William Burtch, in the nose turret, was killed in the attack as he, like Labat, was tracking the other Jap plane.

The second Nip was still in Labat's sights, but he was so intent on hitting him that he wasn't using his sights; a short burst from his twin .50s showed that the Jap was almost in range as he came boring in for a frontal attack.

"I opened up and poured a long burst that seemed like 600 but probably was sixty rounds into the Jap," Labat recalls. "Our nose turret wasn't firing at the *Zero;* I wondered why. My guns were so hot the turret cut out; I hit the reset button and threw more lead at him as he kept coming in at our nose until I was sure he was going to pull one of those 'For-the-Emperor' tricks and ram us.

"The terrific crash of an explosive shell, flying glass and debris around my legs, the rush of cold air, and a burst of flame from the Jap as some of my shells exploded his gas tanks—all happened simultaneously. When it seemed too late, the *Zero* pulled up just enough to miss us, hurtling over my guns like a Roman candle on the Fourth of July.

"I knew we were hit bad now; our wing still was burning. Before I could get out of my turret to see what had happened, the right wing dropped, and we slid off in a skidding dive underneath the other planes in our formation. Then I couldn't get out of my turret because the negative G had me plastered against the top. By reaching down to the ammunition boxes, I finally managed to pull myself down out of the dome as our radio-command set was screeching, 'Bail out, bail out before it's too late . . . bail out, you don't have a chance, bail out.'

"I never had thought much about hitting the silk before, and I didn't have time to think about it then for something was wrong in the cockpit and I had to know what it was. It was bad. Blood was splattered over everything, and maps and papers were flying around in the blast of air coming through a shell hole in the windshield. Kurth was slumped forward over the stick, Graves was wavering in his seat, and we were dropping fast."

Graves said, "For God's sake, get him out of there."

Labat unbuckled Kurth from his chute, and dragged him out of the seat. It didn't take a second glance to see what had happened. A 20-mm shell had pierced the windshield and exploded in Cy's face; he was dead—the quick way.

Labat clambered into the empty pilot's seat, captured the loose controls, and gradually dragged the diving *Liberator* out of its plunge. Graves, suffering from shrapnel wounds and shock from the shell explosion within a few feet from his head, still clung to consciousness and the controls. The plane responded and leveled off at 8,000 feet, still over enemy territory but far out of formation.

The wing fire had put itself out—the self-sealing fuel tank apparently having sealed off the gasoline after the first splattering from the explosive shell. The plane was riddled; two *Zeros* had followed *Old 26* most of the way down and had peppered it with shells. Both waist gunners had watched bullets pierce the fuselage where they had been a fraction of a second before as they were tossed about by the falling plane, but they had ducked them all; their numbers hadn't come up yet.

The hydraulic system was perforated in half a dozen places, and the prop governor on number three was frozen at 2,300 rpm. But the plane still was flying and had made its way back into another squadron's formation for protection. Graves, though still fighting off unconsciousness, told Labat he could hold the plane, so Labat took over his turret again.

Navigator Lt. Grant Erwin had been calling out *Zero* clock positions from his dome in front of the cockpit but couldn't get any responses on the interphone. He climbed up to the flight deck to investigate. When he saw Graves was wounded and flying by himself, he patched up his wounds with first-aid bandages and then slid into the empty seat to help fly the plane. Although he wasn't a pilot, Erwin had picked up copiloting time.

A Jap started coming in from twelve o'clock to finish off the crippled *Liberator*. Graves threw the ship into violent evasive maneuvers, but Labat held his guns on the Nip and drilled with short bursts until the Jap finally slid off in a dive (the action was witnessed by other crews and scored as a probable for Labat).

Despite the protection of two other ships that stayed with *Old 26,* another *Zero* came in for a pass, but the guns from all three planes played a tune on him. Without pressing his attack, the *Zero* pulled away and headed for home. Another *Zero* made a pass, but the tail guns of one of the protecting ships scared him homeward too.

At last feeling free of the Japs, Labat slipped out of his turret and discovered that Lieutenant Erwin was helping fly the ship. He then checked the gas supply and found it adequate for the long haul back home.

Bombardier Lt. Cecil Day and S/Sgt. Robert Block (radio operator and waist gunner) broke through the glass of the jammed nose turret and found Burtch with his guns pointed in the direction of the *Zero* he never got a shot at. His death grip on the interphone button had kept the system from operating.

S/Sgt. James McKernan, in his belly turret, had been doused by fluid from the ruptured hydraulic lines but had kept playing his guns to make the Japs think he was still in action, although he couldn't see through his glass enclosure.

After checking the gas, Labat relieved Erwin at the controls, so he could return to his navigating job. During the fight, Erwin had mentally noted headings and speed and now was able to determine the location of the plane after the protecting ships pulled away. Lieutenant Day, the bombardier, who had been circulating through the ship, bolstering the spirits of the rest of the crew, now took over the top-turret position.

Behind the controls again, Labat mentally projected the entire return trip. "I even pictured myself on the approach to our field and went to the extent of worrying whether I could clear the wires at the end of the field on landing, even to the point of foolishly thinking of flying under them."

As Graves, still in a semiconscious condition, continually made instinctive adjustments of the controls, Labat patiently corrected them and eased the ship back on course. Although number-three prop had been a drag with its frozen governor, it was a help at cruising speed, so it was not feathered.

"*Zero* at five o'clock at 2,000 yards," came barking over the interphone from waist gunner Sergeant Block, and a grim tenseness settled down on *Old 26*. Another attack might be the last straw. A second *Zero* appeared, and both started to follow the wounded ship. The crew sat and waited, a wait of years that ended when Erwin told Labat to head for an emergency landing at a nearby field. When the plane nosed down for its approach to the field, the *Zeros* turned away.

On the downwind leg of the landing approach, Labat learned that the crew couldn't get the landing gear cranked down. He turned the controls over to Erwin with instructions not to go in for a landing until the gear was reported down (the nose wheel had dropped down OK, but one wheel wouldn't lock into position). The plane was on its final approach, hardly fifteen feet above some sailing ships, before the wheel finally clicked into place.

Swinging back to the flight deck, Labat saw a dike looming up ahead of the plane—too high to clear. All he could do, as Graves was shooting the landing, was talk into his ear. "Haul back, haul back, haul back." The big plane eased up a bit, but the wheels dug into the dike and before anyone could catch another breath

Graves had recovered and set the ship down perfectly on the runway.

With only 800 pounds of hydraulic pressure remaining, Labat again resorted to repetition as he warned Erwin and Graves to keep their feet on the brakes, not to let up for an instant. There was only one application of brakes left in *Old 26*.

The brakes held, and as the battered ship rolled to a stop, Graves, who had been flying on spirit and instinct all the way, passed out completely. Ambulance and crash truck came to a wailing stop as Labat and Erwin carried out their wounded pilot.

B-29 RAID ON JAPAN

LOU STOUMEN, SERGEANT

USAAF

A Forward Air Base in China [By Radio]—For three weeks I had sweated out a ride on one of the B-29 Superfortresses that were going to bomb Japan. Luck finally came my way just two hours before take-off. I was given the chance to flip a coin with a British civilian correspondent for the last seat. "Tails," I called, as he tossed an Indian coin in the air. Tails it was. He tossed the coin again. Tails a second time. I grabbed a parachute and rushed to the field.

Brig. Gen. Kenneth B. Wolfe, the homely, smiling commanding general of the XX Bomber Command, was sitting in a jeep in front of Operations and looking unusually glum. He had just received orders from Washington not to fly with the mission he had planned for so long. Brig. Gen. La Verne G. Saunders, wing commander of the XX, who has a lot of South Pacific B-17 combat flying time under his belt, was going to fly this mission to represent the higher brass.

Soon I was drawing my equipment. I replaced my parachute with another, because mine had no jungle kit attached. I also drew a helmet with earphones and an oxygen mask, a rubber Mae West life jacket, a plastic-boxed survival kit (fishhooks, dextrose tablets, first-aid materials and other stuff), a pointie-talkie book of Chinese and English phrases in parallel columns, a heavy steel-filled flak suit and certain confidential material.

They told me that, except in an emergency, there was no need to take oxygen; one of the secrets of the B-29 is its sealed pressure cabin, which makes possible normal breathing and movement without oxygen at any altitude. I was also told the target: Yawata, the juiciest industrial center in all Japan, home of the Imperial Iron and Steel Works.

"Crew inspection! Let's go!" Capt. R. A. Harte of Lafayette, Ind., plane commander and pilot of our B-29, was speaking. The enlisted crewmen lined up in front of the silver Superfortress and alongside the big black letters K-26 on her nose. Each man showed his dogtags to Capt. Harte; each said yes, he carried an extra pair of socks. Then the captain, unsmiling, made a brief speech.

"We have," he said, "a pretty fair ship and a pretty good chance of coming back without a scratch. We are going to take as much cover as possible from the clouds. We won't take cover at the expense of hitting the target. If any plane pokes her nose near us, you know what to do. We take off in about 10 minutes. Man your stations!"

The B-29 needs a longer runway for take-off than any other plane. I stood on my knees during the take-off and looked out of a side blister as the ship, the world's heaviest aircraft, pounded and blasted her way down the runway. The strip unfolded like a never-ending drive belt of a factory motor, going by in slow motion until it seemed we had been roaring along for a full 10 minutes and were still not airborne. Then there was the green end of the runway, and we were skimming a few feet above trees and rice paddies.

During the take-off I also watched Sgt. D. L. Johnson of Rio, Ill., the right gunner; Sgt. R. G. Hurlburt of Gaines, Pa., the left gunner; S/Sgt. A. (for Algernon) Matulis, the chief gunner, and 2d Lt. Tash of New York, N. Y., the bombardier. They held on tight. When we were airborne, their faces cracked in smiles and their bodies eased. "She's a good ship," said Johnson, as he wiped a wet hand across his face. "But some good guys get killed in take-offs."

That was the first of several sweating outs. A few miles out and a few hundred feet up, someone noticed the No. 2 engine smoking and reported it over the interphone to Capt. Harte. "Probably the fuel mixture's too rich," said Lt. Tash. And that's what it turned out to be; the smoking soon stopped. But the men sweated it out anyway. They were afraid the ship might have to turn back. As anxious as they were to return home safely, the dangers of the mission evidently meant much less to them than the danger of missing out on bombing Japan.

One ship did have to turn back, we learned later. The men returned only four hours after take-off, both GIs and officers with tears in their eyes, some of them openly crying and all of them cursing. The pilot kept repeating, over and over: "God damn the engines! God damn the engines! God damn the engines!"

After getting the plane commander's okay over the interphone, I followed Lt. Tash forward on hands and knees through the long padded tunnel over the bomb bay. Lt. Tash took his position in the greenhouse nose, and I kneeled over the hatch cover behind the pilot and next to the engineer, 2d Lt. G. I. Appognani of New York, N. Y. The engineer sits before a four-foot panel of dials, flashing lights, switches and control levers. He handles the main throttles for the four engines, controls the fuel supply and mixture, regulates the ship's electrical system and operates the pressure cabin's mechanism.

There was still light in the sky as we crossed the border of Free China into Occupied China, flying higher now, and began our next sweating out—waiting for interception by enemy fighters. There was a large force of B-29s on the mission, but we saw only an occasional plane ahead of us through the clouds or above and to the left of us. A B-29 needs elbow room to fly, to shoot and to bomb. This was not a formation flight.

Still no Jap fighters. It was dark now, and we were approaching the coast of China. Each man was wearing a Mae West over his parachute. The plane groaned on at terrific speed. There was practically no vibration inside and very little noise. In the cabin, the ride was as comfortable as a Pullman—a design for the airliners of the future. But the Jap fighters—where were they?

"We are four and a half hours from Japan," said 2d Lt. E. K. Johnson of Portland, Oreg., over the interphone. Then came the voice of Matulis: "No. 3 engine throwing a lot of sparks." The engineer, Lt. Appognani, looked out his window and confirmed this. No. 3 engine kept throwing sparks most of the way out and back. That was something else to sweat out.

The radio operator, Sgt. E. A. Gisburne of Norway, Maine, broke open a carton of rations and handed a candy bar to each man in the forward compartment. We were one short, and the engineer shared his bar with me. Candy never tasted so good. We downed it with long swigs of water from canteens. The engineer and the navigator also took benzedrine tablets, the same drug I remembered using back in school to keep awake for my final exams. By this time I was comfortably stretched out on the hatch cover in back of the pilot's, using my parachute and jungle kit as a bed. We were flying over the Yellow Sea toward Japan, but the sea was not visible; the weather was too dark and too cloudy.

At last a voice came over the interphone: "We are approaching the target." Everyone began to struggle into his heavy flak suit, putting it on over the parachute, strapping it securely at the sides and pulling the bottom flap down over the thighs like a baseball catcher's chest protector. Only Capt. Harte and the co-pilot, Lt. Haddow, busy at the controls, didn't put on their flak suits.

We were over Japan now. Through breaks in the clouds I could see the ground below. The Japanese blackout was perfect.

Then dead ahead, a faint white globe—Jap searchlights over Yawata, the target city.

The sharp voice of Matulis, the chief gunner, came over the interphone: "Tracers. They are coming right past the ship." There was a pause, then someone said: "Tracers, hell. It's only No. 3 engine throwing sparks again." He was right. Over the interphone came a chorus of wry laughs.

The searchlights were brighter now, but their dangerous pointing fingers were diffused through the undercast of clouds. The tail gunner, S/Sgt. F. G. Hodgen, said our tail was caught several times by lights. Apparently we were not seen through the clouds, and the lights moved on. Still no Jap fighters.

The target was just ahead. There was no fiery glow through the clouds to show it had already been hit. We had been the fourth plane to take off from the field and were evidently one of the first over the target.

Flak! The gunners said the sky was full of exploding ack-ack shells, some close, most of them beneath us. Intelligence reports confirmed this later, calling the ack-ack "moderate to intense." But I saw no flak.

Later we learned that searchlights caught one of the last planes over the target, the one on which Bill Shenkel, *Newsweek's* correspondent, was a passenger, and held it in a firm bracket of light until gunners shot it down with all four motors streaming fire.

Our bomb-bay doors were swinging open now, without noise and without making the rest of the ship vibrate. The bombs dropped, one by one, one by one. . . . Then, over the interphone: "Bombs away!" The doors closed.

The K-26 seemed to sprout an extra set of engines and props. At a terrifically increased speed, she made a sharp left turn and headed back toward the Yellow Sea. Over the interphone, tail gunner Hodgen yelled: "I can't see very much through the clouds, but there's a big glow over the target."

The clouds were still below us. B-29s that came in later could see, from 50 miles away, columns of smoke and fire rising 5,000 feet into the air. Yawata, the Pittsburgh of Japan, had been hit hard. This was no token raid but, as Brig. Gen. Wolfe put it, "the beginning of the organized destruction of the Japanese industrial empire."

We were still tense after the bomb run. The Jap fighters had not come up to meet us yet, and the sweating out continued. We left Japan without interception and flew out over the Yellow Sea.

An hour out and radio operator Gisburne broke into the ration box. For each man there was a large can of grapefruit juice, which we opened with jungle knives, and chicken sandwiches, not too expertly made. The bread was too thick. Good, though. We chewed gum and smoked.

Over the China coast—Occupied China—not a single fighter came up. 2d Lt. E. M. Greenberg of Brooklyn, N. Y., combat observer, had by this time crawled forward to his station amidships and was helping the engineer make fuel-tank adjustments. "You know," said Lt. Greenberg, "the Fourteenth Air Force must have done a hell of a good job with their B-24s over the Jap fighter fields in China." Being a last-minute passenger, I had missed the briefing, so he explained: "The Fourteenth went out yesterday and bombed the Jap fighter strips we're flying over now."

But still, the raids could not have knocked out every Jap plane in the area, and even if they had, that wouldn't explain why there were no fighters over Japan. Either we really caught them flat-footed or they were plenty scared of B-29 firepower. Probably both.

Time marched on like a crippled snail. We had been flying almost half a day. With the flak suits off again, we were more comfortable. The No. 3 engine was behaving well enough. My parachute-bed was soft. I slept.

Dawn over Free China: a wild, gray sky of tumultuous clouds, empty of aircraft. I crawled back through the tunnel and batted the breeze with the gunners for a while. Then I returned to the forward compartment. Capt. Harte and Lt. Haddow looked plenty different from the eager beavers who had coaxed the K-26 off the ground so many hours ago. Now their bloodshot eyes hung heavily over pouches that looked like squashed prunes. You'd have thought that someone had been beating them about the head with a rubber hose, judging by their appearance toward the end of this longest bombing mission in history.

"Fighters!" exclaimed Lt. Tash. He put his binoculars on them. They were ours—fast, high-altitude American fighters flying top cover over the B-29 fields. At last, at the dead center of our course, the home field came into sight. It looked miles long, even from our altitude. Loud flopping, banging noises came from the No. 3 engine. "Engineer to pilot," said a voice over the interphone, "don't count on No. 3 engine for landing." "Maybe," said Sgt. Gisburne, "we got hit by ack-ack after all. It sounds like No. 3 was hit." There was a burst of sparks from No. 3's exhaust, and the engineer said he was afraid the engine would catch fire.

We made a long, sharp bank and approached for the landing. No. 3 continued to bang and throw sparks, but it didn't get any worse. We came in fast, about 20 feet above the end of the runway. Gently Capt. Harte set her down, like a mother placing a child in a crib. We rolled a great distance, about the speed of a fast car on a U. S. highway. Then slower, without stopping, we turned and taxied to a parking strip. The crew piled out through the bottom hatches, limp and happy. Ground crewmen and intelligence officers were there to greet them.

While the handshaking and congratulations were still going on, M/Sgt. Herb Coggins of Nashville, Tenn., chief of the K-26's ground crew, was already walking around the ship with Lt. Appognani, the engineer, looking for flak holes.

Later, in the interrogation room, A-2 officers gave each man some egg sandwiches, coffee and suitable refreshments. Then the questioning began. When the intelligence reports were finally tallied up, it turned out that four B-29s had been lost—one shot down over the target, one unreported and two lost in accidents. The entire crew of one of these planes, which made a forced landing just this side of Occupied China after completing the bombing mission, came back two days later. The pilot was wounded in the eye when Japs strafed and bombed his grounded plane.

Back in the barracks, still sweating out their unreported buddies, the weary flight crews turned to their sacks. From beneath the mosquito-net cover on a bed came a last crack: "Somebody tell me a spooky story. I love to hear a spooky story before I go to sleep."

A Superfortress Base, Western China—Half a million Chinese laborers, working from dawn till dusk and getting about 10 cents and a bowl of rice a day, built the vast system of forward airfields in China that made possible the first B-29 raid on the industrial heart of Japan.

Lt. Col. Waldo L. Kenerson of the U. S. Army Engineers, a native of Marblehead, Mass., supervised the construction of the air-base system, together with officials of the Chinese Ministry of Communications. The bases form a great Chinese fan covering many square miles of former riceland. Several of the fields are oversized and extra hard, so they can take the B-29s. Others are fighter fields, housing new high-altitude pursuit planes. Still others are outer-ring emergency fields.

Army engineers here compared the job with the building of the Burma Road and the Great Wall of China. But they said this project was so vast and so quickly accomplished that it has no parallel in history. Construction of the airbase system cost 6 billion inflated Chinese dollars (about 150 million dollars in U. S. currency).

On Apr. 24, 1944, just 90 days after the first dike was broken to drain the water from the rice paddies, the first B-29 landed on one of the airfields. It was piloted by Brig. Gen. Kenneth B. Wolfe, commanding general of the XX Bomber Command, and co-piloted by Brig. Gen. La Verne B. Saunders, a wing commander of the XX.

Exactly 26 American officers and enlisted men, plus a large corps of Chinese engineers and government officials, supervised the half-million Chinese coolies. Individual U. S. GIs, such as T/Sgt. Aaron Jones of Shelton, Conn., Sgt. Henry B. Dresen of Seattle, Wash., and T-5 B. W. Harwood of Laredo, Tex., had as many as 23,000 men working under them at one time.

Behind the building of the superbases was the epic building and proving of the B-29 Superfortress. Behind it was much sweat and long-range global planning by the General Staff in Washington—for the XX Bomber Command is accountable not to the local China-Burma-India command but directly to Gen. H. H. Arnold, CG of the AAF, and to the Joint Chiefs of Staff.

Target dates for completion of the bases were set by President Roosevelt and Generalissimo Chiang Kai-shek at the Cairo Conference in 1943. These dates were met and in some cases bettered.

Lt. Col. Kenerson, his small American staff and Chinese engineers began paper work in January 1944. Working 18 hours a day, they finished this part of the project in 20 days.

While the plans were still on the drawing boards, the preliminary draining and clearing of the land was already in progress, and the governor of "Air Base Province," under orders from Chungking, was already conscripting Chinese farmers for the heavy labor ahead. About 360,000 laborers were drafted.

The other 140,000 were employed as workers by private Chinese construction firms which had contracted to do various specific jobs, and as rice carriers, pay clerks, Red Cross workers and administrators servicing the armies of laborers.

Only in patient, hard-working China, with its manpower reservoir of 400 millions, could this job have been done in such jig time. "I doubt very much," said Lt. Col. Kenerson, "if we could require a job of similar magnitude in the States to be completed within the time allowed, even with the skilled labor and mechanical equipment available."

The air-base labor draft hit the Chinese farmers hard. Already millions of China's fittest young men were in the Army, and many were dead. Old men, young boys, heads of families, women and young girls had to leave their homes and their growing crops in the hands of neighbors while they went to do unaccustomed manual labor on the airfields. These people were farmers, and they had to be taught the construction trade.

Families were broken up, crops were lost, the work was harder than any they had done before, and incomes dropped almost to the vanishing point in China's spiraling inflation. But the farmers of Air Base Province responded to the need with patience and good humor.

They moved out to the field sites in armies, as many as 110,-000 on a single field. They smiled smiles of curiosity and genuine good-fellowship at the few Americans they met there, and exchanged thumbs-up signs and the words *"Ding Hao! (Everything's okay!)"* with them. And, best of all, the Chinese understood why they were working so hard—working all the time they were not eating or sleeping. Chinese propaganda units from Chungking explained to them why the Americans had come to China.

Specifications for the China air-base system were exceptionally rigid, for these fields were designed for the world's heaviest military planes. Slight dips and ridges that were okay on a B-24 or a B-17 field could not be tolerated here. And the high landing speed and long take-off run of the B-29 meant that the fields had to be longer than any forward combat fields ever built, so long that a man at one end could scarcely distinguish a man at the other.

The rice paddies were drained. The soft century-old mud,

sometimes six to nine feet deep, was carried away in the picturesque shoulder-borne tandem baskets so common throughout
Asia. Tons of stones, worn round by the water, were carried
from river beds to the strips in the same useful baskets. Larger
boulders were patiently crushed with small sledges, the fragments were crushed again into gravel, the gravel was carried in
the baskets to the strips. Acres of dirt were dug up with iron
Chinese tools, a cross between a pick and a shovel. The dirt was
carried to the strips in the baskets by never-ending queues of
workers—men, women and children doing the job entirely by
hand.

And then 10-ton rollers, some carved by hand from sand-
stone and others made of iron, were pulled on ropes by many
hundreds of workers the wearying length and breadth of the
strips. No bulldozers or other mechanical equipment had been
flown across the Hump to do the job, although there were a very
few trucks with very little gas on hand.

When the strips had been rolled, black tung oil—a tarlike
substance that comes from a Chinese tree—was spread out to
bind the dirt and gravel and help keep down the dust.

More than 80 Chinese workers lost their lives in construction
accidents. The most terrible of these deaths were caused by the
10-ton rollers, which could not be stopped quickly. If an un-
lucky worker stumbled and fell in the path of one of these
rollers, he was squashed into a bloody pancake—and the roller
went on, for the work could not stop. Some 25 men died this
way.

As barracks, built for the Americans at the expense of the
Chinese government, went up, and as more U. S. administrative,
ground and maintenance men flew in over the Hump to prepare
for the coming operation, a new level of Chinese-American
friendship was established. The Army and the U. S. Office of
War Information brought American movies with Chinese titles
to the laborers and townspeople. As many as 30,000 Chinese,

few of whom had ever seen a movie before, craned their necks at one time on one flight strip to see an American film.

The Chinese reciprocated. Those who could afford to do so invited Americans to their homes, making no distinction between officers and GIs.

And when the B-29s roared back from Yawata, word of where they had been and what they had done spread quickly. Shouts of *"Ding Hao!"* were almost as loud as the motors of the B-29s, and Chinese grins of welcome to the flyers were almost as broad as the landing strips the Chinese had built with their own sweat and blood.

MEN OF THE B-29s

KENNETH B. WOLFE, BRIGADIER GENERAL

USAAF

When the time came for our first B-29 outfit to move overseas we were falling short of our own training standards, but by any other standards we had the best-trained heavy bombardment organization ever to leave the States.

This merely means that the standards we had set for the B-29 program were virtually out of reach of both men and machines. It is doubtful that we would have accomplished our mission if we had not raised our sights that high.

Our directive from the commanding general was to commit the B-29 to combat without delay. To carry out his orders, we supervised and expedited all production, flight-tested the experimental planes, flew acceptance tests on all new-production aircraft, effected modifications while prescribing changes in equipment for later models, determined the flight characteristics and limitations of our aircraft, established tactics best suited for combat, trained air and ground crews, and prepared all squadrons for combat service overseas.

Eleven months after the first combat B-29 rolled off the production line, we had bombed the Japanese homeland.

Much has been said and written about the planes of that first outfit—the 58th Very Heavy Bombardment Wing—but I look back on the preparatory phase of the B-29 program primarily as a struggle of men against unique engineering, production, training, and tactical problems.

When D-Day came for the 20th Bomber Command in China, and our B-29s took off to bomb the Jap steel center of Yawata, the bombers carried veterans of many air campaigns, including men who had first challenged the enemy after Pearl Harbor as members of the 19th and 11th Bombardment Groups. Men who had helped engineer the B-29 through production also were there, some flying as regular combat crewmen. At the bases were hundreds of ground men who had pioneered their jobs and become specialists at them. In the background were hundreds of thousands of Chinese coolies who had carved out our airfields by hand. Back home there were more thousands of aircraft workers who had given us our planes. How these men—working together—made that first B-29 mission possible is the manpower story behind this three-billion-dollar gamble on long-range heavy bombardment aircraft.

We started from scratch. We began with what was still, by military necessity, an incompletely designed, experimental airplane—more complicated than any ever before used in aerial warfare. When the 58th Bombardment Wing was activated on June 1, 1943, we had no personnel, no planes, no precedents.

As our first step, we moved in with the Boeing company at its Wichita, Kansas, plant and we brought along some of the top engineers of the Matériel Command. Our test pilots were experienced command pilots; our crew members were high-ranking experts who had helped develop the equipment we were to fly. Our production men had been working with the B-29 since the aircraft was on blueprints in 1939. Our training instructors were veterans of more than a year of combat operations.

Officially, we received our first experimental XB-29 from Boeing on May 28, 1943. Two weeks later, the first production-type plane was flown successfully. The first of the combat B-29s rolled off the line in July.

While we were flying continuously to test all of the capabilities and idiosyncrasies of the new bomber, we organized the staff of the 58th Wing, which later was to become the 20th Bomber Command. Brigadier General Laverne Saunders, former CO of the 11th Bombardment Group and air adviser to Admiral Halsey during the Solomons operations; Colonel Richard H. Carmichael, who had formerly commanded the 19th Bombardment Group in the Southwest Pacific; Colonel Leonard F. Harman, B-29 project officer from the Matériel Command, and others of equal caliber were selected as staff members.

Already we had started ground-crew training in the Boeing factories, with our mechanics working side by side with the men and women who were building the B-29s. Our men worked on the flight lines of Boeing at Wichita and Bell at Marietta, Georgia, where we were flying accelerated service tests. At the same time, subassemblies were being shipped to train new factory workers in B-29 construction at the Bell plant.

New crews were checking out in the B-29s while they were being flight-tested. As rapidly as these tests uncovered "bugs," engineers took the problems to Wright Field's laboratories and worked them out. Their expeditious handling of our design and mechanical problems continuously contributed to improve the performance and reliability of our new plane. We were rolling because we had to roll. We were accomplishing a week's research, testing, modification, and training every twenty-four hours.

Near the Bell plant, on an unpretentious Georgia estate, we set up the first headquarters of the 58th Wing. The area was officially the Cobb County Army Air Field, and it was the logical choice for our headquarters at that time since modifications and most of the Army's B-29 flight-testing were scheduled for Marietta, Georgia. From this headquarters, on June 21, 1943, General Order No. 1 was issued, announcing my assumption of command of the "58th Bombardment Operational Training Wing (Heavy)."

In September, to be near tactical units then undergoing training, we moved to Smoky Hill Army Air Field at Salina, Kansas—a post so forlorn that our GIs jokingly asked for theater ribbons for serving out of the States. We had only a few B-29s for flight training, but we had to instruct our crews in long-range, high-altitude formation and instrument flying. We decided to answer our immediate problems with other bombardment aircraft.

Fifty B-26s were obtained to familiarize pilots and copilots with tricycle-gear landing and glide characteristics of a high-wing-loaded airplane. Later we secured B-17s because of the similarity of its mechanical parts to those of the B-29 and because reasonably long-range, high-altitude missions could be flown with these planes.

At Salina we benefited from the experience of the Second Air Force in training of heavy bombardment groups. Although our problems were different, training methods essentially were similar. Selection of personnel specifically qualified for B-29 work necessitated constant review of training schools and individual requirements, particularly since about 50 per cent of the personnel supplied at this time proved to be physically disqualified for high-altitude combat-crew duty. Fortunately, many of the rejected men were found suitable for ground-crew work.

While trying to speed up production of the B-29s' new 2200-horsepower engines, which was falling behind schedule, and trying to stimulate the slow operation of modifying B-29s with unskilled personnel, we also had to organize our tactical units and solve the logistics problems of moving all units overseas and providing for their maintenance in the theater of operations.

After full study of possible maintenance and supply plans, we prepared to set up a maintenance squadron at every field to be used by B-29s. Such squadrons would be able to keep the planes in operation at forward as well as rear bases. The training of these advance squadrons was a priority project because we had to ship the men and their equipment by boat at least two months before our air units left the States. The final decision required the movement of ground units in January and air units in March of 1944. How to house these men and how to set up our bases in India and China, and how to operate and maintain our planes once we arrived there were added worries. We were continually sending various staff members from our organization to the CBI to lay the groundwork for our movement to the theater. And at this time the fact that we were to operate from bases in India and China was still highly secret information.

While this work was progressing, we were attending to one of our most vital assignments: the drafting of our recommendation to General Arnold on how we proposed to use the B-29 tactically. Thus, long before we had any tactical squadrons trained or equipped, we had worked out with the Air Staff the plan of attack which our aerial task force was committed to accomplish.

Progress of the training program upon which the success of our missions hinged was discouraging at this stage. We didn't have enough planes for complete training of flight crews, and our crew specialists and ground personnel had to be given extra training to measure up to the high standards we had set, despite their completion of specialized courses in AAF schools.

After hundreds of hours of semioperational flying, we had determined that most efficient use of the plane could be attained with a crew of eleven men. The pilot and plane commander and the copilot were assigned the conventional responsibility of flying the airplane, except for operation of the power plants. This task was assigned to the flight-engineer officer, who would adjust the carburetor mixture, regulate manifold pressure, transfer fuel, and, in general, control the power output of the engines at all times, subject of course to instructions from the pilot.

At first, our new flight engineers were eyed suspiciously by pilots as surplus personnel usurping some of their own functions. However, as crew-team training progressed, the value of keeping one man's complete attention on power and fuel-system problems was proved, and the flight engineers were accepted in good standing with the combat team long before our planes left the States.

Because there was no background whatever in the AAF for training personnel on any type of B-29 equipment, our policy was to insist that every man who was to have any responsibility in operation or maintenance of the plane had to know its structure and equipment from wing tip to tail fin, including all of its capabilities and limitations under combat conditions.

Colonel Harman, who had grown up with the plane from the drafting board, summed up the AAF attitude this way: "We think a hell of a lot of knowledge about the B-29 is necessary before any man can develop all of the capabilities that have been built into the airplane by the hundreds of engineers and scientists who created it as a military weapon."

When we entrust eleven men with a million-dollar weapon, we have a right to expect them to use it to the maximum of its effectiveness. Every man had to be an expert.

Now and then, we established new training aids and methods to attain our high standards. In addition to his many engineering contributions, Colonel Howard H. Couch, chief of the technical staff, who later disappeared on a routine flight over the India-China "Hump," introduced a pocket-size picturized training manual that enabled our men to learn in about fifty minutes the same information that previously had required some two hours with standard training manuals.

Our men were enthusiastic in their training, eager to learn their tasks, itching to be on their way to combat. They liked their planes. They liked their organizations. Each and every one of our GIs and officers had contributed to the building of our first tactical B-29 unit. As training progressed, excitement about our combat assignment increased.

A conference was held in General Arnold's office on December 21. After outlining our progress to the General, who was to be in command of the Twentieth Air Force, I was on my way when he said: "You had better get over there yourself. Think you can make it by Sunday?"

After my arrival in India, the entire staff back in Kansas was officially apprised of our theater of operations and our mission for the first time. We would operate from rear bases in India, forward bases in China, and our targets would include the islands of Japan and some areas in Manchuria.

During the next few weeks, our maintenance squadrons and the depot group for our rear-echelon bases were shipped out of the States. Supplies were 98 per cent at the embarkation port by the middle of January, when a letter reached me, advising: "You have coming to the theater enough supplies to cover about 150 acres piled 100 feet high. . . ." And this represented only our initial requirements.

To expedite delivery of needed supplies from India to China, a number of C-87s were assigned by ATC as cargo carriers for the B-29s. C-46s later supplemented this force. However, the supply requirements of the advance China bases were so great that, after their arrival in April, B-29s flew thousands of tons of gasoline, bombs, and supplies over the "Hump" for their own use.

In February a depot group, assigned to the B-29s for work at our rear bases, arrived in India. Maintenance squadrons docked during the following two months and prepared for the arrival of our air echelon at bases being rushed to completion by engineers and Indians.

Back at Salina, late in March, the last of our quota of planes was delivered to the crews. As rapidly as planes could be loaded with engines and spare parts, they began sifting out of the country, each with a complete combat crew.

First plane to reach India was that of Colonel Harman, who settled the big plane down on the runway of our dry and dusty base on April 2. As others arrived on succeeding days, we again resumed our training program.

Keeping our planes in commission was a major problem. During the day they were peppered with hot, dry, dusty winds, and at night they were drenched by the humid atmosphere. Air crews joined ground crews in their constant maintenance and repair work, for all were eager to put in more flying time before the big show started.

Whenever possible during the next two months, we would load up the Superfortresses with bombs and gasoline and fly nonstop to our bases in China, building up a reserve of supplies for our first missions. This flying—a distance of more than 1000 miles at an altitude above 22,000 feet—provided crews with excellent operational flying experience in the theater before our first mission was scheduled.

Only once did Jap fighters attempt interception. Five of them made passes at a B-29 over the Hump, but they inflicted no damage. When under fire, one of the enemy planes fell out of control and in flames into the clouds below. The B-29 was credited with a probable.

By the first of June, just one year after our B-29 unit was activated, we were ready to fly our first tactical mission. Bangkok, Thailand, the rail and shipping funnel for Jap military supplies to Burma, was selected as our target on the shakedown mission. This was the dress rehearsal, the critical mission that would give us the final information on the capabilities and limitations of our crews and planes.

Early on the morning of June 5, scores of B-29s roared down the runways, soared into the hot, humid air of a monsoon daybreak over India. Weather was bad, making formation flying virtually impossible. Navigators and pilots and flight engineers sweated out one of the toughest flights they had ever made. Over the target, they found 7/10 cloud cover. They dropped their bombs and fought off a small attacking force of nine Jap fighters between 20,000 and 25,000 feet, scoring one probable and two damaged. Flak was heavy, but only one B-29 received a minor hit, in the tail.

The mission was an operational success. We were ready to launch our attacks on Japan.

On June 15, 1944, as summer twilight settled down, our B-29s lifted their wheels off the runways of our Chinese bases, with bombs for Japan. Many of our crews personally were avenging the Jap attacks of December 7, but strategically we were doing even more—we were ending forever the immunity of the Jap homeland from destruction by our bombs.

Many hours later, our radio operator at the home base waved his arms and shouted, "Betty! Betty! Betty!"—the code word we all were waiting to hear.

Our B-29s were over the target. It was bombs away on Japan.

FROM KANSAS TO TOKYO

MILTON R. KRIMS, MAJOR

USAAF

This is the story of how one B-29 and its crew became operational. It could be the story of many B-29s and many crews now hitting Japan.

The Superfort grew up somewhere in Kansas. In another part of Kansas, at practically the same time, eleven men were learning to become its crew. First there was the airplane commander, a West Point graduate, class of '43. His name was Capt. Russell J. Smith. Three corporals were added as gunners: Edward Zita in the right blister, Charles E. Boland in the left blister, and Joseph P. Bohan in the tail. Later were added 2d Lt. Robert Dean as copilot, 1st Lt. Carlysle E. Schnelle as bombardier, 2d Lt. James E. McLain as navigator, 2d Lt. Raymond Yeager as special equipment operator, Cpl. Sam Schulman as radio operator, Cpl. Boyd Mericle as central fire control operator, and Cpl. Hayden F. Washington as flight engineer.

This was the crew. They flew navigation missions to Cuba and Puerto Rico. Once they lost an engine about an hour out of Puerto Rico and got back with a new confidence. They went to a B-29 plant, watched an airplane being built. But always they wanted a plane of their own. Even when they began processing for overseas duty—straggling from office to office making out papers, getting sore arms from shots, kidding about infectious diseases—they still didn't have their own plane.

Then one day their airplane was sitting on the ramp. Separately, they wandered down to admire the shiny new B-29. One by one they went inside, handled controls and guns and instruments, each man especially concerned with the tools of his job.

When the time came for the overseas hop, takeoff was delayed by a leak in the relief valve to the debooster. Standing around on a cold, windy morning, waiting for the valve to be replaced, they grumbled about it being a hell of a way to get started.

The seven-hour flight from Kansas to Mather Field, Calif., Port of Aerial Embarkation, was routine except that number-one engine carburetor acted up, making it necessary to operate on auto rich most of the time. At Mather the maintenance boys installed a new carburetor, and, while they were at it, replaced a cracked glass in the bombardier's pane.

The schedule was rigid at Mather—checking and processing, briefing on everything from navigation to tropical diseases. And they had time to wonder about their B-29. The flight engineer wasn't at all sure about the wisdom of keeping cowl flaps closed down to within temperature tolerance; he'd always believed a reasonably low cylinder-head temperature was easier on the engines. But he appreciated the cruise control charts. Time and again he'd been told that if he adhered to their established requirements, he would get maximum efficiency with minimum fuel consumption. The plane had been washed and steam-cleaned at Mather, and they wondered how many mph this would add to the previous speed.

From the time they left Mather to arrival in Hawaii, the radio operator, navigator, and engineers were constantly busy; pilot or copilot occasionally adjusted the turn control on the automatic pilot to correct a tendency to drift to the right. The navigator was determined to find Hawaii on no more than three readings.

The airplane commander, the group flight engineer, 1st Lt. John L. Stevens, who was flying with them as a passenger, and the flight engineer were holding within the exact specifications of the cruise control charts and flight plan.

A perfect landing was made at John Rodgers Field in Hawaii. They felt better with a long overwater hop behind them.

On their way again, forty-three hours later, there was a noticeable change in the crew. For one thing, they were no longer troubled by overwater flying, although Kwajalein was a landfall over ten hours away. About 200 miles from Kwajalein, the navigator called for a slight change of direction. Then, once again, Lieutenant McLain called his shot. Kwajalein was straight ahead, a hairpin-shaped atoll, and the pilot brought them in with another perfect landing.

The next morning there was some trouble with the oil pressure gauge, and the men were impatient, anxious to beat the noon deadline that would keep them another day on Kwajalein. Then at 11:16 they took off for the last step on their journey to an island in the Marianas.

For the next six hours the men speculated about their future home, about living conditions, climate, but mainly they wondered about their first mission. When would they fly it? What would it be like? They felt ready for a mission, and, thinking back, they tried to remember what they had learned on this journey. The navigator had learned to trust his instruments. He had flown day and night over water, and he knew he had both the confidence and the tools to guide the airplane to any desired destination. The men knew that an airplane must be kept as clean as possible inside and out; washing and steam-cleaning the plane had added five to seven mph to their airspeed. The engineer was finally convinced he must run his engines at the indicated maximum temperatures. And pilots and engineers had proof that the airplane should be flown according to specification of the cruise control charts.

The voice of the navigator came over the intercom. "Navigator to pilot. You should be seeing that island any minute now."

It was only their second day in the Marianas when one of them said, "I came over here to fight, and they've got me going to school again." The whole crew was annoyed. They had taken their plane across 6,000 miles of water and were ready to take her into combat, and here they were in school—eight hours a day of it.

Maj. Gen. Curtis LeMay, commanding general of the XXI Bomber Command, put it this way, "The idea that training days are over when a crew arrives in a combat zone is absolutely false. The basic training in the States is excellent, but it can't help but be a little behind because we learn new things every day over here, and we can't possibly get the information back fast enough. Training continues right through combat operations, letting up only a little in direct ratio to the combat experience of the crew."

The crew of this B-29 went to school for ten days. General LeMay gave their class its first lecture and introduced them to air discipline. He said crews must reach a point of proficiency where procedures become automatic, must become thoroughly at home over the target, know the way there and back as well as they knew the way to the mess hall, must learn to fly exactly as briefed.

On the fourth, sixth, eighth, and tenth days of school they flew practice missions, and it felt good to get back to their plane. They dropped bombs on Jap-held islands, and the first time they returned a little disgruntled. They hadn't even hit the target. There were all the intricate problems of allowance for turn to be solved. They were flying new and very close formations. In the States they had paid little attention to fuel consumption.

They felt differently now about the training.

Lieutenant Schnelle, the bombardier, said, "High ballistic winds really present a problem. At home you've got an average wind of about thirty mph. It's not unusual, I'm told to run into 150- and 200-mph winds over Japan."

Lieutenant Yeager, the special equipment operator, smiled happily. "One thing I like about this school. They explain my problems to the rest of the crew."

Added Lieutenant Dean, "They say copilots in the States don't get enough chances to function as pilot. Here they expect us to get more time so we can lighten the load on the pilot. Suits me fine."

Lieutenant McLain, the navigator, said, "We're going to fly through all kinds of weather, fly doglegs to miss Jap islands. I got to be sure to get a fast reading as soon as we come out of an overcast. I got to make sure the pilot goes into the wind to make landfall. I got to worry about 180-degree wind shifts and constant altitudes on the way to the target and varying altitudes on the way back."

Precision instrument flying, almost split-second timing, tight formations for perfect bomb patterns—these they found added up to air discipline. And these they thought of in terms of the first mission.

Then suddenly it came. March 8, 1945, was no different from any other day at first. They had planned to do some work on their huts, check the airplane. But they had no time for casual activities that day. Captain Smith was informed there would be a briefing for all crew members.

The briefing hut was overflowing into the white coral path. At the long end of the hut there were maps on the wall, maps of Tokyo. Smith and Dean and Schnelle and the others grinned a little; not bad—Tokyo. And then a quiet, unemotional voice was talking to them. "You will come over the target at an altitude of 5,000 feet." There was more, but for the moment that was enough. Their first mission—Tokyo—with the lowest stack at 5,000 feet.

Then they were suddenly very busy. Col. Carl R. Storrie, CO

of their group, gathered them together for a talk. The colonel had a long record of combat in Europe and he spoke with the quiet assurance of a man who knows. They listened as he told them the tricks of flak evasion, warned them about making precision turns and maintaining altitude, told them how to evade fighters. There would be some 300 airplanes over the target, and each must be in its assigned place at the proper time. If not, there would be air collisions as well as planes hit by friendly bombs. And wear amber glasses so as not to be blinded by lights and flak. Finally Colonel Storrie said, "And don't go for the Emperor's palace. It's not named as a target. There's only one place for your bombs to land that's on your target. Good luck— I'll see you all tomorrow when we get back."

They talked excitedly as they left the briefing hut. "Holy hat . . . 5,000 feet . . . incendiaries . . . five to seven tons of bombs in each airplane . . . and at least 300 airplanes."

After dinner, Captain Smith and the crew returned to the briefing hut. They wanted a man-to-man briefing. Never before had a B-29 been flown at such a low altitude over an enemy target. Quietly they studied the maps, reviewed their problem.

They slept late the next day, and they slept well. A late breakfast was arranged. There was a final air-sea rescue briefing, a weather briefing. "Got a hack coming up," said Capt. Joe Byrtus. "Fifteen forty-four in thirty seconds." They bowed down over their watches. Five . . . four . . . three . . . two . . . one . . . hack."

Following a 5:39 p.m. takeoff, Captain Smith was guiding the plane carefully over the cliff that dropped abruptly into the blue sea. The intercom was busy. Schulman at his radio . . . Mericle, Zita, Bohan, Boland at their gun positions . . . each had his own way of answering "RRRRodgeRRR." Somehow you always recognized them as soon as they spoke. The tenseness was gone.

Each man tested everything he could think of, tested it again. Gradually the chatter on the intercom died down, and it became very quiet. The sun was setting, and it seemed the whole world was gradually turning gray. Then suddenly it was dark. All around, the darkness was crowded with airplanes. General Power, Colonel Storrie, Colonel Wheless, Lieutenant Colonels Mason, Martin, and Strouse, Majors Baird and Evans, and others. The sky was full of rank flying with the men they commanded—and trained. As Colonel Storrie said, "The only way I can pick my lead crews is to fly with them." He had flown every mission so far.

Time passed; gradually, the values of air discipline began to show. Maintain proper altitude and airspeed and you needn't worry about other airplanes nearby in the dark. Set power according to the specifications at the cruise control charts and you needn't worry about running out of gas. Maintain a proper military organization in your crew and you knew everyone would function efficiently and calmly, quick to respond to every command. Everything seemed to be working as planned. Finally, quite incredibly, they began to feel as if this were just another flight.

It was getting pretty close now. They struggled into their flak suits. They put on their amber goggles. They seemed to be able to remember everything they had been told without even trying.

Yeager sighted land. McLain had guided the big airplane over 1,300 miles through darkness and changing weather and made landfall only three miles off course. Already, he was plotting the course away from the target.

The Japanese homeland was hidden under a perfect blackout. The weather, as predicted, was CAVU. They were over the IP, turning into the axis of attack. Smith increased his airspeed, and the airplane surged forward.

Suddenly, off a little to the right, there was an oblong of yellow flame. In another moment, it was crossed by another, forming a perfect X. The first incendiary bombs had been dropped on Tokyo. Colonel Storrie, flying with Captain Russell, was first in.

Lt. Col. Gene Strouse, with Captain Douglas, crossed his bomb pattern.

A split-second later, the darkness over Tokyo was cut by daggers of searchlights. They sliced up and down, searching the high altitudes for airplanes that were thousands of feet lower. They slashed across the sky, came closer.

Smith looked straight ahead, never deviating from course. Bob Dean leaned a little to the left, watching, adjusting altitude. Schnelle crouched over his bombsight, counting off the seconds on his stop watch. There were four bursts of flak near the tail, some heavy flak ahead, low, inaccurate. But the searchlights were coming closer. Washington never turned from his instrument panel.

Another oblong of flame spread over part of Tokyo. And at the same time light from a searchlight flooded the cockpit. All of a sudden it went out . . . and a few moments later an airplane spouting a tail of blue flame shot past and up at a terrific speed. No searchlight picked them up again; only once had been enough to teach Smith how to avoid them. The flak improved as they made their turn around and away from the target. Bohan, in the tail, spoke very steadily. "Night fighter coming in at six o'clock." They waited for the burst of fire, their guns tracking him as he came within range. The Jap veered off. To the right, a B-29 was coned in a pyramid of searchlights. Somehow, they forgot their own danger, begged for her release. A great ball of fire plunged toward them, then dipped under them. A B-29 burns big at night.

The searchlights ringing the city frantically searched the sky. Ack-ack ran in yellow and red and white bursts in desperate pursuit of targets. And through this pattern flew some 300 B-29s, each maintaining a planned course, speed, and altitude.

They were away from the target now, looking back at the growing fire that was sending a faint streak of red to thin clouds 10,000 feet above. They watched sudden bursts of new fire added to the old. And even as distance made the fire grow smaller, a great plume of black smoke grew higher and higher over the city.

It was a beautiful fire.

They chattered over the intercom, excited now by the spectacle below and behind. But they were still over Japanese land and they were abruptly quiet when Zita broke in with "Flak below!" A few moments later Boland called, "Night fighter coming in at four o'clock." Smith called for auto rich. Seconds passed and they were like hours. "The crazy guy is blinking his lights," said Boland.

Mericle's voice was a little bored. "Two bits says there's another fighter at about five o'clock." There was. The one blinking his lights was probably acting as a decoy, trying to draw the fire so the other could shoot into the blaze of the B-29 guns. There was no shooting. The Japs went away, probably thoroughly annoyed at the unwillingness of the stupid Americans to fall into a trap.

So at last they were on the way home from their first mission. Neither the airplane nor its crew had been hit. But it was a long way home, over nothing but water. Smith checked McLain, got the course. Then he checked with the flight engineer. Gas? Hell, they had plenty of gas to get home. In fact, their fuel consumption had been a little less than predicted in the cruise control charts.

For a while they chatted among themselves.

Then it became very quiet, and there was only the roar of the four engines taking them home. Hours passed. The clouds began to turn gray with the first light, then a brilliant white as they were touched by the morning sun.

Bob Dean looked at the light and said, "This is the most beautiful morning I've ever seen."

ACTION IN THE SOLOMONS

HULBERT BURROUGHS, LIEUTENANT

USAAF

The B-17s rolled down the Henderson Field runway early that October morning, on their way to drop a few eggs on a Jap airbase at Buka and an enemy shipping concentration at Shortland Harbor. The targets were located at opposite ends of Bougainville Island.

The Zero base at Buka was visited first, and from 12,000 feet the B-17s laid a beautiful pattern of 1,000 pounders right down the middle of the runway. Five Zeros moved in to attack, but they were turned back in short order.

The B-17s then turned south to Shortland and found thirty-eight Jap ships, including battleships, cruisers, and destroyers, not to mention troop and cargo transports, all gathered together for a nice bombing. The ack-ack was heavy, but from about 11,000 feet the bombers made their runs and scored direct hits on a cruiser and a transport.

Ten Zeros came up to intercept. Two were shot down. Three B-17s collected a few routine perforations. Another was hit by a 20-mm shell that failed to explode. One of the navigators was killed by a stray 7.7 Zero bullet. A radio operator was hit in the ankle.

The B-17s turned for home. They arrived offshore near Henderson Field just as a flight of twenty-five Jap bombers was pounding the runway. It was easy to see that the B-17s couldn't land on the pock-marked strip, so they began circling high above the area to await developments. From their grandstand seat the B-17 boys saw quite a show.

US warships near the island filled the sky with heavy antiaircraft fire. Long condensation streamers curled high in the sky as Marine Grumman fighters dived on the attackers. American landing boats in the process of unloading troop reinforcements cut the water with their white wakes as they chugged rapidly away from their mother ships.

Exploding Jap bombs kicked up huge clouds of dust and smoke on Henderson Field. Finally the enemy bombers were driven off.

The B-17s flew low over the field, but the runway had been hit twice. In a moment, however, Marine construction crews swarmed about like ants repairing the strip. Nearby a Navy dive bomber, which had been hit on the ground, sent up clouds of black smoke. Other bomb craters dotted the adjacent area.

For two hours the B-17s circled. Then, when the Marines had finished their job, the bombers landed. And just in time to get right in the middle of a repeat performance of the show they had witnessed from the air.

Within fifteen minutes another wave of Jap twin-engined bombers was spotted heading toward the field. For most of the Air Force flyers, the receiving end of a bombardment was a new position. A similarly new experience was their wild scramble for Marine foxholes.

The twenty Jap bombers, flying at 20,000 feet in their usual V formation, dropped their bombs. Three hit the runway, one failing to explode. One B-17 was hit, but only slight damage resulted. Most of the other bombs fell wide. Again the indefatigable Marines scrambled onto the runway and, with shovels and crowbars, trucks and rollers, repaired the damage.

By evening of that day the men were ready for a bite to eat and a night's sleep. But that's a little out of routine for Henderson Field.

At 6:30 p.m. a battery of Jap guns from the hills to the west began shelling the field. Five-inch projectiles whistled intermittently for an hour and a half. Red tracers from Marine coastal batteries rocketed back into the hills in reply. All was quiet at 9:00 o'clock, and some of the men turned in for the night. They were optimistic.

Two hours later, the Jap land batteries opened up again. At 1:30 in the morning a Jap plane, probably a cruiser catapult type, dropped a flare behind the field and in a few seconds a sixteen-inch shell from a Jap battleship exploded overhead.

Then for two hours enemy battleships, cruisers, and destroyers shelled Henderson Field and Marine emplacements with five-, eight-, and sixteen-inch projectiles. Some Air Force personnel sought protection in open foxholes; others crowded into covered dugouts. Throughout the rest of the night many lay on their bellies on the ground behind logs or in bomb craters.

One Jap shell exploded near a dugout in which six Air Force men were lying. The walls caved in and buried five of them. The sixth, S/Sgt. Sebastian Maraschiello, of Buffalo, N. Y., extricated himself and, during the height of the shelling, managed to rescue three of the others.

At 3:30 a.m. "Maytag Charlie," an enemy plane so dubbed by the Marines because its engines sounded like a washing machine, dropped a flare just short of the runway and then laid two big bombs down the field.

Four more times before dawn enemy planes bombed the runway.

Shortly before sunrise Air Force officers inspected the runway and cleared it of shell and bomb fragments. Miraculously, only two B-17s had been hit, neither damaged badly enough to keep it from flying.

But the runway was damaged, particularly on one end. A conference was held with the B-17 pilots. Could they take the heavy bombers off the shortened runway? They agreed it was worth a try rather than have their ships go through another pasting on the ground. More Jap shells from the hills broke up the conference.

The first B-17 taxied to the end of the runway in the face of the bombardment. The pilot locked his brakes, gunned the motors to full rpm and let her go. The B-17 hurtled down the pitted runway, dodged two craters, and leaped into the air just in time to miss three others. A half hour later all the planes were off the ground.

Another day had begun on Guadalcanal.

The Japs aren't the only headaches for the men in the Solomons. There is the little matter of weather, for one thing. A "front" in the Solomons is nothing less than a cement wall.

Then on the ground in the daytime there are flies by the millions. Malaria-loaded mosquitoes work the night shift, and they come in similar numbers. Mosquito bars are an absolute necessity.

There are no luxuries on Guadalcanal. The men sleep in tents on canvas cots with neither pads nor sheets. Officers and enlisted men usually wash their own uniforms. A few have made deals with ex-cannibal Melanesian natives for laundry service—provided the flyers supply the soap. There is no hot water, of course, no fresh meat or vegetables, no sweets, no cokes, not much mail from home. And when the mail does come to the South Seas it's usually a month or so old.

Transportation, mostly via jeeps and two-and-a-half tonners, is "rugged." When it rains—and the yearly rainfall is about 120 inches, most of which falls during the three-month rainy season—the mud is ankle deep. When the mud dries up, the dust is ankle deep. GI shoes have at last come into their own with the Air Force officers.

Despite these hardships and discomforts a tremendous amount

of work has been accomplished. One Air Force base in the New Hebrides was hacked out of a dense tropical forest and ready for use in fourteen days—thanks largely to that typically American piece of heavy equipment, the bulldozer. On one occasion, before adequate servicing equipment was available, one aircraft crew, anxious to get into combat, filled the big gas tanks by bucket brigade, passing five-gallon "drinks" from the ground to wing.

Out in the jungle bases there is little distinction of rank either among officers or between officers and enlisted men. There is little saluting. A man is taken for what he is really worth. Between officers and enlisted men there is a feeling of mutual respect and great confidence. This is especially true in combat crews, where morale is very high.

Variety is not lacking in the missions which the B-17 crews fly day after day. Lt. Thomas H. Trent, of Hardinsburg, Ky., and his crew were out over Kapingamarangi Island (Greenwich Island) near the Carolines, when they spotted a big Jap radio schooner standing off the reef. Having no bombs and despite heavy machine-gun fire Trent dove in for an attack. For twenty-five minutes his gunners strafed the enemy vessel from as low as fifty feet. By the time the crew had finished its job the schooner was burning and had been beached.

Another of Trent's "routine" experiences occurred on the afternoon of October 15 when he flew to Guadalcanal with other B-17s to bomb a Jap invasion force consisting of cruisers, destroyers, and transports. While making his bombing run from 11,000 feet on a troop ship, four Zeros made a concerted attack upon Trent's plane.

In the first blast of fire he had his right aileron cable severed by a Jap bullet—that one-in-a-million shot. Out of control, the plane fell 3,000 feet before Trent was able to right it. Again the four Zeros came in, this time to finish off the crippled B-17.

Trent's gunners shot down two of the Japs and drove the others off.

Free at last of Jap fighters, Trent faced the almost hopeless task of trying to save his crippled plane. For five long hours he alternately nursed and cursed the faltering bomber. In one stretch of rough weather the plane began to lose altitude. Trent warned his men to prepare to bail out. But again he succeeded in gaining control.

Finally they sighted their home field and were ready to try a landing. In a wide skidding turn Trent made the run for the field, found his right wing dropping too low. It refused to come up even with full left stick. Trent gunned number-four engine, brought the wing up, and made a perfect landing.

On the same flight with Trent was Lt. William S. Cope, Salem, Ohio, piloting another B-17. As Cope was making his bombing run on a Jap transport the antiaircraft bursts grew thicker. Fifteen Zeros waited overhead for our bombers to clear through the ack-ack.

Cope wanted no slipups. Over the interphone he called to his bombardier: "Be ready to get bombs away."

In the excitement of the attack the bombardier caught only the words "bombs away." Thinking that something had gone wrong and that it was an order to dump the load, he hastily jettisoned all the bombs. A few moments later two of the castoff bombs, falling short of the Jap transport for which they had been intended, landed squarely on the deck of a Jap heavy cruiser. Badly damaged, the ship was later sunk by Navy dive bombers.

Capt. Vincent M. Crane, Manchester, Mass., and his crew, spent an interesting twenty minutes over Jap-held Rekata Bay one afternoon. From a height of only 200 feet they strafed ground installations, sank two anchored seaplanes, poured 700 rounds of fire into a couple of hundred Japs scrambling around the beach, got hit by a 37-mm shell which severed one of the control cables in the tail of their ship. By skillful maneuvering Crane made a successful forced landing at Henderson Field, tied the damaged cables together with bailing wire, and made it back to his home field.

Returning from a tough bombing mission of Jap installations in the northern Solomons, three B-17s ran into one of those cement-wall fronts. For hours they sought an opening. Lost and out of gas, they were forced down at sea. Lt. James Van Haur and his crew spent seven days at sea on a damaged raft. One man died at sea.

In another plane, Lt. Col. Philo O. Rasmusen, Salt Lake City, Utah, was knocked unconscious by the force of the water landing. As the ship was submerging, the copilot, Lt. Clyde Shields, of Aberdeen, S. D., himself suffering from a deep head wound, dragged the unconscious Rasmusen through the escape hatch and swam with him to the raft. The pilot of the third plane, Lt. Willard G. Woodbury, Omaha, Neb., and his crew were luckier. Uninjured, they reached shore in a few hours.

Lt. Sam B. White and his crew will have something to tell their grandchildren—if and when. On a mission over Jap territory they were jumped by fifteen Zeros. In a wild fight that lasted about twenty minutes, White's plane was badly shot up. Three hundred and fifty bullet holes riddled the ship, but the crew escaped with no injuries. Lt. Everett S. Turner of Binghamton, N. Y., was struck on the sole of his shoe by a 20-mm shell. "It was a GI shoe," said Turner. "The bullet suffered more than I did."

On another occasion White and his men were out on a search mission. At 8,000 feet they flew into what White described as "an awfully pretty white cloud." A terrific downdraft hit the bomber and turned it upside down. Crew members rattled around in the fuselage like peas in a pod. The controls went limp. White shoved the stick forward, throttled the motors down. For terrifying seconds the plane careened wildly downward. When it finally broke out of the cloud it was in a vertical dive.

"She was indicating 340 miles an hour straight down and with the motors idling," White reported later. "We were at 2,800 feet before I could get the nose up."

The main spark plug for such "routine" operations was tough, but affable Col. Laverne G. "Blondy" Saunders, one of West Point's former all-time star football players and coach [*now retired as a brigadier general and living in Aberdeen, S. D.—*THE EDITORS]. Working long hours with quiet determination, he still found time beyond his regular duties to accompany his boys on dangerous bombing missions.

It was the colonel and his boys who had the hectic twenty-four hours operating out of Henderson Field that early October morning.

HIROSHIMA BOMBED

A Japanese radio broadcast describing the atomic bombing of Hiroshima on the day of the attack. The broadcast was intercepted, and translated by the U. S. Office of War Information.

PD to WA and OWI
P31148 H30752 Japanese Home Service Kon 630 KCS at 6:00
AM *Tuesday 8/7*
   (*Text*) *A small number of B-Twenty-Nines penetrated into Hiroshima City a little after eight* AM *yesterday morning and dropped a small number of bombs. As a result a considerable number of homes were reduced to ashes and fires broke out in various parts of the city.*
   To this new type of bomb are attached parachutes, and it appears as if these new bombs exploded in the air. Investigations are now being made with regard to the effectiveness of this bomb, which should not be regarded as slight.
   The enemy has exposed his cold bloodedness and atrocious nature more and more in killing innocent people by the use of this new-type bomb. It is believed that the enemy, being faced with difficult conditions, is feeling rushed to turn the war into one of short duration. Hence he has begun to use this type of bomb.
   The use of this new type of bomb by the enemy in the future can be expected. As for measures to cope with this bomb, it is anticipated that they will be disclosed as soon as possible. Until these measures are disclosed by the government authorities, it is necessary for the general public to strengthen the present air defense system.
   As frequently pointed out in the past, the people must watch themselves against underrating the enemy simply because he has carried out raids with a small number of planes. The enemy has been carrying out large-scale propaganda on the effectiveness of

this new-type bomb since using these bombs, but as long as we formulate strong steel-like measures to cope with this type of bomb, it will be possible to keep the damage at a minimum.

We must be careful at all times so that we will not fall victim to the enemy's machinations. (JER-TB)
MRS 8/7—1134 EWT

THE ATOMIC BOMBING OF NAGASAKI
(*Official War Department Release*)

WILLIAM L. LAURANCE

WAR CORRESPONDENT, *New York Times*

With the Atomic Bomb Mission to Japan, Aug. 9 (Delayed) —We are on our way to bomb the mainland of Japan. Our flying contingent consists of three specially designed B-29 "Superforts," and two of these carry no bombs. But our lead plane is on its way with another atomic bomb, the second in three days, concentrating in its active substance an explosive energy equivalent to 20,000 and, under favorable conditions, 40,000 tons of TNT.

We have several chosen targets. One of these is the great industrial and shipping center of Nagasaki, on the western shore of Kyushu, one of the main islands of the Japanese homeland.

I watched the assembly of this man-made meteor during the past two days, and was among the small group of scientists and Army and Navy representatives privileged to be present at the ritual of its loading in the "Superfort" last night, against a background of threatening black skies torn open at intervals by great lightning flashes.

It is a thing of beauty to behold, this "gadget." In its design went millions of man-hours of what is without doubt the most concentrated intellectual effort in history. Never before had so much brain-power been focused on a single problem.

This atomic bomb is different from the bomb used three days ago with such devastating results on Hiroshima.

I saw the atomic substance before it was placed inside the bomb. By itself it is not at all dangerous to handle. It is only under certain conditions, produced in the bomb assembly, that it can be made to yield up its energy, and even then it gives only a small fraction of its total contents—a fraction, however, large enough to produce the greatest explosion on earth.

The briefing at midnight revealed the extreme care and the tremendous amount of preparation that had been made to take care of every detail of the mission, to make certain that the atomic bomb fully served the purpose for which it was intended. Each target in turn was shown in detailed maps and in aerial photographs. Every detail of the course was rehearsed—navigation, altitude, weather, where to land in emergencies. It came out that the Navy had submarines and rescue craft, known as Dumbos and Superdumbos, stationed at various strategic points in the vicinity of the targets, ready to rescue the fliers in case they were forced to bail out.

The briefing period ended with a moving prayer by the chaplain. We then proceeded to the mess hall for the traditional early morning breakfast before departure on a bombing mission.

A convoy of trucks took us to the supply building for the special equipment carried on combat missions. This included the "Mae West," a parachute, a lifeboat, an oxygen mask, a flak suit and a survival vest. We still had a few hours before take-off time, but we all went to the flying field and stood around in little groups or sat in jeeps talking rather casually about our mission to the Empire, as the Japanese home islands are known hereabouts.

In command of our mission is Maj. Charles W. Sweeney, 25, of 124 Hamilton Avenue, North Quincey, Mass. His flagship, carrying the atomic bomb, is named The Great Artiste, but the name does not appear on the body of the great silver ship, with its unusually long, four-bladed, orange-tipped propellers. Instead, it carries the number 77, and someone remarks that it was "Red" Grange's winning number on the gridiron.

Bombardier an 8th A. F. Veteran

Major Sweeney's co-pilot is First Lieut. Charles D. Albury, 24, of 252 Northwest Fourth Street, Miami, Fla. The bombardier, upon whose shoulders rests the responsibility of depositing the atomic bomb square on its target, is Capt. Kermit K. Beahan of 1004 Telephone Road, Houston, Tex., who is celebrating his twenty-seventh birthday today.

Captain Beahan has the awards of the Distinguished Flying Cross, the Air Medal and one Silver Oak Leaf Cluster, the Purple Heart, the Western Hemisphere Ribbon, the European Theatre Ribbon and two battle stars. He participated in the first Eighth Air Force heavy bombardment mission against the Germans from England on Aug. 17, 1942, and was on the plane that transported Gen. Dwight D. Eisenhower from Gibraltar to Oran at the beginning of the North African invasion. He has had a number of hair-raising escapes in combat.

The navigator on The Great Artiste is Capt. James F. Van Pelt Jr., 27, of Oak Hill, W. Va. The flight engineer is M/Sgt. John D. Kuharek, 32, of 1054 Twenty-second Avenue, Columbus, Neb.; S/Sgt. Albert T. De Hart of Plainview, Tex., who celebrated his thirtieth birthday yesterday, is the tail gunner; the radar operator is S/Sgt. Edward K. Buckley, 32, of 529 East Washington Street, Lisbon, Ohio. The radio operator is Sgt. Abe M. Spitzer, 33, of 655 Pelham Parkway, North Bronx, N. Y.; Sgt. Raymond Gallagher, 23, of 572 South Mozart Street, Chicago, is assistant flight engineer.

The lead ship is also carrying a group of scientific personnel, headed by Comdr. Frederick L. Ashworth, USN, one of the leaders in the development of the bomb. The group includes

Lieut. Jacob Beser, 24, of Baltimore, Md., an expert on airborne radar.

The other two Superfortresses in our formation are instrument planes, carrying special apparatus to measure the power of the bomb at the time of explosion, high-speed cameras and other photographic equipment.

Our "Superfort" is the second in line. Its commander is Capt. Frederick C. Bock, 27, of 300 West Washington Street, Greenville, Mich. Its other officers are Second Lieut. Hugh C. Ferguson, 21, of 247 Windermere Avenue, Highland Park, Mich., pilot; Second Lieut. Leonard A. Godfrey, 24, of 72 Lincoln Street, Greenfield, Mass., navigator, and First Lieut. Charles Levy, 26, of 1954 Spencer Street, Philadelphia, bombardier.

The enlisted personnel of this "Superfort" are: T/Sgt. Roderick F. Arnold, 28, of 130 South Street, Rochester, Mich., flight engineer; Sgt. Ralph D. Curry, 20, of 1101 South Second Avenue, Hoopeston, Ill., radio operator; Sgt. William C. Barney, 22, of Columbia City, Ind., radar operator; Corp. Robert J. Stock, 21, of 415 Downing Street, Fort Wayne, Ind., assistant flight engineer, and Corp. Ralph D. Belanger, 19, of Thendara, N. Y., tail gunner.

The scientific personnel of our "Superfort" includes S/Sgt. Walter Goodman, 22, of 1956 Seventy-fourth Street, Brooklyn, N. Y., and Lawrence Johnson, graduate student at the University of California, whose home is at Hollywood, Calif.

The third "Superfort" is commanded by Maj. James Hopkins, 1311 North Queen Street, Palestine, Tex. His officers are Second Lieut. John E. Cantlon, 516 North Takima Street, Tacoma, Wash., pilot; Second Lieut. Stanley C. Steinke, 604 West Chestnut Street, West Chester, Pa., navigator, and Second Lieut. Myron Faryna, 16 Elgin Street, Rochester, N. Y., bombardier.

The crew are Tech. Sgt. George L. Brabenec, 9717 South Lawndale Avenue, Evergreen, Ill.; Sgt. Francis X. Dolan, 30-60 Warren Street, Elmhurst, Queens, N. Y.; Corp. Richard F.

Cannon, 160 Carmel Road, Buffalo, N. Y.; Corp. Martin G. Murray, 7356 Dexter Street, Detroit, Mich., and Corp. Sidney J. Bellamy, 529 Johnston Avenue, Trenton, N. J.

On this "Superfort" are also two distinguished observers from Britain, whose scientists played an important role in the development of the atomic bomb. One of these is Group Capt. G. Leonard Cheshire, famous Royal Air Force pilot, who is now a member of the British military mission to the United States. The other is Dr. William G. Penny, Professor of Applied Mathematics, London University, one of the group of eminent British scientists that has been working at the "Y-Site" near Santa Fe, N. M., on the enormous problems involved in taming the atom.

Group Captain Cheshire, whose rank is the equivalent to that of colonel in the United States Army Air Forces, was designated as an observer of the atomic bomb in action by Winston Churchill when he was still Prime Minister. He is now the official representative of Prime Minister Clement R. Attlee.

In Storm Soon After Take-Off

We took off at 3:50 this morning and headed northwest on a straight line for the Empire. The night was cloudy and threatening, with only a few stars here and there breaking through the overcast. The weather report had predicted storms ahead part of the way but clear sailing for the final and climactic stages of our odyssey.

We were about an hour away from our base when the storm broke. Our great ship took some heavy dips through the abysmal darkness around us, but it took these dips much more gracefully than a large commercial airliner, producing a sensation more in the nature of a glide than a "bump," like a great ocean liner riding the waves, except that in this case the air waves were much higher and the rhythmic tempo of the glide was much faster.

I noticed a strange eerie light coming through the window high above the navigator's cabin, and as I peered through the dark all around us I saw a startling phenomenon. The whirling giant propellers had somehow become great luminous disks of blue flame. The same luminous blue flame appeared on the plexiglass windows in the nose of the ship, and on the tips of the giant wings. It looked as though we were riding the whirl-wind through space on a chariot of blue fire.

It was, I surmised, a surcharge of static electricity that had accumulated on the tips of the propellers and on the di-electric material in the plastic windows. One's thoughts dwelt anxiously on the precious cargo in the invisible ship ahead of us. Was there any likelihood of danger that this heavy electric tension in the atmosphere all about us might set it off?

I expressed my fears to Captain Bock, who seems nonchalant and imperturbed at the controls. He quickly reassures me.

"It is a familiar phenomenon seen often on ships. I have seen it many times on bombing missions. It is known as St. Elmo's Fire."

On we went through the night. We soon rode out the storm and our ship was once again sailing on a smooth course straight ahead, on a direct line to the Empire.

Our altimeter showed that we were traveling through space at a height of 17,000 feet. The thermometer registered an outside temperature of 33 degrees below zero Centigrade, about 30 below Fahrenheit. Inside our pressurized cabin the temperature was that of a comfortable air-conditioned room and a pressure cor-responding to an altitude of 8,000 feet. Captain Bock cautioned me, however, to keep my oxygen mask handy in case of emer-gency. This, he explained, might mean either something going wrong with the pressure equipment inside the ship or a hole through the cabin by flak.

The first signs of dawn came shortly after 5 o'clock. Sergeant Curry, who had been listening steadily on his earphones for radio reports, while maintaining a strict radio silence himself, greeted it by rising to his feet and gazing out the window.

"It's good to see the day," he told me, "I get a feeling of claustrophobia hemmed in in this cabin at night."

He is a typical American youth, looking even younger than his 20 years. It takes no mind-reader to read his thoughts.

"It's a long way from Hoopeston, Ill.," I find myself remarking.

"Yep," he replies, as he busies himself decoding a message from outer space.

"Think this atomic bomb will end the war?" he asks hopefully.

"There is a very good chance that this one may do the trick," I assured him, "but if not, then the next one or two surely will. Its power is such that no nation can stand up against it very long."

This was not my own view. I had heard it expressed all around a few hours earlier, before we took off. To anyone who had seen this man-made fireball in action, as I had less than a month ago in the desert of New Mexico, this view did not sound overoptimistic.

By 5:50 it was really light outside. We had lost our lead ship, but Lieutenant Godfrey, our navigator, informs me that we had arranged for that contingency. We have an assembly point in the sky above the little island of Yakoshima, southeast of Kyushu, at 9:10. We are to circle there and wait for the rest of our formation.

Our genial bombardier, Lieutenant Levy, comes over to invite me to take his front-row seat in the transparent nose of the ship and I accept eagerly. From that vantage point in space, 17,000 feet above the Pacific, one gets a view of hundreds of miles on all sides, horizontally and vertically. At that height the vast ocean below and the sky above seem to merge into one great sphere.

I was on the inside of that firmament, riding above the giant mountains of white cumulus clouds, letting myself be suspended in infinite space. One hears the whirl of the motors behind one, but it soon becomes insignificant against the immensity all around and is before long swallowed by it. There comes a point where space also swallows time and one lives through eternal moments filled with an oppressive loneliness, as though all life had suddenly vanished from the earth and you are the only one left, a lone survivor traveling endlessly through interplanetary space.

My mind soon returns to the mission I am on. Somewhere beyond these vast mountains of white clouds ahead of me there lies Japan, the land of our enemy. In about four hours from now one of its cities, making weapons of war for use against us, will be wiped off the map by the greatest weapon ever made by man: In one-tenth of a millionth of a second, a fraction of time immeasurable by any clock, a whirlwind from the skies will pulverize thousands of its buildings and tens of thousands of its inhabitants.

Our weather planes ahead of us are on their way to find out where the wind blows. Half an hour before target time we will know what the winds have decided.

Does one feel any pity or compassion for the poor devils about to die? Not when one thinks of Pearl Harbor and of the Death March on Bataan.

Captain Bock informs me that we are about to start our climb to bombing altitude.

He manipulates a few knobs on his control panel to the right of him and I alternately watch the white clouds and ocean below me and the altimeter on the bombardier's panel. We reached our altitude at 9 o'clock. We were then over Japanese waters, close to their mainland. Lieutenant Godfrey motioned to me to look through his radar scope. Before me was the outline of our assembly point. We shall soon meet our lead ship and proceed to the final stage of our journey.

We reached Yakoshima at 9:12 and there, about 4,000 feet ahead of us, was The Great Artiste with its precious load. I saw Lieutenant Godfrey and Sergeant Curry strap on their parachutes and I decided to do likewise.

We started circling. We saw little towns on the coastline, heedless of our presence. We kept on circling, waiting for the third ship in our formation.

It was 9:56 when we began heading for the coastline. Our weather scouts had sent us code messages, deciphered by Sergeant Curry, informing us that both the primary target as well as the secondary were clearly visible.

The winds of destiny seemed to favor certain Japanese cities that must remain nameless. We circled about them again and again and found no opening in the thick umbrella of clouds that covered them. Destiny chose Nagasaki as the ultimate target.

We had been circling for some time when we noticed black puffs of smoke coming through the white clouds directly at us. There were fifteen bursts of flak in rapid succession, all too low. Captain Bock changed his course. There soon followed eight more bursts of flak, right up to our altitude, but by this time were too far to the left.

We flew southward down the channel and at 11:33 crossed the coastline and headed straight for Nagasaki about 100 miles to the west. Here again we circled until we found an opening in the clouds. It was 12:01 and the goal of our mission had arrived.

We heard the prearranged signal on our radio, put on our arc-welder's glasses and watched tensely the maneuverings of the strike ship about half a mile in front of us.

"There she goes!" someone said.

Out of the belly of The Great Artiste what looked like a black object went downward.

Captain Bock swung around to get out of range; but even though we were turning away in the opposite direction, and despite the fact that it was broad daylight in our cabin, all of us became aware of a giant flash that broke through the dark barrier of our arc-welder's lenses and flooded our cabin with intense light.

We removed our glasses after the first flash, but the light still lingered on, a bluish-green light that illuminated the entire sky all around. A tremendous blast wave struck our ship and made it tremble from nose to tail. This was followed by four more blasts in rapid succession, each resounding like the boom of cannon fire hitting our plane from all directions.

Observers in the tail of our ship saw a giant ball of fire rise as though from the bowels of the earth, belching forth enormous white smoke rings. Next they saw a giant pillar of purple fire, 10,000 feet high, shooting skyward with enormous speed.

By the time our ship had made another turn in the direction of the atomic explosion the pillar of purple fire had reached the level of our altitude. Only about forty-five seconds had passed. Awe-struck, we watched it shoot upward like a meteor coming from the earth instead of from outer space, becoming ever more alive as it climbed skyward through the white clouds. It was no longer smoke, or dust, or even a cloud of fire. It was a living thing, a new species of being, born right before our incredulous eyes.

At one stage of its evolution, covering millions of years in terms of seconds, the entity assumed the form of a giant square totem pole, with its base about three miles long, tapering off to about a mile at the top. Its bottom was brown, its center was amber, its top white. But it was a living totem pole, carved with many grotesque masks grimacing at the earth.

Then, just when it appeared as though the thing had settled down into a state of permanence, there came shooting out of the top a giant mushroom that increased the height of the pillar to a total of 45,000 feet. The mushroom top was even more alive than the pillar, seething and boiling in a white fury of creamy foam, sizzling upward and then descending earthward, a thousand Old Faithful geysers rolled into one.

It kept struggling in an elemental fury, like a creature in the act of breaking the bonds that held it down. In a few seconds it had freed itself from its gigantic stem and floated upward with tremendous speed, its momentum carrying into the stratosphere to a height of about 60,000 feet.

But no sooner did this happen when another mushroom, smaller in size than the first one, began emerging out of the pillar. It was as though the decapitated monster was growing a new head.

As the first mushroom floated off into the blue it changed its shape into a flowerlike form, its giant petals curving downward, creamy white outside, rose-colored inside. It still retained that shape when we last gazed at it from a distance of about 200 miles.

KOREA

The United States forces in South Korea were ill prepared for the onslaught when hordes of Red North Korean troops came screaming across the 38th Parallel—the arbitrary artificial boundary between North and South Korea established by the Soviet Union and the U.S. at the end of World War II. The Communist North, sharing a border with Red China, as indicated by its name held the territory north of the parallel. South Korea maintained that portion of the peninsula below the line.

The unsuspecting and outnumbered South Korean forces reeled back before the surprise blow from the north. Slowly they were pushed back south to the Pusan perimeter defended by American forces. From here like a snake recoiling, they lashed out. Reinforced they began a steady drive northward. The South Korean cause had become a United Nations cause and token units from twenty-one nations including U.S., Greek, Turkish, and British joined the South Koreans and the U.S. to help push back the Communist invaders. Under United States command the UN forces were successful. A dramatic landing behind the Reds was made at Inchon, on the Korean west coast. The drive north, supported by aerial bombardment of enemy troop concentrations and supply depots, continued as the UN troops forced the retreating North Koreans deep into their own territory toward the Yalu River, North Korea's natural border with Communist China.

Without warning wave upon wave of bugle blowing, screaming Red Chinese "volunteers" came thundering across the border
to reinforce the North Koreans and pounce upon the advancing
UN troops. Now once more the tide of battle turned against us.
The advance turned into a retreat as American and Allied troops
fought their way back down the peninsula, in the dead cold and
ice of winter.

U.S. and other UN fighter and bomber aircraft supported our
ground troops. Chinese MIG-15s took to the air but generally
sought sanctuary beyond the northern bank of the Yalu when
challenged by American F-86 *Sabrejets*. American fliers were
under orders not to violate this sanctuary by pursuing the enemy
or bombing his airfields so that the Chinese were able to find
safety on their side of the river. If our B-29s were going to be
denied the right to destroy the Chicom airfields they would—
and did—cut the bridges over the Yalu thus cutting supply lines
and the sources of troop replacements. General Douglas Mac-
Arthur objected to this privileged sanctuary, dictated by higher
authority, and it was this difference of opinion that was the
principal reason for his removal from the UN command by President Harry S Truman. He was replaced by General Matthew
Ridgway and the war continued. In fact the Korean war never
really ended, continuing in a restless quasi peace along the original 38th Parallel where representatives of both sides meet constantly, at Panmunjon, to debate the uneasy armistice.

The stories in this section are representative of the type of
combat action engaged in by the USAF bomber crews during
the "hot war" of the Korean "police action."

66)   German ground crew load bombs on a World War I Gotha GV bomber bound for England.

67)   U. S. Navy crewmen load a bomb on a carrier based bomber headed for a Japanese target during the Second World War.

68)　An Army Air Force ground crew ready a load of bombs for a B-24 **Liberator**

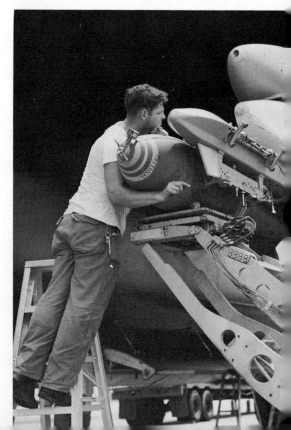

69)　750-lb. bombs being loaded on a B-52 destined for targets in Vietnam.

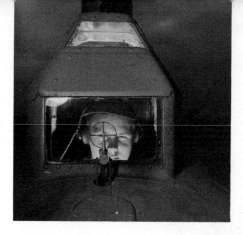

70) B-17 tail gunner.

71) Waist gunner.

72) Bombardier and the Norden bomb
sight aboard a B-26 **Marauder.**

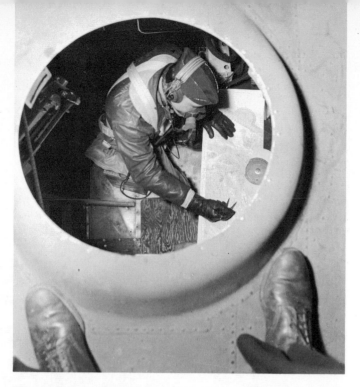

73)   Navigator of a B-17 charts his course en route to bomb German targets somewhere in Europe.

74)   Radio operator on a **Flying Fortress.**

BOMBING THE RED HORNETS' NEST

ROBERT B. ALMACH, LIEUTENANT

USAFR

It's a big jump from selling stationery to dropping bombs on Commies, but I was ready for it. I was ready the day the war started in Korea. The Air Force called me back to duty in August 1950, and from then on I moved fast.

I got a one-month refresher course at Mather AFB in Sacramento, Calif., to brush away the cobwebs and get back into the swing of things. I met my crew at Fairchild AFB, in Spokane, Wash., and we took off together to MacDill AFB, Tampa, Fla., for five weeks of combat training in B-29s. Then back to Fairchild for more training in weather more like the kind we would run into in Korea. By then it was November and colder than blazes.

For me, the transition to B-29s from the B-17 we flew from England during World War II was easy. The equipment I used as a bombardier was just about the same, and the '29 was a lot more comfortable than the old "Forts."

Finally, they figured we were ready and we got our travel orders for Japan. We arrived on March 8 and were assigned to the 98th Bomb Wing operating out of Yokota Air Base near Tokyo. Two days later we flew our first mission in *Heavenly Laden,* a B-29 we had inherited from a crew that was going home.

I don't remember where we went that first time. I was too excited. It brought back a lot of memories of Eighth Air Force days in England, days when we were bombing the Jerries in Berlin and Frankfurt.

I've flown twenty-five missions here since that first one, and most of them have been pretty much the same. There's one, however, that I'll remember as long as I live. Even as long as the time we had two engines shot away over Germany and barely limped back to Belgium before bailing out. That one is the big raid on the bridges over the Yalu River at Sinuiju on April 12.

We knew it was a top-priority target even before the target-study briefing the night before. We could feel it in our bones. The crews gathered in the briefing room at 1700, and when they pulled back the curtains and showed us the maps with the crayon streaks marking the target you could hear a murmur run through the room. We were headed for the hornets' nest at the mouth of the Yalu.

Our mission was to knock out the two railroad bridges that connect North Korea and Manchuria. The Communists were funneling all their supplies for the western front across those bridges. It was our job to stop them.

They didn't have to tell us it wouldn't be easy. We'd heard stories about Sinuiju. About big concentrations of antiaircraft guns there, and, more important, those flashy MIG jets based just across the river in Manchuria. We heard a lot about those MIGs. The intelligence officer's report that we'd probably run into swarms of them didn't make us feel any better.

To complicate our job, we had to hit the two bridges between Antung and Sinuiju without violating Manchurian territory. It wasn't going to be easy.

We hit the sack early that night. As usual, I slept like a baby, despite the forecast for a rough one the next day.

We were up at 0200 for a breakfast of eggs (cooked to order), bacon, toast, and coffee.

The final combat briefing on the latest weather information, intelligence reports, and the front-line situation was at 0300. The crews were joking back and forth, and I needled our copilot, Lt. Courtland Moore, "Don't forget to hit the right switches today, you truck driver."

It was chilly riding out to the *Heavenly Laden* in the two-and-one-half-ton truck. The sky was inky dark, and the stars twinkled like bright candles at the far end of a room.

We were carrying one-ton demolition bombs so I put the fuses in and armed them myself. Shortly before takeoff at 0500 we lined up for personal equipment check, and each man inspected another's chute. I checked my survival kit in case I had to walk home. The kit contains maps, a compass, and gold coins for bartering purposes. I made sure I had my knife and .45 pistol.

Our pilot, Lt. Junior Jamison, a lanky Southerner who has the perfect physical and mental combination to be a bomber pilot, said: "Boys, where we're going today we might get hit hard. Let's all keep our eyes open."

That's all he said, but it was enough.

The planes took off at one-minute intervals, and by 0530 we were all in the air, headed for the rendezvous over Korea. We hit the meeting place right on the nose and swung into formation. All I had to do was keep track of where we were and make sure my equipment was working properly.

We began a slow climb to 21,000 feet, the bombing altitude for the day.

From my spot in the nose, in front of and between the two pilots, the whole panorama of Korea spread out in front of me. As the morning wore on the first flush of dawn crept up out of the Sea of Japan, and finally the sun began bouncing orange rays off the snow-capped mountain peaks below us.

Some distance from the target—I can't say how far because it's classified—we picked up our fighter escort. We had both F-86s and F-84s with us. They looked good out there, with the sun flashing off their silver sides and wings when they banked for a turn around the formation. They were flying the "buddy system," protecting each other's tails, and they flew like they were tied together.

I ate my in-flight lunch and drank some coffee and hot soup. I figured that if we were shot down I'd bail out with a full belly.

The 19th and 307th Bomb Groups from Okinawa were a few minutes ahead of us. They were scheduled to attack in the first wave. We were to hit the bridges in a second wave. I could see their rear-echelon planes ahead of me through the nose.

A few moments before we got to the IP (the initial point, or start of the bomb run) I got up and put on my sixty-pound flak suit, flak helmet, and immersion suit.

Just before reaching the IP, I checked the wind. Then, as we passed over the start of the bomb run, I made a quick wind drift reading. I threw in the bombsight, taking over control from the pilot, and said to Junior, "I've got it, boy."

I began searching for the target with my binoculars and found it quickly. After all, you can't miss a thing like the Yalu River. I got the bridges in the sight and began "killing course" by adjusting the controls.

It was about 1100 as we began the bomb run.

The plane was entirely under my control, and I flew it by moving the knobs and switches of the bombsight to alter course. We were bombing visually.

The Communist flak and MIGs hit the formations about the same time. The boys from Okinawa were getting hit hardest because they were already over the target and making their final approach. They couldn't evade because to shift course would have thrown their bombs off target and made the whole mission useless.

They stuck to their course and made a good run of it, but they paid for it with blood, lives, and planes.

The sky around them was pitted with ugly, black balls of flak.

Some of it was striking home. The Commies don't throw up as much as the Germans did, but it is just as accurate. Don't let anyone tell you those babies can't shoot.

I still think that "One-Eye Charley," the same guy who taught the Jerry gunners at Berlin and Leipzig, must have tutored those Communist gunners at Sinuiju. The Chinese and North Koreans can't be that good.

They were throwing up big stuff—105 and 155 mm. It was good shooting.

Dozens of jet fighters streaked in and out of the bomber formations. Some were ours. Some were Communists. I don't know. It's hard to tell the difference between a MIG and a Sabre in the air. Some of them went down flaming.

I saw a bomber wing burst into flame and the plane flutter down. Another '29 lumbered back through our formation, smoke trailing from its body and wings. I saw five parachutes and no more. A B-29 carries more than twice that many men.

The MIGs would make long, swooping passes at the bombers, starting from the Manchurian side of the river, and then scoot back to where our boys couldn't follow.

By then we were on the final approach, and I concentrated on the bombsight. I didn't have much trouble keeping on course. There were a few near flak bursts that threw us slightly off, but I quickly shifted back onto the right track.

When the bombsight marker touched the bridges the 2,000-pound blockbusters let go automatically. There was no upward surge like we had with the Forts because the '29 is so much heavier.

I had a clear view of the bridges, and I watched my bombs walk right down the middle of them. A perfect strike. And not one hit Manchuria.

While the bombs were falling I punched the button to shut the bomb-bay doors and unlatched the bombsight from the automatic pilot so the pilot could take over and fly evasive maneuvers.

We made a sharp turn to pull away from the river and started the long trip home. The flak and the MIGs followed us a short distance, but there wasn't much they could do once we got away from the area. The MIGs scuttled back to their fields across the river at Antung.

If our fighters could have crossed the river after them and if our light bombers had been able to hit them while they were all jammed up landing, there would have been some tears and broken hearts at the Chinese air force headquarters that night. We would have smeared them good. But we couldn't help that.

After we got safely away I took off the flak suit and helmet and the rubber immersion suit. It was good to stretch away the tension of the last half hour.

It was good to be alive.

I did a lot of thinking on that ride home. About how I had joined the Air Force to be a pilot and how I washed out. I remembered my feeling of pride when I graduated from bombardier school at San Angelo, Tex.

We fought a tough war in Europe. I flew thirty-five missions over Germany, lost one plane, and had to walk out from the Belgian countryside. We stayed three days in Brussels that time and could have stayed a week because we had been reported shot down in flames over the target.

I was discharged after three years in the Air Force. I got married and have a beautiful daughter, "Lynnie," who is five and one-half now and named after her mother, Madeline.

I'm from the Bronx in New York originally but for the past five years I've been living in San Francisco. I had a good business worked up out there, selling stationery wholesale to business offices.

But I don't think I'll go back to it. I've found my spot. The Air Force is spreading out in a big way, and I would kind of like to be a part of it.

I WAS A KOREAN SHARPSHOOTER

BILLIE G. BEACH, SERGEANT

USAF

I'm just a farm boy from east Tennessee. And before I got into this war business the fastest thing I ever shot at was a squirrel scampering up a hickory tree in the Blue Ridge Mountains. Of course a squirrel can't shoot back, but outside of that it's a lot like hunting for MIGs. They're both greased lightning, and you've got to be fast to get them. If you miss on the first shot you generally don't get a second chance.

You only have a split second to spot your target, draw your bead, and fire. But you've got to be cool and deliberate. I never saw a jumpy, excited guy drop a squirrel. And I don't think I'm off base when I say that goes for jet airplanes, too.

I was just an extra gunner when the 19th Bomb Group got a hurry-up call to move from Guam to Okinawa last June. When we first started working over the Commies, I didn't get a chance to go along unless a regular crew member was sick or had some other duty. As a matter of fact, I didn't get a permanent assignment until three missions before my big day.

Those first months of the war were just so much flying time for us gunners. We sat and watched—maybe ate an apple or read a book or a comic magazine—while the bombardiers and pilots did all the work.

There was some flak, but all a gunner could do was help pray that it wouldn't find us.

We came into our own early this year when the Reds brought in their jets. At first it was an off-hand pass here and there. The Commie pilots were skittish and wouldn't get close enough to get our range.

But they kept getting bolder and bolder. They started shooting up the Superforts. It got so you hadn't lived if you didn't come back with a few bullet holes in your plane.

So we got fighter escort for the big missions. And the aerial gunners on the bombers were back at war—something more than excess baggage for the first time.

I decided I wanted to knock down one of those MIGs. We used to have a lot of arguments about whether a gunner with a .50-caliber machine gun on a propeller-driven bomber could bag a jet fighter flying at maybe twice the speed.

I said it could be done, and I promised myself I'd prove it. I didn't realize at the time, though, how near carrying out that pledge would take me and the crew to our deaths.

It happened on my nineteenth mission (I now have twenty-six), my third flight out as the regular right gunner on the B-29, *No Sweat*.

The briefing officer told us it would be one of the most dangerous missions of the war. Our targets were those bridges across the Yalu over which the Chinese were shipping all their men and supplies.

We were told the flak would be thick and accurate and that MIGs would be on our tails in large numbers. Our targets were in sight of the big Red air base just across the Yalu River—in the deep end of "MIG Alley."

Twelve Superforts, in flights of four, were assigned to the mission. A cover of F-84s and F-86s was scheduled to rendezvous with us over Korea before we headed out for enemy territory.

They loaded the *No Sweat* with 2,000-pound bombs.

We took off at dawn. The day broke bright and clear—perfect for flying. We could make a visual drop.

About forty minutes out we test-fired our guns. Mine was working smooth as clockwork.

Then we settled down for a long ride.

I pulled out a book from my hip pocket and settled down to enjoy the flight.

I wasn't thinking about anything in particular, certainly not MIGs. In the back of my mind I was sort of wondering about the flight lunches. I was hoping I would get one with boned chicken in it—most of them are not so tasty.

After about two and a half hours we began to climb. We pulled up to 21,000 feet before leveling off. The planes pulled into formation, and over Korea we picked up the fighters according to schedule.

It was about noon when we got the alert that we were approaching the target area. Everybody got ready for the bomb run. We were less than five minutes away from the bridges.

The sun was shining brightly. Although it was thirty-five degrees below zero outside and the mountains below us were snow-covered, we were comfortable in the pressurized cabin. I had on only my flight suit and my fur-collared B-15 jacket.

Then the tail gunner shouted into the interphone:

"MIGs, about thirty of 'em, coming in at six o'clock!"

I had just taken a big bite out of a juicy apple I had tucked into my jacket. I don't know to this day what happened to that apple. It just disappeared.

They were MIGs all right. They were coming in fast at six o'clock and breaking away at four—right in line with my sights. They shot for the tail first and then swung to hit us amidships.

They were coming so close I could see the orange fire spit from the barrels of their 20-mm cannon.

I started firing as soon as I got one in range.

I caught my first MIG on the breakaway. I tracked him and kept firing short bursts. He got out about 900 yards before I saw he was out of control.

The last I saw of him he was spinning like crazy—straight down. One of the crewmen saw the plane crash.

Still they came.

Three minutes and four passes later, I spied this other baby coming in at one o'clock, low. I picked him up 1,200 yards away. I chopped into him with short, steady bursts.

That MIG got out about 400 yards and keeled over on one side. I watched it go into a headlong dive and crash and explode on the mountain below.

That was the last shot I've had at a MIG. And I had about 100 rounds of ammo left in my belts.

The fighters moved in and got the MIGs off us. But in the eight minutes they were on us they hurt the *No Sweat* plenty bad.

Both the number-two and -four engines were shot up and had to be feathered. The right aileron was shot out. The interphone conked out. The number-two gas tank caught fire.

Our formation was broken up. Two of the four planes went down in flames. I saw one of them explode into the side of a mountain. Nobody saw anyone bail out.

The third ship had to turn back, but it made it to Okinawa OK.

The fighters were gone, and we were all alone. The pilot rang the alert bell—three rings, the signal for "prepare to bail out."

All of a sudden I realized I was scared, plenty scared. I'd never jumped before.

Then the Commies on the ground started throwing flak at us. I couldn't hear it, but I could see the little black puffs jumping up at us. Bursts caught us along the wings and engines.

But the bailout signal didn't come.

It dawned on us that we were going to make our bomb run

anyway. The pilot tried to catch up with the flight in front of us, but with two engines gone we couldn't make it.

We went it alone. It seemed we were suspended there in space. Like a big bird with a broken wing, we limped in over the bridges.

But we got them—direct hits, smack on the nose.

The "Old Man" sent word back that he was going to try to make it back to the lines, or as close as he could get us to them. But he told us to be prepared to jump on a second's notice.

The next hour was the longest I've spent in my young life.

I was shaking. I chewed my fingernails into the quick. I broke out in a cold sweat.

I prayed.

We lost altitude. The captain had to depressurize the cabin. It got so cold we nearly froze.

With each ticking minute we dropped closer and closer to the mountaintops. They looked like big hands, reaching up to pull us down. I thought for sure that we were goners—if not killed in the crash, then doomed to capture behind the enemy lines.

It was the most spectacular flying I've ever seen. We were just barely in the air when the plane broke out over the Han River flats and over an advance fighter strip.

The runway was much too short, but we went in anyway. It was the last chance, and we made it. The landing gear had been riddled, and it collapsed when we touched down.

We slid in on the belly and nose wheel.

HOW KOREAN CLIFF DWELLERS CALLED
THE SHOTS

LOUIS W. DAVIS

WAR CORRESPONDENT

A console like a big pipe organ filled most of the trailer. In the organist's seat was a lanky Air Force officer, pencil and pad in hand, watching a large, back-lighted control board mounted vertically above the center of the console.

An instrument pen on a long metal arm operated by a hidden hand left a thin red track on the white surface of the board. It traced pencil lines, previously plotted, marking the course or bomb run of a high-flying bomber about to "play a tune" on a frontline Red position just 800 yards north of entrenched friendly forces.

In this case, the radar controller was the "organist" and would call the tune. His attention never wavered. All action was concentrated on the creeping plotting pen which responded to electronic fingers reaching out from the trailer for miles to measure and record the precise movement of the plane.

The bomber was an Okinawa-based Boeing B-29 Superfort, flying above 20,000 feet, out of sight and out of hearing. The crew may not have known tonight's target before leaving home base some four and a half to five hours before. With radar direction from the ground it was not necessary.

Lt. William H. Gill, Washington, D. C., was the USAF officer controller on duty at the console. He checked and rechecked all calculations as he monitored the '29's progress on the base leg. Airmen stood by to double-check his figures and to furnish data on drop speeds, trajectory of bombs, outside air temperature, headings, etc. He, not the B-29 bombardier, would give the signal to toggle the Superfort's forty 500-pound fragmentation bombs.

Distance closed fast. The red track approached the first pencil line tangential to the bomber's course. It marked the northern boundary of friendly troops. At this point, Gill called for bomb-bay doors to be opened.

The B-29 complied.

Outside the mobile trailer, the night was blacker than a Communist heart. Boiling clouds of solid overcast sailed by just a few feet above the trailer's antenna saucer. Still locked onto the B-29, the saucer began to pan slowly downward toward Red-held Sniper's Ridge.

Only seconds remained. The pen trailed across no-man's land and approached the "ready" plot, about five seconds to the drop point. Gill tensed as the pen made contact. Slowly he gave the count to the bomber pilot:

"Five . . . four . . . three . . . two . . . one . . . BOMBS AWAY!"

Ripping off his earphones, he said, "Let's watch this."

He doused the lights and opened a side window. It afforded an unobstructed view of the front lines across the width of Kumwha Valley. Lights of friendly vehicles bobbed along the winding Korean roads without fear of enemy air attack.

You could see miles in each direction. Tracers painted brilliant red trails in the sky. Reflections from exploding artillery shells danced up and down the ridges. One whole section of no-man's land was bathed in the blue-white light of giant US searchlights.

Gill checked his wrist watch and estimated the drop time of

the 20,000 pounds of explosives to be about twenty seconds. He said the target was on the reverse slope of Sniper's Ridge, at the foot of 3,900-foot Papa-San Hill.

Then it came. A series of blasts bathed the front in orange light as smoke billowed skyward. The underside of clouds seemed to catch fire as fragments from forty bombs ripped through the night. Silhouettes of dark, ragged ridges between the station and the blast enabled Gill to estimate the point of impact.

The former fighter pilot said, "That's close enough for me—should've singed their thick skulls a little." He looked at his watch. "Well, I guess I'd better get ready for the next one. It's a B-26—he'll be calling in about three minutes. This goes on all night, every night, you know—in the daytime, too, when the weather socks in or when we have to hit targets on the front line."

From Gill's Tadpole station to all corners of South Korea and many islands in the Sea of Japan and the Yellow Sea, USAF tactical air control facilities probed with radar and radio to give UN air forces all-weather capability and to aid maximum combat effectiveness.

Fifth Air Force's 502d Tactical Air Control Group numbered more than 3,000 men. They had two big jobs. First and foremost, an offensive service, which gave around-the-clock flexibility and direction to interceptor, fighter-bomber, bomber, and all-weather fighter operations; secondly, defensive or early-warning functions in case of enemy air attacks plus coordinated communications and direction-finding assistance during rescue operations.

About the 502d, Gen. Otto P. Weyland, commander, Far East Air Forces, said:

"You can't fight an air war without being able to direct planes to and from their targets. This service, which is essentially electronic and the heart of any tactical air operation, raised its control potential by more than 100 percent during the last year of the war (1952–1953)."

He explained that this was achieved in spite of the fact that most available electronic equipment (especially radar) was of World War II vintage. He said, "Our men just developed better ways of using it."

Col. Ernest White, jet fighter pilot and commanding officer of the 502d, explained that the change in the application of tactical control from a ground-controlled interception function to that of an offensive weapon, was largely responsible for the high rating his organization received from Lt. Gen. Glenn O. Barcus, Fifth AF's commanding general, during the last year of the war. He added:

"When you remember that we had no tactical control organization at all in the Far East when the Reds attacked and only one in the United States, then you'll agree with me that the Five-Oh-Deuce has come a long way."

A typical station was the one called Mongoose, 120 miles north of the battle line and eight miles off the mainland, on Cho-Do Island in the Yellow Sea.

A special mission force set up Mongoose last winter. It was operated around the clock until after the truce when USAF had to move it south of the truce line. It was a typical Tactical Air Direction Center (TADC) of the 502d. It used radar research equipment and air-to-air, air-to-ground, UHF, and VHF radio systems to control and track friendly aircraft operating in the Yalu area as well as fighter-bomber and night intruder planes hitting at those targets north of the bomb line.

Mongoose also monitored several VHF channels and one emergency channel. In addition to voice, VHF direction finders provided friendly planes with directional bearings in case of emergencies or when radar traffic was too heavy to carry all of the load.

Men at Mongoose were occasionally shelled by Red mainland-based artillery. Once or twice there were minor damage and casualties. Fifth Air Force mounted air cover at all times against sneak raids.

Beyond Mongoose's prime mission of giving tactical air control and direction, it was the core of our Yalu air rescue system for the scores of pilots who bailed out over the frigid Yellow Sea. Helicopters, Grumman SA-16s, and Air-ResCAP (usually fighters or fighter-bombers) orbited over the area whenever daylight interception missions were laid on.

In the MIG-killing department, Mongoose controllers showed just as much pride and interest as they did in helping to retrieve a jet pilot from the water.

First Lt. William G. Rohm of Van Nuys, Calif., a B-24 crewman during World War II, had more than two years' experience in control work in Korea. He worked as a controller at Mongoose for seven and a half months and played an important part in many kills made in the Yalu area.

Rohm said, "Every time we vectored friendly fighters into a hassle that got a MIG, we'd celebrate. Sometimes pilots flew up to thank us and to see what a scope-happy controller looked like. Often they'd ask for the same men to work with them every time they flew up to the Yalu."

Lieutenant Rohm participated in one of the first night kills made by Lockheed F-94s of the 319th, an all-weather interceptor squadron, when they started flying combat missions last January.

It was the night of January 30. The moon was full, and the night air was crystal clear. Rohm huddled over his radarscope because "this kind of weather was for Red raiders." He picked up a blip around Angu and, after tracking it for a minute or two, found its course pointed for Pyongyang.

An F-94 had just reported in at a point south of Mongoose on its way north to sweep the Yalu. Rohm diverted the night fighter and vectored it toward the bogey. By now there were more blips in the hostile cluster. They were moving at LA-9 speed, and between 500 and 1,000 feet altitude. Rohm, using preestablished code words, directed the '94 on an interception letdown over the water and positioned the jet behind one of the Red prop planes. As the '94 closed in, its own radar made contact, and the pilot, Capt. Ben Fithian, reported the enemy visible at one mile. As the jet fired, Rohm watched the LA-9 blip fade from the scope. A moment later the F-94 pilot announced jubilantly, "Splash one."

The other LA-9s headed for Mongoose and revenge. Fithian's plane was short of ammo and turned homeward, but two companion F-94s closed in to chase the enemy craft back to Manchuria.

"After that," said Rohm, "we broke out a can of pineapple juice, and my name was ceremoniously inscribed on the honor roll with other Mongoose radar aces."

Col. Ernie White's theory was this: "We may be cliff dwellers, but we can be tigers, too. We're important even though we don't shoot guns."

To promote this spirit, controllers paid overnight visits to interceptors and fighter-bomber wings—and combat personnel returned the calls at Cho-Do. Through this exchange system, understanding of each other's capability helped develop teamwork and technique while some of that tiger spirit rubbed off.

Sometimes Mongoose control was so good that our own fighter-interceptor pilots complained. One Sabrejet pilot came back from a Yalu sweep in a very unhappy frame of mind:

"I was on a MIG's tail. I didn't know where I was. Didn't care. But I wanted that MIG. Then that blasted controller at Cho-Do breaks in. 'Squawking Red Leader, you're on the fence (meaning the Yalu). Uncle won't like. Be a good boy now and come back.'

"Even a fighter pilot can't have privacy any more. Everybody's getting into the act."

Our radar equipment in Korea was neither modern nor adequate. It developed holes and range limitations under certain conditions which made the job a "guessing game" for the most alert controllers. Through chatter with men in the Sabres, downright deduction, a full knowledge of their own limitations, and the right amount of ingenuity and teamwork, gaping holes were covered. "Educated guessing" made up for mechanical shortcomings.

Individual incidents make good listening, but it was the everyday, routine tactical control operation of stations like Mongoose that made it possible for Fifth Air Force to mount as many as 2,400 combat sorties in one twenty-four-hour period and to shuttle night-flying bombers and fighters to and from North Korean targets regularly and safely, good weather or bad.

It was like running a railroad but tougher, and more fun. Trains have tracks, automatic signals to warn engineers, and preestablished schedules. Aerial tracks are invisible. They overlap, and schedules are never fixed. Planes are only numbers and call signs. Controllers never see them fly by and seldom hear them.

As one Korean cliff dweller put it, a radar controller should have gotten flight pay for helping night-flying B-26s, F-94s, B-29s, and F-84s. He said, "A lot of them wouldn't make a move without position checks and bearings from our radar stations."

Or take the April morning when Capt. Clarence Bell, ex-pilot, Van Horn, Tex., was working the early morning shift at TADC station Wildfire.

Just before daybreak, when fighter-bombers were heading out for first-light strikes, Bell heard a shaky, mumbling voice of a pilot asking for directions. At first he thought it was a kid on his first mission, a little nervous and "clanked-up." But it was Thunderjet pilot Lt. Richard L. Spaulding, Iona, Mich., who was on his thirty-ninth mission.

When Spaulding's Thunderjet developed a faulty oxygen regulator, he began to black out, and his fighter-bomber bucked all over the sky. Bell watched the crazy flight pattern on his scope and fought hard to "get through" to Spaulding, urging him to reduce power and let down to lower altitudes. After seventy long minutes, Bell got Spaulding to drop his bombs over enemy lines and coaxed the guy to lower altitude near a forward air base where he was barely able to land before collapsing from exposure.

Said Spaulding, after recovery, "I'm alive today because a scope watcher knew what he was doing—in my book, Captain Bell is an ace any day."

Many controllers were experienced pilots. Some got radar assignments before leaving the States. Others were given the "happy" news after they arrived in Korea, ready for the MIG hunt, only to find they were declared surplus. Reassignment officers said they were "fortunate in receiving such choice duty."

Naturally, some disgruntled tempers flared, and their attitudes were, understandably, bad. But once they got into the thick of it, they did a good job.

Lt. Norman Green, Philadelphia, who was training for controller duty, flew twenty missions with the 4th Fighter-Interceptor Wing before he was assigned temporarily to a TADC station. In fact, on one mission, his plane was damaged by MIG fire. After many attempts to make home base—and through the aid of radar—he was finally plucked out of the Yellow Sea by an SA-16.

Most 502d equipment was not only weary but scarce. Backup equipment was not to be had, so mechanics and maintenance officers had to make the best of what they did have.

Men of the 502d employed ingenuity, talent, and "even miracles" to keep equipment running. They wound their own armatures, fought moisture during the rainy seasons, and dust and wind in dry weather.

In some cases, maintenance men needed eight hours a week for preventive maintenance but instead got continuous operation.

During rough Korean winters TADC and TAD posts were

often snow- or ice-bound. Many stations had to be supplied through air drops. Spring thaws made muddy mountain roads dangerous and often impassable. Wind and storm played havoc with antennas and living quarters. Occasionally, roving bands of guerrillas used isolated radar posts for target practice.

Here are some points TAC men want to make sure you remember:

Close-support bombing in Korea was primarily by ground control, using radar equipment.

When you hear a fighter pilot tell about tangling with a flock of MIGs, remember that radar may have led him to them.

When a fighter-bomber pilot talks about letting down through the overcast to bomb a target, ask if radar led him through the soup and positioned him for the bomb run. This was the case during one F-84 raid on Toksan Dam when radar vectored the jets through the overcast to the breakout point and the start of the bomb runs, at 8,000 feet altitude.

When a jet fighter-bomber struck a target its pilot couldn't see, you can be sure the bombs were toggled at the direction of an experienced controller, like Lt. Bill Gill, who ran the mission from a mountaintop TADC station beneath the overcast.

When you hear a Korean veteran describe his rescue from behind enemy lines, try to visualize how radarscopemen and radio operators guided the retriever plane to him.

When a B-26 pilot tells of weather flying on nearly every night mission in Korea, ask him how radar and radio helped make his missions just a little safer.

How do these men behind the scopes feel about their work?

Lieutenant Gill's answer is typical.

"Next to flying, I like doing this. It's just as hard on the nervous system—if we hit, that's expected, but if we miss, we catch hell.

"But it's one mountaintop after another. I can't say it's a good life for a family man."

Under Korean truce terms, the UN air forces lost a vital advantage when they were forced to move all tactical control stations south of the truce line. The early-warning capability at Cho-Do Island was one example.

Now the Reds are free to rebuild North Korean fields and are stocking them with MIGs. Monitoring MIG movements is now tough, and many experts believe that surprise attacks against our own front-line forces would be almost impossible to detect beforehand and in time to mount effective interception.

This one sure fact remains, however. Should the shooting start again in Korea or should there be other MIG Alleys to sweep, cliff-dwelling scope watchers must be there to call the shots.

VIETNAM

In the relatively short history of the United States, soon to celebrate its 200th anniversary, war has played a significant part. It
is sad but true that this is the case for most nations of the world,
many of which were born to the sound of drums and gunfire. So
it was with the U.S. We are not a particularly belligerent people,
no more so than other people. Yet we have precipitated conflicts
with Mexico in 1846 and Spain in 1898. And war has been thrust
upon us as in the War of 1812 and World War II. In recent
times, as in the case of Korea and Vietnam, the U.S., under its
newly found mantle of leadership of the Western World, and a
strong sense of obligation dictated by treaties, has felt it necessary to act swiftly and with determination. In Korea U.S. forces
were attacked by the Communist North Koreans. In Vietnam the
U.S. was asked by the South Vietnamese government to help, and
to fill the vacuum left by the French.

At first the United States furnished arms and equipment to the
South Vietnamese. Americans served primarily as advisers to the
ARVN (Army of Vietnam). Special Forces (Green Beret)
teams trained South Vietnamese units in the "boondocks" (hin-
terland) and did a great amount of civic action, furnishing the
local populace with sorely needed medical assistance, and helping to build roads, bridges, improve local water supplies and
sanitary conditions, etc. The USAF furnished aircraft, both
propeller and jet, and American pilots trained the South Vietnamese Air Force. But the war dragged on and on, and finally

American fighting men, ground and air, were committed to direct action against the Viet Cong and the North Vietnamese forces.

Paradoxically, in this fast moving age of the jet it was found that often the conventional, propeller-driven aircraft was able to do a better job locating and hitting hard to find Viet Cong targets and on other type missions where "stay power" was needed. The jet moves too fast and cannot stay in the action for any length of time.

To solve the problem the U.S. furnished the North American T-28, a prop driven trainer with slower speed and lower ceiling than the World War II P-47 and P-51 but with a greater range and capable for use as a fighter-bomber. We also brought out of "mothballs" the rugged Douglas *Skyraider*. A considerable number of these planes were given to the Republic of Vietnam and our own Air Force and Navy used them in Vietnam as well.

There were "jobs," too, where the special attributes of the jet bomber were required, and the particularly powerful punch of the eight-jet Boeing B-52 cannot be denied. The Vietnam conflict was the first time that the mighty *Stratoforts* of the Strategic Air Command were used in anger, and though limited to conventional bomb loads they packed a mighty wallop.

Smaller jet aircraft like the F-4C *Phantom* and F-105 *Thunderchief* performed exceptionally well as tactical fighter-bombers against bridges and supply lines.

In addition to the USAF fighter-bombers and heavy eight-jet B-52 *Stratoforts* that pounded North Vietnam military targets daily, sleek Navy attack aircraft and fighter-bombers roared off the decks of our giant aircraft carriers, in the Gulf of Tonkin, to strike at the heart of the enemy.

With the possible exception of the Second World War there has never been a war in which the U.S. has engaged that there has not been a strong opposition and a loud public demand to "bring our boys home." Opposition to the Vietnam War is probably no louder or stronger than any previous demands but the more widespread and more powerful means of mass communications have made it appear so. Perhaps if the same thing happens in other countries our planet may yet see an end to war.

MISSION TO QUANG TIN

BRIAN SHEEHAN, CAPTAIN

USAF

Up came the landing gear.

Bomb-laden, the B-52 lifted skyward through the dark Pacific night as wind and rain pummeled its aluminum surface.

In the pilot's seat Lt. Col. Eldon Jamison, a powerfully built six-footer, used every ounce of his skill to keep the eight-jet *Stratofortress* climbing under its maximum load of fuel and bombs.

Everything went well for 15 seconds after takeoff for aircraft commander Jamison and his crew, on their fourth combat mission in 12 days. Then the 16th second struck.

Fire Warning

"Fire warning light on number seven engine," called Lt. Richard Jones, the copilot. Four aircrewmen in other sections of the aircraft tensed.

In a small, packing-crate-size room near the cockpit, Capt. Don Milner, electronics warfare officer, reached down instinctively and pulled his parachute straps tight.

Downstairs in another compartment, Capt. Edwin Jones, the radar navigator, looked quizzically at Capt. Merrill Freeman, the aircraft navigator.

At the same time MSgt. Don McElliot, the tail gunner, spun his head around to peer at engine seven. "No visible fire yet!" he said over the intercom.

Meanwhile, Colonel Jamison instantly pulled back the throttle on engine seven. Mockingly, the red fire warning light continued glowing.

Intently, Jamison eased the throttle up a bit, then back, up again, and back once more. For five long seconds the red light shone like a lighthouse beacon. Then it died out.

Jamison inched throttle seven forward. All engine instruments responded normally. The fire warning stayed black. "Faulty circuit," he told his crew. "Everything's okay."

Now the huge B-52, picking up speed like a long-distance runner, reached for its assigned altitude. It was speeding in trail formation toward a target in Quang Tin Province, South Vietnam.

There Viet Cong troops were dug into a mountain ridge against advancing United States Marines. The enemy stronghold contained a command post, network of underground tunnels, food and arms storehouses, and a communications center.

As 45-year-old Eldon Jamison leveled off his 430,000-pound bomber at cruising altitude, his thoughts of the target turned his mind for a moment to the mission briefing three hours before.

To him, it was like all the others during World War II—and Korea, where he flew B-26s into combat 65 times. There were the same kind of serious young crewmen. There were the concise briefings by intelligence, weather, and operations officers. And there was that somber moment when the chaplain said a prayer.

The crackle of radar navigator Capt. Edwin Jones' voice interrupted Jamison's thoughts. "Pilot, we're now 30 minutes out. Radar shows we have proper aircraft separation, and altitude difference."

"Roger," said Jamison.

In another B-52 eight miles ahead, this mission was led by Col. William "Bill" Cumiskey, combat commander of the 454-320th Bomb Wing (a composite of SAC units from Columbus AFB, Miss., and Mather AFB, Calif.).

Flying behind Colonel Cumiskey's jet bomber were other *Stratofortresses,* including the one flown by Lt. Col. Jamison.

Five Hours to Target

When the fluorescent hands on Jamison's watch showed 0400 hours, his aircraft had been airborne one hour. Flying time remaining to the target? Five hours.

During the next 60 minutes Jamison and copilot Lieutenant Jones continued their checks of each cockpit instrument. Everything read "green." Even engine number seven purred.

The other combat flyers were equally busy. Captain Milner read through the check list for his incredibly complex electronic warfare devices. Navigators Freeman and Jones cross-checked the B-52's airspeed (now up to 440 knots), position, heading, and altitude. Tail gunner McElliot tested his four .50-caliber weapons. His guns were "go."

As these men completed their important tasks, all thoughts focused on the mission. It had to go right. US Marines were depending on them.

Crack went the intercom. "Pilot, this is navigator. Estimate refueling point in six-zero (60) minutes."

"Roger."

Peering into the black of night, Colonel Jamison could just see the flashing red beacon of another B-52 flying ahead. It was his single outside reference point. Soon a formation of KC-135 tankers should appear.

Forty-five minutes dragged by. Then time took on new tempo.

"Pilot, I've got the tankers on my radar," said Capt. Edwin

Smith. On his radar screen one "blip" after another quickly appeared. They were the tankers, flying a parallel course.

"Going down to 26,000 feet for rendezvous," spoke Jamison.

With precise control he confidently pulled back the B-52's eight throttles, putting the bomber into a shallow dive until refueling altitude was reached.

The formation of tanker aircraft, equipped with red flashing beacons and navigation lights, looked like distant fireflies. Soon they came closer, then fell into the proper positions among the speeding B-52s.

"Got mine in sight," snapped Jamison. "Here we go!"

Mid-Air Hookup

Cautiously Jamison approached his KC-135 from below and behind. Distance closed rapidly. Both aircraft flew in formation —nearly touching.

Nudging into contact position, Jamison held the giant B-52 steady with a firm grip. Simultaneously the KC-135 boom operator extended the tanker's long, metal refueling probe.

Clank! The tanker's probe locked into a steel receptacle behind the cockpit atop the B-52. Time and space seemed motionless.

"You now have contact," said copilot Jones on the intercom.

Fuel raced from the tanker into the *Stratofortress* as copilot Jones advised Jamison of the fuel levels taken on board. "10,-000 pounds . . . 20,000 pounds . . . 30,000 pounds . . ."

Several minutes passed.

Nearly 30 tons of fuel had been transferred.

Then the refueling boom retracted up and away.

"We're disconnected," said copilot Jones.

Carefully the B-52 dropped away from the tanker. Minutes later Colonel Jamison took it back to mission altitude, and on toward the target.

For the next 1 hour 27 minutes the *Stratofortress* sped south.

Near the Philippine Islands dawn finally broke—pink, white, and finally blue. Now the bomber was 21 minutes from South Vietnam's coast. The Viet Cong? Seventy-five minutes away.

"Check your personal equipment." Jamison's order struck a grim note in crewmen's hearts. Each man looked over his .38-caliber pistol. Flares were pulled from zippered flight-suit pockets and examined. So were maps, rations, medical packs, and ammunition.

Within a quarter hour South Vietnam came up green against the South China Sea. The B-52 held its heading, swiftly passing over Ham Tan, an agricultural community near the coast and 50 miles north of Saigon.

Six minutes crept by. Then Eldon Jamison swung his bomber north. "Forty-eight minutes to target," navigator Merrill Freeman announced.

The moments quickened. At 0848 hours the *Stratofortress* was boring in on the Viet Cong. Captain Smith flipped the "bomb arming" switch.

Each of the fifty-one 750-pound bombs—under the wings and in the bomb bay—was ready.

Now the navigator and radar navigator mentally ran a nerve-wracking race against time. The mechanism to open the bomb-bay doors checked okay. So did radar. And bombing systems. The first aiming points—critical in importance—were identified.

Just seven minutes to go!

Time flashed past.

Now Eldon Jamison's crew was three minutes from bomb release. Airspeed and altitude were perfect. Below, an overcast spread out like a white blanket hiding the target from everything but radar.

"One minute out."

The bomb-bay doors were opened.

Radar navigator Smith called the countdown. "Five, four, three, two, one.

"Bombs away!"

The bombs streaked through the sky toward the jungle-covered mountain ridge. On the ground the Viet Cong were unaware of the impending attack. Then suddenly the devastating 750-pound bombs ripped their camp. The command post splintered like a matchbox when two bombs struck it dead center. A network of underground tunnels collapsed. Marines waiting three miles away heard the ammunition warehouse blow up.

"How close did we hit?" asked Jamison.

"Estimate within 200 feet," said the navigator. A cheer resounded over the intercom.

Ninety seconds after bomb release the B-52 was turned southeast toward the coast. Then electronic warfare officer Don Milner shouted into the intercom.

"Pilot, I have indicators on radar."

"Roger," said Jamison.

"Ops," cut in tail gunner McElliot. "Got two unidentified aircraft at 10 o'clock on my radar. Confirm, EW?"

"Roger," said Milner.

"They are friendlies," someone called.

"Stay alert," said Jamison.

For several minutes Milner and McElliot tracked the enemy radar. Each second seemed like a century. Then Captain Milner spoke again: "Off radar. No sign of unidentified aircraft."

Away from South Vietnam, toward the open ocean and safety, the B-52 dashed. The sun rode high. Cloud cover was broken at 3,000 feet. Shortly the Philippine Islands slipped beneath, and were left behind.

The Unsung Heroes

Meanwhile, back at home base the weather was getting worse by the minute. Winds were up to 35 knots. Rain pounded down. Visibility was almost zero, and Maj. Gen. William Crumm, commander of SAC's 3d Air Division, monitored progress from his command post.

More than anyone else, General Crumm knew the unbelievable amount of work necessary to get those bombers into the air and over their targets.

"There are a lot of unrecognized heroes in this type of operation," he once observed, "and they all don't wear flying suits."

Who are they? Cooks, drivers, air policemen, maintenance men, bomb loaders, crew chiefs, intelligence planners, weathermen, and administrative clerks. Each played a vital role. Today he didn't want *anyone* let down.

In General Crumm's division command post, information about the air strike began trickling in from South Vietnam. Every bomber had dropped its bombs right on the target area. The Marines stormed the VC camp. They took it after a brief fight. They reported that B-52 bomb damage was "awesome."

An aide interrupted General Crumm, "Sir, the B-52s are now 35 minutes out."

"Thank you."

It was 1405 hours—11 hours 5 minutes after the mission was launched—and in the air Lt. Col. Eldon Jamison heard the weather report from his base. It wasn't good. Rain was still coming down in sheets. Clouds covered the island.

Instrument Approach

At 1420 hours Jamison went on instruments, and minutes later began his descent. Now air traffic controllers took over. Down through thick clouds and rain came the B-52. Following precise directions from the air traffic controllers, Jamison turned and twisted his *Stratofortress*. The B-52 kept working down through the weather.

Now Jamison was on final approach, and ground-controlled approach (GCA) gave the instructions. "Two miles from touchdown. On course . . . on glide path." Black clouds still shut out sky and earth.

Suddenly Jamison's bomber broke out of the thick weather. There was the field—straight ahead—coming up fast.

Moments later the aircraft's tires squealed as they touched the long concrete runway. The *Stratofortress* crew—11 hours 40 minutes after takeoff—was home from its war.

Epilogue. Two hours later, after completing their intelligence and maintenance debriefing, Colonel Jamison and his crew walked toward their fenced, guarded quarters for a crew rest. After taking a few steps they met Col. Bill Cumiskey, the wing commander. "You are scheduled as 'spare' for tomorrow's mission. Can you make it?"

"Sure," responded the crew.

They did. But not as spare. They flew.

I EJECTED AT ALMOST THE LAST MOMENT

BRIAN E. WESTIN, LIEUTENANT

USNR

Pulling out of our bombing dive, I heard a loud, popping explosion and tiny particles seemed to hit me in the face—a little like the light spray you sometimes get when people are talking to you. I think I felt some decompression.

We were climbing out pretty steeply and I looked at Bill. He seemed to be hurt and I figured the impact of the small arms bullet—if that's what it was—made him jerk the stick back. He ripped off his mask and his face looked drained. I asked him over the ICS (intercom) if he'd been hurt. But he didn't answer. His left arm was limp and completely incapacitated, resting on the throttles where his ICS button is located, but he couldn't key the switch to talk. He could hear, though.

Our flight path was pretty erratic. We were at military power and had a lot of acceleration from our dive. We must have been going through 6,000 or 7,000 feet when I realized Bill was see-sawing in and out of full consciousness. I grabbed the stick and started the airplane descending in the right direction over the water. Soon afterward he started coming out of his initial shock and seemed to be getting the A-6 back into the right parameters to head away from the coast of North Vietnam and back towards the ship. I tried to help him with the stick and radioed that he had been hit and that we were trying to get back to the *Kitty Hawk*. I could see our section leader in a tight orbit to the north as we sped out to sea.

Bill managed to pull the throttles back and get the speed brakes partially deployed, for we were accelerating past at least 450 knots. During this period I kept talking and trying to get him to talk to keep his attention on our flight. I remembered a small bottle of medicinal brandy, issued by flight surgeons to flight crews, that I had in my navigation kit. I offered it to Bill and he took a couple of swallows. It seemed to increase his consciousness. He kept shaking his head, trying to clear his mind. He often seemed to be fainting. Finally, I heard him yell "eject" and blow the canopy. The fresh air and burble in the open cockpit served again to momentarily revive him. I kept talking to him and coaxed him to fly on toward the carrier as long as he could last. Again he tried to get me to eject, but I indicated that I would wait until after he ejected.

Our skipper in the other A-6 shot overhead, trying to slow down with his speed brakes, after trying to catch our airplane at our initial high speed. At that instant Bill ejected and the CO banked off sharply to circle the parachute. The rush of fresh air into the cockpit had probably helped revive Bill and now I found it doubly refreshing. I'm a Bombardier/Navigator, not a pilot, and with the skipper probably orbiting over Bill, it flicked through my mind that our survival chances might be better if I tried to head for the *Kitty Hawk* and eject. That wouldn't split the Search and Rescue effort. During those few seconds alone in the aircraft I radioed the *Kitty Hawk* that I was 60 miles out. My mind stumbled over the back end of the tacan needle and I momentarily had trouble figuring my bearings from the ship.

But the fresh air was stinging my mind into a more reasonable course of action and probably at almost the last moment, I ejected—at about 800 feet in a 20-degree bank. The ejection proved to be no problem, except that my left rocker jet fitting came free, leaving me dangling awkwardly in the descent. In 20 seconds or so I hit the water. I saw the skipper orbiting about 1½ miles west and tried to contact him on my radio. No luck.

After what seemed an eternity, a couple of "Spads"—Douglas A-1 *Skyraiders*—coming from seaward missed me, but when they circled back nose-on to me—I fired a flare. They apparently saw me and roared down low and directly overhead.

Pretty soon along came an SH-3 (Sikorsky twin-turbine *Sea King*) and hauled me aboard, after I knifed off some of the lanyards connecting me to my raft and other equipment. I got out of a lot of wet gear, including my harness with its flotation gear, and sat down on the step between the helo pilot and copilot.

After a short conversation with the helo pilot I realized Bill was not in definite contact and that there was some confusion as to whether one or both of us had ejected. I gave the helo pilot a short vector to where I thought Bill would be, and we headed in that general direction. A few minutes later, the pilot told me that they had sighted Bill. Apparently he had become separated from his raft assembly and survival gear, and the orbiting A-6 had been following the empty inflated raft. Bill was tuckered out but smiling. The helo crew dropped the sling. But the rotor downwash and fatigue were too much for Bill. I remembered reading in *Approach* magazine about the possibility of an injured survivor falling out of the sling. So I got in it and went down in the water with Bill and hooked the line up to the helo hoist ring on his torso harness, after unhooking the sling from the hook assembly. After some difficulty, they pulled him aboard. Bill fainted as the first tug on the line started pulling him out of the water.

Aboard the helo, I had taken off my Mark III Charlie flotation gear and torso harness. In my hurry to get down to Bill I had grabbed an old-fashioned Mae West and put it on wrong. Now the darn thing was forcing my face into the water as I tried to get into a makeshift sling they lowered for me. For a few minutes, I was suffocating and about to drown. I think I almost gave up. But finally I began to think rationally again, got my head up, and blew up my anti-G suit. I found I could rest quite comfortably in the water with just my G suit and the small Mae West slung under my left shoulder. I waved the helo off to take Bill to medical aid because the secondary sling was too small for me to fit into. I knew my struggles were taking too much time and that they should fly Bill back to the Search and Rescue ship before he lost much more blood.

Man, it was lonely out there—just me in my green suit in that dark blue water! My white hands seemed to provide the only contrast for searchers to spot and I figured they'd probably blend with the whitecaps. But the helo had dropped a smoke flare to mark me. I put my G-suit tube in my mouth and managed to blow up the suit a bit. At least it kept my face from pitching over into the water again.

After about five minutes, another rescue helicopter found me. A crewman was standing in the door, pointing at something and shouting. After they hauled me aboard, he said it was a shark. I never saw it.

"SKYRAIDERS" AT THE BATTLE OF
LONG MY

HEADQUARTERS, U. S. MILITARY ASSISTANCE COMMAND, VIETNAM

1 January 1965

For the insurgent in any guerrilla war, success depends upon how well he is able to cancel out his opponents' technical superiority. If he can force his opponent to fight on his terms using his weapons, his battle is won. The war then becomes one of ambush, hit and run strikes, attacks on outposts at night, sabotage of trains and installations. The insurgent has the advantage because he can conceal himself in a countryside he knows well and pick his own time and place of battle.

For the counterinsurgent, the opposite is true. Unless he can find and discriminately destroy the enemy in his own environment, with superior weaponry, there can be no victory. This is the central core issue in the military phase of the war in Vietnam.

That the United States is not coming out second best as the struggle increases in intensity is becoming more and more apparent. One battle fought on December 11 in the flat delta land of Chuong Thien Province about 110 miles south of Saigon shows what coordinated air activity can do to an enemy who is committing larger and larger forces to actions of his own choosing.

On that day, 18 Vietnamese Air Force A-1E and A-1H *Sky-*

raiders, plus U.S. Army helicopters, teamed up to decisively smash an enemy who had committed two battalions in three separate attacks on government installations.

Before nightfall, an estimated 400 Viet Cong lay dead in the rice paddies, banana groves and mangrove swamps of this flat and rice-rich land.

Even more important, air strikes—according to U. S. Army advisors and Vietnamese ground commanders—averted what could have been a major disaster.

December 11 started peacefully enough. At about 0900 Major Asa N. Chandler, of Cambridge, Maryland, advisor to Vietnam's 21st Infantry Division, was moving eastward along a dirt road with two Regional Force companies. Their mission was to deliver a 155mm howitzer to an outpost about 8 kilometers south of the district capital of Long My. The outpost had been attacked by the enemy the previous night and the powerful artillery piece would help them fight off future attacks.

About 1,000 feet overhead, in a U. S. Air Force light liaison 0-1F plane, Air Force Captain Stanton R. Musser of Gettysburg, Pennsylvania, with his Vietnamese observer was patrolling the route the companies would travel, looking for signs of the enemy, especially anything indicating a possible ambush.

The two Regional Force companies were moving along a road running parallel most of the way with a major canal that was intersected every couple of kilometers by smaller canals.

Chandler, suspecting an ambush not far from Long My, asked the O-1F to take a look. Captain Musser and his VNAF observer dropped low to look and found nothing unusual. The lead company moved forward and the observer in the plane overhead kept a close watch for any signs of Viet Cong activity.

Four VNAF *Skyraiders* flying cover overhead were ready to strike if the enemy showed himself. The A-1Es had their radios tuned in to Paddy Control, the radar control for the delta. Paddy Control was also in contact with Musser.

By 1130 hours, the lead company had moved to within about five kilometers of its destination. The *Skyraiders* overhead were nearing bingo fuel and would soon have to return to base. Then almost suddenly, the first contact in a deadly hide and seek game was made.

Just a few hundred yards east of the ground force, the O-1F pilot noticed some sampans sunk in the canal, a Viet Cong tactic for hiding these supply vessels. He also saw what looked like foxholes, but he couldn't be sure. Dropping down to under 500 feet, he flew over the suspected area and drew no fire. This was unusual, he thought, but if a main force Viet Cong unit was hiding below, it wouldn't fire at the liaison plane since the Viet Cong knew fighters would be in the area.

Musser reported to Chandler, who replied that there were no signs of Viet Cong activity on the ground. Just to be safe, the Army ground officer told the observer to fire a rocket smoke marker into the suspected area, a tributary canal which lay just ahead of the lead company.

Musser described what happened next. "I rolled in and marked the target with a smoke rocket and, boy, as soon as the smoke came, everything busted wide open. Automatic fire from .50 calibers came reaching into the sky and a string of muzzle blasts could be seen all along the canal. We had stepped on a rattler."

Almost immediately, Musser was directing the four A-1Es in strikes against the Viet Cong concentration and in ten minutes of bombing, the enemy ranks were shattered. With Musser calling the shots, the *Skyraiders* dropped 18,000 pounds of napalm and high explosive bombs onto the enemy positions. "It was a beautiful job of precision bombing," Musser says. He counted 35 dead on the ground, "but there must have been a lot more" he added.

Taking advantage of the Viet Cong confusion, Chandler accompanied the Regional Force company in pursuit of the bombed Viet Cong. The unit moved past the enemy bodies, picking up weapons and searching for any survivors. At first, it looked like the air strike had done the trick. But unknown to both Chandler and Musser, the main force of the Viet Cong battalion was on the west side of the main canal about 100 yards away. During the bombing strikes they had laid low, waiting the right time.

Suddenly, the enemy opened up with small arms, automatic weapons and 57mm recoilless rifles. The small force which Chandler was accompanying was getting fire from several directions. The second of the two companies retreated back toward Long My with their precious 155mm howitzer. In the confusion of the battle which followed, Chandler soon found himself with only 14 men from the lead company.

Chandler and the 14 soldiers took cover in an abandoned triangular fort which they had passed earlier and jumped into trenches running from each corner to the center. The fort had 50 foot sides with a five foot high earth mound on the perimeter. It wasn't much protection, but the best available.

As the Viet Cong prepared to move on the fort, Chandler radioed for more air support. He estimated they could hold out for ten minutes.

In the air about 40 miles north were four more A-1Es which were scheduled for a routine air cover mission. The planes, with a full load of napalm and bombs aboard, were diverted to support the outpost defenders. Musser was told it would take 20 minutes for the planes to arrive over the target.

Six armed U. S. Army UH-18 helicopters, sent up from the nearby base of Soc Trang, held off the enemy until the fighters arrived. The helicopters, flying against heavy anti-aircraft fire, smashed 2.75 rockets and machine gun fire into the enemy positions but the well dug-in guerrillas were able to withstand the attacks.

Tod 31, the call sign for the A-1E flight, arrived on the scene in 12 minutes—not 20. Musser told the choppers to clear the area

BOMBS AWAY!

for air strikes. Then, like a quarterback calling the plays, Musser directed individual runs against targets.

"I'm putting a rocket on the first target," Musser radioed, "it's a row of huts across the main canal west of the outpost. Watch for it."

Musser put the light plane into a dive and fired the rocket. The yellow smoke was clearly visible to Air Force Major William G. Plunk of Bethel Springs, Tennessee, pilot in the A-1E picked for the first strike.

Since the area was clear of civilians, the strike pilots had clearance to hit anything within 100 feet except the outpost itself. Plunk put the sturdy aircraft into a dive and slammed several 500 pound bombs smack on the target.

"Perfect," Musser yelled, "now just north of the small canal. A banana patch and two rows of houses. All filled with Viet Congs."

It was now the turn of Air Force Captain Walter L. Dixon of Opelika, Alabama, flying with a VNAF student pilot. Dixon came in low from the north, parallel with the huts. His 260 and 500 pound bombs obliterated the target area with smoke and dust.

The other two American pilots, Captain Thomas A. Johnson from North Manchester, Indiana, and Captain William H. May of Bakersfield, California, with VNAF pilots at their side, then unloaded their weapons on the enemy. The strike by Johnson's A-1E was made just over the fort and the napalm was dropped so close that the heat singed Chandler's eyebrows. But it had to be that way. The bombs landed on the enemy guerrillas who were on the same side of the canal as the fort. Johnson's plane was hit twice, once at 50 feet and again at 2,500 feet. However, it limped safely into Can Tho.

A total of nine strikes was made on enemy forces all around the fort. The whole thing lasted only ten minutes and Chandler and his Vietnamese cohorts were able to walk out, moving north again to find the second company. The aircraft returned to their base at Bien Hoa.

Although the *Skyraiders* had shattered the Viet Cong positions around the fort leaving more than a hundred dead, this was not the end of the battle. It turned out that the force surrounding the fort was only part of two battalions massed against the government forces in Long My.

A truck convoy had been dispatched by the Province Chief to go from Vi Thanh to Long My to help the ambushed unit. About eight kilometers from the fort, it was ambushed in classic Viet Cong fashion, the lead and rear trucks being hit. The burning convoy was reported to Captain Musser by a radio operator at Duc Long outpost which was also under attack at this time.

Since morning, Musser had teamed up with an Army L-19 radio relay plane, flown by 2nd Lieutenant Robert D. Thorton, of Vicksburg, Mississippi, which was directing supporting artillery strikes. The Army pilot and his Vietnamese observer went to look for the convoy while Musser flew cover over Chandler's unit. When Lieutenant Thorton found the burning convoy on the road, another call went out for air support.

Again, armed *Hueys* attacked the enemy around the convoy until the third flight of A-1Es arrived. Musser learned from a radio operator at Duc Long outpost that the friendlies were north of the convoy and the enemy fire was coming from the south. That's where the bombs would go.

Musser directed these four aircraft as he did the others, placing their weapons along the banks of three canals where the enemy was entrenched with heavy weapons including 57mm recoilless rifles. These strikes, plus the armed *Huey* attacks, saved what was left of the convoy. Numerous enemy bodies were seen after some 20,000 pounds of napalm and bombs were dropped. A-1E aircraft, facing intense ground fire, took several hits. These attacks did much to save survivors of the ambushed convoy although one American was killed and one missing.

Shortly after, two A-1H *Skyraiders* directed to cover Major Chandler's withdrawal, expended against enemy forces armed with several .50 caliber machine guns. One A-1H was shot down and landed in a rice paddy, but the pilot was rescued by an armed chopper called to the scene by Musser. The chopper picked the pilot up under withering enemy fire. The Viet Cong however, controlled the area where the plane went down and kept an explosive ordnance destruction team from getting near it. Here again, the enemy was armed with .50 caliber machine guns and recoilless rifles and air strikes were required.

Tod 51 was called in, another flight of four powerful A-1Es, each capable of carrying the bomb load carried by a B-17 in World War II. Their target was the Viet Cong concentration around the downed plane, possessing at least two .50 caliber guns. The planes were over the target at 1820 hours and by 1830, had dropped some 6000 pounds of bombs on the enemy. The enemy machine guns were knocked out and the Viet Cong withdrew, opening the way for the ambushed group, which had been pinned down. The attacking planes received several .50 caliber hits.

Captain Musser and his Vietnamese colleague had been directing the air action for ten hours and five minutes, stopping only for ten minute intervals to land and refuel the plane. It was a good day's work. In all, the air strikes they directed had accounted for approximately 400 Viet Cong killed. They had saved the company Chandler was with and they had saved the attacked convoy from being wiped out.

Later that night, flare ships and fighters supported the convoy and the area of the downed plane. The next morning, an EOD team got into the area to blow the aircraft up and keep the enemy from stripping it. Also, at dawn, a relief force arrived to get the surviving members of the convoy to safety.

This was one day in the air war over the flat delta land of Vietnam. Eighteen single engine prop planes plus U. S. Army *Hueys,* guided by a USAF Forward Air Controller in a light liaison plane, were able to cope with a highly confused battle situation. "The enemy seemed to pop up everywhere," Musser says. "And I just don't see how we could have averted disaster except by use of tactical air power."

Both Vietnamese ground commanders and U. S. Army advisors backed up this opinion. The close support by *Skyraiders,* involving in many cases the dropping of bomb loads within 100 feet of friendly positions, was a tribute to the highly skilled pilots of the USAF and the VNAF.

The experience at Long My also showed how armed helicopters and the more powerful *Skyraiders* could work together over the battlefield. The *Hueys* with their light weapons kept the enemy at bay until the *Skyraiders* could get into action with the heavy, deadly aerial ordnance.

The enemy paid heavily at Long My as a result of timely and highly effective air action. In a similar action two days earlier some 500 miles to the north near An Lao, air also was employed to drive Viet Cong away from positions they had captured.

In a sense, the experience at Long My was a portent of the future. As the Viet Cong massed battalion size units for large scale attacks, they would become more discernible and more vulnerable. When this happened, tactical air power could be employed much more effectively than when fighting was mainly limited to sporadic acts of terrorism by relatively small units.

RESCUE FROM THE GULF OF TONKIN

JAMES P. COYNE, CAPTAIN

USAF

You're aircraft commander of Mustang Four in a flight of F-4C *Phantom* jets about to launch on a US Air Force strike over North Vietnam, and you stand in front of your bird talking to the aircraft commander of Mustang Lead—Capt. Jack Gravis, of Tampa, Fla. You don't talk about the target, heavily defended Vinh Linh barracks, just north of the demilitarized zone. Instead, you keep the conversation light and discuss the fishing at your home station, MacDill Air Force Base, Fla., and the water-skiing on Tampa Bay. Jack remarks he really needs a haircut and is going to get one as soon as he returns from this flight. You're not clairvoyant, so you don't know that he won't get a haircut this day. When you taxi back in from the mission, the space Jack's aircraft now occupies will be empty.

Just prior to start-engine time, Jack gestures to the other pilot of his bird, 1st Lt. Wylie E. Nolan of Fayetteville, Ark., and the two climb into the gray-and-white, black-radomed *Phantom*—Jack in the front cockpit and Pete in the rear.

You go through the prestart checklist with your own pilot, 1st Lt. Michael Chwan,[1] and start up in a swirl of black smoke. You check the two big engines running smoothly and taxi out in

---

[1] Three missions after the one described in the story, Lt. Chwan was shot down over North Vietnam and is now listed as missing in action.

trail to the arming area beside the takeoff end of the runway. The hard-working armorers, stripped to the waist in the Southeast Asia heat, swarm under the four aircraft in the flight and then swiftly withdraw, each man bearing handfuls of red-bannered, steel-shafted "safety pins." Your load of deadly 750-pound high-explosive bombs is now ready to go to war.

Jack radios the tower for takeoff clearance, taxis onto the runway, checks his instruments. He calls "Mustang Lead rolling," and you see twin shafts of fire spurt from the tailpipes as he engages both afterburners. More than 34,000 pounds of thrust kick the *Phantom* in the tail as she lunges down the runway and up into the burning blue sky. You watch Mustang Two and Mustang Three follow suit, and you bring up the rear. You've got more than 350 hours of *Phantom* flying time, but you still marvel at the way this big, heavily loaded fighter gathers speed and leaps off.

This is a short mission so there's no inflight refueling to worry about. You let Mike do the flying as the flight levels off, and soon you cross the boundary of North Vietnam. No enemy air opposition is expected, but everyone scans the sky, especially at six o'clock. Your pulse quickens, and you feel a little tightness in the throat.

In a few minutes, Jack calls, "Mustang, go mission frequency." Mike dials in the prebriefed frequency on the UHF radio and you hear Jack, "Mustang Flight, check in," followed by the members of the flight: "Two," "Mustang Three," and you say, "Four's on." You take control of the aircraft.

Jack calls the mission commander. "Jackknife Lead, this is Mustang. Five minutes out with four." Jackknife is Maj. Robert E. Olson, thirty-seven, of St. Petersburg, Fla., who led today's first flight into the target. Now he circles to direct the attacks by succeeding flights. "Roger, Mustang. Tiger is just finishing up. We'll be ready for you when you get here."

The flight is now approaching the target area from the south at more than 500 miles an hour. It's near the coast. The Gulf of Tonkin, steel gray and sullen, stretches away to the horizon. You remember the strike briefing. "If you're hit, head out to sea." It doesn't look very inviting, but you know you can be rescued from the Gulf. If you go down over land near the densely populated target area, you will almost certainly be captured.

Tiger has now departed, and you can see the target. The barracks complex is an area about four city blocks square, the barracks laid out in neat, orderly rows. A layer of dingy clouds hangs over the area at medium altitude. Flak! You'll have to roll in for your run right through it. Another cloud hangs lower, just about at pullout altitude. You curse. The flak is thickest right at the two points in your flight path where you will be changing altitude the least, making you most vulnerable. And you know the "clear" area between the two clouds is filled with hot metal from small arms, machine guns, and 20-mm anti-aircraft. "Mustangs, set 'em up 'hot.'"

On intercom, you tell Mike to read off the checklist, even though you know the procedure by heart. You want to make only one pass through the flak. Statistics, it has been drummed into you, show that making more than one pass on a target as heavily defended as this one is inviting the undertaker. If you forget a single step in the arming procedures, your bombs won't drop, and you'll have to go in again. So Mike reads the checklist.

"Sight setting?"

"Depressed, ninety-five mils."

"Weapons selector?"

"Bombs, ripple."

"Bomb arming switch?"

"Arm, nose and tail."

"Intervalometer?"

"Set."

"Station selector?"

"Bombs, all."

"Master arm switch?"

"Arm."

All you have to do now is roll in, line up your target, push the red bomb-release button on top of the stick, and it's bombs away. You know everybody in the flight has been going through the same procedure, and now you're all "hot." You reduce power slightly and slide back into the prebriefed staggered trail position, about 3,000 feet behind number three.

"Mustang, this is Jackknife. We've pretty well cleaned up Area A. Hit Area B. Don't hit north of B. That's where the town starts." You look down at the town. It has turned red as the 37, 57, and other antiaircraft guns concealed there open up at you. You can't keep a wry smile from forming. We don't hit towns because they're not military targets.

"Roger, Jackknife," Jack answers. "Mustangs, hit your briefed targets in Area B. We'll roll in in ten seconds." You peer down through the smoke and pick out your assigned building. It's an H-shaped structure, probably a headquarters. You switch your attention to the rest of the flight. Now Jack is in a screaming dive, a third of the way down his run. The flak seems thicker around him—at least the smoke seems darker. Then you watch Mustang Two and Three roll in almost simultaneously, and you get ready to roll in seconds later. The plan is for all four aircraft to come down the chute at approximately the same time, complicating the enemy's targeting and tracking solutions.

"You're hit! You're hit!" Jackknife calls. Mustang Lead, you're on fire!" You snap your gaze back to Jack's aircraft. A dirty red trail marks the sky behind him. The aircraft hurtles downward in its dive. There is no transmission from Mustang Lead. He's going straight in! Then the bombs separate from the aircraft. Slowly, the nose of the *Phantom* starts up. He's pulling out! As the aircraft regains straight and level flight you see the bombs impact, smack on target. Jack heads for the coast, five miles away. The way his ship is burning, he'll probably blow up before he gets there. In the meantime, Mustang Two and Three have dropped. You're late because you were watching Jack. Now it's your turn, and you'll be a lone aircraft coming down the chute. You don't think about Jack. You ignore the flak around you. The red tracers coming up all seem to be pointed directly at the cockpit. You roll in, then roll the wings back level with the aircraft pointed down in a forty-five-degree dive. In the back seat, Mike calls off the altitudes. "Nine thousand . . . eight thousand . . ."

You check your airspeed. How's the dive angle? What about drift? Your briefed aiming point is the center of the roof of the H-shaped building's east wing. Making small corrections in pitch, roll, and power, you watch the aiming "pipper" move across the ground and onto the roof. You make it reach the center of the roof just as the aircraft passes the computed drop altitude and Mike calls, "Pickle 'em off!"

You ease a little forward stick, stop the pipper on the target, thumb the red bomb-release button, and hold everything while you feel the 750s come off the racks. Then you suck the stick back and the G-suit grips your gut and legs as you execute a six-G pullout. As soon as the nose comes up through the horizon, you plug in both afterburners and guide the aircraft through an evasive, crazy, twisting, climbing dash for the coast. Mike risks vertebra injury to look back over his shoulder, with the Gs still on, so he can spot the bomb impact point. "Right on target!"

Ahead, at only 2,000 feet, in the cockpit of crippled Mustang Lead, Jack Gravis fights to stay in the air. The right engine fire-warning light glows bright; both engine temperature gauges are way beyond safe limits, and the hydraulic pressures for the controls are fluctuating wildly. The aircraft pitches and bucks in its flight path. First Jack has control, then the hydraulic pressure falls, and he loses control. As the nose starts to wobble downward, he pumps the stick. Somehow, the riddled *Phantom* responds—the nose comes up.

The cycle repeats itself over and over in the flight toward the safety of the sea. The flames now lap at the fuel tanks in the aft fuselage section. The other members of the flight are alongside now, not too close, in case she blows, and they watch, unable to do anything else. While he fights the controls, Jack is thinking fast. "Better bail out now, before we blow up . . . no, we'll be captured . . . losing thrust . . . telelight warning panel's lit up like a pinball machine . . . come on, coastline. . . ."

Finally, a strip of white sand flashes by below. Jack shuts down the right engine, the one with the fire-warning light. The precaution is academic. By now, the whole aircraft from just behind the rear cockpit is a mass of orange and red flames. The flight continues on one engine. "Got to get out of small-arms range . . . a little further. . . ."

You see the two parachutes open, a quarter-mile apart, and watch the crippled *Phantom* take its final plunge. Jack and Wylie drift down in their chutes. Jack unsheaths his emergency radio and is talking to us before he hits the water. "I'm okay. Tell Rescue to hurry up. We're drifting inshore." Momentarily, they're safe. Now Rescue has to get to them before the enemy does.

You switch to rescue frequency and contact the nearest radar site.

"Bandbox, Bandbox. This is Mustang Four. Mustang Lead has been shot down over Target 296. Both pilots have ejected and are in the water about five miles off the coast. Send the rescue boys."

"Roger, Mustang Four. Scrambling rescue aircraft. Squawk emergency for a fix." You twist the frequency selector on one of the black boxes in the cockpit. On the operator's screen at the radar site the pinpoint of light that represents you blossoms into a big blip. The operator plots the center of your orbit and relays the coordinates to Rescue.

The two pilots are in their yellow life rafts on the water now, a quarter-mile apart, and you climb higher in your orbit around their position. Mustang Three orbits low to fight off enemy surface craft. You can see an enemy gunboat circling on the water about ten miles away. You orbit at medium altitude, high enough to stay in radio contact with Bandbox and low enough to see what is going on down on the water. Mustang Two orbits high, ready to engage enemy fighters, if necessary.

"Look at those splashes!" Mike calls. You look. Guns on the beach—big guns—are shelling the area. Geysers erupt from the sea, a couple of miles north of the two tiny life rafts. Then the guns fall silent. Because of the waves and the distance, the gunners can't see the rafts. But they will be able to see the rescue plane when it arrives. Time is on the enemy's side, because brisk wind and tide are carrying the pilots nearer the beach.

"Mustang Four, this is Navy 798. We're two F-8s with guns and missiles. Can we be of assistance?"

"Roger, Navy 798, stick around. You can help knock out the big guns on the beach." Camouflaged, the guns will be almost impossible to find until they start firing again and their muzzle flashes give away their position. You watch the two sleek jets take up their own orbit, high above you.

Ten minutes drag by. Mustang Three has already punched off his empty tanks and bomb racks to reduce drag and conserve fuel. You do the same. "Bandbox, where's that rescue bird?"

"Mustang Four, this is Bandbox. Your rescue bird is approaching the area now. He's an HU-16." The HU-16 is a slow, reliable, extremely tough twin-engine flying boat—an amphibian with an outstanding record of pickups at sea.

"Mustang Four, this is Rescue Alpha. We're about ten minutes south. Transmit for a fix." You press your mike button and count from one to five, slowly, and then back to one. The HU-16, with its direction-finding equipment, homes on the radio signals you're sending out.

The next ten minutes pass slowly. On strike frequency, Jackknife Lead has instructed the last strike flight not to expend on target but to orbit at altitude. He knows the guns will open up again when the rescue plane starts in, and he's going to try to silence them. Two more aircraft, propeller-driven A-1Es, have arrived and also are standing by.

Finally, you see the HU-16, low over the water, flying up the Gulf parallel to the coast. "Rescue Alpha, this is Mustang Four. Turn left twenty degrees. The pilots are about ten miles northwest of you." Rescue Alpha acknowledges. You tell Jack to turn on his emergency radio again so the seaplane can home in on it. You watch Rescue Alpha turn and fly over the two life rafts. They have drifted in to about four miles from the beach.

As soon as Rescue Alpha starts his landing pattern, the enemy artillery opens up again. You watch the muzzle flashes. There must be twenty guns, in a long line up and down the coast. They are behind the beach, in a sloping, heavily overgrown area, situated far enough apart so one aircraft can't destroy more than one emplacement at a time. Over the beach, you watch the fighters start in. Shells begin to impact on the water near the rafts. Bombs, rockets, missiles, and bullets begin to churn up the sand on shore.

The HU-16 touches down in a shower of white spray and begins to taxi towards the rafts. As it approaches Wylie, who is closest to shore, the enemy gunners begin to get the range. Geysers spew from the water on both sides of the aircraft and behind it. Your throat gets dry as you realize what a sitting duck the flying boat is as she churns slowly through the swells. One line of geysers begins to track up the aircraft's wake.

At last, you see the first raft disappear under a wing. "We've got one of them, Mustang," the Rescue Alpha pilot calls, "but we can't see the other one. Waves are pretty high, and the shelling's getting pretty thick down here." Just then you see a geyser erupt directly in front of the plane, so close the spray drenches the cockpit windows. You look back on the shore. Where some of the gun emplacements were hidden there is now blackened wreckage, smoke, and fire; but many of the guns are still firing, and the accuracy of the gunners is improving. Above the guns, the planes roll into their bombing and strafing runs, trying to silence the remaining artillery before the rescue plane is blown out of the water.

You see the big plane turn left and lumber toward Jack's raft. A brace of geysers erupts from the spot the aircraft just vacated.

Jack sees the aircraft taxiing toward him over the wave tops and tries to paddle the raft toward it with his hands. The effort is futile; but what the hell, you have to do *something* at a time like this. Finally, the aircraft wing is over him, and he grabs one of the plane's floats.

The whoosh of the shells, the roar of the now almost continuous detonations, and the sound of the HU-16's engines are deafening. Jack jumps off the raft, his orange life vest inflated, and swims toward an open hatch. A frogman, trained in rescue, jumps from the plane into the water to meet him. Together they reach the hatch. Jack is exhausted. His body has been pumping adrenalin ever since he rolled in for his dive-bomb run. This, combined with the emotional strain and the physical effort of ejecting from the aircraft, hitting the water, and climbing into his raft, have drained him of strength. It's just too much effort to pull himself through the hatch.

The pararescueman, A2C Eldridge Neal of Charleston, W. Va., tries to boost him through the hatch. But with nothing except water to push against, he can't get leverage. Looking back from the cockpit, the rescue pilot, Major Donald C. Hollfelder, of Castro Valley, Calif., realizes what the trouble is, unstraps from his seat, leaps to the hatch, and with one hand jerks

Jack bodily through the opening. The copilot, First Lieutenant Joseph C. Kirby of Waterford, N.Y., has everything in readiness when Hollfelder returns to the cockpit, glances back to make sure the frogman is inside, and shoves both throttles wide open.

From the air, you see the ring of explosions tightening around the aircraft as, one by one, the remaining enemy gunners get the range. Then Rescue Alpha starts to move. She gathers speed, and the shells begin to fall behind her. She skips off a wave crest, settles back, skips again, and she's off!

"Rescue Alpha, did you get both pilots?"

"Roger, and they're both okay."

"Roger."

You search for words to say thanks. All you can think of is "You guys did a beautiful job. You deserve a medal."

You check your fuel and head for home. You look back at Vinh Linh barracks and wonder if you'll have to hit the same target again tomorrow.

JET BOMBERS MAKE THE DIFFERENCE

HEADQUARTERS, U. S. MILITARY ASSISTANCE COMMAND
VIETNAM

April 1965

The use of speedy jet aircraft against guerrillas in a counter-insurgency environment has been debated since early 1962 when a U. S. Air Force detachment arrived in the Republic of Vietnam to support the government in its struggle against a communist-directed insurgency.

One side holds that using modern jets is like "hitting an ant with a sledgehammer," that the jets are too fast, too indiscriminate and too uneconomical. On the other side, there are those who argue that the jets can react quicker, carry bigger loads, and have a more terrifying effect on the enemy.

On 19 February 1965, the USAF 2nd Air Division, the U.S. air component command in Vietnam, began using B-57 *Canberra* bombers and F-100 *Supersaber* fighter-bombers for in-country operations. While it is still too early to fully evaluate the effectiveness of these jets, there are strong indications that these aircraft are well-suited to the counterinsurgency task.

Perhaps the best test of the effectiveness of jets came on February 24th when eight B-57s and eight F-100s were directed to cover a U. S. Army force of 36 helicopters in an important rescue operation. The choppers had to extricate a force of 220

Vietnamese with their U.S. advisors who were surrounded and pinned down by two Viet Cong battalions on strategic Highway 19 near An Khe, about 250 miles north of Saigon. The situation of this ground force, caught up in a series of enemy actions which had caused heavy friendly casualties including one U.S. killed and nine wounded, was desperate. Unless the Vietnamese/ U.S. forces could be immediately rescued, they would almost certainly sustain heavy losses.

But getting helicopters into this heavily defended area presented a major problem. For five days previous the Viet Cong, in a series of ambushes and attacks, had mauled units sent piecemeal into action. The Viet Cong now stood ready to ambush a ground relief force or a helicopter force. In addition to having modern Chinese copies of Russian manual and automatic weapons, the Viet Cong insurgents greatly outnumbered government forces.

Curiously, the enemy was using the same tactics in the same area where eleven years ago, he virtually annihilated the famous Group Mobile 100, composed of 3,500 crack French troops equipped with tanks and artillery. His objective then, as now, was to cut off the strategic east-west 102 mile long Highway 19 linking Pleiku in the western highlands with Qui Nhon on the South China Sea coast in central Vietnam. With a series of lightning ambushes and attacks, mainly in the narrow mountain passes on both ends of the 20 mile long An Khe valley, he shattered French convoys, relief forces, and military camps with mortars, bazookas, cannons, and human wave attacks. His tactics of isolation and encirclement were highly successful and in some battles he was inflicting casualties at the rate of a man a minute.

In early February of 1965, it looked like the Viet Cong were planning the same thing. Five Viet Cong battalions in Binh Dinh Province began a campaign to cut Vietnam in half. Their first objective was to gain control of Highway 19, where it ran through the strategically important An Khe Valley. Their first operations were successful.

On the early morning hours of February 20th, Viet Cong main force troops attacked a government outpost in the Mang Yang Pass which guards the eastern entrance to the An Khe Valley. There the enemy carried out a series of ambushes and attacks over a four day period. They succeeded in isolating and chopping up separate units like they had done against the French.

By the morning of February 24th, the Viet Cong had baited the trap and were ready to spring it. A company of Civilian Irregular Defense Group (CIDG) troops, helilifted into an area along Highway 19 about 10 miles west of An Khe, came under heavy Viet Cong attack, and a Ranger Battalion was sent out to relieve it. One Ranger company managed to fight through and link up with the CIDG unit by 10:30 a.m., only to find they were completely surrounded by a well-armed Viet Cong battalion. It looked like almost certain defeat.

At Pleiku, where the II Corps headquarters is located, the ARVN[1] Corps Commander, Brigadier General Co, was facing the problem of how to get his men out. To relieve them by land would open the relief forces to ambush and more casualties. General Co wasn't about to repeat the mistake made by the French. The only way to extricate the trapped unit was by air.

It was a tactical plan which the French never tried—jet bombers and fighters to keep the enemy's heads down while the more vulnerable helicopters moved in and out of the landing zone.

At Pleiku, a USAF Air Liaison Officer, Lt. Col. William L. Janssen, of Decatur, Illinois, climbed into his tiny O-1F liaison aircraft about 2:00 p.m. to fly over the battle area. With him was his Vietnamese observer, 1st Lt. Ha. Their job was to direct the air strikes—to make certain that the weapons in the hands of the enemy were not used against the relief helicopters.

Forty-five minutes later, eight B-57s of the 8th Bomb Squad-

[1] Army of the Republic of Vietnam.

ron and the 13th Bomb Squadron, took to the air from Bien Hoa Air Base. They were joined by eight F-100s of the 614th Tactical Fighter Squadron out of Da Nang. In less than an hour, they were in action.

The plan called for the F-100s to strike the area north of the road in a racetrack pattern covering an area one kilometer north and ten kilometers east and west of the trapped unit. The B-57s would fly a racetrack pattern in the same area south of the landing zone.

Arriving over the area several minutes before the helicopters, the jets, directed by the Air Force airborne forward air controllers, started blasting the area with 500 pound bombs followed by concentrated low-level strafing with 20mm cannon fire. As the helicopters moved in, they found the jets flying level with them, creating an "alley" through which they could move in relative safety. The helicopters literally "bounced in the air" from the concussion of the bombs released from the F-100s and the B-57s.

At 3 p.m. a force of four *Skyraiders* A-1Es arrived and took over from the F-100s, dropping incendijel as well as fragmentation and general purpose bombs. The helicopters made three lifts out of the area, finishing the job in about an hour.

Not a single casualty was experienced during the whole operation. Fewer than ten of the 36 helicopters were hit by even a single Viet Cong bullet.

Said Colonel Theo C. Mataxis, the Senior U.S. Army Advisor to II Corps, "The bombing and strafing by these aircraft suppressed heavy enemy ground and anti-aircraft fire allowing helicopters of the 52nd Aviation Battalion to make three lifts from Highway 19. The records show that 220 officers and men who had been surrounded and might otherwise have been lost were saved in this one operation."

The success of this operation exceeded the most optimistic

hopes. The trapped units were removed to fight again under better circumstances.

Two weeks following this dramatic rescue, government forces decisively smashed the Viet Cong unit, reopening this strategic highway to government traffic.

The three-week long battle reached its peak on 8 March when the communist force attacked the Special Forces camp at Kannack on the Eastern entrance to the valley. Government forces, with air support, drove them off, killing an estimated 300 Viet Cong who were armed with modern Chinese copies of Russian designed weapons. These included the AK assault rifle, the RPG anti-tank gun and the SKS rifle, all standard weapons for Soviet ground forces.

In the later stage of the Binh Dinh engagements, government forces avoided the piecemeal commitment of force which could be mauled the way they were at Binh Gia in December of 1964. After the highly effective use of jets on February 24th in extricating trapped forces, the Viet Cong had to face reorganized groups of government units which were strategically placed and in sufficient strength to beat off attacks.

The jets had certainly proved their worth at An Khe, not only on February 24th but again on March 8th when eight B-57s struck elements of the Viet Cong forces which were in the Binh Dinh area. So long as ground forces knew that these powerful air weapons were on hand to quickly arrive at a battle area, their chances of effective action against the enemy were increased.

The addition of B-57s and F-100s to the existing force of about 100 A-1E and A-1H aircraft greatly increased the contribution of air power to the Vietnam fighting. They were something new to the war—something which the French did not fully employ and something the Americans had foregone prior to 1965. Colonel Mataxis, commenting on the 24 February action, said that if the French ground rules had been employed, the force near An Khe could have been wiped out. "Mobility and air power is saving us from what the French experienced," he added.

"In the month of February," he said, "we have been faced with heavier concentrations of enemy forces. Actually we welcome this change for it provides an excellent opportunity to exploit even further the outstanding air support which we are receiving. This is particularly true since the Second Air Division has been permitted to add jet aircraft to our in-country support."

General William C. Westmoreland, Commander U.S. Military Assistance Command, Vietnam, in a letter to Maj. Gen. Joseph H. Moore, the 2nd Air Division commander, indorsed the commendatory comments of Colonel Mataxis. Said General Westmoreland: "The increased integration of U.S. air power in the counterinsurgency campaign in South Vietnam has been a significant accomplishment. The air support provided by your command as cited by the Senior U.S. Advisor of Army of Republic of Vietnam, II Corps, is typical of the support rendered by the 2nd Air Division throughout the area of operations."

The employment of jet aircraft for in-country close air support, coupled with the air attacks against North Vietnam, threw a new and more optimistic cast on the Vietnam struggle. It was a sign not only of U.S. determination to defend the Republic of Vietnam, but of the great potential of American power which could be committed to the fighting as required.

OPERATION SHERWOOD FOREST—
BOMBERS THAT AREN'T

HEADQUARTERS, U. S. MILITARY ASSISTANCE COMMAND
VIETNAM

6 April 1965

It was reminiscent of a World War II B-17 bombing strike from a base in England. There was the morning briefing in the base theater, United States Air Force crews in fatigues and flying clothes getting the word on weather, communications, navigation and the two-minute prayer by the chaplain.

The excitement and tension and anticipation were there too. This was a strike mission against the enemy's heartland. Then, precisely as scheduled at 1515, Air Force planes took off from Tan Son Nhut, one every fifteen seconds, circling, getting in formation until 24 were in the air, headed for the target.

At exactly 1600, the first flight of three went in for the "bomb run," dropping their weapons while later flights ploughed through the smoke and fire to drop their loads from 2,100 feet altitude.

Only there was a big difference between this and any other bombing raid. The 24 strike planes were C-123 twin-engined cargo planes. Their bombs were 50-gallon fuel drums loaded on pallets—24 to each aircraft. Each pallet was equipped with M-6 night flare rigged to set it afire after dropping.

Led by their commander, Col. David T. Fleming, these duck-shaped airplanes of the 315th Air Commando Group executed on March 31 a bomb raid that is probably unique in the history of air combat.

Their target was a section of the Boi Loi woods, a 48-square mile Viet Cong jungle sanctuary stretching from a point about 25 miles northwest of Saigon west to within several miles of the Cambodian border. Under a 100-foot high tree canopy, the VC for ten years had been using this area as a training and marshaling center.

The area was honeycombed with caves, trenches, tunnels and underground facilities, including communications. Protected by heavy anti-aircraft guns, it was a nerve center for guerrillas operating south of the 17th parallel, having easy access to the Ho Chi Minh trail, the infiltration route from North Vietnam. A hard core VC regiment had been using the area.

The C-123s were to fly in at 2,100 feet and drop their load of fuel drums in a smoke-marked area on the southeast corner of this forest. This was a small part of a 7,500 hectare stretch of dry and dead jungle, defoliated weeks earlier by four chemical spray-dispensing C-123s.

This was a precision mission. The drums had to fall into two rectangular aiming points at about 90 degrees from each other. Each point covered an area about a mile by half a mile. It was hoped that this would create a "venturi effect," starting a terrific blaze which the wind would carry across the 7,500 hectares of defoliated forest.

Each aircraft carried 24 of the 50-gallon fuel drums for a total of 1,200 gallons per aircraft and a grand total of over 28,000 gallons. The fuel would drench the dead leaves and foliage and aircraft flares attached to each pallet would set the fuel ablaze.

The C-123s were complemented by more conventional strike aircraft—A-1E aircraft from the 34th TAC Group loaded with incendijel. The incendijel would help to feed the fire. This mission was also supplemented by B-57 jet bombers dropping incendiary bombs.

Three months' preparation had gone into this mission. Planning began in late 1964 after several months' surveillance of the area which revealed considerable VC activity beneath the thick jungle growth. Initially the area was a rest and recuperation center for the VC, but revetments, AA emplacements, barracks, and camp sites were later pinpointed and eventually it was learned that the VC's main force C-58th Regiment was located in the woods.

Brigadier General Robert R. Rowland, chief of the Air Force Advisory Group, on Dec. 9, 1964, presented a concept for wiping out the area. The plan was to heavily bomb pinpoint targets in the area, then defoliate the 48 square miles of forest which was about twelve kilometers in length. After the defoliation had taken effect, the burning mission could take place. This was timed for late March when the winds were brisk and the temperature high.

The Vietnamese Government and the Military Assistance Command, Vietnam, were involved in the program since the military effort had to be coupled with a vast civic action program. It was important not only to get an estimated 4,000 civilians out of the area but to win them over to the government side and resettle them.

In early January, 1965, loudspeakers in light aircraft broadcast for 40 hours and three and a half million leaflets were dropped announcing the imminent operation and telling civilians to get out. Then on the 18th, 19th and 20th of January, heavy bombing of the area by A-1H and A-1E *Skyraiders* began. In that three-day period, 800 tons of explosives were dropped on pinpointed targets during 139 sorties. This included 24 1,000-pound bombs, the first use of this bomb in Vietnam.

Then, in 95 defoliation sorties flown by four C-123 spray aircraft of the 315th Air Commando Group between Jan. 22

and Feb. 18, about 7,500 hectares of the forest were sprayed with some 82,000 gallons of chemical spray. This was the largest defoliation mission ever flown in Vietnam.

By the end of March, everything was ready for the final phase of the three-part operation. The defoliant had taken effect. The area was at the end of the dry season and the winds were coming from the right direction and at the right speed. All that was needed was to light a massive torch in the right place letting the wind do the rest of the work.

That was where the C-123s came in. After discarding a plan to have refueling tanker aircraft drop the fuel, it was decided to rig the C-123s with palletized oil drums, each fitted with an illumination flare that would ignite the fuel on contact. Successful tests were made of this concept by the 315th Air Commando Group. The C-123s would drop their oil drums in conjunction with napalm strikes by A-1Es. Fitting this preparation into an already full schedule of operation, the group worked day and night. By the end of March, when the "go" signal was given by the Vietnamese government, the Group was ready.

Flying to the target, a distance of only 30 miles, the crews looked down on dozens of little smoke fires traditionally set this time of year by farmers in the flat ricelands to burn their fields. The C-123s had a similar job on a much larger scale.

A smoke marker and flare on the target guided the lead element in—three C-123s led by Colonel Fleming, looking for all the world like bombers on a target run. Right behind them were three more Providers and behind them six more flights all dumping their "ordnance" on the prescribed area. Then the A-1Es and B-57s flew into the huge black column of smoke created by the earlier fires and unloaded . . . . . tons of incendijel and incendiaries in the same area. They left the target a huge circle of flame with a black smoke column stretching up several thousand feet.

Long before this phase of the mission had begun, over a thousand civilians had come out of the forest area in response to government appeals and were being re-settled and looked after. However, several secondary explosions clearly observed during the March 31 "burning" mission indicated that some elements of the enemy forces might still be in the woods.

Unfortunately, despite weather forecasting of dry weather with a fairly brisk wind of five to ten knots, a huge rain cloud formed over the target area. Rain, coupled with a very slow wind, did not let the fire spread as expected and by the following morning, the fire had diminished.

Nevertheless, the Boi Loi woods would not furnish the same safe sanctuary to the Viet Cong that it did before 1965. The "Sherwood Forest" operation, as the project was dubbed, laid open for surveillance several hidden areas.

But the interesting part of the operation was its assignment of a new role to the highly versatile C-123 of the 315th Air Commando Group. These aircraft, operating in Vietnam since 1963, had proved to be one of the most adaptable and effective weapons in the Air Force program for combating the insurgency in Vietnam. Prior to the May 31st mission, Colonel Fleming told his men: "Today's mission takes us out of the troop carrier business and puts us in the air commando business."

Paradoxically, a substantial number of the pilots in the 315th are ex-SAC B-52 and B-47 pilots who served up to ten years in SAC without ever firing a shot in anger. On May 31, they flew a combat mission, dropping weapons on an enemy while flying at 130 knots in a twin-engined transport plane. A far cry from the Arctic patrols at over 500 knots and over 40,000 feet but an ample reminder of the versatility and experience in today's Air Force.

"THUNDERCHIEF" TARGET:
BRIDGES, NORTH VIETNAM

HEADQUARTERS, U. S. MILITARY ASSISTANCE COMMAND
VIETNAM

May 1965

On April 16, 1965, the United States Air Force launched 38 F-105 *Thunderchiefs,* led by Lt. Col. Robbie Risner, on a strike into North Vietnam. Each aircraft carried eight 750-pound bombs and was armed with ammunition for its 20mm Vulcan cannons.

The strike force was airborne at 2 p.m. Within two and one-half hours, these aircraft would recover back at their launch base, and three bridges would be in the water.

The first *Thunderchiefs* hit Kim Cuong Bridge where route 8 crosses a stream about 30 miles southwest of Vinh and 10 miles from the border of Laos. Pilots reported the weather "clear but hazy; visibility four to five miles," as they went in to strike. Anti-aircraft fire from a building near the bridge called for suppression, and a strike support F-105 blasted the building with 2.75-inch folding finned rockets. Within minutes a considerable portion of the 130 feet by 12 feet concrete bridge was in the water. As one of the pilots laconically reported, "when the smoke cleared, it was down."

The next flight was directed to hit the Trai Hoi highway bridge on route 12 where it crosses the Nga San between Vinh and Do Khe. One span of the trussed steel bridge was dropped and the southern approaches were obliterated. Ferry docks by the approaches were also destroyed.

The last target was a railroad bridge made of trussed steel. This was the Dion Chau Railroad bridge over the Song Con River between Vinh and Than Hoa. One third of its 390-foot length was down by the time the *Thunderchiefs* turned and headed for home.

But the day wasn't over for the flight of F-105s, as pilots spotted an engineless train on a siding. A tank car, two bunk cars and four freight cars were strafed by the F-105s.

While it will be relatively easy to build a temporary bridge to replace the first target, the Kim Cuong Bridge, the other two will be difficult or impossible to bypass. The destruction of these bridges means that movement of vehicles in those areas is restricted, and the shipment of supplies vital to the success of the Communist activities in South Vietnam is slowed or stopped.

And the labor of thousands of men who assembled these structures and the expenditure of considerable amounts of North Vietnam's financial asset, has been negated. In a few minutes' time, the F-105s wiped it out with a roar and a splash.

As of this date (April 26, 1965), U.S. aircraft have destroyed 23 bridges in North Vietnam. These bridge targets have been on the main arteries for travel and transport from the industrial complexes around Hanoi through North Vietnam into Laos and South Vietnam. They were constructed of various materials; wood, concrete and iron, and spanned rivers like the Song Co and the Ngan San.

Some were located in valleys, making them difficult targets, and many were defended by anti-aircraft guns and automatic weapons positions. Still, they were hit and knocked down, and the rivers they spanned are once again obstacles to the movement of troops and supplies.